The Arts of Zaire

Volume II
Eastern Zaire

The Arts of Zaire

Volume II
Eastern Zaire

The Ritual and Artistic Context of
Voluntary Associations

Daniel Biebuyck

UNIVERSITY OF CALIFORNIA PRESS
Berkeley Los Angeles London

University of California Press
Berkeley and Los Angeles, California

University of California Press, Ltd.
London, England

Copyright © 1986 by The Regents of the University of California

Library of Congress Cataloging in Publication Data
(Revised for vol. II)

Biebuyck, Daniel P., 1925–
   The arts of Zaire.

   Includes bibliographies and indexes.
   Contents: v. 1. Southwestern Zaire—v. 2. Eastern Zaire.
   1. Art, Zairian.   2. Art, Primitive—Zaire.
3. Ethnology—Zaire.   I. Title.
N7399.C6B5   1986   730'.09675'1   84-21928
ISBN 0-520-05210-2 (v. 1)
ISBN 0-520-05211-0 (v. 2)

Printed in the United States of America
1   2   3   4   5   6   7   8   9

Let them remove his heart of feathers
And with knowledge he will remain

Porcupine does not eat fallen bananas
in full daylight

Lega aphorisms of bwami

Contents

Plates

Photographic Credits

Acknowledgments

This book is based on my fieldwork among the Lega, Bembe, and Nyanga between 1949 and 1958, which was sponsored by l'Institut pour la recherche scientifique en Afrique centrale (Brussels). Data on the Bira, Lega of Mount Ruwenzori, Nande, Pere, Komo, Leka, Bemo, Tembo, Kwame, Konjo, Kanu, Hunde, Havu, Shi, Nyindu, Vira, Furiiru, and Tali were obtained in the field with the support of the same institute between 1958 and 1960, when I served as a member of the Land Tenure Commission for the Congo.

Comparative research on the arts and cultures of Central Africa has been sponsored by the National Endowment for the Humanities, the Samuel Kress Foundation, a Rockefeller Foundation Humanities Fellowship, and a John Simon Guggenheim Memorial Fellowship. Without this assistance, which provided the necessary free time and the opportunity to visit museums and to study archives, and without the continued support of the University of Delaware, long-range comparative study of the heterogeneous and inadequately covered topics in widely scattered sources would have been impossible. The present work is only one of the results of this research.

My special thanks go to the Musée royal de l'Afrique centrale (Tervuren), and in particular to Huguette Van Geluwe, Albert Maesen, and the staff of the ethnographic section. Their cooperation has greatly facilitated my task.

Introduction

In *Lega Culture: Art, Initiation, and Moral Philosophy among a Central African People* (1973*a*), I briefly discussed general aspects of the Lega social and cultural system and analyzed the organization, function, and ideology of the bwami association. I also examined the significance of sculptures and other initiation objects in the bwami context in their interplay with grade levels, statuses, ritual action, and sung aphorisms. Several later publications (Biebuyck 1974*a*, 1976*a*, 1977*a*−*b*, 1979, 1981*b*−*d*) provide additional data on the rites of the bwami association and on specific artistic subjects (e.g., stools, animal figurines, spoons, bifrontal figurines, schematization). *Lega Culture*, however, is the essential background for the detailed study of Lega art undertaken in the present volume. I reemphasize, mainly in the introduction, only those intersecting aspects of bwami history, structure, ideology, and rites which are vital for comprehension of the arts in their socioritual and conceptual framework.

Although I do supply morphological descriptions, the approach is primarily contextual. Lega art in all its manifestations is bound so intimately with the bwami association that no valid interpretation is feasible without stressing the structural and organizational principles, the philosophical outlook, and the performance contexts of bwami. The art is an essential channel through which the basic tenets of the association are illustrated and expressed, and many specific performances require the display and exegesis of prescribed artworks. Bwami is organized hierarchically into a system of complementary grades to which men and some of their wives are initiated, step by step. Initiations to all grades consist of mandatory sequential ritual enactments. Dances, gestures, dramatizations, sung aphorisms, and displays and manipulations of initiation objects are combined to communicate fundamental messages about the moral philosophy and the values, the modes of savoir vivre and etiquette, and the sociojural and ritual principles cultivated by the members of the association. Although the framework for the interpretation of artworks is the graded bwami association with its structure, principles, and goals, the actual contexts vary widely. Artworks form only a part, albeit an indispensable one, of the initiation objects. In numerous rites, at the lowest as well as at the highest grades, no sculptures are exhibited. The primary contexts for the study of the artworks are not the bwami rites as a whole but rather particular ritual performances, mainly at the two top grades for men (yananio and kindi) and at the highest female grade (bunyamwa). A few art objects of a certain type, however, do appear—in some Lega communities more than in others—in rites leading to the lower grades.

The artworks used in the rites are never chosen randomly. Certain ritual observances demand that all participants display wooden or ivory masks, whereas others require the presentation and revelation of collectively owned masks or figurines. In any ritual featuring prescribed artworks, the way they are used may vary. For example, a performance may begin with each partici- pant dancing, holding his own mask in his hand, under his chin, or against his hat. The initiates may then place their masks on the ground, in a row or in a pile; some dancers in solo or duo performance may then pick up selected masks and swing them around, drag them over the ground, or simply point at them. This procedure may be allowed in one ritual context but prohibited in another; one type of mask may be used while another is excluded.

Clearly, the functions and the meanings of sculptures can be understood only through comprehensive observation and analysis of the contexts, the ac- tual performances, the types of artworks, the social backgrounds, the interrela- tionships of actors and owners, and the purposes of each rite. Observation of a particular sculpture or a type of sculpture in a single rite does not necessarily convey the complete meaning of that work. An object used in more than one rite may be treated and interpreted differently in each instance. Although orga- nized in accordance with the same principles and structured on identical themes and goals among all Lega, the bwami initiations are arranged indepen- dently by different socioritual communities. When these communities are his- torically, geographically, and socially close to one another, similarities will emerge; when they are more remote from one another, fewer features will be shared in common. All autonomous communities cultivate originality and uniqueness, which are particularly striking when truly gifted preceptors pre- side over initiations. Thus the contexts in which artworks appear may vary, either slightly or significantly, from community to community.

Initiations are exclusive and secret not only to noninitiates but also to initi- ates, depending on their personal status. Kindi of the highest level may, and usually do, participate in all ritual performances leading to any grade. Yananio at the top level are admitted to all initiations up to lutumbo lwa yananio. Be- cause artworks are the prime initiation objects, they are seen only at the higher grades and levels, and their secret uses and meanings are not revealed to those in the lower echelons. Only initiates entitled to own the artworks know their contextual interpretations, and some preceptors and tutors are more knowl- edgeable than others. Initiates are thinkers; they have learned to find meanings in things that others take only at face value. A needle and its bone sheath are not simply useful objects; they are also symbols of the bond between a man and his wife, a tutor and his protégé. A figurine that looks like a chameleon does not necessarily represent that animal. A figurine that resembles a pregnant woman is not just any pregnant woman; nor is it a sex or fertility symbol. Many figurines superficially similar in form represent different characters; others that vary morphologically may symbolize a single character. The revelation of hidden meanings is an intrinsic part of the initiatory experience. Because the real meaning of an object is defined by its ritual context, its symbolic interpretation varies widely. The exegesis is not limited to its general or specific form, its generic or individual name, or its overt usage; rather, it extends to materials and manufacturing processes, to structural details, to prescribed associations with persons and activities, to the object's position in the rite, and to its complementarity to or its difference from other objects. Lega art is therefore a hidden art par excellence. Artworks are not made for display in shrines, chiefs' palaces, men's houses, or cemeteries. They are not meant to be acquired, owned, manipulated, seen, interpreted, or understood by all.

It is understandable, then, that few Europeans who lived and traveled among the Lega attempted to comprehend the purposes and meanings of bwami and its art. Delhaise (1909*b*), who lived among the Lega around 1903, was an astute observer of Lega culture but provided little information about Lega art. He repeatedly stresses the secrecy enveloping the artworks. When he was finally permitted to view kindi dances in which some figurines were handled, the performance seemed to him to be staged. In later years, when initiates agreed or were forced to reveal some of their secrets, they proved to be masters of the staged performance, interesting to observe but devoid of real content.

Books and catalogs on African art have long treated Lega sculpture in a haphazard way. Until Olbrechts's work was published in 1946, most writers simply ignored the Lega (see, e.g., Einstein, 1920; Fuhrmann, 1923; Vatter, 1926; Hardy, 1927). Lega (incorrectly called Warega) carvings were occasionally illustrated, but no identification or interpretation was provided (e.g., Lega spoons in Clouzot and Level, n.d., pl. 36; a wooden mask ascribed to the Kasai in Locke, 1927, pl. 9; a Lega mask in Chauvet, 1930, fig. 62; figurines and an ivory mask in von Sydow, 1932*a*, pl. 133, 1932*b*, pl. 25; figurines in Frobenius, 1933, pl. 101). Maes (1924, pp. 44–46 and fig. 49) illustrates as Lega a wooden polychrome horned mask collected for Tervuren by Dargent. Using the information given by Delhaise (1909*b*), Maes notes that this and two other similar masks were most likely connected with the highest grade of the bwami association, but they are not representative of the Lega and possibly were made by groups such as Bakwame, Baleka, and Bakonjo, who are transitional among Lega, Komo, Nyanga, and Havu. Clarke (1929, p. 68) mentions an ancient ivory mask and two small ivory figurines "standing back to back on a common pedestal which are now at the British Museum" (Fagg and Plass, 1964, p. 144). He associates the double figurine with bwami because of the headdress and because the mask has "the mark of the mwami on its forehead." The Museum of Modern Art exhibition organized by Sweeney in 1935 included several wooden and ivory masks, figurines, heads, ivory spoons (nos. 440, 446–447, 450, 455, 461–462, 464–465, 504–506, 509–510, 512, 514–516, some illustrated in seven plates), and a rare ivory neck rest (no. 472). The only information given relates to size, material, and collection. The description of no. 455, for example, is "Mask of the Miwami [*sic*] secret society."

Kjersmeier (1937, vol. 3, pp. 33–34, pls. 54–56), finding Lega art to be "l'art le plus spontané du Congo Belge," evokes its technical perfection and its expressive value. There were two types of ivory masks and figurines: those dominated by rounded forms and those featuring straight lines. The "ornamental tattoos" on the sculptures, when present at all, consisted of dots, circle-dots, and short lines; the eyes were often indicated with encrusted cowries. Wooden figurines were artistically less interesting than wooden masks, but there were exceptional pieces. One multifrontal figurine, which Kjersmeier identifies as a dance baton, had a "captivating effect." Wooden masks occurred in so many different forms that division into style groups was impossible. Lega sculpture was closely linked with the rites and ceremonies of the "seven grades" of the "mwami secret society." The ivory masks carried in the hand were symbolic insignia of high dignitaries, but no other information is supplied about their alleged "magical and religious function."

Gaffé (1945, pp. 55–56 and unnumbered plates) reproduces three Lega ivory masks, praising them for the unique blend of simple effects and rigor (severity in some, serenity in others). He thought one mask was the "living portrait of death" (an ancestor come to life again); another depicted "a personage who serenely entered immortality." The Lega, though "the most perfect sculptors in ivory," were less successful in wood carving. Their masks were used as rallying signs by secret societies whose members carried them in their hands on important occasions. The extraordinary patination of the pieces was achieved because their users anointed their bodies and the sculptures with oil. Herskovits (1945, p. 53) merely notes that there was little information on the arts in northeastern and eastern Zaire. Specimens from the Lega and Mangbetu, however, suggested "that these two localities may in the future become designated as the seats of distinctive styles." Several sculptures that had already been illustrated (e.g., the L. Carré and the A. Stoclet ivory masks) were reproduced repetitiously in the few publications that considered Lega art.

In contrast with these crude or subjective analyses, Olbrechts (1946, pp. 37, 39, 64, 84, 87, 90–91, pls. 177–179, 198, figs. 12 j–k, 17, 36) was more objective. He included Lega art in his northeastern style region at the periphery of the Luba style complex, with the Zimba (Binja) forming a gradual transition between Lega and Luba. The general sculptural poverty of the northeastern region was offset in the south by the "rich sculpture" of the Lega, who together with the Bembe had been strongly influenced by Luba styles. The "productive but not extensive" Lega center linked the realistic art of the southeast with the stylized arts of the north. Lega art (mainly in ivory) was characterized by its "consistent and impressive stylization, its patination, and its compactness." Olbrechts divided the artistic output into two groups: ivory and rare wooden masks, and male and female anthropomorphic figurines, mostly in ivory. The oval masks of the Lega had style characteristics in common with the figurines: a convex face in which a flat or concave space was delineated by the eyebrows, the cheekbones, and the lower lip; eyes, nose, and mouth were carved in relief. The heaviness of the swellings between hips and knees or between knees and ankles was striking in the figurines.

It was uncertain whether the morphological diversity otherwise noticeable in the figurines was owing to regional or individual differences. The face was sometimes elongated as in the masks, or lozenge-shaped; the head was occasionally round and heavy like the rest of the body; eyes were often cowrie-shaped or were fashioned of real cowries. Nowhere else in Africa could more blatant disregard for natural proportions (e.g., huge hands, thin arms) be found; fantastic human forms (e.g., huge head on one leg) were frequently seen.

Olbrechts deemed two other stylistic characteristics to have particular significance: the circle-dot motif and the "concave-face" type. The circle-dot was applied to some pieces to indicate the eyes; in other sculptures it was used for decorative (not for representational) purposes. Although widespread in the world, this characteristic motif seemed to be linked with Islamic influence in this part of eastern Zaire. The concave-face type (rendered on a spherical head or a convex mask form) was found from the Lega to the Fang in Gabon, and among the Zande, Mitoko, Ngbaka, Gobu, Togbo, and Bolia in Zaire, but it was absent from the southern Zaire style regions. A great deal of Lega ivory sculpture functioned within the "moami sect," but most of its ritual and social significance was undocumented.

Olbrechts's classification and morphological characterization were significant and innovative in the light of earlier discussions of Lega art. His work obviously dealt with only a small sample of Lega figurines and masks. He understated the importance of wood carvings, overstated the number of ivory masks, simplified the extreme diversity of forms, and ignored other types of sculptures (zoomorphic figurines, spoons, axes, billhooks, knives, hammers, dice, etc.). The most striking omissions from Olbrechts's writing (and a fortiori in those of his predecessors) are the socioritual contexts of the artworks.

Neglect of already documented information about these contexts persisted for many years after publication of Olbrechts's work, and it has not entirely subsided (e.g., Griaule, 1947; Wingert, 1947, 1950; Kochnitzky, 1948; Maesen, 1950; Olbrechts, 1951; Périer, 1952; Radin and Sweeney, 1952; Lavachery, 1954). Many recent works on African art seriously understate or misrepresent the scope, diversity, and significance of Lega sculpture and its context.

It is important to assemble the data available by 1946 about Lega art and its context. The principal published sources are Cordella (1906, pp. 974–975), Delhaise (1909b, pp. 23, 94, 103, 133, 199–201, 209–210, 227–239, 245, 275, 337–343; pls. 23, 94, 103, 133), Maes (1924, 1933), and Moeller (1936). Unpublished documents include the information on collected objects at the Musée royal de l'Afrique centrale (Tervuren, Dossiers, 1930–31 by Ledocte and Corbisier, Baude, and Zographakis; 1938 by Van Hooren) and elsewhere (e.g., Stockholm, Berlin). Less readily attainable are reports written between 1916 and 1931 by colonial administrators (Corbisier, de Villenfagne de Loën, Fassin, Fivé, Laurent, Marmitte, Merlot, Pestiaux, Schwers, Teeuwen, Uyttebroeck,

Voukovitch, Van de Ghinste). The following synthesis is constructed from all these sources. In view of the paucity of data incorporated in catalogs and art books, they offer valuable information.

The central element in Lega culture and society is the bwami association (variously referred to as moami, mwami, or buami sect or secret society), which dates from the beginnings of Lega society. Through an elaborate system of initiations it spread among the component Lega units and also to fractions of neighboring groups (Bembe, Binja, Kanu, Komo). Bwami exhibits structural and organizational features in common with associations of adjoining populations (Songola, Ngengele, Binja, Komo, Nyanga). Bwami consists of a hierarchy of grades for males and females, although the sources differ on the number and the names of these grades. In principle, accession is open to all Lega males and their wives through initiations that are kept secret from outsiders and noninitiates. The rites require the participation of initiates from different villages, long preparations, and distributions of goods. Uyttebroeck (1935) was the first to note the aspects of social structure which are reflected in the bwami organization: the significant role of maternal uncles (mother's and father's mother's group; mother's mother's and father's father's mother's lineages), of the *nenekisi* (master of the land), and of the preceptor (whom Uyttebroeck regards as a guardian of custom and jurisprudence).

The initiations center on dances, songs, speeches, and artworks. The initiates receive paraphernalia and insignia appropriate to their rank. The most frequently mentioned artworks are wooden and ivory masks, anthropomorphic and zoomorphic figurines, ivory spoons, and phallus-shaped ivories. The figurines are male, female, or asexual; they are sometimes multifrontal or extraordinary stylizations (e.g., a large head on a single leg). Masks are worn on the face or on the forehead or are carried in the hands in a dance context. After removing the figurines from a closed initiation house in the center of the village, the initiates hold them in their hands or place them on the ground. Most sources link the manipulation of sculptures with the highest grade (kindi), but at least one author mentions masks in the context of the second-highest grade (yananio). The objects are taken to the initiation house before the dances, but they are usually guarded by initiated women on behalf of their initiated husbands.

The authors call masks *kingungungu, gande, kibome, kalimu, lukungu lwa kindi, binumbi, lukwakongo lwa lubumbu* (sic) *lwa yananio*. Generic terms for anthropomorphic figurines, such as *kalimbangoma, tulimbangoma,* or *nyasombo* (sic), are rarely cited, but specific names (often misspelled) are used: Sakasala, Keitula, Kalaga, Kasisi ya kindi (sic), Kiniembe, Kilinga, Golombe, Yinga. Most of the sources provide valuable but unexplained documentation. Merlot (1931*a*−*b*) gives the most extensive terminology and explanations. He describes figurines (probably wooden, as the author speaks about their whitened faces) used in *mosagi* (sic; probably musage wa kindi): Kakulu ka mpinda (an asexual figurine representing an old man); Muzumbi (a man) and Wayinda (his wife who died while pregnant); Kasongalala (a figurine with raised arm, the hand held in a protective gesture; Merlot thinks it is a divinity); Mwelwa (a man); Kabalama

and Katembo (women); Samukulusongo (a figurine with spread legs; a prosti-
tute); Kimatemate (a bifrontal head on a pole). Merlot also designates other
objects: an ivory phallus (*katimbitimbi*), an ivory pounder (*moketo,* sic), and an
elongated quadruped on short legs representing a dog (*mukukundu,* sic). One
source calls the animal figurines *mugugu* or *mbwa za kindi;* another identifies
twin animal figurines as *wamuse* and *musiramu.*

There is little or no information about the meaning of these terms or about
the songs and dances associated with the objects. Zographakis claims that a
stone head represents the kindi initiate. Delhaise does suggest some meanings:
one sculpture depicts a person who sees everything, one is symbolic of evil, one
is an emblem of hospitality and another of friendly understanding; a female
figurine with swollen belly refers to the dangers of infidelity, while another
suggests an evil and overly inquisitive woman. Although Delhaise applied the
term "fetish" to the sculptures, he notes that the Lega "n'invoquent pas les
fétiches, ils ne leur demandent rien et ne s'occupent d'eux que dans le mpara
[initiation]." Delhaise nevertheless concludes that the fetishes exhibited during
the initiations have certain magical properties: they protect fields, procure
game, punish evildoers, preside over death, and oversee everything. In a similar manner, Ledocte and Corbisier note that the objects are not "fétiches" but
simple insignia that enable kindi initiates to identify themselves. Only noninitiates, who never see the mysterious objects, believe they have an occult power.

Among other carvings, ivory spoons are said to be used either by kindi for
eating or for administering medicines to the sick. Cordella describes phallic
sculptures that women hang from their belts. Delhaise notes that the paraphernalia of a dead initiate (who was buried in the village near or on the threshold of
his house) are placed on his tomb. The skull of a dead kindi is preserved as a
reliquary in the house; when the dead man's son achieves kindi, the skull is
placed in a small shrine built on poles near his house. Hautmann (Tervuren,
Dossier 1045 of 1940) has seen similar constructions in which the reddened
skull was visible; an offering of cassava and bananas was placed before the
skull in an iron pot.

Maes concludes that the bwami rites confer upon initiates the privilege of
owning the highly symbolic sculptures. Moeller, however, speaks about the
display of male and female figurines (with large genitalia) within the enclosure
where the circumcision takes place (note that these rites are organized by members of bwami).

Much of the information given in these pre-1946 sources, although sketchy, is
correct. It is surprising that so little of it was used in publications on African art.

From 1950 to 1981 Lega sculpture has received increasing attention in exhibition and sales catalogs, museum inventories, and handbooks on African art.
Few of them fail to take notice of the Lega, who tend to be placed with other
northeastern Zaire peoples at the end of surveys because most authors follow a
geographical progression from west to east. The range of illustrated artworks
has broadened, in contrast with the period when most of the objects reproduced, mainly ivory figurines and masks, belonged to a very few private and

public collections. Scholars and connoisseurs have come to recognize the diversity of forms and materials in Lega sculpture: maskettes as well as larger masks, anthropomorphic and zoomorphic figurines, and a wide range of other sculptures including spoons, billhooks, knives, ax blades, hammers, dice, pegs, pins, pounders, and phalli, some of which are miniature replicas in ivory and bone of larger objects. Lega artists have not worked primarily in ivory, as has been suggested, but also in bone, wood, stone, resin, copal, clay, elephant leather, and *ntutu*. As the extraordinary diversity of form and of morphological detail within each category of sculpture has been acknowledged to some extent, changes have been made in the characterizations of Lega style and its relationships to other style areas of Zaire. There has been a tendency to categorize the Lega and some related units as a distinctive style group or region. Little effort has been made, however, to place the multiple types of Lega art into morphological and thematic categories. The least progress has been made in incorporating into general works on African art the known data about socioritual and ideological contexts, and about uses, functions, and meanings of the artworks. Some of the old stereotyped generalizations and unverified simplifications continue to plague writers of treatises that include Lega art.

Some authors still prefer the Swahili term "Warega" to the correct spelling of Balega (Lega). They see no aesthetic merit in Lega art and are unable to distinguish genuine Lega art from degenerate, fake, or modernistic pseudo-Lega sculpture. Too many others are still guilty of making loose, unrelated, haphazard, and uncritical statements. In some instances an amazing trend has emerged: a Lega term, sometimes misspelled and certainly misused, is placed as a caption under a sculpture that was not identified in the field situation but was found undocumented in some collection. This feat is apparently accomplished through the method of comparative guesswork. Numerous authors (e.g., Thompson, 1974; Rosefielde, 1977; Fry [Delange], 1978; Anderson, 1979; Brain, 1980; Celenko, 1980; Sieber, 1980) fortunately have incorporated substantive Lega data in their recent works. Because the scope of Lega sculpture is so much broader than the stereotypes and generalizations about African art would suggest, because its analysis requires so many nuanced statements, some authors find it easier simply to dismiss the bulk of the evidence.

PART ONE

The Bwami Association and Lega Art

Organizational Aspects

Sculptures are the privileged possessions of members, both male and female, of the bwami association, which dominates the social and cultural life of the Lega. Spread over three administrative territories or zones (Shabunda, Mwenga, and Pangi) in eastern Zaire, the Lega comprise six subgroupings, herein labeled as follows:

1. Northern Lega: the Bakisi group of the Shabunda zone including subgroups such as Bakyunga, Banangoma, Banangabo, Beigala, and Bamuguba as well as numerous smaller incorporated units. The Liga form the transition with the northeastern Basimwenda (diagrams 4, 5 in appendix).

2. Western Lega: the Beia and Babene groups of the Pangi zone including subgroupings among the Beia: Beianangi, Beiankuku, Banasalu, Beiamisisi, Beiamunsange, Baziri, Banalyuba, Banameya, and Banakeigo; and among the Babene: Banamunwa, Banisanga, Bagilanzelu, Batoba, and numerous smaller units (diagram 7 in appendix).

3. Southern Lega: the Bakabango of Kasambula and Kama of the Pangi zone with the subgroups Babongolo, Banangabi, Banikinga, Banakinkalo, Banasunguli, Banalila, Balambia, Banakasyele, Banamombo, and Banantandu (diagram 6).

4. Southeastern Lega: the Bakabango (of Moligi) of the Shabunda zone incorporating the subgroups Babongolo, Bayoma, Banakinkalo, Basitabyale, Banakasila, Bakusa, Bakila, Bakabondo, Bagalia, Banakasyele, and numerous others (diagram 6).

5. Eastern Lega: the Bamuzimu (of Longangi) of the Mwenga zone with the subgroups Bakuti, Basi'asa, Balimbikyi, Basisemu'a, Bazyara, Banamukabo, Basisunge, Bouse, Bagunga, Basimbi, Basi'umbilwa, and Basitabyale (diagrams 2, 6).

6. Northeastern Lega: the Basimwenda (of Alenga) of Mwenga zone including subdivisions such as Basimwenda, Basi'amena, Bamunda, Basimkobe, Basitonga, Basilubanda, Balimbikyi, Basitabyale, Bagezi, Balobola, and Babundu (diagrams 1, 2).

The Lega have many historical and cultural relationships with subgroups settled among their neighbors: in the north with the Binja, Bemo, Bakwame, Bakanu, and Bakonjo; in the east with the Havu, Shi, Nyindu, and Bembe; in the southeast with the Bembe; in the south with the Batali, Binja (Zimba), and Bangubangu; in the west and northwest with the Binja, Songola, and Babile of Nkumba. Among the northern neighbors (Vira, Shi, Havu, Tembo, Hunde, Nyanga, and farther north to Mount Ruwenzori) of the Lega, various ancient groups are considered to be of Lega stock. These remnant Lega, together with Pygmies, frequently hold important ritual offices in connection with the enthronement of chiefs.

The hierarchical structure of the bwami association is based on complementary grades for men and women. Despite variations in details of the rites, the basic terminology for grades and levels and their hierarchical sequence are remarkably consistent among northern, western, southern, and southeastern Lega. Major deviations mark the northeastern and eastern Lega, the Bembe, and the Nyindu.

The following nomenclature of bwami grades in hierarchical order is used in this volume:

kongabulumbu
kansilembo
bombwa
ngandu
bulonda
yananio
      levels: musage wa yananio
              lutumbo lwa yananio
kindi
      levels: milungu za kindi
              kyogo kya kindi
              musage wa kindi
              lutumbo lwa kindi
bunyamwa

This outline requires explanation:

1. The bombwa, bulonda, and bunyamwa initiations for women, in which men usually participate, are linked inseparably with ngandu, yananio, and kindi.

2. In some communities initiations do not go beyond ngandu or yananio, either because the higher grades were never introduced among them or because they were lost as the result of proscriptions. A score of Bakabango-Babongolo lineages stop at the ngandu grade because, having lost all their *musanga* shell money (necessary for payments and gifts) in early warfare, they were never able to "buy" the higher rites. The Bakuti among the Bamuzimu abandoned yananio because several persons initiated to that grade four generations ago died in rapid succession.

3. In most northern and in several southeastern Lega groups, *mpunju* (or *mpunzu*) is a separate initiation preceding ngandu. Among the Nyanga and some Komo and Lengola, *mpunju*, also known as *mbuntsu*, forms a different association.

4. In some northern and northeastern groups, the *bubake* initiation precedes *mpunju* and ngandu. In other groups *bubake* is a special rite incorporated into kongabulumbu. An initiated man with many wives and sons selects a preferred son (*ngoli*) to be his possible successor. Through *bubake,* he bestows upon *ngoli* the privilege of participating, even though the son is still of low rank, in all higher initiations except for certain exclusive rites, such as *mukumbi* and *kasisi* in yananio and *bele muno* in kindi. The term *bubake* is

related to *mubake,* a title the Nyanga and Hunde give to a ruler who is born of a chief and his ritual wife (a half sister or niece) and selected and enthroned by a college of ritual experts.

5. Initiation to each grade is based on a sequence of rites or ritual phases. In some communities a particular ritual phase is mentioned separately as the final closure of the grade (e.g., the *kasisi* or *yango* rite of lutumbo lwa yananio) or as transitional or preliminary to the higher grade (e.g., the *muzigi* rite between bombwa and bulonda). The actual initiations to the higher grades are preceded by stereotyped ritual activities that are part of the essential preparations. The preliminaries to a lutumbo lwa yananio initiation include *mukano, kimpilinda,* and *musigo.* For *mukano,* after the candidate has amassed the necessary fees and gifts, he and his tutor invite a number of high initiates (agnates, cognates, affines) to make a formal inspection of the goods. These initiates receive shell money and food and usually encourage the candidate to find more valuables. If he is successful the initiates return for a new appraisal; if satisfied, they authorize the building of the initiation house, as the candidate continues his search for more valuables. During *kimpilinda* the high initiates again visit the candidate; they prepare the reed swatters (*masandi*) used by messengers to invite other bwami members to the ceremonies. They also make the *byanda* trails at the outskirts of the village, which function as a ceremonial crossroads. An initiate approaching the village must decide whether to enter it or bypass it. If he crosses the *byanda* he must participate in the coming rites. New payments and gifts are made on these occasions. Special fees are required if the candidate's father died without having been initiated. By the beginning of *musigo,* most of the invited initiates have arrived; *kamondo* dances are held during the waiting period. The candidate then makes prescribed payments to his senior and junior tutors and to the person bringing the collectively owned initiation objects. He also presents *mwikio* gifts to his close agnatic relations. The actual initiations start only after these requirements have been fulfilled. No institutionalized proceedings follow the yananio rites, but after lutumbo lwa kindi the candidate receives *muyolelo* gifts (see below) in his own and other villages.

In principle, all circumcised males and the wives of initiates have access to the bwami association, which sets psychological, intellectual, moral, social, and economic standards for membership. The criteria increase in complexity as one moves from the lower to the higher grades. It is impossible to initiate to a bwami grade an uncircumcised man or a woman whose husband is not a member. A man who has no wife cannot advance to the higher grades. The linkage between husband and wife is so crucial that when a man achieves yananio or kindi, at least one of his wives must be initiated to the corresponding bulonda or bunyamwa grade, except that at the lowest kongabulumbu rites a young kinswoman (called *kigogo* or *mombo*) of the candidate is briefly introduced to a rite that inculcates principles of fidelity, restraint, respect, and moral integrity. Without the support of kinsfolk (members of one's own agnatic group as well as affines and cognates), and without tutorship by an initiated kinsman of appropriate status, one cannot be successful in the quest for membership in bwami.

In traditional society all men aspired to become members of the bwami association. The "things" of bwami are coveted (*kilembo*) by all. Men hope to achieve the highest possible grades, but few get to the summit, for "those who suffer from dizziness return at the intersection of the branches." Reaching the top grades means high status in the society, fame, power and authority, privileges and duties, and quasi immunity; it also holds the promise of wealth: "He will not be poor anymore, he who rests against the yango pole." At all levels, members must keep in mind the teachings of bwami: "Everything goes to sleep, Hole-of-Anus does not sleep." Even at night the initiate thinks about the lessons of the fathers which are the guidelines for his life and actions. The candidate must show restraint, assiduity, and piety. Throughout the rites he must display humility, patience, and equanimity. A depraved person has no chance of success. The candidate must also be able to provide the ever increasing amounts of food and commodities required as gifts and payments.

Behind the decision-making process lie the principles of social and spatial structure. The segmentary lineages and clans of the Lega are historically, spatially, ritually, and socially either linked with one another or completely separate. Lega individuals and groups trace nonagnatic links with several lineages of maternal uncles and sororal nephews, as well as with various sets of affines. They also cultivate, through friendship and geographical proximity, special bonds between individuals and groups. People are settled in hamlets and villages, and villages are organized into clusters. The resulting patterns of autonomy and interdependency affect the priorities and the limitations set by groups and individuals for the initiations. The higher the grade, the more complex the rules that govern selection and induction of candidates. The initiation process always involves members of agnatic lineages, clans, or linked clans as well as initiates of nonagnatically related groups (maternal uncles, sororal nephews, in-laws). In this way the association fosters solidarity between individuals and groups, cutting across historical linkages and bonds of kinship.

The special statuses and functions within the bwami association may be permanent, transitional, or temporary. Each high initiate of kindi traditionally has his own aide-de-camp (*kalombola*); the yananio of an autonomous group share one such person. Usually an aide-de-camp is a close agnatic relative of lower grade (ngandu). *Kalombola* serve as messengers and are charged with whitening or oiling the sculptures; they also supervise the women's work. They prepare the food for some exclusively male rites.

Some initiates act as tutors and sponsors for candidates; at the highest levels a candidate may have several tutors with specified tasks. Other initiates are trusted with temporary or permanent possession of collectively owned initiation objects. Some of them are recent initiates who must transfer the objects during the rites to the new mwami. Others are the most senior living incumbents of a certain grade within a given ritual community. (Seniority is determined not by the kinship structure but by the chronological sequence in which they or their lineage achieved the grade.) Still others are particularly intelligent and trustworthy persons or expert preceptors (*nsingia*) excelling in knowledge of texts, dances, and the usage and manipulation of the objects.

The work of the *nsingia* (also referred to as *kalingania*, thinker) is vital to the success of the initiations. In high-level ceremonies several preceptors and their aides (or apprentices) may cooperate in the actual performance of the rites. The preceptor is in charge of the spiritual aspects, just as the tutor and his aides plan the organization of the rites. Preceptors are of the three highest male grades (ngandu, yananio, kindi); kindi may preside over all initiations, but ngandu cannot function above their own level. A preceptor does not inherit his position; he has to learn how to serve in it. The job requires skill and vocation, yet kinship bonds play a part in the choice of apprentices. In one instance a famed *nsingia*, whose knowledge and skills I admired, had early in his youth shown interest and skill in drumming. Although a preceptor is not primarily a drummer, he does interact closely with drummers, and in certain rites he beats a suspended drum. This *nsingia*'s father, also a preceptor, had helped his son reach the kongabulumbu grade and then had sent him for apprenticeship to a famed preceptor belonging to a group that stands in a perpetual sororal nephew relationship with father and son. The son accompanied the master on all his professional trips and later on became an outstanding preceptor-exegete-dancer himself; he had also reached the kindi grade. At the time of my research he was instructing a sororal nephew, who had already been initiated to musage wa yananio.

In other instances different patterns were followed: one preceptor had been trained by a maternal uncle and by two other experts belonging to separate lineages of his clan; another had learned from a senior half brother, who had been instructed by his father's sororal nephew; the latter had learned it from that man's father, who had continued his own father's tradition. A preceptor is highly respected, and a good one enjoys fame and may lay claim to payments, gifts, and particular rights (e.g., he may own certain objects that others do not commonly have).

Initiation Rites (*Mpala*)

In order to achieve any grade level, the candidate and his kin, with the help of tutors and advisers, make careful and, for higher levels, extremely elaborate preparations. To the noninitiate and candidate alike the initiation process is complex ("The initiates build the little house of many affairs"), difficult ("Little-Knife begins to clear the dense growth of vines"), endless ("Bwami that father Itula has danced is *katondo*," i.e., like a tall tree in which eagles like to nest), and dangerous ("I climb over the back of Ndezi [Big Leopard], I die of fear"). After the preliminary activities are deemed adequate by the initiates of a particular group, the members are ready to start the rites. Whatever grade level is being sought, the rites are structured on common principles. They always include dramatic performances; presentation, interpretation, and transfer of paraphernalia, insignia, and other initiation objects; and distributions of food, gifts, and payments.

During the waiting period that follows the preparatory arrangements and the acceptance of the candidate, the invited initiates begin to gather in his village; for the higher levels the interlude may last several days. During this time the initiates engage in *kamondo* performances, public dances during which aphorisms are sung but no initiation objects are used. The initiations for any grade, whether they last one day or longer, are divided into distinctive phases. Some performances take place during the day; others are set for the very early morning, for the late afternoon, or for the darkness of night. The dramatic performances vary for the different phases, but in general they proceed as follows.

1. Activities outside the initiation house

   Ceremonies begin on the village dance floor with a solemn entry. The male and female initiates in full regalia arrive in the village in one or two groups, carrying shoulder bags, baskets, reed swatters, or wickerwork rattles. Two or four initiates, remaining silent, sit on stools between the incoming initiates and the initiation house, where the candidate and his tutor await them (pl. 6). Then follow dances by all initiates, in small groups or singly; they may be performed by males only, by females only, or by both sexes. Solo and group dances are often combined; initiation objects are manipulated during the dances, usually by one or several preceptors, sometimes by all participants (pls. 12–13). The objects are simply held in the hands or worn on the body; they are passed along from one dancer to another; they are moved around, left on the ground or on a fence, or held by sitting persons while the initiates perform dances or engage in other dramatic activities around them. In some rites objects are taken into and brought out of the initiation house; in others the initiates bring paraphernalia from behind the houses or from the forest. Dances by one or two soloists follow. Specially dressed in hides, cloth, feather bunches, and masks, they vividly represent typical characters (e.g., a person suffering from scrotal hernia, an old man, a hunter). Dramatic action takes place around the initiation house or on housetops (e.g., sitting on the roof hiding something; crossing the roof by means of a ladder).

   A solemn and silent display of artworks is arranged outside the village in the nearby forest. Secret rites, held in a specially built shack or near a brook, may include ablutions or formal inspection of the contents of baskets before they are brought to the village.

2. Activities inside the initiation house

   Most presentations of configurations of objects, as well as the oiling and whitening of sculptures, take place inside this house. Each rite involving configurations begins with the preparation of the display; this task is performed without music or dance and in the absence of the candidate. The tutor then brings the candidate to the house, a procedure that may include a vividly enacted rite of passage. The candidate, received by a leading preceptor, is led or carried around the configuration and then is seated on the ground. The systematic exegesis of the objects is undertaken by the preceptors, who dance and execute various movements with them, point at them, or pass them around, while the other initiates sit along the walls of the house. In certain rare rites assemblages and sculptures are specially displayed. Other rites may include the ritual killing of a goat by suffocating it or breaking its spine, the mock seducing of an unmarried woman (close relative of the candidate), or the enacting of games, divinations, poison ordeals, or burials.

3. Removal to a new village

This elaborate rite of passage is performed only at the end of the highest lutumbo lwa kindi initiation. The ceremonies in the candidate's village conclude with the "skinning of the elephant," that is, with the removal and burning of all leaves placed on the roofs of the initiation house and of other dwellings. This action also signals the departure of all participating initiates. The next morning the tutor leads the new initiate, his wives, and his aide to *nkwaka,* a hunting shack in the forest. Located between the old village and the new one (*ligu, bukumbu*), it has been built by the initiate's kin who have already established themselves there. The tutor goes to the new village, leaving the initiate, his wives, and his aide in *nkwaka.* They stay there for two days, repeatedly bathing, oiling, and rubbing themselves with red powder, for they were not allowed to take care of their bodies during the initiations. At the end of that period the tutor and his wife lead them to the new village, where the initiate and his wife are seated on stools to receive the *musekelo,* valuable gifts offered by all his kin. On the next day the new kindi, his wife, and his aide depart to visit other villages, first those of their own clan and then those of other lineages with whom they have special cognatic and affinal ties.

Most of the initiation ceremonies are accompanied by music, but the prescribed instruments vary from rite to rite. At kongabulumbu (the lowest grade), where no drums or rattles are used, they include percussion sticks (*binkombe,* sometimes replaced by scepters, ax blades, or simple bone blades), anklet bells (made of pods), mirlitons, and a blowpipe (a hollow bamboo stem or reed blown in a pot that is either empty or filled with water). At other grade levels the instruments most frequently used are two funnel-shaped membranophone drums (the main one, *muningati,* beaten with the bare hands; the second one, *kimbili,* beaten with sticks by two drummers, one striking the membrane, the other the wooden side of the drum), a large trapezoidal slit-drum (absent in some areas), and wickerwork rattles (pl. 5). Usually the membranophones rest on the ground and are held between the legs of the drummers; in some rituals the drums hang from a string slung over one shoulder, or they are suspended from a pole. In some rare rites only the sacred mirliton (*kingili*) sings; in others music is replaced by the rubbing of leaves, or by murmuring, shouting, or imitating animal calls. In a few instances the performers are silent.

All the songs that accompany the music consist of short aphoristic statements. The words are repeated by the choir and by the dancers for the duration of a particular dance. The choir, composed of male and female initiates, some of whom shake rattles, sits behind the drummers. One of the choir members is Nyagwamana or Nyawendidungu, usually a woman who has learned to sing in a high-pitched, strident voice. For each separate song and dance sequence, the preceptor and his aides stand in front of the drummers. The *kimbili* drum starts the melody; the choir sings without words to the tune of the drum beat; the preceptor gives the song text; the *muningati* drum picks up the rhythm. When singers, drums, and rattles are in unison (*kilunga*), the preceptor and his aides move away to lead a row of dancers.

The participants in the initiation drama thus include four main categories:

1. The candidate and his tutor(s).
2. The preceptor(s) and aides.
3. The musicians (percussionists in some rites; drummers in others) and the choir of initiated men, some of whom shake rattles, and women, including Nyagwamana (a role sometimes assumed by a man).
4. The other initiates, male and female, of different initiatory level for all grades below lutumbo lwa kindi. They include both close and remote agnates, cognates, and in-laws. For some rites only men are admitted, for others only women, but on most occasions both sexes take part in the dances. Among the initiates is the *mukomi,* who holds the collectively owned objects that will be transferred to the new initiate.

A typical initiation, whether lasting for one day (kongabulumbu) or extending for several (yananio and kindi), is made up of a series of named rites. One of them, which centers on one object, or perhaps more, is characterized by a sequence of dances. Each dance is correlated with an aphorism sung by the participating initiates as they dance around a configuration of objects or collect them one by one to show and interpret them in the dance context. Some dances portray characters, situations, or activities, including an old gambler; a sick person; a seducer; a hunting, trapping, harvesting, or fishing party; a divination or a gambling scene; a poison ordeal; a mock quarrel or fight; a withdrawal from battle; and an ambush. As noted above, a few rites include solemn processions, ceremonial entries of the candidate supported by his tutors, or preparation and observation of initiation objects.

Some ritual performances achieve high comedy or drama, particularly when behavioral excesses are parodied or criticized. In one example a preceptor impersonates an old man hopelessly addicted to the game of dice. Heavily loaded with bags, bells, and paraphernalia (in other words, all his movable possessions), he arrives at the outskirts of the village. Called Isabambabamba (Mr. Stakes-Stakes), he is traveling "in a spirit of provocation" (*kalingi*) to play the game in the village of Nyamunyungu za Baitindi (Arrogant-One of the Passionate Players). The actor supports himself painfully with a walking stick, with a leaf covering a large leg wound. As he approaches the village he anxiously asks where the game is taking place, halting repeatedly to chase flies away from his wound. He arrives in the village of the Baitindi (the village of the candidate), where he wants to establish himself. His voice is raucous and sickly; his fingers are crippled by disease. He immediately starts a brawl with the village head-man. Bystanders quietly advise the old man to settle down, asking: "How will you, an old and sickly man, fight?" The game is now ready to begin, but the old man is impatient and irascible. Chasing flies and scratching his head, he pro-vocatively throws all his possessions down in front of his adversary (the candi-date). When one player is about to throw the dice, the old man interferes, telling the player that he knows nothing about the game. When the dice are thrown the old man shouts, "I win," and takes back his possessions. As the game con-tinues amid confusion and aggressiveness, the choir sings aphorisms castigating the behavior of the old man. He is likened to a chimpanzee and a monkey: "Musile [Monkey] came to the game of the Baitindi, he wanted to argue with the winner, he the sole loser"; "Nsoko [Chimpanzee] came to the game of the Baitindi, he lost; he pursed the lips [in anger] and nothing again came out [of his mouth]." Although the performance had excellent comic effects, its purpose was not simply to amuse. It criticized excessive gaming and quarrelsomeness, and it also warned an initiate not to throw the dice when playing the *mbali* game. The drama, intended mainly to caution the candidate not to be impa-tient, meddlesome, or belligerent, also urged him to be passive and discreet.

Some dances present highly suggestive scenes of mock seduction, including touching, coital movements with or without carved phalli, reaching for each other's penes, flooring and sleeping on a person, and lying on one's back with legs spread wide. Other dances imply anger, challenge, quarrels, and fighting by pulling the lower eyelid, sticking out the tongue, brandishing stools or sticks, or throwing things on the floor. In some scenes scorn and rejection are symbolized by bending the lower lip, turning the back to each other, or snap-ping the fingers; refusal is indicated by shaking the head. Objects placed upside down signify opposition, change, prohibition, or nonparticipation. Zigzag movements depict people who follow the long rather than the short path to achievement of a goal, but zigzagging in loops between standing persons de-notes a sense of continuity. Circling persons, houses, or objects evokes prohibi-tion, trickery, danger, trouble, or a secret pact to kill. Sorrow is expressed by crawling on knees and elbows; climbing and descending mean wealth and pov-erty, impossibility, danger, and dizziness. Walking while holding the big toes or the calves denotes an invalid or a sick person who should not be mocked. Other concepts are expressed in the performances, such as group unity by jointly holding a vine or a feather rope; dispersal of initiation objects because of war by rolling objects over the ground; and scorn and hate by blowing in shells.

Some presentations are inspired by communal activities such as hunting with nets and dogs; gathering honey, termites, or mushrooms; tree felling; smithing; making bark cloth; and harvesting bananas. Animals and their habits, including the sounds they produce, are vividly enacted: a hunting dog, a dwarf antelope, a pangolin, a chimpanzee, a monkey, and a snake.

In most group dances the males, aligned by grade level and always led by preceptors and followed by the women, form a circle or a row. Several dancers or a soloist may move away from the group to perform a separate dance; sometimes the circle is broken when some of the men dance toward the women or the initiation house. At the beginning of the dance the initiates usually perform a slow *nsombi* movement, which gradually becomes faster and livelier, particularly when they start to handle objects. The dancers frequently make half-turns, facing one another's backs, then facing the center of the circle or turning their backs to it. A nervous rhythm accompanied by shivering movement of the hips (*luzanzia*) is highly appreciated. Preceptors excel in dance fantasies (*tungeningeni*). When the dancers are not holding objects they make rhythmic movements with their hands (*kwandizia*), such as pointing their outstretched fingers downward or caressing their aprons (*kupola*) as a sign of joy. A drummer is sometimes honored by a dancer who moves toward him and dries his sweat; occasionally the candidate's limbs are pulled (*kunanuna*) to communicate force.

Dance sequences and rites are interspersed with gift giving, both prescribed and optional, payments of fees, and distributions of food supplies. During the interludes the initiates relax, eat, and discuss matters in small groups. A rite may be delayed because the required supplies of animals have not yet been secured by the young hunters.

Economic transactions are complex in kindi and yananio initiations but much simpler in lower rites. By the time a kindi acquires the masks and figurines, a fortune has been accumulated and distributed among initiates and kinsfolk (agnates, cognates, and in-laws). The major commodities circulated as payments or gifts are shell money, necklaces, bracelets and bangles, packs of salt, packages of resin torches, jars of oil, goats, and game meat (sometimes of prescribed species of antelopes). In addition to meat, oil, and salt, food distributions include plantain bananas and pounded peanuts.

The following synopsis, though lacking details, suggests the exchange procedures in lutumbo lwa kindi.

1. The preparatory period

    The candidate assembles the required goods by his own labor, by playing the *mbali* game, by purchases, and through kinship cooperation. He visits or sends messengers to agnatic, cognatic, and affinal relatives to solicit goods (*mululo*). The goods are given to him as outright gifts or as liens against marriage payments received for his daughters and sisters or as a partial return of the bridewealth he gave for his wives. High-level initiates are invited to make formal inspection (*mukano*) of the quality and appropriateness of the accumulated goods. A powerful, wealthy candidate usually shows only part of what he has, keeping the rest in hiding (*mbiso*). If the goods are deemed insufficient, the candidate has to contact more relatives and then proceed with a new *mukano*. Food and gifts are offered to the inspectors.

2. The actual initiations

Large distributions of various commodities are required:

a. *Kililo* or *kilisio:* food.

b. *Nkindo:* small donations of shell money presented individually to musicians, singers, preceptors, and dancers during performances.

c. *Kukinduzia bana ba tata:* special compensation as recognition of status for close senior agnates (e.g., a senior brother, a little father) of lower grade than the level sought by the candidate.

d. *Mwikio:* prescribed fees for certain ritual phases of the initiations. In kindi, for example, fees are paid for at least thirteen phases, including those in which masks and figurines are displayed. These payments, made in one sum, are shared by the participating kindi according to seniority and individual functions in the rite. When the initiates ceremonially enter the village, a welcome gift (*musekelo we isengo*) is placed on the collectively owned baskets containing the initiation objects.

e. *Musigo:* prescribed fees given to specified individuals the day after the *bele muno* rite (secret display of the figurines). Recipients include *mukomi,* the most recent initiate, who transfers the collectively owned basket to the new initiate; *kakusa,* the experienced tutor who has watched over all procedures and has assured the distributions of goods; *kilezi,* a second tutor who supports (physically and morally) the candidate during the rites; *mwikalizi* (or *kilego*), a powerful kindi (often a maternal uncle or sororal nephew of the candidate) who plays a vital role in expediting the procedures. Smaller payments are made to the *basula,* trustworthy initiates who witness the payments.

f. *Bikulo bya kitampo:* exceptional fines imposed because of a transgression or nonobservance of a kindi prescription.

g. *Minganangana:* a distribution coinciding with the final rite *ibago lya nzogu* (lit., the skinning of the elephant), the partial demolition of the initiation house. The payments are compulsory gifts to close agnatic, affinal, and cognatic relatives who in the preparatory stages helped accumulate the necessary goods.

h. *Kukinduzia:* a dinner for relatives of lower grades who did not assist in the rites but performed such tasks as supplying game, water, or firewood. The female bunyamwa rites are intermingled with those of lutumbo lwa kindi. As no mortuary payments (*idigo*) can be made to her group when a kanyamwa woman dies, the candidate compensates the fathers or brothers of his wives who are being initiated.

3. After the initiations

The new kindi leaves his old village and settles in a new one, where many of his coresident kin are already established.

a. *Muyolelo:* the kindi receives gifts from the villagers.

b. *Kasabalala:* he offers a dinner for all persons who worked to make the initiations successful.

c. *Muyolelo:* the new kindi goes on a tour to visit his dispersed kin, receiving gifts in each village and hamlet.

Initiation Objects

Items from the animal, vegetal, and mineral worlds, either in their natural state or transformed, are used in the rites of all grades. Birds' beaks, for example, appear in their natural form or partly wrapped in wickerwork; scales of the giant pangolin are used plain or perforated, glued or tied together. Ordinary Lega technology supplies bark and raffia cloth, baskets, shoulder bags, pots, plates, mats, nets, fire drills, torches, ropes, feather hats, pipes, necklaces, house beams, and rafters. The iron implements and weapons customarily used are replaced in the rites by smaller wooden, copper, bone, or ivory replicas of knives, billhooks, axes, hammers, spears, arrows, and shields. For bwami rites, however, a special technology produces skullcaps (pl. 8), hats (pl. 9), coronets, diadems, necklaces, belts, aprons, collarets, feather bunches, feather ropes, snakeskins trimmed with feathers or quills, miniature plank doors and dugout canoes, ajouré wickerwork shields, wooden spears (pl. 11), assemblages of natural and manufactured objects, and artworks. It is noteworthy that most of the items selected for the rites have been manufactured by men (e.g., mats, baskets, bags, plates, collarets, nets, bark and raffia cloth). Pots, red color, and oil are produced by women. Shell money, white coloring, and torches are prepared by both men and women.

From the animal world, the initiates utilize exuviae from mammals, reptiles, fish, amphibians, mollusks, birds, insects, arachnids, and myriopodes in the form of hides, skins, skulls, jaws, bones, fangs, teeth, scales, claws, carapaces, shells, pincers, quills, horns, and feathers. Although many animals are mentioned during the rites, the exuviae used most frequently are from the pangolin (scales and claws), aardvark (claws), golden mole (hide), potto (hide), porcupine (quills), dendrohyrax (outer teeth), genet (hide), dwarf antelope (paws), bongo antelope (hide), elephant (tusks, bones, molars, tail), leopard (teeth, skull), *kagelia* monkey (skull), chimpanzee (skull), forest crocodile (skull), viper (fangs), *Clarias lazera* and *Hydrocyon goliath* fish (skull, jaw), aquatic and terrestrial snail (shell), mussel (shell), hornbill (beak), *kakulikuli* bird (beak), and parrot (red tail feathers).

From the large number of animal families in Lega forests, certain ones are selected on the basis of their features. These criteria, explicitly mentioned in the texts, include anatomical and physical characteristics (e.g., scales, claws, long tongue, strong smell of the pangolin), nesting and feeding habits (e.g., the pangolin lives in holes and eats termites), predatory or nocturnal habits, types of movement (slowness, climbing, gliding), sounds produced (e.g., calls of chimpanzees, unison calls of male dendrohyraxes, chattering of birds), qualities of fierceness, strength, or shyness (e.g., the strength of the pangolin or the potto), and the associations among animals living in quasi symbiosis. The ways in which animals are hunted, trapped, and caught, their broad socioritual significance (prohibitions, privileges), and real or perceived resemblances and differences between animals also serve as guidelines. Among domestic animals, hunting dogs, chickens, and goats are selected, respectively, for their skill, their stupidity, and their fighting instinct.

Plant world specimens include bark, leaves, mosses, epiphytes, saps, resins, vines, fibers, roots, nuts, pods, seeds, branches, sticks, beams, and stipes. Plants are chosen for their anatomical and physical properties (e.g., soft or hard wood; a tree that is straight, gigantic, or slippery), the uses of their products (e.g., nuts eaten by humans regularly or only in times of hunger; ficus trees used for bark cloth; resin- or oil-producing trees), the environment in which they grow (e.g., in secondary or primary forest), their associations with other plant and animal life, their life cycles and states of decay (deciduous, dying, fallen, or cut trees), and their medicinal or magical properties. In one rite twenty-two species of leaves were interpreted symbolically. They all came from vines, trees, and shrubs that also served everyday needs: leaves used to cover roofs, wrap packages, and grill food; leaves licked every morning when the hunting nets failed, or burned and rubbed on the nets to fortify them; vines for weaving nets; trees cut for firewood and for making fences, rafters, beams, shields, and ax handles; and trees whose fruits were eaten in times of dire necessity. Banana and phrynium leaves, raffia fibers and leaves, bark from ficus trees, and *mbubi* vines are the most frequently used initiation objects from the plant world.

Fewer items are derived from the mineral world: pieces of termitaria, mud nests of insects, quartz stones, river pebbles, and earth colors. The quartz crystals are said to have been brought into Legaland by immigrating ancestors. Certain river pebbles and mud nests are selected on the basis of form; special clays, because they are coloring agents.

All insignia, paraphernalia, and dance accoutrements are acquired by the candidate during the rites. They function also as initiation objects since they are elaborately explained in dance and song contexts. Except for the candidate, all participants are dressed in full regalia during the rites (pls. 1–2, 12–14). The paraphernalia for men include skullcaps, hats (in hide and in wickerwork adorned with nutshells, cowries, beads, or buttons), necklaces (beads interspersed with teeth of leopards and other animals), belts (of vines and raffia; of bongo antelope for the highest grades), reddened bark cloth used as loincloths, and aprons of *mpaga* or genet hide. The men wear few armlets or bangles, but those that are worn often represent a special status (e.g., copper bangles worn by a man who is *bubake*). Hats in particular indicate rank; they are made of different materials and are adorned with objects (shells, pods, teeth, copper and ivory plates) according to initiatory status (Biebuyck, 1981*a*). In some rites all men may carry reed swatters or wickerwork rattles; they may wear anklet bells, fiber or leaf collarets, or feather-trimmed snakeskins. In rare ceremonies a few men may be dressed in completely white or black-dotted bark cloth that hangs loosely over the body and serves as a hood. The paraphernalia of women include beaded diadems (pl. 3), wickerwork coronets adorned with an upright piece of vine, chest and hip belts (in some areas completely stitched with cowries), reddened bark cloth aprons, feather bunches, and armlets, bracelets, and bangles in copper and iron. In rare instances women wear their husbands' hats. Men and women are rubbed with oil mixed with red powder and perfume; white dots or crossed lines are occasionally marked on a dancer's body.

Initiation objects are kept in baskets and shoulder bags (pl. 11). Baskets are linked with specific grades; in addition to animal exuviae, plants, and minerals, they may contain wooden anthropomorphic and zoomorphic figurines, masks, other carvings (a wooden arm; a miniature game board, dugout canoe, or slit-drum), and occasionally an ivory object such as a pounder or phallus, or a small elephant tusk. The almost rectangular shoulder bags, traditionally made of *lukusa* fiber or antelope hide, hold an individual's private initiation objects, including sculptures.

A single initiation object may be used in more than one rite to present analogous or complementary information; in dance context, one object may be manipulated in many different ways. Most initiation objects, except for the majority of masks and figurines, are used at different grade levels. Particular meanings are not linked exclusively with specific objects. Identical or similar songs may be sung, for example, in connection with wooden maskettes, ivory spoons, mussel shells, and chimpanzee or *nsamba* fish skulls. The overlapping of meanings, however, is never total; in other words, every distinct type of object has a point at which its symbolic connotations deviate from those of other items.

In a single rite one object may have a wide range of meanings. Take, for example, a *lubumba* mussel shell. Its name (*lubumba*) becomes the designation of a place, Kulubumba, or a village, Idambo lya Mbumba (the hunting grounds called *lubumba* shells). The shell is polished until it is white and shiny by the initiates, who say that nothing is whiter than the polished shell. The name of the shell thus comes to stand for the village Lubumba, "where it shines," that is, where the initiates dressed in all their regalia have gathered for the ceremonies. The shell is derived from a water mollusk, which is collected downstream. It is likened to a woman who runs away from her husband, but she is stopped in the village of her husband's colleagues. The shell is a valve with a convex and a concave part; when the concavity is placed upward, the shell depicts an adulterous woman. The polished shell is attached to the front of hats worn by full-fledged yananio initiates and is a distinctive symbol of that grade. It represents a status that is not readily available to any "poor man"; wearing the shell on one's hat is a privilege coveted by all men. The crescent-shaped polished valve displayed on the hat is compared with the waxing moon: just as the waxing moon is widely visible, so the fame of the initiate wearing the shell is widespread. The idea that the shell represents the moon is developed further by the use of two shells, each one held in the raised hands of two initiates dancing some distance from each other. The two shells symbolize Mwezi, the moon, and Nyasana, a star. Mwezi and Nyasana stick together and follow each other endlessly, just as the initiate and his senior initiated wife (*kalia*) are inseparably bound together.

The use of initiation objects frequently has surprising features. In many instances the manipulation of even a simple object shows an unexpected range of possibilities when combined with dramatic action. The sleeping mat (*katanda*), for example, is often used for the display of objects or as a screen to hide a masker. In one rite, however, the rolled-up mat signifies a fish trap (*kigomu*). A preceptor holding the mat under his arm dances around, saying as he displays it that tomorrow he is going to trap in the Kamiluka River. The actor and his aides then arrive near the imaginary river and place pieces of bait in the trap. A dispute develops when some of the participants decide to place the trap with the opening pointing upstream. One participant gets so angry that he threatens to throw his hat on the ground (a major taboo). Restrained by others, however, he pulls the trap out of the water, inspects it, and finds it empty. Then it is put back in the river, this time facing downstream. In the meantime another actor clears (with a leaf!) a spot near the river where the trap can be emptied, while a third gathers wood to grill the fish. A new quarrel develops over who is to remove the trap. One participant finally pulls it out and opens it, while the others stand ready to club the fish (with genet hides!). Falling out of the trap, the imaginary fish slides back into the river. An actor now sets the trap for the third time, but as he steps into the water he rummages for something and acts as if a crab has pinched his hand. He descends farther into the river, plunges his hand into the trap, and howls: a catfish has bitten his penis! The performance ends with this unsuccessful fishing party.

The scene is both a parody and a lesson. Individual traps, in contrast with those that are part of a set, are placed facing downstream. The Lega consider a person who places the traps pointing upstream to be more than stupid. The trappers are likened to a group of initiates journeying to the candidate's village for the ceremonies; some of them get involved in matters that should not concern them and about which they know nothing. The escaping fish suggest initiations that elude a candidate who indulges in self-praise; the crab pinching the hand is Nyakinkende, an arrogant woman who chases her husband's other wives. Women who eat catfish, which is strictly forbidden them, are guilty of sorcery; the image stands for a woman who desires too many men.

Initiation objects are not part of a cult; rather, they are the essential elements in an exclusive system of statuses and teachings. Initiation (*mpala*) and initiation objects (*isengo*; pl., *masengo*) are often used synonymously; initiates say: "Kikulu, the drummer, whenever they go to *isengo* [i.e., initiation] they call him." There can be no initiation rites without the display and manipulation of the appropriate items. The initiation object is thought to be "heavy" and sacred; it cannot be profaned, and it cannot be owned, interpreted, or understood by outsiders. People who lack the appropriate status may not see or touch most initiation objects (whether in use or not). The secrecy and the inviolability of *isengo* are expressed in numerous ways. In the lower kongabulumbu rites it is repeatedly noted that *masengo* are things that may cause pain, things that one must sound out (as if groping about in the dark, one must feel one's way and proceed cautiously). Dancing with a bag filled with the objects, the initiates sing—"I forget my shoulder bag in the house of the sorceress Nyakamuno [Mrs. Trap]"—to warn that a person who illicitly removes the objects from the bag may be treated as a sorcerer. Initiation objects are often compared with the porcupine trap of Kamikele wa Kyanga (Thorns-Son-of-Bent-Stick-of-Snare) or are called *lukabia* (a barricade, a construction erected as a no-trespassing sign). An unauthorized person who views a configuration of objects is guilty of a transgression (*kitampo*) of the sacred rules. *Kitampo*, a state of ritual impurity and imbalance (*lukwo*, a ritual death), means losing one's ritual status. It results from violation of the prescriptions and prohibitions of bwami, regardless of whether or not the act was involuntary, accidental, or unconscious. There is *kitampo* when an initiate's house containing the sacred objects burns, or when the small skullcap worn on the head accidentally falls to the ground. Special rituals to cleanse a person of such guilt require large payments of shell money, game, and goats as well as formal reconciliation expressed by means of the sacred *moza* blowhorn. *Moza* is the ritual instrument par excellence for such occasions (it is also blown at the end of the kongabulumbu rites or when a great initiate dies), and it is sounded after the payment of fines to signify the restoration of balance. *Kitampo* may lead to deferment of the initiations, "forced" induction into bwami, extra payments of goats, and possibly subsequent exclusion of an entire group from a certain grade level.

Other aphorisms evoke the secrecy, mystery, sacred status, and power of initiation objects. Any item selected to be *isengo* has a special fame: "Every kind of fish is [found] in the river, Nsamba [a fish whose jaws are used as *isengo*] is the famed one [the one boasted about; the celebrated one]." The *isengo* has the power to blind the noninitiate: "Know whence comes the darkness that closes the eyes." Like a needle that sews things together, the *isengo* links the past, the present, and the future. As a needle is a precious commodity that must not be lost or mislaid, so the *isengo* left by one's father or predecessor must not be relinquished. The *isengo*, kept in a shoulder bag or a basket, is the "friend" of the initiate; he understands and controls it. In the appropriate context it is his duty to teach others the meaning of the *isengo* and not to keep it for himself: "What is in there? What a man does not know, he asks about it." The truth contained in *isengo* will be revealed at the proper time: "The wife hides the pregnancy; what is in the belly will speak the truth for itself." Except for the insignia and paraphernalia worn by the initiates, all their objects are hidden and made visible only during the rites. The baskets and bags that hold the ritual equipment are carefully stored, usually in the house of the senior initiated wife, whose duty it is to preserve their secrecy and integrity.

When a high initiate dies, some of his secret initiation objects are displayed on his tomb, which is built in the house of his senior initiated wife and is protected by a designated guardian. After the prolonged mortuary ceremonies, some of the deceased's public paraphernalia (hats, aprons, belts, bags, staff, stool) are placed at the immediate outskirts of the village. These objects, untouched by anyone, must remain there as a sign, unless a high-ranking sororal nephew of the deceased decides to appropriate some of them. Except for a mask, the objects still displayed on the tomb are removed by the guardian at the end of the funerary ceremonies. He safeguards them until a successor to the deceased initiate is found; they are then transferred to him during the initiation rites. The tomb, with the remaining mask, is closed off to everyone. If the deceased was a recent initiate who still held trusteeship over a basket of collectively owned initiation objects, someone in his kinship group must immediately be initiated to take charge of the basket.

In time of warfare the *masengo* must not be burned or destroyed; they must be left alone. The same inviolability attaches to a kanyamwa woman, a blacksmith, a pregnant woman, a person taking refuge in the men's house, two kindi sitting back to back shaking their rattles to avert war, a drum, and a beer pot.

From the point of view of initiates who are in full control of the *masengo,* the objects are *kakengezio* (or *kalolesia, kakengelezio*), reminders of their status and signals to convey their messages. The term *kakengezio* evokes a person in trouble who makes marks (with a pangolin claw) on a tree or on the ground to inform his friends. The *masengo* also enable the initiate to obtain valuables, since their display requires payments and gifts. The initiation objects thus are often referred to in the following ways: "The trunk [is] the arm of the elephant to eat banana leaves"; "The ears of the big elephant, it is with the clapping of his ears that he lures them." Possession of certain objects may give initiates special status and immunity; a kindi carrying his wickerwork rattle cannot be arrested or killed. As the possessor-caretaker of some collectively owned objects has ritual seniority, he cannot hold any of the individual insignia characteristic of his rank. Some objects have transcendent powers. One ordeal requires the guilty party to drink water in which the bwami skullcap or an ivory bracelet (worn by an initiate) has been soaked. A method of curing utilizes scrapings of ivory figurines mixed with water.

Sculptures

Sculptures, an integral component of initiation objects in all areas of Legaland, come in a wide variety of types: anthropomorphic figurines and masks; zoomorphic figurines; rare figurines combining animal and human traits; spoons, some anthropomorphic; knives, scepters, axes, billhooks, hammers, phalli, pegs, pins, pounders, mortars, and oblong pieces of bone or ivory; flat dice; chips; imitation forearms; stools; bells, whistles, and horns; miniature canoes, mancala game boards, and bellows. Unusual pieces include a relief sculpture representing a vagina with penis, well-polished wooden canes topped with figurines carved separately, cephalomorphic and other well-carved knife han-

dles, and ornamented small elephant or hippopotamus tusks. Temporary assemblages of anthropomorphic or zoomorphic objects are also put together.
The sculptures are made from a variety of materials: soft, rarely hard, wood;
elephant ivory but seldom hippopotamus ivory; elephant bone; sometimes the
sole of an elephant's foot; stone, clay, termite nest soil, resin (copal), and *ntutu*
(core of dead trees).

The objects found in any local community or larger region within Legaland
may vary widely in abundance and diversity. In one area virtually all the above
types may occur in different quantities, whereas only a few may be found in
another region. This uneven distribution (to be discussed later) results from
the degree of development of grades and grade levels, the number of initiates,
and local preferences and modes of operation. It is also connected with the
geographical distribution of the bwami association.

In areas where the hierarchical structure of bwami has reached the peak of
complexity, some types of sculptures appear in the lower initiations (kongabulumbu, kansilembo, bombwa, ngandu). Disregarding regional variations, in
general the carvings produced for the lower rites are displayed in small groups or
often singly. In different rites of the lower grades, I have observed the limited use
of spoons, knives, scepters, axes, billhooks, chips, miniature stools and doors,
wooden spears, wooden dog bells, wooden figurines, and masks. These objects,
however, are often mentioned in the texts without actually being seen by the
initiates. In other words, the lower initiations center mainly on natural and
simple manufactured objects. By far the largest number of artworks are used in
the rites of the highest male (yananio and kindi) and female (bulonda and bunyamwa) grades, but they are never the sole initiation equipment. And in top
initiations they appear only at specific levels and in certain rites. At the musage
level of yananio, for example, very few sculptures (e.g., a wooden arm; small
wooden figurines) are presented. At the higher lutumbo level of the same grade,
a large number of wooden anthropomorphic and zoomorphic figurines, wooden
masks, and stools, as well as a few wooden axes and ivory spoons, do indeed
appear, though some groups use no anthropomorphic figurines. At the two lowest levels of kindi (milungu and kyogo), anthropomorphic and zoomorphic
figurines in wood, ivory, or bone are occasionally manipulated. Some wooden
and ivory anthropomorphic and zoomorphic figurines are displayed at the intermediate level of kindi (musage). The largest number and the widest diversity of
sculptures are seen at the top level of kindi (lutumbo). Masks and anthropomorphic figurines are also employed in the two female grades (bulonda and bunyamwa). In regions where kindi does not exist, or where the supreme grades
are called by different names (*hingwi, kidasi, biciba*), the number of sculptures
decreases and fewer types are used, but masks and figurines do appear.

The types of sculptures presented in one community during the three-day
lutumbo lwa yananio initiations illustrate the distribution. The following objects were seen in separate rites: small wooden masks (one for each participant
of the grade) with whitened faces and long fiber beards; two large masks, one
completely whitened, the other black with white around the eye sockets; two

large wooden figurines, one bicephalic, one bifrontal; small well-polished wooden quadrupeds (one for each participant of the grade); three large wooden quadrupeds, one of them bicephalic, one wearing a dog bell; an ivory spoon; a wooden arm; spherical stools; a miniature mancala game board; a wooden phallus; and an ax. These carvings were part of a larger array of natural and manufactured items, including stuffed rodent hide, goat hide, wickerwork shield, bark and raffia cloth, baskets and bags, feather rope, feather and quill hats, double-edged copper knives with wooden or ivory handles, sticks, gaffs, leaves, branches, nuts, snail shells, pangolin claws, and hornbill beaks. (Other communities would probably show a different pattern: for example, zoomorphic figurines might be replaced by anthropomorphic ones.)

In the same community, sculptures used during the five-day lutumbo lwa kindi initiations included eight ivory masks (one for each participant of the grade); one big whitened wooden mask; one large blackened wooden mask; three crude wooden anthropomorphic figurines; one wooden and one ivory zoomorphic figurine; an aged small elephant tusk with decorative designs; small ivory or bone figurines and one well-polished wooden figurine; ivory or bone spoons, hammers, and knives. In the bunyamwa rites two ivory masks, small ivory anthropomorphic and zoomorphic figurines, and an ivory hammer and knife were exhibited.

Texts

Bwami initiations at all levels include songs and dances, and most of the texts, called "words of the land," are sung aphorisms. In some rites, however, the texts, instead of being sung, are murmured, whispered, or tonally reproduced on a kazoo, a blowhorn, a membranophone, or a slit-drum. Although the aphorisms are the primary exegetical documents, other types of verbal communication are used in the rites. The ceremonial entrance of the initiates is accompanied by spoken dialogue, stereotyped conversation between the row leader and the tutor, speeches of welcome, and proclamations. In certain rites the initiates and the candidate shout their own drum names or the names of all those who preceded them in achieving yananio or kindi in their own kinship groups and ritual communities. Sometimes a senior initiate recites formulas of blessing or makes hortatory statements. The rite of kansilembo is characterized by riddlelike phrases.

A listing of the functional types of aphorisms, with examples, follows.

1. To try out drums, percussion sticks, or anklet bells: "Let us first find out [try out] the manner in which we are beating the drums"; "Let us check the anklet bells, each initiation, each one is checked out."

2. To call the participants, particularly women, together: "I am calling the Babila of Nkumba, those that have the coronet on the head."

3. To welcome, scare, flatter, or appease the candidate: "The masters of the candidate, the masters of the candidate, they love him."

4. To announce the preparation of a configuration or the beginning of a dance sequence: "Musagi [or Yango, Kabobe, Bituzi, etc.] is dancing on the road."

5. To order the display or the removal of objects or to announce the arrival of a particular object or character: "Everyone his one, everyone his one, Big-One of Kabilundu"; "Mr. Many-Halting-Places is dancing on the road."

6. To order that objects be deposited on the ground or that the carriers of baskets and bags be relieved of their burdens: "Shall I not find [get] a sleeping place; I am carrying the dangerous thing of Bad-Man."

7. To request admittance to the initiation house: "Open up the door, Masters-of-the-Initiation-House, that I may see the manner in which it is adorned there."

8. To invite the candidate to come and view a configuration: "Come and see . . . [this or that]."

9. To order certain people (e.g., women or lower initiates) to leave the initiation house: "Get out, get out from here with your [kind of] thoughts."

10. To signify the end of a rite and the departure of the participants: "Turtle goes to sleep; every man has his sleeping place"; "Rain is falling, the Big-Animals are dispersing"; "The Anointed-Ones go to give a last farewell."

These standard texts are the basis of aphorisms that accompany, illustrate, and explain actions, objects, events, and situations. They are fundamental for the understanding of what is done, said, intended, and implied by each rite.

Conceived and formulated in different ways, the aphorisms may be affirmations, negations, exclamations, exhortations, questions, wishes, orders, warnings, complaints, reflections, expressions of astonishment, critiques, satires, and statements of principle. Many aphorisms are presented in the first person, singular or plural, as if the preceptors and singers were identifying directly with the actions, experiences, and ideas evoked by the texts. Other aphorisms, formulated in the second person, singular or plural, are addressed directly to the candidate or to an imaginary interlocutor. Some texts refer to real or invented persons, groups, and places. Fictional persons may be identified with animal, plant, and object names, or as characters. Thus hundreds of stock characters are presented in the aphorisms as symbols or exemplifications of virtues and vices, fame and infamy, ugliness and beauty, decrepitude and physical or moral strength. The actual texts relate directly to many aspects of Lega life, some of them known to all, some to select groups, and some known to only a few people. Major themes are shown in the following list.

Historical events

Anecdotes about unusual occurrences

A discovery (e.g., of the resin of the *musuku* tree used for making torches)

Activities related to hunting, trapping, fishing, gathering, cultivating, blacksmithing, carving, pot making, bark cloth making, basketmaking, plaiting, house building, tree climbing, and other techniques

Natural phenomena, animals, plants, minerals, and objects from the physical environment, and their properties, uses, and behaviors

Social situations and relationships, social institutions (kinship, family, sociopolitical control)

Cults, divination, poison ordeals, burial rites, witchcraft

Personal statuses, privileges, and obligations

Psychological and behavioral characteristics—good or bad—of men and women, of young and old, of initiates and noninitiates, of leaders and subjects, of the sick and the healthy

Attitudes and obligations of the candidate

The bwami association and its structure, organization, rules, and values

The initiation rites, their organization, principles, demands, and results

The initiation objects, their nature and purposes

The social positions of the initiates and their rights and duties

References to tales, dances, musical instruments, and music

Concepts about beauty, sickness, infirmity, decrepitude, strength, fertility, survival, and death

The ideas expressed in the aphorisms, whether overt or implicit, are directly or indirectly correlated with performances and with the forms, materials, and uses of objects employed jointly with the texts, and with the origins, sources, locations, properties, and associations of these items. The aphorisms pertain to the animal and plant species from which the objects are derived, the technological processes involved, and the names of the objects. Particular dances, movements, gestures, expressions, and dramatic enactments accompanying the singing of the aphorisms, whether or not associated with objects, either are referred to in the text or relate to its interpretation.

Some aphorisms recited in the context of dance action or manipulation of objects refer vividly to realistic actions—a person attacking others; a person playing a game of dice or consulting an oracle; a limper, an invalid, or a sick individual; one who is deprived of the objects he carries—or to actions that are widely known—the nocturnal call and response of dendrohyraxes, the habits of the terrestrial giant pangolin and the arboreal pangolin, the secretion of slime by a snail. Other texts refer to symbolic actions (e.g., turning an object upside down; hanging an object behind one's back) or to the perceived properties of forms, colors, and behaviors (e.g., a black nut with a slit represents the female labia; whiteness expresses glitter, shine, smoothness).

Still other texts make less clear-cut allusions to the forms, functions, and uses of objects; for example, "A mwami [is] a Mr. Lusembe [Shell]; Mubinga [Dendrohyrax] dies because of Mbalo [Waxing moon]." The referents here are full-fledged yananio initiates who wear the outer teeth of dendrohyraxes and affix polished, slightly crescentic, oblong shells to the fronts of their hats. Dendrohyraxes are trapped for their teeth, which are part of the insignia; the yana-nio seen wearing the shell and teeth is compared with the waxing moon, which many people can see and admire.

Actors in the aphorisms are personified plants, animals, phenomena from the natural environment, ordinary people, and people who maintain a certain social position and status, engage in specified activities, or exhibit certain characteristics. A large number of symbolic characters, both real and invented, are also central reference points. The names of the characters are often introduced by the morphemes *(i)sa-* (lit., father of; translated as Mr.) and *nya-* (lit., mother of; translated as Mrs. or the equivalent of *na-,* owner or master of); examples are Isamalomengi, Mr. Many-Sleeping-Places; Isabulumbu, Mr. Obscurity; Nya-malendelo, Mrs. Who-Likes-to-Run-Away. Among the numerous other designations for characters are Kakuliso, Something-in-the-Eye, and Kyasula kanwa, What-Has-the-Mouth-Wide-Open.

Some aphorisms occur in identical formulations and contexts across Lega-land; others are found in different versions (e.g., substitutions of words). Reversal of the word order in varying contexts sometimes seems to affect the meaning of an aphorism. In a yananio initiation, for instance, the initiates, shaking their reed swatters, sang "Kimpe [bird] listen! In Deciduous-Tree Ax sounds" to announce the sound of music accompanying the arrival of the initiates. In a kindi rite the initiates sang, without using objects, "In Deciduous-Tree where Ax sounds, Kimpe listen!" The aphorism refers to witches who threaten the life of a young man unwilling to take over the initiations from his dead father.

Most texts are direct or symbolically phrased statements about the values, rules, expectations, thought patterns, knowledge, and activities of bwami initiates. Several themes that are developed at great length throughout the initiations are formulated, visually illustrated, and dramatically expressed in many different ways. Some of the major thematic focuses may be summarized as follows.

1. The origins, universality, structure, organization, purposes, roles, and requirements of the bwami association are evoked by numerous images. Bwami has no inventor: it is "the fruit that came from above." It spread all over *malinga* (the lowlands) and *ntata* (the highlands); old and durable, it is the greatest and most famous of all institutions. Although bwami rites are exclusive and for the most part secret, membership is open; it is not restricted to seniors or to wealthy people. Bwami is big, high, and powerful: it brings its members greatness, honor, fame, and, above all, a "change of heart" leading to moral and spiritual excellence. Bwami, based on cooperation and harmony, provides order and solidarity and counteracts all forms of behavior that produce dissension, strife, violence, and war. Among the many membership requirements are personal effort, kinship support, character, and high morality as well as material goods to be given as fees, gifts, and rewards. To outsiders bwami looks awesome, but insiders are fully aware of its benefits and blessings.

2. The initiation rites preceding induction into bwami grade levels not only are long and arduous, but they also require elaborate preparations, close

consultation, and plenty of labor. Their ultimate purpose is "to straighten what is bent, what has a hunch." They take place in an atmosphere of *kubonga* (harmonizing, smoothing, pleasing, functioning well) and *kwanga* (to be in good order, to be well-shaped, to sound well). Nothing must disturb this harmony, and so strict observance of the rules of bwami is necessary. Always present are the impossibility of predicting the outcome of the rites and the uncertainty as to the reactions of initiates. The initiations lead the successful candidate from a state of "wildness" and "ill fate" to one of *busoga* (anthropism, humanity).

3. The initiates glorify the magnificence of their paraphernalia and the power of their positions. In numerous texts they speak of themselves as the Anointed-Ones, the White-Binyangi-Birds, the Dendrohyraxes, the Ones-of-the-Elephant-Tail, and the Ones-of-the-Walking-Cane (with reference to physical appearance). They also evoke the eminence of their social position as Big-Ones, Heavy-Ones, Unifiers, Elephant-Folk, Bat-Folk (building their houses one by one; bringing together what was dispersed), Guinea-Fowl-Folk (finding their things in their nest), Nkamba-Fish-Folk (who do not carry those who are not of their group), Mbubi-Vine-Folk (ramifying everywhere), and Ridge-Pole-Folk (supporting the structure). Initiates praise their high morality: they are not fighters or quarrelsome people, nor are they seducers, slanderers, or hypocrites. Top-level initiates speak about the state of plenitude, immunity, and quasi immortality they have reached.

4. In contrast, the noninitiate is shrouded in darkness that prevents him from seeing and understanding. He has no intelligence and no heart, or simply a "heart of feathers," and he is unwise because of meddling in things that do not concern him.

5. The candidate is alternately exalted, criticized, and humiliated because of his character, his attitude, his preparations, and the goods he provides. He is warned about nonobservance of rules and prescriptions.

6. The initiation objects and the paraphernalia are celebrated for their beauty, the status they provide, and the dangers they contain. They are described as durable goods that create linkages across generations; they are objects to be inherited, owned, displayed, and interpreted.

7. Throughout the initiations the texts and the actions lay heavy stress on the position, attitude, mentality, and power of women. Remarks are made about particular women, such as the initiated wife, the senior initiated wife, senior and junior wives, and witches, as well as about those who are adulterous, meddlesome, arrogant, quarrelsome, unsettled, easy, talkative, and competitive. Obsessive concern is expressed about disruptions caused by female witches and by adulterous and quarrelsome women. Innumerable dramatic actions and objects have sexual and erotic overtones, either criticizing immoral behavior or stressing the positive aspects of sexual relationships. The accompanying texts are subtle allusions to, or overt statements about, these matters. The emi-

nent position of the initiated wife and the indissoluble bond with her initiated husband are also placed in perspective.

8. Men are reprimanded for inactivity, laziness, irascibility, violence, hypocrisy, double-talk, bragging, interference, indiscretion, and lack of generosity and solidarity; the opposites of these attitudes and behaviors are praised. The achievements of men, such as raising children, attaining bwami, and securing wives, kin and followers, and wealth, are strongly underscored.

9. Children are criticized for the same reasons as men and also because they are inconsistent and lack filial piety and motivation. Particular emphasis is placed on a son's duty to perpetuate his father's role and position in bwami.

10. Support from and harmonious relationships within kinship groups are a central concern in the texts, as initiations require the support of many kin. Especially important are maternal uncles, sororal nephews, and in-laws; their privileges and duties and the help they can give are stressed. All factors that might diminish or strengthen the unity, cohesion, and spirit of cooperation prevailing in kinship relations are examined. There is a preoccupation with everything that preserves the well-being, harmony, and continuity of the group. The aphorisms depict the many characters whose attitudes disrupt the smooth in-group relationships and solidarity (e.g., Isakabitabita, Mr. War-War; Isabumania, Mr. Desire; Isakasumo, Mr. Spear; Sanzugunzugu, Mr. Callousness).

11. The qualities and weaknesses of persons with special occupations and functions are evoked in the texts: hunters and trappers; males and females engaged in fishing; gatherers, mainly of honey, mushrooms, and termites; tree climbers; makers of bark cloth; potters; blacksmiths; initiates in the special roles of preceptors, tutors, or guardians of the tomb; diviners; gamblers and game players (dice, ball, and mancala); and persons administering or receiving the poison ordeal.

12. A few historical and legendary characters, groups, and places of Lega or non-Lega origin appear in the texts. The Babile, Songola-Binja, Komo, and Twa (Pygmies) are noted among foreign groups; and the Bembe, Batali, Bouse, and Enya, among related and incorporated peoples. Except for the Banamuningi, Batoba, and Banamombo, few Lega clans are mentioned. Most of the place-names mentioned in the aphorisms are purely symbolic and invented, but a few denote the locations of important Lega migrations and battles. Europeans are not mentioned, but some texts criticize the Europeanization process. Although the Europeans took away the strength of the initiates, they will not destroy the latter's secrets, for nothing can wring the words of bwami from the heart. Europeanization is compared with *kigunda*, the emptiness and heartlessness of the noninitiate.

An enormous number of texts center on these institutions, customs, activities, situations, and interpersonal and intergroup relationships. By illustrating principles of the social, legal, and moral code, both positively and negatively, they also increase the knowledge of animal habits, characteristics and uses of plants, techniques, and mores.

No mention is made of nature spirits or divinities, but there are occasional references to the dead, the shades, and the ancestors. Some texts are, in fact, directly concerned with the concepts of death and survival. These are extremely important in furthering the understanding of the ultimate role and purpose of the bwami association and of the paraphernalia as the privileged possessions of the initiates. Although the Lega regard witchcraft, ritual pollution, transgression of major taboos, and strife as the immediate causes of death, they hold a rational view of death itself:

Death has no owner; it is "the fruit that came from above"; it is universal and threatens "every possessor of a body."

Death is the "Master of the Imminent" (*kyongama,* what hangs above the head); it is inescapable: "I look down into the grave; I shall go in it, into the tomb into which the Dead-One went."

Whatever one's status, one cannot know how or when death will come: "Mr. Affairs-Affairs, Mr. Shrewdness-Shrewdness, the death which one will die, one does not know it."

One by one the people die "like the fruits of the *muzombo* tree swallowed by the river." People die every day; there is no mercy since "little children precede old persons in death." Death carries away everybody, the Beautiful-One and the Big-Ones: "Gusts of wind, Shrewd-Ones, tease the young banana trees."

However powerful one has been and however large the number of followers, one goes alone into the grave.

Death is always bad; it is compared with the back of a snake: "Wherever one bites, there are but bones."

Death is final: "He who dies is no longer seen."

The name and the works of a deceased person, however, survive if he had gone through the bwami initiations and also had fathered sons: "The grave of He-Who-Was does not rot; it is always a heap" (i.e., it is taken care of by the sons). A man's ultimate life goals, therefore, are to achieve high rank in bwami, to marry many wives in order to have many sons, and to create and maintain a broad spectrum of kinship relationships. The grave of a high yananio or kindi initiate is treated with special care. Placed in the house of his senior initiated wife, the grave is guarded for months and later is closed off by the sacred feather rope. In ancient custom the skulls of yananio and kindi initiates were carefully preserved. Some of the principal insignia were displayed on the tomb; a few objects were left there as permanent reminders, while others were removed at the end of the mortuary rites and kept in trust by the initiated guardian of the tomb. As soon as possible the latter were transferred in an initiation context to a close agnatic relative, preferably a son or a brother of the deceased. Whenever feasible, or if necessary because the deceased held collectively owned initiation objects (in addition to his personal ones), induction of the successor into the relevant grade was performed "on the tomb." The major insignia and initiation objects were transferred during the rites, and the texts strongly emphasize that they are the perpetual extension and the lasting contribution of the dead: "What remains of the Dead-One: the limb of the arms"; "Everything rots: the limb of the arm does not rot"; and "Muntonko [tree of whose wood masks, stools, drums, etc., are carved] has no imputrescible core [i.e., it rots easily]; Adz is its hard core." The artworks and other initiation objects presented to the successor are identified as "Hammers which Those-Who-Were [or Those-Who-Died or the Ancestors] left behind [or forged]" to stress the ideas of permanence, continuity, and linkage.

PART TWO

Anthropomorphic
Figurines

Materials and Sizes

Perhaps two thousand Lega anthropomorphic figurines are known in world collections. Carved in different materials, they show varying degrees of finish and artistic skill. Many writers on African art tend to group the figurines into one category and to characterize them by a set of stereotyped descriptions. In doing so they fail to see the wide diversity in forms, materials, semantic categories, uses, modes of presentation, ownership and transfer, functions, contexts of occurrence, and meanings of Lega figurines.

Anthropomorphic figurines are carved mainly from wood, elephant ivory, and bone; the use of other materials such as stone, *muntita* termite nest clay, baked clay, copal, and *ntutu* is rare (pls. 15–17; see also Allison, 1968, pl. 87; Altman, 1963, pl. 14; de Kun, 1966, pls. 15, 23; Sotheby and Co., 1960, pl. 101). Figurines in *ntutu* and *muntita* are found in only a few regions and are limited in function and usage. Some temporary anthropomorphic assemblages are made of banana stipes, hides, and feathers and enhanced with hats, necklaces, and masks (Biebuyck, 1973a, pl. 47).

Two major categories of sculptures are made of wood (mostly soft). The large, usually voluminous figurines in the first group are rarely more than 38 cm tall; they have crude, unpolished surfaces and dull, dark patinas. The figurines are sometimes reddened and often have white coloring, at least on the face. Illustrations of figurines of this type appear in Bascom (1967, p. 72), Bassani (1977, pls. 49–50, 463–467), Biebuyck (1973a, pls. 23–24, 27–33, 65, 67–70), Cornet (1972, pl. 138; 1978a, pl. 189), de Kun (1966, pls. 18–19, 26), Fagg (1968, pl. 271; 1970, p. 93), Fagg and Plass (1964, pp. 37, 82), Kjersmeier (1967, vol. 3, pl. 56), Krieger (1965, pl. 45), Leiris and Delange (1967, p. 359), Maesen (1967, p. 54), Olbrechts (1951, p. 10), Plass (n.d., pl. 40B), Société générale de Banque (1977, pl. 71), Sotheby and Co. (1960, pl. 130), Sweeney (1935, pl. 446), Van Geluwe (1967, pl. 40), Wardwell (1970, p. 34), and Wingert (1962, p. 178). Some large wooden figurines ascribed to the Lega (e.g., Bassani, 1977, pls. 468–469; Leuzinger, 1963, pl. 203; Robbins, 1966, pl. 199; Sotheby and Co., 1967, pl. 90) are not Lega, but they do fall into the broad area of Lega-related styles. The second group of wooden figurines comprises small, slender ones in the size range of the ivories; their smooth, well-polished, dark body surfaces may be decorated with geometrical designs. Figurines of this kind are illustrated in Altman (1963, fig. 17), Biebuyck (1973a, pls. 71–72), Delange (1967, pl. 165), Fagg and Plass (1964, pp. 38, 50). Wooden figurines in both categories are less numerous than those carved from ivory and bone. As few wooden figurines were known in world collections before 1955, their significance has generally been underrated.

Most anthropomorphic figurines are carved from elephant ivory (*mulamba*) or bone (*ikwa*). Hippopotamus and warthog tusks, which are rarely used for carving, are found in only a few regions. In places where the kindi grade exists, elephant ivory has gradually become the exclusive possession of its members, who are sometimes called *nenemulamba* (owners or masters of ivory). Sculptors use the top parts of the tusks, especially the finer, lighter ones of female elephants, and thus some figurines are hollow and others are solid. The kindi use other parts of the elephant for decorative and sculptural purposes: the tail that adorns the hat of the kindi; the ears to make a belt occasionally replacing one of bongo hide; the wedge-shaped pad of the foot soles for rare kindi masks; and the huge oval-shaped molars rubbed with white clay and exhibited in the *kasisi* rites. In monopolizing the elephant, the kindi are inspired by its majestic power, which turns into awesome destructiveness when the animal is disturbed. They are also impressed by the elephant's keen sense of smell (*Encyclopedia Americana*, 1978 ed.) and its retentive memory (*Encyclopaedia Britannica*, 1969 ed.).

The smooth surfaces of elephant tusks are enhanced by polishing and oiling. Tusks of the forest elephant (*Loxodonta cyclotis*) are darker than those of the savanna elephant (*Loxodonta africana*; Schouteden, 1947). When the ivory is fresh, the pores are filled with an oily substance that makes carving easier and brightens the natural sheen (Penniman, 1952, p. 14). Ivory tends to become yellowish brown when frequently handled or when worn against the skin. The initiates rub their skin with *mwambo, ikumu,* or *kinkinda* oils (the last two used mostly on head and hair). Women prepare these oils from certain kernels, which they dry, split by pounding, steam, and knead, and may then mix with red colors. Different red hues are derived from *mukusa* clay, *kibonge* stones, and the *nkula* tree. Women put powdered red stone in their hair; men use it in their whiskers. Bodies are also rubbed with *bulago* perfumes, produced by combining resins, *makoma* leaves, *lungo* bark, and charcoal from the parasol tree. The sculptures are not only manipulated by oiled and sweaty hands during the rites; they are also polished with the same oils and perfumes (see De Kesel, 1980, p. 106). The mixtures may be darkened by adding the saps of certain vines and trees. Lega ivories thus show an incredibly rich spectrum of patinas ranging from light honey colors to yellowish brown to deep red and brownish red (Cornet, 1972, pls. 147–149, 151–152; 1978*a*, pl. 193; Maesen, 1960*b*, pl. 40). Figurines are also carved from elephant bone, mainly the thick parts of the rib or the joint bones that are flat in the articular areas. These sculptures have porous surfaces that preserve the natural brown-gray colors of the dried bones. Their patinas are varied but are duller than those of the ivories. The bone figurines may be so well polished and coated with oily and resinous mixtures that it is hard to distinguish between them and ivory sculptures (see Penniman, 1952, p. 31).

All Lega sculptures are small—wooden ones are seldom more than 38 cm high; ivory ones, more than 22 cm—but size ranges vary widely. Of thirty-eight wooden figurines in the Tervuren collection, the smallest is 8.2 cm and the two largest are 43 cm and 44.7 cm, the rest ranging from 8.2 to 38.4 cm. Eighteen are below 20 cm and eighteen are above 20 cm; only three are more than 38 cm; twenty-four are in the 10- to 30-cm range.

Ivory and bone figurines are all less than 30 cm tall. Of 391 such figurines in the Tervuren collection, the tallest (which I collected in southern Legaland) measures 28.9 cm and is an unusually elongated figurine ending in a sharp point. Following is a detailed breakdown of the 391 pieces.

Size in cm	Number of figurines
5.1	1
6.1–6.8	6
7–7.9	14
8–8.8	17
9–9.8	21
10–10.9	49
11–11.9	40
12–12.9	49
13–13.9	49
14–14.9	41
15–15.9	34
16–16.6	18
17–17.9	17
18–18.9	13
19–19.9	8
20, 20.5, 20.8	3
21–21.2	5
22–22.3	2
23.1	2
26	1
28.9	1

As the listing indicates, more than half of the figurines (280) measure between 10 and 16.6 cm and together represent all intermediary steps between those two sizes. The number per size bracket decreases gradually as one approaches either of the two extremes.

The size ranges do not correlate with types of artworks; for example, the peg-shaped ivory figurines I collected measure from 7.9 to 28.9 cm. The sizes, however, do correspond to measurements taken on the outstretched hand for the ivories, a method also used for arranging perforated fragments of snail shells on raffia fibers (Biebuyck, 1953a). Three sizes are critical: *kanue*, length of the middle finger; *ibungakwanga*, from the top of the middle finger to the base of the knuckle; *magombelo*, from the top of the middle finger to the wrist joint (considered double the *ibungakwanga* measurement). Although many of the smaller figurines clearly fit the *kanue* and *ibungakwanga* sizes, most of the sculptures fall between *ibungakwanga* and *magombelo*; very few are larger.

Wooden figurines are all below *kilunga*, which extends from the tip of the middle finger to the joint of the upper and lower arm. *Kilunga* is the most important measurement as far as shell money is concerned. It is noteworthy that wooden sculptures of more than 21 cm usually have different functions from those that fall in the size range of the ivories.

The materials used and the sizes of figurines are related to a large extent to modes of ownership, methods of use, and functions. The boundaries, however, are not absolute.

Forms

Ivory and Bone Figurines

Anthropomorphic figurines are striking in their stylization and schematization. Forms are reduced to a succinctness and a parsimony of expression which also mark the accompanying aphoristic texts. Anthropomorphic representations reveal very little about the messages they convey. Unlike other arts in Africa, Lega sculptures have few distinctive signs—as expressed in poses, gestures, hairstyles, caps, tattoos, carved or added status symbols—to point to their purpose or significance. The cryptic character of the form admirably fits the mystery surrounding the uses and meanings of figurines in a closed initiation context.

If a large number of ivory and bone figurines, collected over several decades in different parts of Legaland, were randomly placed together, their diversity would be striking, despite overall resemblances. The differences are not limited to material, size, and volume but include variations in finish, color, morphology, and stylistic features. A cursory glance at the plates in this and other books instantly reveals the many divergences.

Some pieces are much more refined than others and show smoother surfaces, a characteristic obviously linked in some degree to the quality of craftsmanship, local preferences, and time periods. As carving traditions declined abruptly in the twentieth century, poorer sculptures were produced by carvers who worked hastily or who were poorly trained. Some figurines, however, are deliberately made rough, a trait correlated with the characters they are meant to represent. When turned out by the artists, the ivories are white to slightly yellow brown. They gradually achieve their warm patinas, their "velouté de profondeur" (Bonew, 1974), in initiation contexts, as they are rubbed with oils mixed with differing quantities of colorants (resins, reds, ashes, saps from vines). The variations resulting from these repetitive treatments are so wide that virtually each piece that has actually been used has a distinctive patina and gloss.

Some ivory figurines are hollow. The cavity may extend partly or entirely through the image, depending on whether the top of the tusk or its upper hollow part has been used. In some figurines that are completely hollow the hole in the skull is covered with resin and a cowrie; in others the cavity extends to the lower part of the head, the chest, or the belly.

Heads are rounded or flat. Viewed frontally they may be ovoid, rounded, or angular (lozenge or polygon shape). From the back the heads look rounded, slightly convex, and almost flat, or there is a second face. The flattened, rounded, or pointed skulls are broad or narrow, and usually they have no skull-cap or hairdo. Cowries may be glued to or carved on the skull; skullcaps are sometimes carved in low relief or marked with striations and dots, and some pieces have small wickerwork caps with or without cowries and buttons.

Many figurines have the concave, heart-shaped faces that are generally con-sidered the hallmark of Lega sculpture. The concavity may cover the entire face below the forehead, or it may appear only around the eyes and the nose. In other sculptures the convex-concave face is replaced by a straight plane of the entire frontal part of the head or by two sloping planes joined together at the nose bridge. Some sculptures have no forehead; in others the forehead is slightly convex and either bulging or flat.

Single morphological features show wide variety. Eyes are very large or small, though a few pieces are eyeless (Bonew, 1974, p. xi). Eyes may be repre-sented by glued-on cowries or pieces of shell; they may be engraved in the form of a circle-dot or a simple dot. Carved eyes differ considerably. Some consist of two conically shaped holes or of a fairly deep and wide oblong groove. Most eyes are carved in light or strong relief in the form of a cowrie (with narrow or wide slit), a coffee bean, an oblong protuberance without slit, a lozenge, an irregular polygon, or a circular bulge with a fine delicate slit. The pupil is some-times indicated. The eyes are placed horizontally at equal height, or they are uneven or slanting. In some figurines only one eye is indicated; others have a third eye in the form of a cowrie fixed above the carved eye, and some pieces have two superposed sets of eyes.

In many models noses, in low or high relief (flat or ridged), are straight and sharp-ridged with no nosewings or nostrils. They end squarely or, because of merging with an open V-shaped mouth, may give a beaklike impression. In rare specimens the massive, flat nose forms a narrow rectangle making the face look like a snout. In others the narrow nose ends in a lozenge shape that marks the nosewings, with two holes indicating the nostrils. Some noses are high-bridged in a face with no forehead; in other examples, the nose root combines with the upper indentation of the heart-shaped facial outline. When the nose is so long that it reaches the pointed or rounded chin, there is no mouth.

Ears, though usually absent, may be rendered in various ways: a circle-dot design, a dot, a ridge, a concave ovoid, a deep groove, a lobe, or a flap on each side of the head (a half circle in relief filled with a cone). Ears are evenly placed in the normal position or near the rim of the face.

Some figurines have no mouths; in other specimens the mouth is suggested by an open V-indentation just below the nose. Sometimes the mouth is marked in a more realistic position by an oval or trapezoidal groove or slit, or by a slight protuberance. A circular hole, a circle-dot, or a deep-cut lozenge may also define the mouth, which is placed horizontally or slants upward. Filed teeth are sometimes indicated by notches carved on the lips. The open mouth may be very close to the point of the chin; it may be exceptionally small or so large that it reaches from one jaw to the other.

Many sculptures lack a well-defined neck, as the head and torso separation is marked by a carved necklace, a deep line, or falling shoulders. Necks may be very short or disproportionately long, slender or stocky, and angular, flat, or cylindrical.

Torsos—rounded or angular, pole-shaped or flat, thick or shallow—vary in details. The upper chest sometimes stands out as a plane separate from the rest of the torso. Some have arms and legs, others legs but no arms, and still others arms but no legs. Legless torsos may end like a bust on a small socle or may taper into a peg, a pin, or a haft. Pole-shaped figurines have no backs; in the others the backs are mostly erect, flattened, or rounded. In some instances a face is carved on the back of the figurine. Rounded or angular buttocks occur occasionally in strong relief and show excessive development.

Breasts or nipples appear on only a few figurines. When they do, they are usually carved in low rounded relief or as polygonal knobs, and they are sometimes formed by circle-dots. In the few pieces where navels are indicated, they are rounded, oval, conical, pointed in light relief, or long and protuberant to merge with the genitalia.

A large number of figurines have no genitalia, but the Lega may still identify them as male or female. In double or double-faced figurines, for example, the sexual difference is suggested by the relative sharpness and elongation of the face. Genitalia are frequently absent in peg-shaped figurines, busts, and other legless pieces, as well as in the smallest ivory figurines. Male genitalia—suggested by a realistically carved penis, a cone, a polygonal knob—are less commonly sculpted than the female ones. In extremely rare instances the scrotum is marked by a rounded excrescence sometimes combined with a penis, and the anus by a hole. The female sex is indicated by a cowrie or circle-dot motif, a V-shaped proclivity, a hole, or a slit with or without two lateral ridges. In rare examples the female genitalia are depicted on the short belly by the akimbo position of the arms and a central protuberant lozenge (e.g., Tervuren, no. 55.3.104), or on the chest itself by a concave chevron, a vertical slit, or a ridge.

The arms, when carved at all, occur in numerous forms and positions: short stump arms in relief against the chest, or carved ajouré or slightly slanting; full arms affixed to the body or ajouré, hanging along the body, placed akimbo near the hips, the flanks, the pubic region, or the lower belly. Arms may appear as stumps that are pulled sideways, full arms curving outward and resting on the back, full arms bent inward touching the lower chest or chin, and arms raised upward touching the temples or the skull. The arms are placed asymmetrically, or there is only one arm. Hands are carved realistically or suggested simply by indentations at the ends of the arms. The outer line of the arms may be straight, but often it is scalloped, crenellated, or curvilinear.

Many figurines are legless. In others the legs may be straight, with or without feet, or massive with swellings and folds to indicate not only the joints but also tumescences caused by the wearing of iron and copper bands. They may closely suggest the pillarlike form of elephant legs and the clublike appearance of elephant feet. The zigzag-shaped, crenellated, scalloped, tumescent, and curvilinear outlines of the legs are conspicuous, but there are also more realistic legs with joint markings and sometimes with slightly bent knees. Very short stump legs are seen on many specimens. Legs are usually carved in ajouré, parallel to each other, sometimes slanting outward. In rare examples the legs are joined entirely or only at the feet. Bases usually are not carved under the legs. Toes are marked by indentations and lines.

Ivory and bone figurines display few accumulations. Cowries, pieces of shell, or buttons are used occasionally to mark the skullcap, the eyes, or the genitalia. A piece is sometimes adorned with a wickerwork skullcap, a beaded necklace, a belt, a bracelet, or an anklet. Some hollow sculptures with a filling of resin and wood were probably broken from a wooden staff. In rare instances a figurine, at least temporarily during a rite, is dressed in a genet hide or in monitor lizard skin.

Many sculptures have no surface decoration at all. When they do, the decoration is restricted to a few basic motifs: blackened dots, engraved circle-dots, and linear designs. These are found in various combinations on almost any part of the face and the torso, more often on the front than on the back of the figurines. The amount and variety of designs differ considerably. In some specimens the surface ornamentation is limited to rows of dots or circle-dots, or to lines that are slanted, crossed, or arranged in triangles or in a herringbone motif. Some sculptures have bands of designs circling the neck, the arms, or the legs.

Some pieces exhibit an unusual amount of surface decoration. One side of a double-faced ivory figurine (Tervuren, no. 55.3.120) is adorned on the chest with a series of triangles and herringbone motifs; the other side has linear herringbone designs. Another small figurine (Tervuren, no. 55.3.76) has intricate linear patterns on the forehead, the temples, the chest, the belly, and the back. On the head and the temples there are three reversed triangles or parallel lines; on the chest, a triangle of indented lines; on the belly, a double triangle; on the sides and the lower part of the torso, a double line filled with dots; and on the back, a cross-shaped motif.

The following recurring categories have been determined by classifying the ivory and bone figurines on a purely formal basis.

1. Heads. The few heads among Lega sculptures occur in different sizes and may be bifrontal, trifrontal, or quadrifrontal. Pure heads are rare (Biebuyck, 1973a, pl. 98) and most rest on an incipient neck, a short pole, or two stump legs (Tervuren, nos. 35406, 38705, 38751, 51.11.4, 51.11.37, 55.3.82, 55.3.147, 55.134.164, 56.3.19; Elisofon and Fagg, 1958, p. 243; Museum of Primitive Art, 1969, pl. 448; Sweeney, 1935, pl. 514). There is wide diversity in size, volume, and patina. Tervuren specimen no. 56.3.19 (pl.

18), an extraordinary product of Lega creative inventiveness, is a massive, deep reddish-yellow sculpture with four faces looking in four directions. One set of opposing faces has cowrie slit eyes, a massive triangular nose, and a small oval mouth; in the other set the hollowed-out eyes are rectangular, and the nose is close to the lozenge-shaped mouth. One face of the second set has, instead of a chin, a phalluslike relief in a large oval concavity; the other face tapers into a sharp chin.

2. Head on a pole (Baltimore, 1954, pl. 98; Biebuyck, 1973a, pls. 86–87; Carnegie Institute, 1969, pl. 302; Cornet, 1972, pl. 154; Elisofon and Fagg, 1958, pl. 309; Fröhlich, 1967, pl. 135; Leuzinger, 1963, pl. 202; Museum of Primitive Art, 1964, pl. 5; Olbrechts, 1946, pl. 179; Vogel, 1981, pl. 134). The Lega have carved numerous heads on poles. The simplest form is a single head with more or less prognathic face surmounting (or hanging from) an unadorned straight pole that flares slightly near the bottom (Tervuren, nos. 34180, 38696, 55.11.21, 52.29.20, 55.3.109). The figurines sometimes have two heads or are multifrontal. The structure becomes more complicated when a short neck connects the head with the pole (Tervuren, no. 38640). Poles may be tubular or angular to form a lozenge. In certain examples the pole rests on a small oval base or on a pillarlike elephant foot or a stool, or the end of the pole may be carved as a head. In other examples the pole narrows so that the piece looks like a scepter. Other possible elaborations are the superposition of two or more faces or crenellation of the pole. Arms are carved only occasionally in relief on the pole. The many hollow carvings in this category are ideal for affixing to the top of the *matakale* stick carried by high initiates (Tervuren, nos. 33184, 38589, 38628, 38631, 38638, 38640, 38687, 38695, 38704, 38712, 52.29.20, 55.3.32, 55.3.130). The specimens measure from 7.1 to 21 cm, but most of them are less than 18 cm.

3. Head on a peg-shaped body (Krieger, 1969, pl. 348; Willett, 1971, pl. 212). The simplest example is an unadorned single head standing directly on a sharp peg. The peg may be flattened to resemble a typical double-edged Lega knife. The arms are carved in relief against the body or in ajouré with a short neck and falling shoulders (Tervuren, nos. 35404, 51.13.8, 53.29.14, and 55.3.20, 23, 25, 35, 54, 55, 87, 104, 121, 124, 132, 134, 148). A variation is found in small sculptures that end in a short pin (Tervuren, nos. 38708, 52.12.2). The pieces I collected measure from 7.9 to 28.9 cm; no one size predominates, but most pieces measure between 10.9 and 22 cm.

4. Busts and busts with a scepterlike or handlelike body (Agnuzzo, 1968, pl. 97; Bassani, 1977, pls. 65–66; Biebuyck, 1973a, pls. 74, 77, 81, 85; Kochnitzky, 1948, p. 61; Laude, 1956, p. 38; Noll et al., 1972, pl. 268; Segy, 1969, pl. 18; Sotheby and Co., 1960, pls. 100, 105; 1965, pl. 12). Busts range widely in size (from 7.2 to 19.6 cm among those I collected) and in their relative flatness or roundness. Some end in a peg or a short pin. They may have up to four faces; arms may be sculptured in relief or ajouré and hang straight or touch the hips (Tervuren, nos. 38623, 38629, 38632, 51.11.28, and 55.3.10, 37, 38, 46, 83, 112, 115, 120, 139).

5. Armless figurines standing on two legs (de Kun, 1966, pl. 16; Frobenius, 1933, pl. 101b; Parke-Bernet Galleries, 1967, pl. 111; Sotheby and Co., 1960, pl. 106). The pole-shaped or tubular torsos (sometimes hollow) of the armless figures stand on two short or long legs. Some are bifrontal; in others two bodies are joined at the back; others may show two additional faces at the height of the shoulders. Many of these sculptures have sexual markings, particularly female (Tervuren, nos. 32873, 33179, 33183, 38641, 38666, 51.11.34). Those I collected (Tervuren, nos. 55.3.7, 27, 36, 39, 123) fall into the 12.3- to 18.5-cm range.

6. Full-standing figurines. By far the largest category of sculptures comprises the full-standing figurines (those I collected range from 10.3 to 21 cm) with arms and legs. (Among the many examples, see Biebuyck, 1973*a*, pls. 75, 82, 84; Chernova, 1967, pls. 156–157; Cornet, 1972, pls. 147–152; Frobenius, 1933, pl. 101; Krieger, 1969, pls. 325, 352–353; Maesen, 1959, pl. 54; Sweeney, 1935, pl. 447.) These figurines also display the largest number and the widest variety of "optional" features, such as breasts, navels, genitalia, and arms. There are several types of legs (straight, jointed, elephant legs) with or without feet and toes. The most remarkable differences are in form and position of the arms. Some have stump arms carved against the body or in ajouré; others have full arms touching the hips or the belly. This category also shows unusual arm positions: arms placed between belly and chest, arms touching the chest or the head, and arms bent angularly at the chest so that the hands reach the belly. There are also uncommon asymmetrical poses: the right arm raised to the cheek and the left placed between chest and belly; the right arm raised to the chin, and the left hand placed near the right hand.

Two style groups stand out among the many heterogeneous sculptures in this category. The first includes pieces that have a lozenge-shaped flat or round head (pl. 19; see also Biebuyck, 1973*a*, pl. 84; Hôtel Drouot, 1965, pl. 102). All have circle-dot eyes and small straight noses in light relief with nostrils. The arms hang along the body in relief or ajouré. All are adorned with black dots that run over the front and back of the torso; there are striated designs on the arms. The second distinctive set of pieces show very round heads and bodies but otherwise exhibit many diverse features (pl. 20; see also Chernova, 1967, pl. 156; Cornet, 1972, pls. 149, 152; Jacquot, 1977, p. 416, pls. 1–2; Krieger, 1969, pl. 325; Leiris and Delange, 1967, pl. 433; Lunsford, 1969, pl. 128; Maesen, 1950, pl. 52; Olbrechts, 1946, pl. 177). One important subgroup, however, is characterized by circle-dot eyes, a small rectangular nose, a toothed mouth, protuberant breasts and navel, female genitalia, hanging ajouré arms with fingers, and massive tumescent legs with feet and toes.

7. Unusual figurines. Limitless imagination, a tendency to extreme schematization, and creative originality have led Lega artists to produce many unusual figurines. These pieces cannot easily be placed in a particular morphological category. Those with a zigzag or a frog-shaped body are transitional to certain types of animal sculptures (Biebuyck, 1973*a*, pl. 76).

Others show an uncommon feature: a child carved in relief on the flank or the back (Roosens, 1967, pl. 256; Sotheby and Co., 1960, pl. 106); a large realistically carved penis (Tervuren, no. 38680) or a penis hanging down from the chest (Elisofon and Fagg, 1958, pl. 309); small breasts placed below the stump arms on the abdomen (Tervuren, no. 38615); a triangular lower torso (Biebuyck, 1973a, pl. 81); a doll-like form (Tervuren, nos. 28098, 38661, 55.3.136). Other figurines are unique in their general appearance (Jacquot, 1977, p. 417, pls. 1–2; Krieger, 1969, pl. 324; Leuzinger, 1963, pl. 204).

One of the most striking morphological features in Lega ivory and bone (and also wood) sculptures is the recurrence of the multifaced motif, which appears in all the above-mentioned types (Biebuyck, 1981d). In the few double figurines, the two sculptures merge back to back or are connected at the buttocks and sometimes also at the heads. Both sides may have common morphological features. In one example the eyes are formed by a circle-dot design; the full ajouré arms touch the belly at the joint of the thighs; the navels and genitalia are not marked but in the area between them there is a protuberant stump that could be interpreted as a navel, a penis, or a clitoris. One side has two small falling breasts; on the other side two circle-dots are marked at the height of the nipples. Other sculptures have two separate heads on a common trunk, which may be carved simply as a pole and have four arms and four legs, or carved on each side of a pole. Multifaced figurines form a distinctive group. In the simple type the back of the head is also carved with facial features. More complicated pieces have a second face carved underneath the head; in others a face may occur on the back, two faces may replace the shoulders, or the entire sculpture may be composed of six faces. These faces may vary in size, length, and degree of prognathism. Different kinds of eyes are found, such as protuberant polygonal eyes on one face and two types of eyes on the other, one carved in the form of an open cowrie and one as a lozenge.

The morphological features and categories of the figurines described cut across different regions and autonomous communities in Legaland. Similar forms recur in different regions and groups. Distinct types of figurines and morphological features are found within the same region, and, as noted above, diverse formal characteristics may occur on a single multifaced figurine.

In an autonomous western Lega community I collected sixteen ivory and bone sculptures (pls. 21–36) from sixteen kindi. There are no heads among them, but all other categories (heads on a pole, busts, peg shapes, armless figurines with legs, and full figurines) are included. Sizes range from 7.1 to 21 cm, and the morphological details vary considerably. Faces are concave heart-shaped, straight, or convex; eyes are carved as holes, polygonal knobs, cowries, coffee beans, or ridges with a slit; some figurines have no mouth, others have a large open ovoid mouth, and in still others the mouth is placed under the nose like a chevron. Some figurines have a single face; others are bifrontal (two faces in opposition or superposition); still others have three, four, or six faces.

This group of sculptures reveals the geographical continuity of Lega carving traditions. If certain morphological features were invented and preferred by some groups, as may very well be true, they spread rapidly to other parts of the country because persons, sculptures, and rites traveled. A person could inherit figurines from remote maternal uncles or sororal nephews; groups also obtained figurines when acquiring new grade levels from other areas. The initiates also often went on journeys. Although the high initiations were organized by large ritually autonomous groups, initiates from other communities were frequently invited because of affinal or cognatic relationships, friendships, or simply geographical proximity. During the rites they could see other models and be inspired by them if they were carvers. Lineages moving away from their clan groups settled among and were incorporated into other units, creating an incredible territorial mix of fragments of social units with diverse regional and historical origins. In addition, any community needed a variety of functional and semantic types of carvings, which added to the heterogeneous demands for local output.

The differences observed for the group as a whole also apply to its constituent units. As shown in the diagram, the sixteen kindi who owned the abovementioned figurines belonged to six out of seven lineages recognized in the Munwa clan. Five of the lineages (Kanyongolo, Kyondo, Nondo, Katumpu, and Bulambo) are agnatically related to the common ancestor Munwa; two other lineages (not indicated by name) are incorporated into the Munwa group.

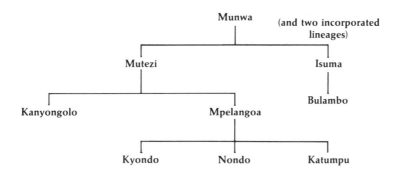

The Banakanyongolo, although living in four adjoining villages, acted as a contained ritual unit; they had their own kongabulumbu bag and yananio, *kasisi,* and kindi baskets. A member of this lineage had acquired the kindi grade seven generations ago among his maternal uncles, the Banameya, who are also western Lega. Descendants of Mpelangoa and Bulambo subsequently had been introduced to kindi by the Banakanyongolo, who therefore held seniority rights. The Banabulambo, settled in two villages, also had their own collectively owned kongabulumbu bag and yananio, *kasisi,* and kindi baskets. The situation among the Banampelangoa was more complicated because its Katumpu branch functioned to some extent as an autonomous ritual community; the Katumpu had their own village, kongabulumbu bag, and yananio basket, but they shared the *kasisi* and kindi baskets with two other related branches of Kyondo and Nondo. Each of the two lineages incorporated with the Banamunwa lived in a separate village, but they shared the collectively owned initiation objects with the Banakanyongolo and the Banabulambo, respectively.

As illustrated in the following listing, three figurines came from members of the Kanyongolo lineage, four from the Kyondo, three from the Katumpu, four from the Bulambo, and none from the Nondo; a member of each of the two incorporated lineages contributed one figurine.

1. The figurines of Kanyongolo (Tervuren, nos. 55.3.120, 121, 123):
    a. A bifrontal bust, the two faces in opposition (pl. 21).
    b. A peg-shaped (broken) bifrontal figurine with two faces in superposition (pl. 22).
    c. An armless quadrifrontal pole-shaped piece on zigzag legs; the two sets of two faces are placed in superposition and the faces in the first set look in the same direction as those in the second (pl. 23).

2. The figurines of Kyondo (Tervuren, nos. 55.3.127, 128, 139, 140):
    a. A large head on a flaring armless pole, ending in a clublike elephant foot (pl. 24).
    b. A head on a straight, hollow pole (pl. 25).
    c. An elongated bust with one face, the arms carved along the body, the hands touching the sides (pl. 26).
    d. A full, slender figurine with one face standing on pillarlike legs, with arms akimbo in very light relief (pl. 27).

3. The figurines of Katumpu (Tervuren, nos. 55.3.122, 125, 137):
    a. A full figurine with one face, standing on stump legs, the slightly rounded arms carved in ajouré but the hands touching the hips; elongated pointed breasts in high relief and female genitalia (pl. 28).
    b. A three-faced armless figurine standing on long crenellated legs; the two supplementary faces are placed on each side of the tapering torso, near the height of the upper arm (pl. 29).
    c. A figurine on a tubular armless pole ending in a rounded base (pl. 30).

4. The figurines of Bulambo (Tervuren, nos. 55.3.130, 132, 133, 141):
    a. A figurine with a tubular, armless body resting on a tubular base on which large female genitalia are marked (pl. 31).
    b. A peg-shaped figurine without arms or legs; the peg bends slightly inward (pl. 32).
    c. A small stocky bust (pl. 33).
    d. A slender figurine on a pole-shaped body that rests on a trapezoidal base (pl. 34).

5. The figurines of the incorporated lineages (Tervuren, nos. 55.3.124, 138):
    a. A slender figurine with an armless polar body that rests on a pin (pl. 35).
    b. A figurine consisting entirely of three sets of bifrontal faces, the faces of the central set looking in a direction opposite to those of the upper and lower sets (pl. 36).

Little information is available about the sculptures collected among the Lega in the late nineteenth and early twentieth centuries. The material, though sparse, demonstrates the diversity of figurines probably collected in a single area as well as the continuity of formal patterns. Two ivory figurines acquired in 1898 by a young Danish officer serving in the Belgian army (Jenssen-Tusch, 1902–1905, vol. 1, p. 123) measure 17.2 cm and 17.8 cm. They were obtained in Nyangwe, the great market south of Legaland to which slaves, traders, and refugees flocked. Both are full female figurines, most likely carved by the same hand, with breasts, navels, and chevron-shaped wedges between the legs; they are sculpted in the rounded style found in different parts of Legaland. The few ivories illustrated by Delhaise (1909b) were apparently collected among the northern Lega in the area between Shabunda and Mulungu. The figurines show the wide diversity of forms that are found everywhere in Legaland: busts, full figurines on stump legs or full tumescent legs, stump arms and full arms carved along the body or in ajouré, angular and rounded sculptures, straight and concave faces, eyes in the form of circle-dots or real cowries. The earliest Lega pieces registered at Tervuren (all collected before 1917) include wood, ivory, and bone sculptures such as busts, heads on poles, and full-standing figurines of varying size with different patinas and morphological details. Figurines in wood, ivory, bone, and stone collected by Arrhenius (a Swedish captain in the colonial army) are busts with or without arms, armless figurines, and full-standing ones. Some have lozenge-shaped faces and others are rounded; all fall within the classic size ranges (9.2 to 15 cm). Sculptures collected by Brissoni in 1900–1901 (Bassani, 1977, pls. 64–66) and by Giglioli in 1912–1913 and Tagnini in 1922 (ibid., pls. 478–480) show a range of morphological and typological differences.

Wooden Figurines

The types of sculptures and most of the morphological details already described for the ivory and bone figurines also characterize the wooden anthropomorphic statues. There are busts (pl. 45) and scepterlike pieces (pls. 43–44), pole and peg-shaped figures; some have legs but no arms (pl. 46); others are full-standing figurines (pls. 47–49). Rather than tediously recounting the morphological features of the ivory and bone carvings, it is better to focus on specific aspects in comparing them with the less numerous wooden anthropomorphic figurines. The most striking differences relate to size, finish, surface decoration, and accumulations, as well as to form. Although many wooden sculptures fit into the size range of the ivories (nineteen were between 8.2 and 21 cm), others are much larger (up to 43 cm and 44.7 cm). The surfaces of these pieces (showing adz marks) are generally cruder than those of the smooth and well-polished smaller pieces. Some of the larger sculptures are highly suggestive: a figurine with a distended belly (Biebuyck, 1973a, pls. 67–68) and another with a flat, perforated body (Leiris and Delange, 1967, pl. 420); a pole with several faces in superposition or opposition (Fagg, 1968, pls. 271–272; Kjersmeier, 1967, pl. 56; Museum of Primitive Art, 1966a, pl. 25; Roy, 1958, p. 12); a full figurine wearing a cap of monkey hide (Biebuyck, 1973a, pl. 69; Cornet, 1972, pl. 138; Olbrechts, 1951, pl. 5; Sieber and Rubin, 1968, pl. 124; Van Geluwe, 1967, pl. 40); a figurine with one or two raised arms (Radin and Sweeney, 1964, pl. 98; Sotheby and Co., 1960, pl. 123; Wardwell, 1970, pl. 7), with one hand touching the chin (Laude, 1966, pl. 127), or with two hands placed on the skull (Plass, n.d., pl. 40B). Of the rare smaller and well-polished wooden figurines, busts with or without arms appear most frequently, but there are also exceptional pieces such as an armless zigzag-shaped torso without legs (Biebuyck, 1973a, pl. 72).

The surfaces of the wooden sculptures range from black to dark or light brown and some are reddened. Most exhibit traces of white clay either in the faces only or over the entire body. Otherwise there are few accumulations, but some pieces are adorned with a cap (made of monkey hide) that falls down in the back. Surface designs, though rarely found, are formed by parallel and crossed striations, holes, waffle-shaped designs, and infrequently by circle-dots. The bifrontal, multifaced (faces in opposition and superposition), and bicephalic motifs of the ivories are also found in wooden sculptures.

What significant conclusions may be drawn from these morphological classifications? Do they overlap with other groupings based on Lega terminology, modes of ownership and usage, function, and meaning? These questions are examined in the following pages, where it is noted that size and material are important criteria for ownership, that meanings are only partly determined by general shape and morphological detail, that functions and uses cut across the categories, and that no Lega generic terminology specifically relates to each of the formal categories.

Lega Terminology

The western and southern Lega classify all anthropomorphic figurines under three headings—*kalimbangoma, katimbitimbi,* and *iginga*—a grouping based to some extent on function, use, and size.

In the *kalimbangoma* category (pls. 51–52) the Lega include small anthropomorphic figurines in wood, ivory, and bone, little polished animal figurines and other miniature sculptures in the same materials, and assemblages made up of natural objects. Some areas have no anthropomorphic figurines identified as *kalimbangoma,* a term whose meaning is obscure. One interpretation—"What guards the drum" or, personified, "Little-One Guarding Mr. Drum"—emphasizes a functional attribute: every initiate of a certain degree has a protector or a guardian who replaces and represents a real companion (i.e., a spouse after his/her death). In another explanation, *kalimbangoma* means "What Mr. Drum pursues," that is, an object left behind by a deceased kin which exercises a compelling force of attraction on a possible heir.

The carvings and assemblages in the *kalimbangoma* category are owned as insignia and initiation devices by men of the lutumbo lwa yananio grade and by women of the highest bunyamwa and sometimes of the lower bulonda levels. Figurines owned by musage wa kindi are occasionally also called *kalimbangoma*. In some areas women, though not permitted to own their personal *kalimbangoma*, may use one of their husbands' sculptures (e.g., an ivory knife or hammer) in appropriate rites.

Most types of small ivory, bone, and wooden sculptures may be identified as *kalimbangoma*: busts, pegs, heads on poles, figurines with legs but no arms, and full figurines. There is no absolute rule as to size, but it is safe to assume that most of the figurines below the *ibungakwanga* size (i.e., less than 11 cm) are considered to be *kalimbangoma* by their owners. In general, persons entitled to possess *kalimbangoma* because of their grade level have only one such carving.

The carvings known as *katimbitimbi* (lit., little phallus; pl. 53) in ivory, bone, and sometimes in *munsemunsemu* wood really constitute a functional subcategory of the *kalimbangoma*. Including some of the smallest carvings made by the Lega, they are distinctive insignia of women of the bunyamwa grade. *Katimbitimbi* are carved in various forms: a small phallus; a little bust; a full figurine shaped like a peg or a pole; or simply a flat ellipsoidal or helical piece of ivory.

The largest group of sculptures in all materials, forms, and types, mostly larger than 11 cm, are identified as *iginga* (pl. *maginga*), which literally means "what sustains," "what keeps from falling." The term is sometimes applied to women of bunyamwa grade to call attention to their vital role in initiations and to emphasize their inviolability. *Iginga* is used commonly among the western and southern Lega, but in other parts of Legaland different terms may be substituted: *kitumba* among the Liga- and Kuti-related groups, *nyansompo* among the Liga, *kate* among the Bakabango, and *alenge* among the Basimwenda. Similar figurines among the Nyindu and Bembe are called *alenge* or *a'inga*. Wooden *maginga* are associated with kindi and yananio initiations and sometimes, when there is no kindi, with the ngandu and bombwa rites; ivory, bone, stone, and copal *maginga*, with kindi and, in groups that do not have kindi, with other grades; pieces in *ntutu* and clay, with the *kasisi* level of yananio. There are no named *iginga* subcategories, but old, bulky ivory carvings (sometimes replaced by a large, carefully finished wooden figurine) may be referred to as *nina* (mother) in the context of the rites.

Ownership, Acquisition, Transfer, and Modes of Keeping

Anthropomorphic figurines are owned individually or collectively by men, and individually by women of extensive initiatory experience. Men of the highest lutumbo lwa kindi grade and, in some regions, of the lower musage and kyogo levels in kindi each own at least one *iginga* figurine in ivory (or sometimes in bone, stone, copal, or polished wood). These figurines are an intrinsic element in the insignia to which these men are entitled by rank. They are kept with other insignia in shoulder bags by a man's senior initiated wife in her house. At least one figurine in a man's possession is inherited from an agnatic kinsman of equivalent grade level, but he may commission additional pieces. In communities where an unusually large number of persons are initiated to the supreme level, or where strong ingroup tensions exist, statues may have been acquired from sororal nephews or maternal uncles in other groups. A figurine may be ordered especially for an initiate by his tutor. The experienced initiate who has served as tutor and as "guardian of the tomb" may temporarily keep in trust figurines left by a dead kinsman. He has, however, no final claim to such pieces, which must ultimately be transferred to the rightful successor of his deceased colleague.

The new initiate receives the inherited images from his tutor during the climactic rites of kindi. The tutor, himself a kindi, possesses the sculptures because he acted as guardian of the tomb of a deceased kinsman or because he had received them from such a guardian shortly before the initiation of his protégé. Decisions to induct into kindi a member of an autonomous community are made by all the kindi of that group in consultation with related colleagues who will also attend the rites. As collective solidarities are expressed in the rites, and as many preconditions limit the number of choices, a person who becomes a kindi does not necessarily succeed his father or his uterine senior brother who was kindi. A man thus may take the place of a deceased classificatory father, a grandfather, a consanguineal half brother, or a patrilateral parallel cousin.

The account of an actual transfer of a particular *iginga* reveals distinct patterns. For example, an owner inherited a figurine from a consanguineal senior brother, who had received it from a patrilateral parallel cousin (his father's senior brother's son). The latter had obtained it from an even more remote patrilateral cousin (his grandfather's senior brother's grandson), who had acquired the image in another clan from a classificatory sororal nephew, who in turn had inherited it from his father. One sculpture I received was traced by its owner to seven previous kindi belonging to three different clans, but all owners were linked by agnatic or cognatic ties. Heterogeneous examples could be cited, but ideally *iginga* sculptures remain in the closest possible agnatic lineage group. It is also important to remember that in the ancient tradition one of the figurines possessed by a kindi was abandoned on his grave, after the guardian of the tomb had removed all other objects displayed there. The house in which the kindi was buried (the grave hidden by a screen) continued to be inhabited by his most senior kanyamwa wife. Even when the house and the village were abandoned, the figurine remained on the grave.

Acquisition of *kalimbangoma* follows the same patterns as acquisition of *maginga* by kindi, but women obtain them from other women who have preceded them in the grade, mainly through their husbands' agnatic relationships. Each man of yananio grade has only one *kalimbangoma;* a woman of bunyamwa owns several, most of them worn hanging from a belt.

Nearly all large wooden figurines and some bulky ivory ones are owned collectively by the initiated members of well-defined groups. Wooden figurines are kept in baskets, some of which are associated with lutumbo lwa yananio and others with the musage and the lutumbo levels of kindi. Besides the human figurines (I have seen as many as eleven in one basket), the baskets may also contain animal figurines, a wooden arm, a miniature canoe, a slit-drum, a mancala game board, a miniature wooden door, a small elephant tusk adorned with circle-dot designs, a wooden or ivory phallus or bark pounder, a large wooden mask, as well as natural objects such as hornbill and ibis beaks, chimpanzee skulls, pangolin scales, giant snail shells, epiphytes, and bark used for making fish poisons. Some groups do not include anthropomorphic wooden figurines in their baskets either because they are not used or because they have been distributed among initiates for safekeeping. For both kindi and yananio, the baskets are held within the autonomous community by the most junior member of the grade, and they change hands when a candidate is initiated. If a recent initiate dies while still in possession of the basket, it is returned temporarily to the closest agnatic relative of the appropriate grade. When Yala of Kabongelo lineage died after just being initiated to lutumbo lwa kindi, the basket passed to his classificatory brother, a kindi of Mwenda lineage, who kept it in trust until another classificatory brother at a lower kindi level in Wanyunga lineage was ready to take charge of it. The three kindi belonged to a single maximal lineage.

Baskets holding initiation objects are also linked with the highly secret *kasisi* rite of lutumbo lwa yananio. In most areas the baskets contain, instead of sculptures, quartz stones, feather ropes, and hoods and mantles in dotted bark cloth worn as disguises, though sometimes they do hold curious elementary figurines made of *ntutu*, copal, or clay from termite nests. *Kasisi* baskets, although owned on behalf of a lineage community, are usually transferred in an almost direct agnatic line of descent. They are passed on when their keeper moves up to kindi rank, or when he dies, to a close agnatic relative of appropriate rank.

Autonomous communities that have the kindi grade collectively own a single bulky ivory figurine (only rarely replaced by a finely polished wooden one) which has special functions. Some of these large ivories seem to be very old. As far as memory serves, certain figurines were entrusted to members of a group through nine generations. Such sculptures symbolize the introduction of kindi into an independent community, the privilege to hold kindi rites autonomously, and the unity of the kindi ritual. Ownership of the figurine is usually entrusted to a kindi representing the lineage that first acquired the grade within the local group. The owner keeps close watch over the figurine, placing it near his head when he goes to sleep. The figurine is transferred only when its keeper dies or when he becomes very old and weak. The recipient, who must hold kindi, is not necessarily a son or a brother of the previous keeper, but he must be a member of his maximal lineage. If a full-fledged kindi is not available in that group, the figurine passes temporarily to another kindi of the local community. He must surrender it to its rightful heir as soon as the latter achieves kindi.

In exceptional circumstances the figurine is no longer kept by the originating lineage, as in the following example. Misenga, a member of Sinda maximal lineage in the Beianangi community, had received the large ivory figurine from his maternal uncles, the Banamulunga-Babongolo. The Babongolo and the Beianangi were constantly feuding. To settle the quarrel the Babongolo gave a wife to Misenga, but dissension lingered on and members of Simulama lineage in the Beianangi killed Misenga's father-in-law, a kindi who was visiting his daughter. The Simulama group thus was forced to take the kindi grade or they "would die under kindi." Acting as *mukomi,* provider of the initiation objects, Misenga initiated a certain Nyamangalu of Simulama lineage. Misenga's figurine was transferred to the new initiate and remained in Simulama lineage, since the "figurine went from the *mukomi* to the *mutende* candidate and cannot be returned." No one among Misenga's five generations of descendants ever again achieved kindi.

Modes and Contexts of Presentation

The manner in which figurines of different types are presented during the initiations varies according to region, rite, and functional category.

The way in which wooden figurines contained in the baskets are used and displayed is the same in yananio and kindi rites. At the beginning a majestic procession of male and female initiates (the men followed by the women) enters the village, accompanied by the sound of rattles or bulrush swatters, dialogue between preceptors and the candidate's tutors, and the beating of suspended drums. The first woman in line carries a covered basket; if more than one autonomous group is participating in the ceremonies, as many as four women may each bring a basket. After marching through the village the initiates, often in bent and reverse positions, enter the initiation house. There, in the rite called "opening of the baskets," the objects are removed, inspected, placed on a mat, and touched up with white color. The coloring matter, provided by the candidate, is applied by the *kalombola* (an initiate of lower ngandu rank and aide-de-camp to the kindi). The process, called *kubongia* (to harmonize), is necessary whenever initiation objects are transferred (*kisomba*) from one place or person to another. In kindi rites the entire operation is accompanied by Kingili, the secret mirliton of the circumcision ceremonies. At the end of this preparatory rite, initiates in some groups strike the ground with seven sticks (from a raffia tree) to represent croaking frogs.

The figurines are later displayed in a row indoors or outside. The preceptors pick them up one by one, or sometimes two or three at a time, and dance with them. As drums are beaten, aphorisms relating to the images and the context are sung by the preceptors, the choir, and other dancers. The preceptors dancing with the figurines hold them in both hands or let them rest in their clenched fingers against their forearms. Sometimes the action is more specialized: the figurine is initially hidden between the legs under the loincloth; it hangs from a string; it is pressed against the belly, the dancer simulating pain; a stick is held against the buttocks of the figurine as if an enema were being administered. Two figurines frequently are paired, the texts referring to the oppositions or complementarities of the characters they represent. An image may also be used jointly with a chimpanzee skull or a turtle carapace. When the figurines and other objects contained in the baskets have all been danced with, they are put back in the baskets, not to be seen again during the initiations.

Male and female rites differ in the presentation of the *kalimbangoma* figurines, and there are slight regional variations. In yananio the dancers leave the initiation house, each holding his *kalimbangoma* in his cupped hands or wearing it tucked into his belt. Singing "Every mwami has his *kalimbangoma,*" they dance in a broad circle and then place the objects on the ground in a long row for display. A preceptor picks up a figurine and, followed by the women, dances around showing the image. The same action may be repeated several times by the preceptor as he is followed by either men or women. In some dances the preceptors caress the images as if they were fondling a woman; in others the figurines are placed on their backs "like old initiates lying in their long chairs." The presentation of the *kalimbangoma* in yananio usually follows the dances with the wooden figurines; some groups combine the two rites, after an interlude in which the *kalimbangoma* are displayed.

In the women's bunyamwa grade the *kalimbangoma* are used in the *kasumba* or *byanda* rite, which is part of the lutumbo lwa kindi initiations. The rite is held outside the village in a specially built shack. The images are displayed in either of two ways: lying on the ground with other women's paraphernalia in the center of a circle of sitting women, or standing against the women's diadems in a structure made of four poles from which their other insignia (feather bunches and wickerwork discs surmounted by erect vines) hang. In either display the assemblage is called *kanembwe eite mizigo,* the "greatest of bwami who carries all the burdens." After the presentation men and women return solemnly to the village, the men shaking their rattles. Proceeding slowly to the initiation house, they hesitate as if they were traveling in a fearsome place. But when the dances start the initiates enter the house and display the *kalimbangoma* on a mat. Then they come outside and dance without images; the aphorisms warn that one must avoid places where one does not belong and must fear unknown things.

Presentation of the individually owned *iginga* ivory and bone figurines in kindi varies slightly from one community to another. The *iginga* figurines are brought to the initiations hidden in the men's shoulder bags. Before displaying the objects the men dance, each carrying his shoulder bag and complaining that it sticks to him as *kabumbu* insects stick to the elephant and saying that he wants to get rid of it. The kindi then enter the initiation house. Mats, oil, salt, peanuts, and bananas are brought in by the candidate's tutors. All participants are then ordered (always in song) to open the bags and to place the objects on the mats (sometimes done by the wives of the kindi). When the images are ready, looking like "a shining mass of white mushrooms," the kindi aides proceed with the oiling while the forbidding Kingili (secret mirliton) sings and tutors distribute handfuls of shell money. At last the initiates pick up the figurines (simulating the gathering of mushrooms) and put them back in their bags as if to spur the impatience of the candidate ("The initiates are clever, they show you, they do not give you"). A long dance sequence focusing on the mats follows.

Kindi initiations reach their apogee in a massive display of figurines (and other sculptures owned by the kindi) at the musage wa kindi level, in a rite called *kinsamba,* and at the lutumbo lwa kindi level, in rites called *kinsamba* and *bele muno.* The climax has been building up gradually: first there was the exhibition of ivory masks on a fence, followed by the "opening of the baskets" containing the wooden sculptures and then the awesome interludes of Kingili's singing. Then came a new revelation of ivory masks and the presentation (outside the village) of the women's *kalimbangoma* figurines and several other paraphernalia belonging to both men and women.

In communities that perform the *bele muno* rite, it precedes *kinsamba.* Several examples illustrate the procedures followed by different groups in organizing *bele muno.* In the first one, the rite takes place outside the village in a specially built shack of leaves (*kasumba*). Anthropomorphic and zoomorphic figurines in ivory and bone stand against kindi hats arranged in a circle. Inside the circle are snail shells and chimpanzee skulls; at the very center is an unusually bulky ivory figurine (only one such figurine for each autonomous community). The configuration is covered with hides. Lying a tergo on a preceptor's back, the candidate is brought in and seated near the display. The objects are uncovered without music or dance, but all images are identified with the appropriate aphorisms. The figurines are called Mwango, Kankubungu, Musongelwa, Kalonga, Nkiti ya kubili, Kandende, Kakinga, Nyamasola, Kuboko kumozi, or by other names. The candidate is given one or more of these images left by a deceased colleague. After everything has been identified, the figurines are put back into the shoulder bags and the kindi return solemnly to the village where the *kinsamba* display is to be held.

In a second example, *bele muno* takes place in the initiation house. The *iginga* images rest against a circle of kindi hats with a large bulky figurine standing in the center. In front of the statues are *aneikozi* pebbles used for secret kindi messages that communicate objections to an individual's participation in kindi. The configuration is covered with hides when the naked candidate, carried on the back of a naked preceptor, is brought into the initiation house. They circle the configuration and twice jump over it, shouting their praise names. All objects are uncovered and identified. The figurines are called Kabukenge, Kasegasega, Mwami we Idungu, Nyanzinzinzi, Kilinga, Kakinga, or by other names.

In a third example, the same arrangements are made, but as the candidate enters the initiation house the kindi rub the ground with dried leaves, as if he were entering the lair of wild pigs. The figurines are identified as Nyantuli, Sakwanyona, Sakimatwematwe, Kabukenge, Wansongo, Ndumbe, Sakatwe ka Mbubu, Kagalama, and Nyaweita meiga.

The *kinsamba* display in musage wa kindi usually marks the final rite of that grade. It is simpler and less spectacular than that of lutumbo lwa kindi, in which it precedes the "skinning of the elephant," that is, the pulling down of the initiation house. The rite is performed consistently in different communities. The drummers and choir call the initiates to remind them of their duty to exhibit their objects: "Even if you do not like your colleague, you must show him the thing you have come with." Then kindi men and kanyamwa women arrive and dance with their shoulder bags. (One song speaks about a hunter whose shoulder bag contains nothing but dog bells.) After the dancing the initiates are ordered to display the images: "Everyone his one, everyone his one, Big-One of Kabilundu"; "Take your children, Little-Pusher has arrived." Both men and women sit down on their *kisumbi* stools either in a long row or in a circle. They remove the sculptures and place them on the ground, usually in front of themselves but sometimes before the new kindi and kanyamwa. Except for the collectively held large ivory figurine seen in *bele muno,* all other sculptures owned by individual kindi and kanyamwa are displayed: spoons, billhooks, axes, hammers, and phalli in ivory or bone; human figurines in ivory or bone or occasionally in stone, copal, or polished wood; animal figurines in ivory or bone. Subsequent actions may differ to some extent. In the musage wa kindi rite, preceptors pick up one or several figurines at a time and dance with them while singing appropriate aphorisms. In lutumbo lwa kindi, preceptors also dance with at least some of the pieces. In communities where there is no dancing, the initiates pick up the sculptures and pass them along behind their backs, from the last initiate to the first and then back. When the order is finally given to remove the images, they are put back into the shoulder bags.

Other than these major presentations in yananio and kindi, few figurines are observed except in regions that do not have yananio and kindi or have only recently acquired them. There a few figurines are shown in exhibits similar to those in *bele muno,* during initiations leading to the highest grades: ngandu, *hingwi, biciba,* and *kidasi.* In groups with yananio and kindi I have sometimes observed special kinds of exhibitions, always with a limited number of figurines. The following examples illustrate some of these special uses.

In the female bombwa rites a wooden figurine tucked into a genet hide was passed around like a child by dancing women; the aphorisms spoke about a young woman who is "freed" when she bears a child. In another bombwa rite women danced in a long row, the first two carrying a male and a female wooden figurine, respectively; some of their female colleagues were drumming inside the initiation house (a rare instance of women obtaining the right to drum). The row was led by a preceptor representing a good and beautiful person who attracts others.

In a male ngandu rite, two ivory anthropomorphic figurines and one wooden animal sculpture were used in a superb dramatic performance. The objects, placed inside a fence of porcupine quills, feather rope, and feather-trimmed snakeskin, were then covered; initiates sat in a close circle around the fence. First, two preceptors engaged in a mock fight, during which they made faces, pulled their lower eyelids down, tugged at loincloths, and threw hats. Two by two, the initiates seated in the circle turned their backs to each other (representing scorn) and then faced each other (harmony, understanding). The objects were uncovered; the animal figurine symbolized Mugugu, the great initiate who sends a message that must be heeded. The male and female ivories were placed on a hide. A preceptor turned one figurine on its back; a second dancer rolled it over. The second figurine was not disturbed, but the dancers stuck out their tongues at it. In another ngandu initiation two preceptors showed male and female wooden figurines; there was no dance or song but simply the beating of aprons on the ground.

In a kyogo kya kindi initiation an ivory figurine with its head down hung from the ceiling, and below it a banana stipe was held in place by a feather rope; two snail shells were placed atop the stipe. The structure, depicting an eagle's nest, symbolized the highness and the visibility of kindi; the figurine represented Mulima (Bat), hanging his head down "because of the bad words said to it by Sun."

I witnessed a curious use of ivory figurines in a musage wa kindi rite equivalent to *bele muno* (rattles were the only musical instruments). Inside the initiation house figurines, whitened or reddened pieces of termite nest, aardvark claws, snail and mussel shells, and a lizardlike ivory figurine were displayed inside a fence made of sticks (some topped with porcupine quills) and a feather rope. Behind another fence four kanyamwa were seated on a low bed, hiding ivory figurines firmly clasped in their hands between their thighs close to the genitalia, and shaking their heads. The actions represented a woman who indicates refusal by sitting on the side of the bed where her husband sleeps.

In a few communities human and animal sculptures in *ntutu* and *muntita* form a part of the *kasisi* baskets used in lutumbo lwa yananio rites. These figurines are displayed with other items (knotted vines, monkey skulls, porcupine quills, epiphytes) and interpreted in proverbs that are murmured rather than sung. The major action in the highly secret *kasisi* rite is connected with the ritual killing of a billy goat by initiates dressed in spotted bark cloth to represent leopards.

All patterns of use show the secret and exclusive character of Lega figurines. They are not displayed publicly but are viewed and explained only in initiations. Noninitiates and initiates of lower levels have no access to them. During the performances the figurines are not merely shown but are also carefully oiled or whitened, exhibited in configurations, and used in dances; some are bestowed upon the new initiate. Like other initiation objects, during the dances they become vehicles of information about the values and the aims of the bwami association.

Functions

Discussions of form, terminology, patterns of ownership and transfer, and methods of presentation have already pointed to functional properties of Lega figurines. The figurines are not cult objects, images of ancestors, divinities, or nature spirits, or dwelling places of mystic powers. Rather, they are vital, but not exclusive, initiation devices on which displays and dramatic performances are centered during the rites leading to specific levels and grades. Initiations are not simply occasions for entertainment, expressions of friendship or kinship solidarity, frameworks for economic transactions, or means to acquire status and to heighten prestige; they are also schools of learning. The initiates are trained to become better men and women through absorption of the great moral, social, and legal precepts that form the basis of a happy life and a smoothly functioning society. Emphasis on the didactic aspect of the initiations and on the moral character of the individual is continually illustrated in the proverbs. The initiates are concerned with "the interpretation of good teachings," with the "words of the land," words that are "high," that "bind people" and "transform" them. They practice the *idimbia lya bitondo,* the seduction of the words, and not the seduction of the apron, *idimbia lya nsulu.* Briefly, the figurines are visual aids in a performance-oriented didactic system that aims at elucidating the values and sociojuridical principles of bwami. They function as an iconic expression of these concepts, which are always stated antithetically; that is, they are expressed either in positive terms or as oppositions to and negations of the code. In this role figurines have the same function as other manufactured and natural objects exhibited and interpreted to suggest moral, philosophical, legal, and social prescriptions, but are not merely repetitive. They constitute, rather, a higher level of abstraction and condensation of symbolism, as is shown by their use in the climactic rites.

As initiation and teaching devices, figurines function in a closed context; their symbolic references are not meant to be understood by outsiders. ("Noninitiates, even though you see our loincloth you do not see our testicles.") They serve as a secret script that can be deciphered only through initiation, even if its basic messages constitute a universal truth and not an esoteric set of information. ("Those who have drummed for Kitindi have understood him.") As initiation devices that are small, portable, and easily hidden, figurines help to establish the recondite and cryptic character of the rites. They are stored in bags and baskets and viewed only during performances from which noninitiates are excluded. The forms they take, even seemingly descriptive ones like multifaced, one-eyed, one-armed figurines, or those with distended bellies or raised arms, are not "readable" by outsiders. Figurines maintain their secrecy until their symbolic meanings are revealed in the ceremonies. If the candidacy of a person aspiring to become a high initiate is accepted, he is certain to have the mysteries of the figurines unraveled for him. ("What is this here? What a man does not know he must ask for it.") During the rites each figurine is associated with at least one aphorism that establishes the character it represents. Objects and texts are inseparably linked. Like other initiation objects, figurines are not only re-minders (*kalolesia*) of precepts but also mnemonic devices (*kakengelezio*) that fa-cilitate the memorizing of an enormous number of texts and actions.

Bwami members, using their secret system of communication, send envoys (of at least kongabulumbu grade) to colleagues to invite them, to warn them, to urge them not to accept a candidate or delay the ceremonies, to inform them that the necessary goods for payments and exchanges are either available or insufficient, or to charge them with a duty (e.g., to poison a person who would have committed homicide). Such an envoy takes with him an object that be-longs to bwami: a reed swatter, a giant snail shell, a wickerwork rattle, a neck-lace made of small polished discs of snail shells, a genet hide, certain species of leaves, chicken feathers, goat's hair, and sometimes knotted or looped raffia strings (the number of knots and the way the loops are to be undone are sig-nificant). There is no evidence that figurines were used in this way.

Figurines are restricted to certain grades, grade levels, and statuses. They are privileged but obligatory insignia of certain male and female initiates. A kindi and a kanyamwa, and in some communities a yananio, must possess figurines. The initiation itself implies the acquisition of objects such as masks, figurines, distinctive hats, belts, and natural objects. The initiate participating in ceremonies held in his own or in other communities must display the figurines at the appropriate time as proof of his qualifications. A ritual commu-nity that has no collectively owned figurines is not autonomous. Whenever two independent communities decide to merge their collectively held baskets, they lose their autonomy and thereafter act as a single ritual entity.

Individually owned figurines are inherited from deceased kin; others are trans-ferred from person to person when a member of the community moves up from yananio to kindi. Collectively owned baskets with figurines are surrendered by a recent initiate and given to the newest one; a single collectively owned figurine is passed along to a kinsman when the keeper dies or becomes too old. This transfer of sculptures creates special bonds of solidarity among the living as well as a sense of continuity between the living and the dead. Initiates are acutely aware of these bonds, which they can trace back through several generations. Figurines thus fos-ter interdependency between individuals and coherence and perpetuity within lineages and clans. The feeling of belonging fits well into the ideology of the bwami association, whose eternity is always emphasized: "Fruits of Mpoko [banana tree] are destroyed, but not Mpoko."

Particular figurines also have accessory functions. Large bulky ivory figurines (and their rare wooden replacements) symbolize high status in kindi. They are kept in trust by the descendants of the persons thought to have intro-duced the kindi rites into the local community. Keepers of such objects are treated with reverence and respect as guardians of group solidarity. They, and the image they protect, must be present when a kindi initiation is held. Opposi-tions, unities, cleavages, and alignments of lineages within large communities are expressed by ownership of different figurines. In one clan composed of seven maximal lineages I found two wooden figurines owned by two "very intelligent" kindi, one on behalf of three linked lineages of the clan and the other on behalf of four. Through six generations these images had been guarded by kindi belonging to sublineages in each of the two segments. Kindi initiations for any member of the group required the presence of both figurines.

When yananio and kindi owners of individual figurines die, the statues and other insignia are displayed on their tombs. Months later, after certain rites have been performed, the objects are collected by the "guardian of the tomb"; some are transferred to a successor, some are exposed permanently near the entrance to the village. One figurine, however, is left on the tomb as a sign, a reminder, and a part of the deceased's being. Exposure of the figurines on a tomb gives them a mystic dimension. As they are inherited, not only do they evoke pleasant memories (*kasina*) of the dead, but they are also impregnated with the vital force of the deceased. When an initiate is seriously ill and the normal pharmacopoeia fail to save him, he is given water to drink in which surface dust rubbed from the figurines has been mixed. The patient is said to "drink the *maginga*" in order to absorb some of the vital force contained in the statues. This force is not the result of some magical action; rather it is in the very being of the figurines, in the fact that they are what they are: sacred and privileged objects intimately associated with their living and dead owners and symbols of continuity.

Special functions are reserved for the small *katimbitimbi* figurines that belong to initiated women. Hung from a ring or a beaded strap attached to the belt near hips or buttocks, these sculptures signify the unique status of the kanyamwa woman. She is a socially prominent person who wields great influence in the polygynous and extended family; she participates in men's councils and deliberations, and she accompanies her husband to all initiations. Through special rites an indissoluble bond is forged between the kanyamwa and her husband. The *katimbitimbi* sculptures thus mark, on the one hand, her virile status (*katimbitimbi*, lit., what shivers passionately, means phallus) and, on the other, her inviolability and inalienability. She must not be coveted or seduced by other men; severe penalties, including death by poison, are imposed for violations. To show the inalienability of a goat reserved for the initiations or of an object (e.g., a stool that might be appropriated in joking relationships by a sororal nephew), a *katimbitimbi* is attached to the animal or to the object.

It is not easy to define the aesthetic functions of figurines, partly because concerns for beauty, morality, and character are intermingled, and partly because the artists who produced the figurines had disappeared from Legaland by the time of my research. The Lega's sense of beauty is strongly expressed by initiates, as when they refer to the "shining splendor [*lunyangala*] of the children of the bami." They take good care of their bodies, oiling them with red color mixtures; Banamombo, Anointed-Ones, is one of their preferred terms of reference. In ordinary life they wear fine, impressive hats, necklaces, diadems, belts, loincloths, and aprons to which they add feather bunches during ceremonies. The male initiate traditionally had his skull shaved and wore his conical hat far back on his head to show the continuity of forehead and head. Physical deficiencies were disliked and were often used metaphorically to refer to an evil character. The ideal of male beauty is a smooth (*kolokolo*), spotless (i.e., without pimples and sores; *bakoma*), well-oiled, and well-dressed body (the term *-ela* signifies, among other things, a place that is bare, a body that is dirty, not oiled and reddened, or bare without clothing). The initiation objects are described as *kyenga kikulangala*, shining whiteness, not in the literal sense but to denote light-coloredness and cleanliness, as when they say that the village place is white (*-enga*).

The same standards of beauty are sought for in women. In addition, the Lega admire the female qualities of straightness of the back marked by the spinal column's concave wedge (*kasamba kasoga*), the heavy, rounded buttocks (*bilimbio*), the tumescences on the upper arms and legs caused by tightly worn bracelets (on the upper arm and wrist) and bangles (between the knee and the ankle; the terms for bracelets and leg rings are used as synonyms for women), and the flat stomach (*idago*). In the ideal pose for women walking or dancing, their arms hang straight down along the body, the hands open but the fingers slightly bent inward. This posture is so important that the term *kusikasika*, which designates it, is used to refer to women in drum praise names; the usual word for a young woman is *musika*, which surely is related to the verb *kusikasika*. In dance contexts the men, when not carrying objects, hang their arms loosely along the body or bend them so that the hands are near the lower belly, at the height of the hips, or close to the chest. As they dance they also keep their bodies straight or lightly curved with slightly bent knees.

Undoubtedly many of these aesthetic ideas about the body and its movements are translated into the forms of the figurines. One must keep in mind, however, that bodily beauty and moral excellence are combined in Lega thought, and that figurines illustrating morally depraved persons tend to de-emphasize the ideal features and overemphasize undesirable physical aspects. In other words, there is a code of the ugly, and it must be thoroughly understood in its context. A female figurine with dimorphous belly, a statue with one arm, and a darkened figurine probably represent characters that are criticized, but meanings read into the forms are ambiguous. It is also obvious that certain poses, such as arms in other than pendulous positions or a bent back, may be inspired by particular but not necessarily negative concepts about moods and expressions. In general, the majority of the figurines reflect the body codes: a smooth shiny surface; a large forehead and a bare skull with a carved skullcap (realistic or symbolized by a cowrie); a straight back and an erect posture; pendulous arms, sometimes captured at the point of forward movement near the thighs; tumescent or scalloped arms and legs. It would be erroneous, however, to think that sculptors were inspired only by codes of beauty and ugliness. The strong emphasis in many figurines on the large head and on the massive legs and feet seems directly related to philosophical ideas cherished by the initiates: they are thinkers and they are elephants (i.e., solid and powerful).

Initiation objects are compared with traps or with elephant ears that catch insects. All initiations to a grade level require fees, presents, distributions of food, and certain physical activities (hunting, house building, making shell money, extracting oil, preparing salt, planting and harvesting bananas and peanuts). Every rite in the initiation, and sometimes every phase in a rite, demands prescribed payments and gifts to all participants with special supplements going to certain performers, status holders, or kin. The following example gives an idea of the payments and gifts made in lutumbo lwa kindi in rites during which artworks are displayed. Certain rites demand an even larger outlay of valuables.

> *Kampumba:* the actors are two masked women, two helpers, four female drummers, and other participants. The maskers and the aides receive one *kako* (four double lengths) each of the *kilunga* size (tip of medius to fold of arm) of shell money strung on raffia fibers. Of the four drummers, each of the three who perform on the main drum, the second drum, and the slit-drum gets one *kako* of the *kilunga* size; the fourth female drummer, who beats the side of the second drum with sticks, receives one *kako* of *magombelo* size (from top of middle finger to wrist). The other participants share ten *kako* of *magombelo,* one antelope, one pack of salt, one jar of oil, and a large bunch of bananas.
>
> *Kasumba* of the women (on this occasion the female initiate gets a figurine and a coronet): the participating kanyamwa share ten *kilunga,* three or four antelopes, a large jar of oil, and a pack of salt.
>
> *Kasumba* of the men (the new male initiate gets a *kikoku* snail shell): the participating kindi divide ten *kilunga,* four or five antelopes, one billy goat, one large jar of oil, and one pack of salt. (A lavish dinner in the forest is prepared at the end of the rites by a male kindi aide; part of the meat and other food is consumed, but the rest is sent in packages to relatives in the home villages.)
>
> Display of figurines for women: handfuls of loose money are given to every participant.
>
> *Ibugebuge* (display of ivory masks on a fence): women get small handfuls of money; each preceptor and each helper receives one *kako* of *kilunga* size.
>
> *Bilimbi* (a mask fixed on a high pole): the group of men and the group of women get ten *magombelo* sizes each.
>
> *Bele muno* (display of figurines): ten *kazigi* sizes (from tip of medius to biceps) for the keeper of the large figurine; three or four goats, six or more whole animals (only intestines removed), two jars of oil, and one large pack of salt with which to prepare a lavish meal.
>
> *Kinsamba* (display of kindi-owned sculptures): handfuls of loose money to every participant.

The kindi rites begin with the ceremonial entrance (*lukenye*) of all male and female participants carrying individually and collectively owned initiation objects. At the end of the procession each kindi receives ten *kilunga* sizes of money and each kanyamwa, two *kako* of *kilunga* size. When the collectively owned basket is opened the junior initiate (*mukomi*) who keeps the basket transmits it to the candidate and receives the important *musigo* payment: a female goat, twenty *kilunga* sizes of money, large packs of torches, and a new bark cloth. On several occasions food is distributed for communal dinners; it includes five or six game animals (mostly antelope), oil, salt, and bananas.

Meanings

Bwami initiations at all levels are based on dramatic performances, dances, and sung aphorisms that accompany the display and interpretation of objects. Thus initiations not only are a way of acquiring status, prestige, and wealth, and of wielding power and authority in social groups; they are also a system of teachings (*lunkungu, yano, lusungu*). In fact, an individual cannot hope to rise in the bwami hierarchy if he or she is unacquainted with and does not live by the principles and values expressed in the teachings of bwami. The noninitiate is a *mutuza*, one who has not received the revelations and is ignorant of causes and meanings. The initiate, on the contrary, from the lowest to the highest level gradually acquires *izu*, the ineradicable understanding of the initiation code, through *kizio*, the absorption of exclusive knowledge derived from social interaction with the Big-Ones.

Any rite in which objects are shown is a form of privileged revelation of things otherwise unseen, "whose secrets are unknown," and of the ultimate truth. The neophyte will learn the real nature and purpose of things about which he previously had misconceptions or superficial information: "I thought Saluzugu [a small bird that has many feathers and imitates the human voice] to be a human being, and lo! it is a little bird that fools me with its many feathers." Any rite that demands gift giving and fees is a form of warfare, a *bita bya mwembe*, that is, a war in which a group of people insist on material retributions for the revelations they have made. Songs remind the kindi that he has traveled on a long and dangerous path: "The trail of the teachings: a difficult trail on which one does not pass a second time." He must now be cautious and must avoid making mistakes.

As noted earlier, the initiation objects (*masengo;* regionally also called *bitungwa, bi'o'o, bilugwe, bilu'we*) are numerous and diverse; they are hidden, secret, and dangerous; and possession of them is coveted (*kilembo*) by all men and women. Figurines form only a part of these objects, but ownership, display, and interpretation of the anthropomorphic sculptures is linked with top-level initiatory experience. Large numbers of them are used in the culminating rites leading to lutumbo lwa yananio, bunyamwa, and the kindi levels. At the end of a long and trying progression to the heights (*igulu*) of personal achievement

("Bwami that father Itula has danced is *katondo*," a tall tree in which eagles nest), the initiate receives the supreme reward of the right to see, possess, and understand the figurines, which represent the highest synthesis of bwami ideals. The teachings, revealed more abstractly than those about other objects, do not center on an esoteric code of knowledge but rather on the moral, social, and legal principles thought to be the very foundations of harmonious and virtuous social life. The actual association between figurines and ideas is secret: it cannot be comprehended by persons of lower rank or by noninitiates ("Let me explain to him the whispers of the teachings").

Each figurine represents a well-defined human character. As already pointed out, animal figurines, masks, spoons, and many other manufactured and natural items also stand for human and real or anthropomorphized animal characters. Most of these have flexible meanings that depend not only on the type of object displayed but also on the ritual context, the configuration, and the accompanying dance action. Many of the simple manufactured and natural objects depict, not a character, but an idea or a principle. The tibia of a cercopithecus monkey used as a sheath to protect a sewing needle or a needle threaded with a raffia fiber, for example, illustrates the companionship of a man and his wife, particularly the bond between initiated husband and wife. These objects, however, also express other ideas: bwami joins people together; problems and litigations afflicting a father are inherited by his son. A broom made of bulrush (used to clean the house) symbolizes the role of bwami as "a cleaner of hearts." Small disk-shaped pieces of hide or raffia adorned with cowries, beads, or chicken feathers are the "shields of the initiates," who no longer need real shields because they are not warmongers and because they have immunity in warfare.

In the minds of their owners and independent of performances, these objects differ from anthropomorphic figurines. The latter intrinsically have a well-defined, permanent meaning. Although there are several iconographic prototypes, the names given to individual figurines are purely symbolic. The naming of figurines is similar to the naming of people. Although a personal name may reflect a particular physical trait, it is commonly derived from social position and status, social situations prevailing in the family group at the time of birth, and local traditions of recurring cross-generational naming. The names of many individual figurines are specific to them, that is, they are not used in conjunction with other initiation devices; others, however, may reflect characters that are illustrated by other means as well. Some of these, such as Kakulu, Katanda, Kasagula, Kabukungu, Mwango, Keitula, and Wankenge, are also the personal names of individuals, and some extend far back in genealogical recitations to the ancestral founders of lineages.

Similarly named figurines of almost identical or of dissimilar form are found across Legaland. Some names recur frequently, whereas others seem to be rare; one figurine occasionally has two names. A character's name is usually mentioned in the aphorism associated with the sculpture, except when the text implicitly points to a certain personage, such as a hungry old man or a stranger asking for hospitality. There are two types of names: specific names, often but not necessarily preceded by the morphemes *ka-*, *(i)sa-*, or *nya-* (*nye-*); and generic names (e.g., *kakinga*, young woman), sometimes identified by a further specification (e.g., *mwami we idungu*, an initiate from far away) or by a relative verb form (e.g., he who has seen the initiation objects).

Figurines have implicit meanings formulated in aphorisms that are traditionally and inseparably associated with them. They are given a less kinetic interpretation than other sculptures and manufactured and natural initiation objects. Whereas figurines individually owned by yananio, kanyamwa, and kyogo kya kindi and those in the baskets are presented with dance action, usually no dancing accompanies the display of figurines owned individually by musage and lutumbo lwa kindi.

The small *kalimbangoma* figurines, tucked into the dancers' belts or held in cupped hands to denote that every high initiate has a companion-protector, seldom have individual names. Dance action, however, may give precise meanings to groups of figurines. In one dance performance a preceptor, followed by the women, holds a *kalimbangoma* figurine, while two other images lie on the ground. A few male dancers then start chasing the women and succeed in catching them. The action refers to a junior initiate whose initiated kalonda wife was taken by others. The two images lying on the ground represent the seducer and the kalonda woman. In another sequence all *kalimbangoma* pieces are placed on their backs to symbolize the elderly—"The old initiates, the children of Bark Cloth, who lie leisurely in their long chairs waiting for food"—that is, old initiates visit a junior who tells his wives to prepare a lavish feast for them. The old initiates, rejoicing in the good treatment they receive, decide to support the candidacy of the junior.

The *kalimbangoma*, in areas where they are assemblages of natural objects instead of anthropomorphic figurines, are likely to designate characters closely linked with the objects. Examples of assemblage articles and the relevant aphorisms include a *kabugi* antelope paw: "Kabugi stands on one leg; he will not arrive"; an aardvark claw: "Aardvark enters the lair; no other animal enters there"; the toothed jaw of the *ntonge* fish: "Those with filed teeth: in laughing there is something big"; the fangs of a *mpoma* viper: "In the fallow land where Mpoma lays its eggs, there is no mouse left."

Wooden figurines from the baskets may be danced with singly, in groups of two or more, or with other objects. The order in which they appear and the action they elicit affect their meaning. For example, dancers holding all the figurines from one basket and following a preceptor dancing with a cercopithecus monkey skull represent Kabamba (lit., a monkey species) and Isabusio, the forefighter followed by his people. In another instance, two women dancing with wooden statues and followed by a long row of initiates illustrate Keitula wa Yimbo, the Beautiful-One (Son) of Singer (i.e., a good and noble person) and his many followers. In another example, two preceptors dance with the representations of Kakulu ka Mpito and Mukobania. Kakulu symbolizes an unwise person who, attracted to a beer party given by Mukobania, runs into trouble. In other sequences a figurine is rolled over the ground to mark the movements of a sick person or to portray a person who is afraid to turn the corpse of a kinsman whom he wronged.

The same kind of dramatic action is seldom undertaken with the *maginga* (ivory, bone, or polished wood figurines) owned individually by kindi. In a rare rite one such figurine was hung from a string with the head downward to symbolize Mulima (Bat), who was wronged by his kin or his peers.

Characters Seldom Represented in Sculptures

At all initiation levels and in hundreds of aphorisms, characters with human attributes are identified in a wide variety of ways. Generic and specific terms for plants, animals, and objects, as used in a verbal and dramatic context, become thinly disguised metaphors for human beings. *Nsinge* is not merely a term meaning "needle" but also the name of a person called Needle; *kinyo kya nsyenge* is not just the tusk of a warthog but Tusk-(Son)-of-Warthog; *lukusa* is not simply a vine used in making nets and bags but Mr. Lukusa. Names of characters are also derived from words that describe social status, kinship positions, occupations, physical and moral attributes, abnormalities, attitudes, and habits. In this way many compound names that directly define or implicitly suggest a person are coined.

The following list shows how some characters enacted or mentioned during the rites but not represented by sculptures were illustrated. Virtually all of them, however, could have been typified by sculptures collected among the Lega. Merlot (1931b), for example, identifies a female figurine with widespread legs as Isamukulu. I heard this character cited in an aphorism connected with Ikaga (Pangolin): "Ikaga, the acquisition of goods [*isongo*] makes me Isamukulu [Father-Walking-Stick] fight with the children of my father." The name Isamukulu can hardly be associated with a female figurine, but it is possible that Merlot heard the text in a slightly different version, such as "Isamukulu, Isonga makes me fight with the children of my father." Thus to him the figurine represented Isonga (Marriage, i.e., the woman I married), who caused trouble among her husband's kin.

> Idimbia (verb, meaning to seduce, used as substantive): "Idimbia would not have died, [because] of fondling Idimbia kills herself." This role is danced by two preceptors touching a pile of bags, becoming wild, and reaching for each others' penes to suggest an adulterous person.

Idumbi (a tuft with quills only used in opposition to a tuft with red parrot feathers stuck in among the quills): "Idumbi who has no heart is a [sheer] mass of feathers." Idumbi symbolizes a person with a nice body but a bad heart.

Ikili and Ikilingania (simply danced): Ikili is one who pretends to surpass others in intelligence but encounters Ikilingania, who is smarter. The characters are mentioned in conjunction with a needle and raffia thread and represent two tutors, one stronger than the other.

Isabulema (mentioned in a song), Mr. Stupid, Mr. Bad Heart, Seducer: "Isabulema, fondling has killed him." He is also identified as one who always wants to talk back to his father, or as Isakati (Mr. Barricade) who cuts ax marks in a *musuku* tree to prevent others from using the wood.

Isabulumbu, Mr. Obscurity, Mr. Inner-Blindness, Mr. Thoughtlessness: "I go chasing *mikala* [small animals that bite fiercely; always used as synonym for women], I Isabulumbu." The role is danced wildly by preceptors shaking bells attached to their wrists and ankles, shivering, and executing coital movements near each initiate.

Isabumania (cited in a song), Mr. Desire, Mr. Lust: "Even if you are an Isabumania, [know that] on the road a child is not born."

Isakabitabita, Mr. War-War, Fighter. He is advised in a song that it would be better first to find out with whom he fights.

Isawambulambula, Mr. Remover-Remover, who likes to take people's belongings. A song warns him not to take things from a dead person he finds on the road because he would be accused of having killed him.

Itamba. See Kalingi and Itamba.

Kabamba Isabusio (lit., a monkey species): "Kabamba Isabusio dies in the very early morning" (i.e., he dies a bad death). He is a master of the land but, against all the rules, acts as Isabusio (Forefighter), one who is too keen on violence. The character is illustrated by a monkey skull with eye sockets filled with cowries and a monkey tail attached to it.

Kabigabiga, Wrong-Wrongdoer: "Wrong-Wrongdoer, child of my sister, wrongs me." This characterization applies especially to a sororal nephew who wrongs his uncle; the uncle does not retaliate, but he hangs his head without looking at anything. The character is depicted in a dance in which the candidate is carried upside down on the back of a preceptor.

Kagelia (a species of monkey): "Kagelia is not [one] of the clan; beat him with a club." A group of dancers with sticks attack a stuffed genet hide that is carried by a preceptor. Kagelia is the arrogant person who visits people of another group, meddles in their affairs, and is beaten. The character is also presented by a chimpanzee skull with one of the eyes closed with leaves or resin: "Kagelia grunts against [other] people; he does not grunt against his [own ones]."

Kalingi, an instigator, teaser, provoker, and Itamba, a moderate person: "Kalingi and Itamba are of the same size of waist [but] they do not resemble each other" (i.e., they do not have the same manners or knowledge). These two serve to contrast the noninitiate with the initiate.

Kamanwa, shrewd person of bad habits. He is compared with "lice running around on what is bought for goats" (i.e., a woman's genitalia). Kamanwa is also a clever person who seeks outside help against one who wants to outsmart him: "Kamanwa follows Kambimbi [Shrewd-One]."

Kansinsi, Wagtail. Presented by a preceptor holding a feather tuft in front of his penis, Kansinsi is one who likes women too much.

Kasegesege, who has a "tough heart," is not concerned about anyone; he does not even look at anyone: "We spend the night at Kasegesege's; we sleep in the place of people with an implacable heart." The character refers to a person who does not care about his kin.

Kasumba, a person with whom one can take refuge, a protector: "To kill a person: to flee to the maternal uncles' group, to Kasumba."

Katutumbi, Who-Shivers-of-Sickness: "He fights with sickness, Katutumbi"; "Katutumbi fights with Bondo [death; lit., a place where one will not be seen again]." The character refers to women who refuse to listen and is symbolized by shaking a feather rope or gaffs planted in the ground.

Kigamba, a physically strong person: "They load him with a bundle of house poles, they do not floor him."

Kikwankondo, a woman who always turns her head away when someone talks to her or when she is asked a question: "My wife Kikwankondo does not speak without shaking [moving away] her head." A crouching preceptor shakes his head and moves his hands in a gesture of rejection.

Kiluku, a person of bad disposition: "Kiluku, my wife, Kiluku hides herself from me in the crowd of males." This woman always runs away from her husband to be courted by other men. She is represented in dance by women who crowd around an overdressed woman and start a quarrel about her.

Kingungu or Kingungungungu (lit., apron of woman): "Kingungu dies because of the labia of Nyansubi [Mrs. Copper Rings]" is about a seducer; "I hate the embracing of Mombo [Oil] of Kingungungungu" is about kin who always act badly toward someone who then leaves them.

Kinumpi, person with a bad smell. The name is given to a man suspected of not having informed the initiates about the death of a pangolin. Severe sanctions are imposed for nonobservance of this practice.

Kisapupa, a strong person: "Kisapupa, the young man, has died for having lost the trail," is about an individual who does not listen to advice.

Kisesa, a slanderer or seducer who destroys the village. The character is portrayed by a preceptor holding a *yango* pole.

Kisibula, Destroyer. Symbolized by a warthog tusk held in the preceptor's mouth, the character refers to a witch or to a headman who inappropriately accuses others of unverified misdeeds: "Tusk-of-Warthog, Destroyer, destroys the village of Mulangwa."

Kitandala, Rambler who has no house, no fixed place. He is always running around; he will die in a foreign land.

Kitwemugumbu, Big-Bald-Head, the young initiate who begins to search for the path his father traveled.

Kyabugogo: "Kyabugogo you cut your father's child an arm; you thought that war would not come." Bold and aggressive Kyabugogo injures a kinsman, not realizing that the latter might help him in time of war.

Kyengengwa, an arrogant woman who refuses to sleep with her husband when he wants her.

Minna, a person speaking hypocritically and in a low voice; a backbiter.

Mulumbu (lit., a person suffering from hate): "Mulumbu calls me Mbagu [Mouse], I am Mukumbi [Golden Mole], I am the junior of Aardvark." This aphorism is sung while the candidate is being pushed around. Mulumbu is a stupid, thoughtless person who easily forgets advice given to him and who scorns his benefactors.

Mwami wa Batoba, the initiate of the Batoba clan: "An initiate does not hang himself; among the Batoba an initiate has hanged himself." Men must not commit suicide by hanging (as women do). The text also means that a person who speaks in this manner is certain to kill someone in the near future. The hanging scene is enacted by a preceptor putting a vine around his neck, or simply by hanging a piece of bark cloth from a feather rope attached to the ceiling of the initiation house.

Mwenia or Mwenia wa Mpego, Unfortunate-One, Child-of-Cold, victim of a troublemaker. If danced with a warthog tusk: "Warthog muddied the river upstream while Mwenia was drinking downstream." When danced with a mat as if it were a shield to indicate one despised in his group: "Mwenia, Child-of-Cold, does not parry the shield in a place where there is no danger."

Nyabukolo, Mrs. Harvesting: "Nyabukolo open the door for me that I may see how it is adorned inside." Dancing with a miniature door, the character portrays a woman who refuses to open the door when her husband knocks, and tells him to sleep elsewhere.

Nyamalendelo, a woman who likes to run away from her husband: "Nyamalendelo will break the child." The characterization refers to a woman with child; when she leaves her husband, there will be many disputes about the social identity of the child. In contrast: "There is no sadness because of the running away of one who has no child."

Nyambambaluka, one who suddenly jumps up and leaves without listening; resembles a bad child.

Nyamilyalya za nkula, Mrs. Eating-Eating of camwood powder (i.e., a woman heavily rubbed with red powder): "Let us greet each other [I] Mombo [Oil] and [you] Nyamilyalya za nkula"; "He who tattooed Nyamilyalya with the *tokembe* tattoos knew how to tattoo!" This beautiful but superficial woman succumbs easily to flattery.

Nyamusili: "The young woman Nyamusili, her belly does not bring forth strong children." Swinging a resin torch tied to a string, this character represents a woman who always has a vine tightened around her belly, which constantly aches.

Nyanegenege, an old, fat, small, unliked woman who waddles like a duck: "You marry Nyanegenege, the masters of Hunting-Ground do not like her."

The character may depict a weak young woman—"Nyanegenege each limb laments"—and is illustrated by squatting preceptors who shake forked sticks planted in the ground while trying to stand. She may be portrayed by a pit in which a *kyombi* stick (symbol of a phallus) is moved. Nyanegenege is also the woman who has no strength left because she has slept with others in many different places.

Nyatulondo twa nsulu, Mrs. Rags: "Nyatulondo, who has called you up for the journey?" An initiated woman dances with a long strip of bark cloth floating on her buttocks; other women who are chasing her try to catch the cloth. The character represents an evil wife; the initiates ask who will go to the ceremonies with her.

Nyawatandala, Rambler, Vagrant Woman: "Nyawatandala, you will encounter danger ready for you." She is depicted by a preceptor dancing along a feather rope until he falls into an imaginary snare.

Nyeidegelege, Mrs. Noisy, Talkative (like certain birds). She causes many difficulties in the village.

Sabigombo, Mr. Big-Arms. He is strong, but "it is in the *ngobi* cradling rope that your mother has carried [rocked] you." This person is represented by strips of banana tree bark tied together with a vine. Another aspect is symbolized by a preceptor unsuccessfully rubbing the fire drill: "Sabigombo is surpassed by Buza [Fire Drill], look at the size of his arms!" Sabigombo is strong but stupid; a smaller or weaker person may be smarter.

Sabikongo, Cougher: "He does not sleep, he is still smoking tobacco." A preceptor circles around a configuration and coughs: "I circle around with Big Yango, I carry a *mutondo* pipe."

Salugi, Lazybones. He is also a jealous person to whom the initiates mockingly say: "Salugi, hide yours [i.e., your wife], Elephant wears the *bilondo* aprons." Here he is admonished not to be suspicious of his wife when she eagerly looks at the well-dressed dancers.

Saluzugu, Mr. Bluff, Deception, Camouflage: "I thought Saluzugu to be a man and lo! it is a bird with many feathers" (or, "It is a little bird that fools me with its many feathers"). The character is enacted by a preceptor who wears a collaret and waddles.

Samukumangwa: "Samukumangwa dies in the last net." All people consider him to be bad, and he will die abandoned.

Sanzugunzugu, Mr. Callous, Hard-Hearted: "Sanzugunzugu [child] of my father, his implacable heart has made his body dry up." This person is represented by a hornbill beak; he cannot shine because he has a bad heart, and he will not have good fortune.

Satugombo, Mr. Arms. People remember this character at the time of the harvest of termites and talk as if he were still alive. When preceptors have difficulty attempting to open a covered pit, they recall Satugombo, a father or a senior who, if he were now alive, would quickly help to resolve the problems.

Sawabuzumbu (lit., *buzumbu* is what hangs down because of its weight): "Sawabuzumbu dies on the side road." This characterization signifies the master of the land who did not go to the front lines in war but was ambushed in his village. The character is described in a mock attack with a wooden spear.

Sawakisuka, Mr. Big Penis. The leader who is a seducer cannot keep a village together.

Sawambombo, Who-Has-Understood: "Sawambombo died among the Babinza [another ethnic group], he had enough of being sent back and forth." A person lacking intelligence falls victim to many evils.

Seikumba, Mr. Bent-Over-Himself: "Mr. Bent beats [on the drums] the dance of initiation and the dance of war." A person with bad intentions calls the initiates together for the rites but then makes trouble.

Seyombombo, Mr. Mercy: "Seyombombo goes to the Batoba without seeing [encountering] one prohibiting the road [the passage]." The character, danced by a preceptor holding a collaret of dried leaves over his head, stands for a young man who is sent by his father to unknown places; he does not object but simply goes.

Temeteme wa Kyanga, one who looks on stupidly and indifferently. The son of one who engages in surreptitious actions, this person magnifies a small piece of news to excessive proportions.

Wakasili, One-with-a-Spear-That-Kills-Right-There: "Let Wakasili who kills me with hatred, let him be with ten wounds." This aggressive person is depicted by a preceptor who attacks the candidate with a wooden spear.

Walimbia wa Mukulu, he who seduces the wife of a Big-One: "Walimbia wa Mukulu eats an egg with rotten odor." This aphorism refers directly to a man who would seduce a kanyamwa woman. In a particular dance the initiates used a light bulb and an aluminum plate (one of the rare occasions when modern foreign-made goods are used as initiation objects) to signify that everything had changed with Europeanization; kanyamwa women could now remarry, a practice forbidden in the old tradition.

Wesatu, Mr. Three (Fingers): "Wesatu died without finishing the yananio initiations." One who is not physically strong enough to assemble all the goods necessary for the initiations cannot be successful in his quest. This character, simply evoked in this song, may also be represented by a trident.

Characters Illustrated by Anthropomorphic Figurines

The following list presents only a sample of the characters associated with anthropomorphic figurines. I have named only those I actually saw in the initiation context. These figurines, of different forms, sizes, and materials, have diverse functions and patterns of ownership.

Bakwampego, Those-Dying-of-Cold (Biebuyck, 1973, pl. 65): "Those-Dying-of-Cold, to be made a fire is what they hate." The character has a double meaning. It refers to an old person who is well cared for by a younger man, whose own father is dead. The young man provides the older one with food and builds a house for him; but the old man begins to dig up old differences he had with the young man's father and finally chases his benefactor away. The character may also represent a young man who is supported by his father's junior brother after the death of his own father. The youth scorns his uncle, who wanted "to make a fire" (i.e., help him into bwami), but the young man spoils the relationship. In other contexts the character of Mwenia mwana wa Mpego (Unfortunate-One, Child-of-Cold) bears on a person who is despised by others in his group.

Bananini (in combination with Bana-, members of the group so-and-so, the Swahili-derived *nini* means Those-Not-Mentioned-by-Name, the Who's): "Those-Not-Mentioned-by-Name who are gnawed by hunger are the first to call for food [Oh! Give me!]." Strangers arriving in the village must receive food; the villagers must not dismiss them and say that they have no food here or that they do not eat.

Beikalantende, Who-Do-Not-Sleep-Fast (Biebuyck, 1973, pl. 81): "Those-Who-Do-Not-Sleep-Fast ponder about many things." This character is the great initiate who holds the teachings of bwami forever in his heart.

Gonda [the correct text is missing from my notes], a person persisting in his quest for a woman or for bwami. Although not liked initially, Gonda will achieve his goals and his tenacity will induce others to help him.

Isakasumo, Mr. Spear: "Mr. Spear ready to throw; once under the shield one no longer knows how the land will be destroyed." He represents a person who changes his attitudes after being initiated. He thinks that no one must follow him in bwami and prevents ("under the shield") other kinsmen from being initiated. A person with a bad character should never be initiated.

Kabongelo, Anointed-One: "Anointed-One hears [words said] behind the back." This and other characters express the idea that the high initiate is well informed through constant communication with his colleagues.

Kabongi Kabongelo, Oiler, Oil-Calabash: "Kabongi from Malinga [the west, the lowlands], Kabongelo does not [go to] sleep without being oiled." Kabongi is the great initiate who always has a well-oiled (well-cared-for) body. There is also a clear-cut sexual allusion in this text.

Kabukenge, Nice-One (pl. 21): "The Nice-One, the woman with fallen breasts, has four eyes"; "The Nice-One, the woman with fallen breasts, shines on the face." Kabukenge symbolizes the supreme qualities of the high initiate as a person exemplifying *busoga*, a goodness that is reflected in his or her moral behavior and physical appearance. The term Kabukenge in itself does not indicate the sex of the character. The texts collected specifically refer to a dignified female ("woman with fallen breasts"), although the sculptures may also be asexual. The femininity of the Kabukenge figurines in the observed contexts was related to their functional role: they were collectively owned objects placed centrally as "mother" images in the display of figurines to depict the introduction of the kindi grade in the autonomous group. Some Kabukenge figurines were bifrontal, two-headed, or double (two full figurines carved back to back from one piece of ivory). Hence the reference in one of the aphorisms to "four eyes" (*meiso manazi*), a symbol of superior vision and knowledge. A double figurine with male indications on one side and female markings on the other suggests that Kabukenge and Kagunza are two distinct characters, Nice-One and his wife Woman-with-Fallen-Breasts, to represent the bond between the initiate and his wife.

Kagalama, Who-Lies-on-the-Back: "Kagalama, master of the men's house, is the first to see things." The men's house is in the center of the village, and strangers and invited guests arrive there first. The old men who lie in their long chairs and watch over this house are often represented as the guardians of village affairs.

Kakazi ka Mungu, Little-Wife-of-the-Senior-Initiate: "She lets herself be seduced by Tongue." An almost obsessive concern with the fidelity of women is frequently expressed in texts and dramatic action. This character is the opposite of what an initiated wife should be. In "Kakazi ka Mungu, her lying on the back will kill the children," Kakazi represents a wife who, though initiated to bulonda or bunyamwa, seduces young men. The aphorism warns young men not to let themselves get caught in this trap. Kakazi symbolizes an initiated woman who is overly fascinated by flattery: "Kakazi ka Mungu, Tongue does not go away from the threshold." In this context Tongue (Kulubanga) is a man who tries to seduce his junior brother's wife.

Kakinga, Young Maiden (pls. 33, 37–42; Biebuyck, 1973, pl. 77): "Kakinga was beautiful; she perished because of adultery." When the figurine has only one arm, the text sometimes reads: "Kakinga was beautiful; adultery cut her an arm" (i.e., she lost an arm because of adultery; she destroyed herself). Numerous figurines portray a licentious woman (married or unmarried) who creates problems in her group. The initiated woman is of a different nature. In fact, Kakinga can evoke the faithful woman who does not succumb to sexual temptations. According to some spokesmen, Kakinga was the Pygmy wife of the ancestor Idega (Lega), with whom she had four sons and one daughter. Her son Isimbio derived his name from his mother's fidelity. Lega's wife excelled because of *kusimbia*, a verb referring to the attitude of a woman who stays with her husband instead of always going elsewhere.

Kakosi, Little-Neck (Biebuyck, 1973, pl. 71): "May I die today; may Kakosi be cut by a claw." The character describes an elder who is desperate because of the bad treatment he receives.

Kakulu, a diminutive form of Mukulu, Big-One (the prefix *ka-*, here and elsewhere, seems to have an affective value, like Poor Big-One). The character, male or female, is expressed from different points of view:

Kakulu kakumba mulomo: "Big-One who bends the lips [i.e., lets the lip hang], it is not I who have scorned you." An initiate is dissatisfied and angered by the behavior of a protégé or colleague who cannot be expected to give him much help. A person should act in ways that please the elder initiates to guarantee that a person achieves his dream of being initiated.

Kakulu ka Mpinda: "Big-One [son] of Mpinda [buttress; metaphorically, a hard and implacable person] sets out [on a journey] in the very early morning." The character represents a kindi with evil intentions. Although he has completed the high initiations, he tries to convince his colleagues to refuse as candidates younger kin who are aspiring to the same honor. Mpinda seems also to refer to dangerous consequences (e.g., sickness) resulting from anger and obnoxious conduct. The term "very early morning" (*nindunindu*) is generally used to denote harmful actions or intentions.

Kakulu ka Mpito (pl. 47; Biebuyck, 1973, pl. 69): "Big-One [son] of Mpito [lit., a hat worn by old initiates made of the black hide of a cercopithecus monkey] dies in the very early morning." The character represents an initiate who runs into trouble, becomes sick, or dies because of his pregnant adulterous wife, Wayinda, or because he accepted without circumspection an invitation to a beer party hosted by Mukobania, Divider. It is usually used together with another figurine symbolizing Wayinda or Mukobania.

Kakulu ka mulubungu: "Big-One of the men's house, the guardian, has no eyes." Somewhat similar to Kagalama, this character refers to an old blind initiate "whose heart is his eyes." Lying in his long chair, he watches over the affairs of the village, while younger men and women are engaged in forest activities.

Kakulu kamwenne kumasengo (or Kakulu kamonne masengo; Biebuyck, 1973, pl. 64): "Big-One who has seen [i.e., who is in possession of] the initiation objects is bent [or bends himself] under them [i.e., under their weight]." The old initiate guards not only his own initiation objects but also those of dead kinsmen and eventually the collectively held ones. He is old and bent but he wields great power; younger men are advised to take good care of him.

Kakulu kengila mumpita: "Big-One who enters into the mix-up [brawl, ritual impurity] dies in the very early morning." An initiate becomes part of the problem instead of being its arbitrator.

Kakumba, Bent Person: "Kakumba I shall not teach you the drum [i.e., how you must drum]; you drum in the manner you like." The famed tutor or preceptor arranges things somewhat in his own manner and style. No one is going to criticize him since he is the expert.

Kakumi, Maiden: "The breasts of Kakumi shine; they will fall and desiccate." An initiated woman (or man) must not be a vagrant because vagrancy will ruin her (or him); vagrancy is a wasting away.

Kakungu, Little-Old-One: "When you encounter Kakungu on the trail do not push him." Old persons must be respected.

Kalemba, Junior-Wife (pl. 22): "Kalemba of the initiate sleeps on the back with widespread legs." This figurine presents the image of a seductive woman. An initiate should avoid being enticed by such women, particularly if they are the wives of high initiates, tutors, or close kin. The character also represents the junior wife who has the privilege and the burden of carrying the bags or baskets of initiation objects to the ceremonies: "Kalemba of Mungu [great initiate] carries Isengo [the sacred object]."

Kaligala, Who-Is-Used-Carrying-Burdens: "Kaligala is not overcome by burdens that bend him who has broken limbs." Kaligala is the high initiate who has the know-how and the status enabling him to confront difficult problems and the power to solve them; a weak person must not get involved in problems that are beyond his ability to solve.

Kalimbangoma (lit., who follows drum; pls. 51–52): "Everyone has his Kalimbangoma, the one of the body [flesh] is dead." Kalimbangoma stands for a man's initiated wife. He has one wife and does not require another; when he has his "protector" to whom he is bound through ritual he needs no other women. "Kalimbangoma finishes all the Big-Ones" refers to an initiate's wife who treats her husband and his peers badly.

Kalonda, Initiated-Woman (of bulonda grade): "Kaungukana [a junior initiate of yananio grade], they have taken his Kalonda on the road." The figurine represents the initiated wife Kalonda. While her husband was journeying to the rites, she was abducted and seduced by others. The character is sometimes presented in the plural: "Batulonda, why do they show you [point at] the wrinkles." The reference is to old, bent women who are toothless and have wrinkled skin. People make fun of them, yet old age is the inevitable fate that will befall everyone. Another text—"Batulonda, why do they show you the snail shells?"—implies that they show the old woman the shells from which shell money is made, but not the money. The widowed Kalonda is told that she must no longer expect to receive valuables at the initiations.

Kamukazi, Poor Woman (pl. 30): "Kamukazi is poor [i.e., sick] with hunger; in her village there is wealth of food." Kamukazi really alludes to a man who runs into trouble in his quest to be initiated. He either has an insufficient supply of goods for fees and gifts, or he was fined for transgressing a prescription and fails to secure the necessary payments. People in his own group have contributed what they could, and his wealthy maternal uncles, who are normally supposed to help him in time of trouble, do not honor their obligations.

Kanunalongo (lit., name of a river; metaphorically, a woman's genitalia): "Kanunalongo the little river destroys the large pots." The reference is to an adulterous woman.

Kanya, Who-Stares-Upward: "Kanya looks at the sky; those looking skyward are dead."

Kasagula, Penis, a male figurine used together with the female Nyabilimbio, Mrs. Buttocks: "Kasagula and Nyabilimbio, senior and junior twins." The two characters symbolize an initiated husband and wife linked by an inseparable bond. In the same dance context, however, Nyabilimbio becomes the evil seductress, and Kasagula her victim: "Nyabilimbio whom father Kasagula has married kills him in Mulemba, their village; where she went, she died on the road." The term "on the road" implies vagrancy.

Kasegasega, Asker-Asker (pl. 24): "Kasegasega, him who was given is being asked again." Kasegasega seeks initiation to a high level. His grandfather or great-grandfather was a kindi, but for one reason or another their immediate descendants did not reach this status. In the meantime the initiation objects had been transferred to guardians outside the group. There is now a candidate who relentlessly asks the keepers to return the objects.

Kasungalala (lit., what shoots up straight in the air, like a tree; Biebuyck, 1973, pl. 66), Who-Stretches-the-Arm(s)-Upward: "Kasungalala, I have stopped [forbidden, arbitrated] Igulu [Sky], I have stopped something big." The character designates the high initiate as an arbitrator, a moderator, and a peacemaker.

Katanda, Mat (Biebuyck, 1973, pl. 63): "Inconstancy [random, unreflective behavior] kills the Good-Ones, it has killed Katanda"; "I used to like you, inconstancy destroys the Good-Ones, it has destroyed Katanda." Katanda, depicted by a flat figurine riddled with holes, refers to a person who some people thought was qualified for kindi, but his behavior and character turned out to be bad. The character may reflect a person who brags about an achievement not yet realized.

Katemene, Lazybones (also person of short stature): "Katemene speaks to himself during the planting season; the masters of the dry season refuse him everything." Katemene is a lazy person, lacking initiative and incentive, who embarks upon a task when it is too late.

Katetele (lit., a badly forged iron tool such as an ax), Poor Devil: "Katetele praises himself during the planting season; the masters of the dry season refuse him altogether (or, cultivate for him in vain)." This personage resembles the preceding Katemene, one who lags behind in his work.

Katindili, Lazy Weakling (Biebuyck, 1973, pl. 75): "Katindili calls [people] for [i.e., to make] the new field; those of the dry season will refuse him." Like the two preceding characters, Katindili lacks the perseverance and strength needed to bring a task to a good end. It applies to a person who claimed he would do the initiations but lacked the strength to accumulate the necessary goods and the patience to endure the wait.

Keida mazi, Who-Lacks-Water: "Keida mazi has placed the lips near the puddle." A seasoned initiate cannot find a candidate to tutor: "He will die without getting his goats." Initiates invest large quantities of goods in their initiations and expect to be rewarded by tutoring new candidates.

Keitula (lit., what forges itself; pls. 48–49; Biebuyck, 1973, pls. 81, 84), Strong Person: "Keitula son of Yimbo [Good Singer], a beautiful person to be seen." To be strong-willed but good is the outstanding quality of one "who has set [acquired] the wickerwork rattles [i.e., the kindi]." If a person acts properly, all will join him, and he becomes the head of a large group.

Keyamba, Stranger-Coming-from-Far: "Keyamba is smooth [he has no scabies; his body is well oiled and reddened]; he who comes from far is not dirty [or, he knows how to take care of himself]." Keyamba is a person who is considered in his own group to be morally and physically ugly, but other people think he is good and beautiful.

Kibazonga, Stupid-One: "Kibazonga, drummer of the drum drums for me in the manner I want." In this context Kibazonga is the candidate. However prominent he may be in the village, during the initiation he is treated as if he were of no importance. If he acts with humility and circumspection, he is praised for not committing any errors; he is the joy of his tutor because he has followed all the latter's suggestions.

Kikulu, Big-One: "Kikulu who beat the drum for me now covers the arms." Kikulu is a tutor who always helped and supported his protégé in earlier initiations and was richly rewarded for it. Now that the protégé is reaching the kindi level, however, the tutor withholds his support (i.e., covers the arms).

Kikulu, Big-Turtle: "Kikulu that passes and passes depletes our mushrooms." Kikulu is the old initiate whose presence is desired even though he no longer performs any major tasks and does not participate in the dances. As an honored guest he gets his share of goods wherever he goes; even if he stays home, gifts are sent to him.

Kilinga, Pigeon (pl. 32): "Kilinga inflates the chest; on the village place will come yours [i.e., your death, destruction, demise]." Kilinga is an initiate who meddles in every small affair and looks for trouble. Although often represented by a zoomorphic figurine, the character is also associated with a human statue.

Kimatwematwe, Big-Heads-Heads. *See* Sakimatwematwe

Kimbayu, Evil or Destructive Person (pls. 26, 50): "Kimbayu with the dead heart"; "May he not come back from [the journey] he undertakes, he Kimbayu with the dead heart"; "Do not look down at Kimbayu with this kind of heart that has killed him." In these aphorisms Kimbayu is presented as a person who fails to listen to advice and teaching because his heart is dead and his mind is not receptive to counsel or warnings. Kimbayu is a killer; people wish that he would disappear completely. The initiate is advised not to retaliate against Kimbayu, who "killed" his kinsman, but rather to search for reconciliation "because at any rate Kimbayu will also die one day."

Kitende, Frog (pl. 27): "Kitende Kituku [a frog species] does not play with children." Kitende is the image of the great initiate who does not engage in lighthearted adventures because he is of a separate breed.

Kuboko kumozi, One-Arm: "You have cut the arm of your father's child, you thought revenge would not come." Kuboko kumozi is a person who lost an arm because of fighting in his group. The character reminds those who cause strife and harm in their own groups about their fate: they will be abandoned by the others, remain alone, and be killed by strangers.

Kwangwakwa or Kongwakwa, Bird: "Kwangwakwa, little bird that sings for Muluma." Although represented usually by a highly stylized bird figurine (a neck with a beak) or by the actual beak, this character may also be carved in human form. Kwangwakwa symbolizes the master of the land or the most senior kindi whose voice, like that of the bird, can be heard at a long distance. He counsels in the presence of all. The version "Kwangwakwa, the bird that sings for the termites" may refer to a sorrowful master of the land who remains the only kindi in his group and cries out for others to follow his example.

Kyamitoe, Big-Heads. *See* Sakimatwematwe

Kyegelela (lit., the thing descending with the water), Drowned Person: "Kyegelela died, he did not see [find] one to save him." Kyegelela is a person who fails to find a tutor for the initiations.

Kyengengwa (lit., who does not forgive): "My wife Kyengengwa, you treat her well, she is merciless." A woman searches relentlessly for the means with which to "kill" her husband.

Milemba, Phrynium: "The Myoli [a variety of phrynium; here, the fighters or warriors] fall down [are slain]; Milemba fled from being cut down." Milemba, the initiate and the master of the land, avoids engaging in battle.

Mpelempele, Scabby: "Even if he is Mpelempele, the child of your mother is not thrown into poverty." Mpelempele, a person with a physical or mental defect, must not be rejected by the group. Mpelempele is the principal symbol of the *kikongolo,* a man who is mentally disturbed and therefore was not admitted to the circumcision or the bwami rites. Such people are treated as "sororal nephews" by high initiates. There exists a mild jocular relationship, from which the *kikongolo* derives extraordinary privileges. I have seen *kikongolo* fully dressed with the paraphernalia of one of their kin participating in public dances of the kindi.

Mpimbi, Latch: "Mpimbi, the Strong-One who is not overcome by things that climb [i.e., difficulties]"; "Mpimbi will say to Door the things that are in the house." Mpimbi is an ambiguous character. He is a person who reveals "inside" things to outsiders, like one who would divulge the inner secrets of bwami. Mpimbi is also the great initiate who knows hidden things, who sees and looks in all directions.

Mpondo: "Who will turn Mpondo rotting on banana leaves?" The male Mpondo image is used with the female Nyabikuba figurine. Mpondo is sick because he seduced Nyabikuba, wife of his father, senior brother, or maternal uncle; he scorned the words of the elders, and nobody will help him. Mpondo also represents the corpse of the father, senior brother, or maternal uncle. The person who seduced his wife will not dare to come into contact with the corpse because he might die as well.

Mubile Muzumbi (Mubile is the singular of Babile, a name the Lega use to designate their western neighbors, the Songola; *muzumbi* is one of several terms that refer to a dead person): "The dead Mubile in the earth of *malinga* [the lowlands; a dynamic concept used in contrast with *ntata,* to denote the western or southern part of Legaland]." The character typifies a person who dies in a foreign land; the high initiate who has "witnessed the depth" must not be a vagrant.

Mubimubi, Bad-Bad-One: "Mubimubi arrives at the outskirts of the village; in a place where there are people, there others are used to arriving." Mubimubi is a person suffering from a serious disease such as leprosy. When he arrives in the village, people must not reject him but rather proffer hospitality, "knowing that tomorrow he will leave again."

Mubumbu, Backbiter: "We were going on the road and Mubumbu [one who sits hidden near the road and is angry with travelers] hears me [understands what I am saying]." Mubumbu is a kinsman of bad intentions; he listens secretly to conversations and then goes to divulge them to others. He abuses one's confidence.

Mukinga, Young Woman: "Mukinga was beautiful; adultery has cut her an arm [i.e., has made her lose an arm; has caused damage to her]." The character, like Kakinga, is a woman who sleeps haphazardly with many men and as a result gets sick. The term is combined in the plural with *nyatwiso:* "The *bakinga,* the *benyatwiso* in the joy of the dance they all perish." The character stands for a woman who has a nice body but whose inner world is filled with witchcraft and adultery.

Mukobania, Divider: "[The bananas] which Kamukobania has sliced [for making beer] are the cause of Kakulu ka Mpito's [which see] death." The two images are used together. Mukobania indiscriminately invites people for a beer party, which ends in a brawl. He is an evil person who causes people to quarrel.

Mulima, Bat (Biebuyck, 1973, pls. 72, 76): "Mulima hangs upside down because of the bad word Sun has told him." Mulima, an obscure character, is a high initiate who is wronged by a junior, or a maternal uncle wronged by a sororal nephew. When a sororal nephew repeatedly says bad things to his uncle or abuses the privileges of his position, the maternal uncle "gets cold"; he is angry and refuses to help. Mulima may also be a braggart who is embarrassed by others; for example, a person who brags that he achieved kindi all by himself is the laughingstock of everyone.

Mulinga Mukulu, Tracker, the Big-One: "Mulinga Mukulu encircles Mpombi [lit., an antelope] with one eye." Mulinga is so fine a scout that even if he has (or uses) only one eye he still finds the animal that is his quarry. Mulinga is a senior, a father, an initiate; if one attempts to fool him, he will rapidly discover the misdeed.

Mumbia: "Mumbia mumbles mumblings against me; I die in it [i.e., I die of fear]." Mumbia is the master of the land, the high initiate who rejects (i.e., by mumbling) someone because of his bad actions. That person suddenly realizes that nobody is going to help him.

Mungu, Great-Initiate: "Mungu who does not speak does not give one hundred of shell money." Mungu is the exemplary initiate: he does not abuse words or talk excessively, and so he cannot be accused of witchcraft.

Mutu Nyabeidilwa, Hornbill-Overcome-by-Night (Biebuyck, 1973, pl. 70): "Mutu Nyabeidilwa, to whatever place she goes, she is being called back." She is a married woman who always wants to go home to her own people and will not return to her husband unless she is forced to do so. An initiated woman must not always want to visit her kin and remain with them.

Mwami Isamikesi, Initiate, Mr. Early-Waking: "Mwami Isamikesi you will encounter a group of people sitting in a circle." Isamikesi is one who enters into a place, mixes with people, and gets involved with things that do not concern him.

Mwami Ntanagamboe: "Mwami Ntanagamboe in the back of the head he hears." An initiate is not talked about behind his back. The initiate is not only well informed, but when he hears people talking behind his back he simply passes by as if he had heard nothing.

Mwami we Idungu, Initiate-(Son)-of-Far (pls. 25, 36): "Mwami we Idungu, why have you come, what are you doing here?" An ambiguous character is depicted here. When an initiate arrives in one's village or at the ceremonies, one must not demand his purpose in coming; to ask that question "is like killing me." An initiate, however, usually does not go where he is unknown, unwanted, or uninvited: an initiate "must not lease his body, running from one place to the other."

Mwanga, Mwangi, or Mwangu, Bringer-of-Joy-and-Prosperity: "Mwanga would not have died; *kyatomutomu* has killed Mwanga." The term *kyatomutomu* refers to something that is full or overflowing (e.g., a cresting river) and, metaphorically, to evil, witchcraft, and thieving. Mwanga, a leader, has caused his own destruction because he chose the path of evil. *See also* Nyakabumba

Mweloa or Mwelwa, Glittering-One (Biebuyck, 1973, pl. 87): "Come to see Mweloa and [all] that beauty." The character is presented together with Wankenge (which see). If used by itself, the statue indicates one who was beautiful but has lost an arm: "Mweloa, behind Mweloa there is a nice youthful crowd." People laugh at him, but he has many helpful kin.

Nduma za Kyanga (the term *nduma* literally applies to the length and weight of *kyanga*, the green banana leaf; the young leaf shoots up straight but soon bends because it grows so long; *nduma* also refers to ill nature, toughness, and callousness): "Nduma za Kyanga: Lubula [Hail] has broken his back." Nduma stands for a callous youth whom the elder Lubula refuses to help. In the text, "Nduma za Kyanga is used to making him bend his neck," Nduma signifies an initiate who extorts goods from a candidate without aiding him during the rites.

Ndumbi: "Ndumbi, may I die today, may the little neck be cut by a claw." This complaint is directed at an old initiate who is the guardian of a young man but who has no strength left; he is afraid that the youth will kill him. Ndumbi also still wants to achieve kindi, even though he knows he must die.

Ngeze, Rat: "I go begging to Ngeze; I shall not eat a [single] ripe banana." Ngeze is selfish and reserves food for himself. The character informs a candidate that he must not rely exclusively on others (close or remote kin, agnates, cognates, or in-laws) to secure the goods and foods necessary for initiation. The candidate must show initiative in preparing his own fields for sowing crops.

Nkumba (lit., a basket; also a coronet worn by a kanyamwa woman): "Nkumba, Miserable-One, carried the basket without knowing what is in it."

Ntombo, Group: "Even if you kill Ntombo, the child left in Mugumo [lit., a tree; a village called Mugumo] will give you Ntombo." The character emphasizes the continuity of the group: one Ntombo dies, another is born; one initiate disappears, another replaces him.

Nyababa, Mrs. Senior: "Nyababa keeps the ears [bitula] open; she does not sleep." The character represents an old initiate, male or female, who is the watchful guardian of the family or the village.

Nyabilimbio, Mrs. Big-Buttocks: "I was Nyabilimbio; the pulling out of peanut plants has made my buttocks flat." If "the pulling out of peanut plants" is understood literally, then Nyabilimbio is a woman who has lost her beauty and power because of hard work. If taken metaphorically, however, the character represents a woman who has had many affairs.

Nyabisabusabu, Mrs. Necklaces-Necklaces: "Nyabisabusabu and her necklace and her stupidity." She is a person of poor taste and bad manners; she wears too much clothing or too much red powder on her body.

Nyakabumba, Bent-Woman: "Nyakabumba, come to beat her! Mwangu dies of poverty." Nyakabumba is a stupid old woman, but that is no reason to reject her. Mwangu is the master of the land; he must govern with a "strong heart" and take care of all his people, good and bad. Mwangu, lacking respect for the weak in his group, may soon find himself without people.

Nyamilenge (lit., *milenge* is the screaming of wild piglets): "Nyamilenge, child of Ngulube [pig], cannot die of one spear thrust." She is the promiscuous woman: "five or six men made her pregnant."

Nyaminia, Mrs. Black (Biebuyck, 1973, pls. 78–79): "Nyaminia, my good and beautiful one, every man has his good and beautiful one." The text stresses the goodness and companionship one gets from a wife or, more broadly, from a kin. The name Nyaminia is chosen deliberately because "blackness of skin" is often symbolically associated with "darkness of heart" or witchcraft. The derogatory meaning implied in Nyaminia is immediately offset by "my good and beautiful one" (*musoga*) to imply that character is not revealed by outward appearances. Through this character the initiate is told that he must never despair and must never say that all people in his group are bad or noncooperative; one can always find a person of good disposition.

Nyamulengelenge, Mrs. Baby: "The young woman gives birth to children, Nyamulengelenge [or Banyamilengelenge]."

Nyandende, Mrs. Stork: "Nyandende, her tongue sticks out beyond the lips." Nyandende is a blabbermouth.

Nyanjinjinzi or Nyazinzinzi, Mrs. Black-Black (pl. 28): "Nyanjinjinzi the old woman may be black [but] she is not with witchcraft." Nyanjinjinzi has an unattractive or decrepit body, but her heart may be good. A double meaning is revealed in this character: people must not be judged only by their appearances, and a great initiate never rashly accuses others.

Nyankinkinde (lit., *kinkinde* is a species of large crab): "Nyankinkinde enters the fish trap, no other Crab still enters in it." Nyankinkinde is an example of a troublesome and egotistic woman (mainly a senior wife); she does not want her husband to marry other wives.

Nyantuli, Mrs. High-Buttocks: "Nyantuli weeps for preferred status [saying to the other wife] your buttocks are flat and emaciated [because of work]." Nyantuli represents a junior wife who is jealous and covets a preferred status (*bulanga*) in the polygynous family; she scorns the senior wife.

Nyatulondo twa nsulu (lit., a woman wearing only small pieces of bark cloth as an apron): "Nyatulondo twa nsulu, who counsels you for the trip?" Nyatulondo is a woman who goes to the initiations with seductive intentions; in general she is a wife with bad habits. An initiate should avoid taking such women with him to the rites.

Nyatwiso, Mrs. Small-Eyes, Mrs. Twinkle-Eyes (pl. 35): "Nyatwiso, in the search for joy it is that she will perish"; "The Benyatwiso [plural] in the joy of the dance, in it, they all perish." Nyatwiso wants to be part of everything; when there is a dance she wants to participate; when people sit chatting she enters into the conversation; and when she travels with her husband and somebody calls her, she stops and lingers.

Nyaweita meiga (lit., who kills herself with mixings): "Nyaweita meiga, emptiness gets hold of her." The character refers to an adulterous woman "who mixes the sperm." *See also* Wayinda

Nzogu, Elephant: "What Nzogu has built for himself is not beaten by rain." Nzogu is a person who desires to be a kindi; as he has built up strength and satisfied the requirements, he cannot fail in his quest.

Sabitwebitwe (de Kun, 1966, pls. 16–17). *See* Sakimatwematwe

Sakakuliso or Sakuliso, Who-Has-Something-in-the-Eye: "Sakakuliso has told Leopard [about] the place where to take Goat." Sakakuliso is a person who acts badly; he is a divider who sets people against one another.

Sakimatwematwe, Mr. Many-Heads (pl. 45; Biebuyck, 1973, pl. 74): "Sakimatwematwe has seen Elephant on the other side of the large river." Sakimatwematwe is the high initiate who sees in all directions and notices things that others do not. He has surpassing knowledge; he is so well informed that nobody can fool him. If there is talk behind his back or a plot against him, he will find out by himself, but he will also have the help of his colleagues. As part of their bond of solidarity, high initiates have developed an intricate system of secret communication. In order to emphasize the penetrating vision, the aphorism sometimes reads: "Sakimatwematwe has seen with one eye Elephant on the other side of the large river." Sakimatwematwe or Sameisomabili—always symbolized by a multifrontal figurine—occasionally represents two persons, such as a father who did not become kindi and a son who did (an outstanding achievement), or a senior who is wronged by his junior and says: "May I die today, let the little neck be cut by a claw." When the bifrontal figurine has only one arm, the exegesis may center on both features. Sakimatwematwe, a master of the land, a person who is supposed to be wise, went to war as a protagonist; he was speared in the arm and lost it. The physical damage becomes a reflection of moral failure.

Samatwemabili, Mr. Two-Heads. He exhibits the same characteristics as Sakimatwematwe. There is also the aphorism: "Samatwemabili, Muzanzalo kills a good and beautiful one."

Sameisomabili, Mr. Two-Eyes (Faces). Same as Sakimatwematwe.

Sawamazembe (lit., *mazembe* are the plaited strands of hair of initiated women; *sawamazembe* is a blackened hat of raffia imitating the women's coiffure and worn by kindi; pl. 34): "Sawamazembe does not hear well." This person does not listen to advice; he is encouraged to pay more attention to what he is told, but he continues to ignore the teachings.

Simweli mwenge, Smart-Person: "Simweli mwenge has seen Elephant on the other side of the large river." Similar to Sakimatwematwe.

Tukungu, Old Men: "Two Tukulu, where they fight with each other there Mutala will die." Seniors and elders must not quarrel for it leads to disruption of the group; elders must be of one mind.

Wabalenga (lit., who surpasses them; e.g., a kindi surpasses a yananio): "Wabalenga open the door for me that I may see how it is adorned there." Only with Wabalenga's help can a person witness the secrets of the highest initiation.

Walemba (lit., one who is being revenged): "You destroy Walemba, behind Glittering-One there is a large crowd"; "You destroy Walemba son of Nyombo, but they [i.e., those coming to revenge him] follow in the wake." These stress the solidarity of kinsmen and of initiates.

Wankenge (lit., son of bongo antelope), Beautiful-One: "Do not kill Wankenge, Mweloa has many [people] behind her." Wankenge portrays a kindi surrounded and protected by his kin as well as a man who has many juniors and children. Such a person is an ideal initiate because he will surely have all the fees, gifts, and food needed to satisfy the needs of the other initiates.

Wansongo, One-Eyed Person: "Wansongo with one eye does not see well."

Wasakwa nyona, One-Who-Has-Tattoos-Carved (on the body; pl. 23; Biebuyck, 1973, pls. 73, 82): "Everyone who had [linear] tattoos carved on the back no longer is as he or she used to be." This character represents an old person who was beautiful in youth but is now decrepit and ugly. It is shameful to laugh because he or she was once beautiful, and the transformation does not differ from the fate that awaits everyone. The text alludes also to a woman who is a man's favorite wife but who then changes into a contemptuous and arrogant person. The aphorism quoted sometimes reads: "He or she who had the tattoos [i.e., signs of beauty] engraved on the back is now in the place of *ezagwa* [one remaining alone in his group]."

Wa(i)yinda or Weyinda, Pregnant Adulteress (Biebuyck, 1973, pls. 67–68). One of the most frequently recurring characters, Wayinda is identified in different ways: "Weyinda died of *mpindi;* she did not arrive at the birth house where her mother was"; "Weyinda died of *mpindi;* of laughing died the males"; "Wayinda died of *mpindi;* [her vulva] is laughed at by the seducers who encircle her"; "Wayinda is mocked by the seducer"; "Wayinda died with the pregnancy [fetus]; the enema is still between the buttocks"; "Wayinda died with *mpita;* the funnel is between the buttocks, in searching for the penis of the males"; "Wayinda died and in the belly there was no fetus"; "Wayinda has killed herself with ritual pollution; she removes herself from life."

In general, adultery (*meiga*) is thought to have detrimental social and physical effects. When a man falls sick, the oracles sometimes attribute the cause of his illness to his wife's adultery. If the man later dies, the initiates subject his wives to the *kiloba* ordeal in one of its forms: the accused must drink water with which the husband's corpse was washed, sleep on his tomb, or eat from an antelope hung above the corpse. It was thought that the culprit would either reveal her misdemeanor or fall sick if she engaged in such an action. The pregnant adulteress exposed herself to imminent sanctions: she and her baby, or she alone, would die in labor. A *confessio parturientis* and appropriate ablutions might save her. For a woman who died with her baby, all marriage payments received by her family had to be repaid to her husband, in addition to the regular *idigo* and *kaginga* mortuary fees. If the woman died but her baby lived, the marriage payments were not reimbursed.

The various aphorisms all point to the same character: Wayinda, a pregnant adulterous woman who causes her own destruction because of ritual pollution to which she exposed herself. The image of Wayinda sometimes is presented together with that of other characters called Kakulu ka Mpito, Sakimatwematwe, or Simweli mwenge (see above). These characters all depict high initiates who are married to Wayinda. Wayinda hoped to fool them, but they were quickly informed about her conduct; or she caused the destruction of her unwitting husband. A wooden phallus occasionally is held against the genitalia of the figurine.

Weida mukulu kumazi (lit., a Big-One to whom an enema is administered):

"When you administer an enema to a Big-One you must look discreetly: the anus is dizziness." The text alludes to a person who seduces his father's wife.

Wikalaga na kabimba (lit., he who sits with a swelling): "Wikalaga na kabimba, in the belly there will come his or her [death]." The aphorism refers to a bad character such as Wayinda; sooner or later his or her punishment will come.

Zogozogo (lit., a species of monkey): "The hat of Zogozogo has destroyed the dwelling place of Mbezi." Zogozogo, a kanyamwa woman and the wife of Mbezi, ruins her husband's house because of her bad behavior. Wherever the kanyamwa goes, her husband keeps guard: "The place where kanyamwa has gone I keep my arrow aimed at." The character also refers to a person who meddles in places where he does not belong: "He goes [and it is not his place] with the Tubamba [monkeys], Zogozogo, he goes with the Mbezi [monkeys]."

Some characters represented by figurines are not named directly, as the preceding ones are; rather, they are implied by the aphorisms and their interpretations:

Flat-Belly: "I came without eating, the belly is flat [hollow]." A childless woman is indicated here.

Generous Host: "Give a stool, a stranger does not go [travel] with his one." The initiate is generous and hospitable.

Imprudent Person: "Pot does not go above [i.e., on the head]; in the little pot in it goes the thing of your colleague." The reference is to a person who leaves another's house carrying a pot on the head. The practice is dangerous because the person may be accused of theft.

Maternal Uncles: "Where the agnatic kinship is dead, I will show you those who are with mother." Maternal uncles provide help. A person who is good and shows respect toward his mother's kin will obtain a wife and go through the initiations with their support, even if he has no agnatic kin or is abandoned by them.

Restrained-One: "I have not spoken my words; I have clasped the back of my head." The character represents a person who abstains from presenting arguments when faced by an important event (e.g., a secret rite).

Watchful Father: "I thought that my father was asleep, and lo! he is looking at me with one eye." An old man seems to be asleep in his long chair, but he is discreetly watching over the people. Specific reference is made to old men who remain in the village as guardians while the other people are in the forest.

Youthful Sorcerers: "Sorcery that was with the Big-Ones was sorcery that listened to words; the one [i.e., sorcery] that remains with the youth is sorcery that does not listen to words." Two images—a classic Lega piece and a modern imported figurine—accompanied this aphorism, which is a complaint. Under Europeanization more people died than previously, and there was more inter- and intragroup conflict. Earlier, traditional methods had contained sorcerers and witches, but evildoers were now rampant because of the breakdown of authority.

Form and Meaning of Anthropomorphic Figurines

The names of the characters represented by the figurines are derived from many sources. Some are common terms used for persons of a particular status in the bwami association (Kalonda, Mungu, Mwami) or in the social system at large (Kakinga, Kakulu, Kalemba). Some refer to a physical characteristic (Nyabilimbio), an injury (Kuboko kumozi), a defect (Wansongo), a particular behavior (Kimbayu). A few names come from animals (Kilinga, Kitende, Nzogu), plants (Milemba), and objects (Mpimbi). Most of the names are invented to bring to life good or evil characters as defined by the bwami association. Nearly all names begin with the morphemes *Ka-* (pl. *Tu-*), *Nya-* (pl. *Banya-* or *Benya-*), or *(I)Sa* (no plural used). *Ka-* is a nominal prefix (class 12) with several possible denotations. It serves as a diminutive, an expression of tenderness (like Dear . . .) or of compassion and sorrow (like Poor . . .). The prefixed morpheme *Nya-* occurs under two semantic forms. *Nya-*, as an equivalent of *nina*, means "his or her mother" and is often translated as Mrs., that is, a person showing this or that characteristic. *Nya-* in Lega, Nyanga, and Bembe also means the same as the widespread morpheme *na-* (*nga-* in some areas), which when added to a substantive or verb expresses respect, a quality, or a status. This form relates to both males and females. *(I)Sa-* means "father of." In combination, *(I)Sa-* indicates a person afflicted by a disease or by turpitude, or one who is in control of something good or bad. The morpheme is often translated as Mr.

What relationships exist between the forms and the meanings they convey? Forms fall into two distinct categories: those that visibly relate to meanings and those that do not. The first group includes some frequently recurring types of figurines. Kakulu ka Mpito and Zogozogo are symbolized by a wooden figurine whose head and back are covered with a piece of monkey hide. Kasungalala has one or two raised arms; Kakulu kamwenne kumasengo is symbolized by a stooped figurine; Nyantuli has heavy buttocks. Kuboko kumozi characters are depicted by one-armed figurines; some Kakinga also may have one arm. Sakimatwematwe and Sameisomabili are represented by multifaced, multiheaded, or double figurines, regardless of the number or position of heads and faces. Not all multifaced sculptures, however, are identified as these two characters. If the figurine has an additional special feature, such as one arm or one eye, or if it lacks facial details, it may symbolize others, such as Kabukenge, Kimbayu, Kuboko kumozi, or Wansongo. Wansongo has one eye or an extra eye in the form of a large cowrie glued above a carved eye. Wayinda, probably the most stable iconographic type, is represented by an ugly wooden or ivory female figurine with a distended belly. Imported modernistic figurines also show direct relationships between form and meaning (e.g., a drummer; one holding a spear).

The iconography of some characters shows the connections between form and meaning less directly, at least to outsiders. Katanda, Mat, is represented by a flat body that is perforated with holes, the symbols of evil and the stylized representations of the joints in a mat. The figurines Wasakwa nyona and Keitula usually have elaborate circle-dot, dot, or linear designs; Wankenge has a wickerwork skullcap or one formed by glued-on or carved cowries; Nyaminia or Nyanjinjinji are usually figurines with deep red-brown patinas.

Many figurines show no obvious link between form and meaning; the relationships between the verbal and iconographic features are purely arbitrary. The hidden connections, known only to the owners and to some astute preceptors and tutors who have seen the figurines presented in the rites, are to a large extent intended to enhance the mystery surrounding the sculptures. These random correlations may also result from the replacement of objects. Some figurines are abandoned on graves; others decay or are lost in fires. A new object retaining its original meaning for the owner may, however, have been carved by a sculptor who lacked a model and may therefore only vaguely resemble the piece that was replaced.

The arbitrariness of verbal and iconographic associations is best illustrated by examples. During kindi initiations held in seven different ritual communities among the western Lega, I collected seven figurines, each identified during the rites by its owner as Kakinga. The owners knew one another as members of adjoining and frequently interacting ritual communities. They nevertheless fully accepted the fact that identical meaning was conveyed by heterogeneous forms. Only two slightly different aphorisms were quoted for the seven figurines: "Kakinga was beautiful, adultery is the cause of her death"; "Kakinga was beautiful, adultery has cut her an arm." The forms of these sculptures are widely divergent. A brief description of each follows.

Plate 33 (7.1 cm). This compact figurine consists of a large spherical head with sharp chin set on a stocky armless and legless tubular bust. The short bust rests on a trapezoidal base; there are some vertical lines at the intersection of bust and base.

Plate 37 (14 cm). A pole-shaped, slender, armless torso stands on zigzag legs with the feet barely indicated. Between the legs the pole ends in an open V-shape. There are no surface designs.

Plate 38 (12.3 cm). This armless figurine has a pole-shaped upper torso suggesting a long neck; the lower torso is tubular with parallel striations; the straight legs, with knees bent outward, stand on massive toeless feet; an oval depression is marked at the bottom of the torso between the legs.

Plate 39 (8.3 cm). This bustlike figurine is formed by a huge oval head that stands on a flaring armless and legless torso, which has a large vertical oval slit.

Plate 40 (13.8 cm). An elongated ovoid head with barely visible facial features tops a very short angular body with only an ajouré right arm. The very long crenellated legs slant slightly outward, and the feet are barely indicated; the torso between the legs ends in an ajouré V-shape. Dots are engraved all over the face.

Plate 41 (11.6 cm). The elongated ovoid head stands on a flaring armless and legless pole that rests on a trapezoidal base. A horizontal depression marks the intersection of pole and base.

Plate 42 (10.7 cm). This rounded figurine has a spherical head and torso; pendulous arms slightly bent at the elbows are carved against the body. The figurine stands on massive, barely curved legs and feet. The large tumescent pubic area between the thighs is marked by a vertical slit and dots. A waffle design is placed on the chest like an open V, and parallel lines are carved on the abdomen.

A single type of figurine is not necessarily limited to one set of meanings. The best example is provided by the multifrontal and multiheaded (rarer than multifrontal) figurines, a distinctive motif in Lega art. Multifrontal figurines come in all sizes and forms, with the faces placed on the body in various ways. I have observed that whenever Sakimatwematwe, Samatwemabili, or Sameisomabili (Mr. Heads-Heads, Mr. Two-Heads, Mr. Two-Faces) was associated with a figurine, the sculpture was multifrontal, and neither the position nor number of faces mattered.

Not all multifrontal figurines, however, represent this type of character. Personages suggested in other contexts by two-faced statues were Kimbayu, Mukobania, Mubumbu, and Kyegelela. Kimbayu was depicted by a multifaced wooden figurine used together with an animal figurine. The preceptor rested the image against his forearm and placed his fingers between the legs of the image: "Do not look at what has killed him, Kimbayu with this [kind of] heart." Kimbayu stood for a person who sows discord by his hypocrisy and bad conduct (a seducer). The horned animal figurine, symbolizing the *lungaga* antelope, was interpreted as "what is with horns is being hooked where there are no vines." *Lungaga* portrayed a person with an evil tongue, one who surely will not be admitted to the initiations. For the depiction of Mukobania (Divider, Slanderer, one who sets people against one another), a two-headed figurine was used with a representation of Kakulu, the Big-One who leaves early in the morning. He has been called by Mukobania for a beer party and does not realize that Mukobania is looking for trouble.

In other contexts where bifrontal figurines were used singly, one head represents a speaker and the other is one (Mubumbu) who overhears the former's conversation, or one head is the drowning person (Kyegelela), the other his savior. In other instances the focus was not on the plurifrontal aspect of the statues but rather on additional features, such as one arm or a body riddled with holes.

These multifaced and multiheaded sculptures differ from the few double figurines in which two full bodies are carved back to back, either joined fully or only at the heads or buttocks. Double statues emphasize primarily the frequently restated idea of the indissoluble link between a kindi and his kanyamwa wife. Such sculptures are often collectively owned emblems of the beginnings of kindi in a specific group.

As has been noted, many of the characters associated with figurines are invented. It is remarkable that in the course of the initiations as a whole, few historical personages or groups are noted. The great names from the Lega migrations, those of the founders of clans and lineages, or those of the first great initiates are neither mentioned in the aphorisms nor illustrated in the performances. The only exception seems to be Katima or Katimi, the legendary first initiate, who is cited in texts but not represented in figurines. The protagonists from the Lega epics—Bungoe, Museme, Wabugila, Mubila, and hundreds of helpers and antagonists—are also missing, save for Kagelia (a monkey species), Kabungulu (Genet), and Wansongo (person blind in one eye). The texts and the dances occasionally refer to a historical or legendary character or to persons of outstanding fame, beauty, or skill, or to those of infamous reputation, such as the Mwami of the Batoba who hanged himself, the man who went to die among the Babinza (a foreign group), and the Banamuningi who were defeated in Katondo. Few of the characters represented in anthropomorphic figurines have animal names, except for Kilinga (Pigeon), Kitende (Frog), Mulima (Bat), and Nzogu (Elephant); even fewer are depicted by masks or other sculptures.

Many characters denoted by figurines, as well as some of their peculiarities and the concepts associated with them, may be clarified in danced performances, with or without the use of initiation objects, as in the following examples.

> Kakulu kamwenne kumasengo, the old initiate who bends under the weight of the initiation objects, and Kakumba (Bent-One), an able tutor. The bent or stooped position is used by initiates when they dance holding wooden masks or initiation baskets to symbolize the "spiritual weight" of initiation objects.

> Katanda, a person of limited intelligence who acts stupidly. In kongabulumbu, Katanda is illustrated by two initiates who try to roll up a mat, starting at opposite ends, to illustrate the character's lack of intelligence.

> Kakinga, a woman who surrenders to *lubabato* (touching, fondling, caressing), which leads to *butazi* (adultery). Many scenes danced by men vividly evoke the *lubabato* of a woman. In the kongabulumbu rites a naked preceptor covered by a bark cloth lies comfortably on his back. Others, who represent the seducers, touch him discreetly; he wakes up and places his legs on the cloth. A dancer approaches and engages in mock coitus with him: "What has started at the sole of the foot, the fondling will kill the marriage." In bombwa a similar idea is illustrated by dancers who touch a pile of covered bags, then go wild and reach for one another's penes.

> Kaungukana, a junior initiate of yananio whose kalonda wife is taken by a "man of nothing" but who is physically stronger than the latter. The scene is enacted in yananio as follows: a bundle of reed swatters lies on the candidate's legs; a dancer starts pulling at the swatters and finally frees one for himself and passes it on to a second dancer. A third dancer protests and, unable to catch to seducers, throws his hat on the ground to place a ritual prohibition against the impostors.

Liso limozi, the person who has only one eye or who sees with only one eye. As the meddlesome Wansongo wa liso limozi and the irascible Kagelia, this ambiguous character is represented in kongabulumbu by a dancer who simply covers one eye or by a chimpanzee skull with one eye closed with leaves or resin. In a yananio rite the impertinent Munyungu wa liso limozi is depicted by a mask with one eye covered by a leaf: "He does not let pass the manner in which there is being spoken." As Mulinga Mukulu, who tracks an antelope using only one eye, he is a person who takes care of others but neglects his own people. He is also the "father," the old man who seems to be asleep but is really watching with one eye the conduct of the villagers. An initiate lies in a long chair apparently unaware of what is going on around him, or a preceptor points at a seated initiate who holds his hand in front of one eye. In kongabulumbu the dancers illustrate the danger of throwing things at people. Dancing with a hard *nkumbi* nut, the preceptors sing: "The *nkumbi* nut that Ntambue has thrown breaks [perforates] him [i.e., the person at whom it is thrown] the pupil." Throwing things is a sign of impatience; a young man or a candidate must be patient, composed, and undemanding.

Mulima, Bat, the elder and great initiate who is wronged by a junior and "lets the head hang down like a bat." In kongabulumbu the character is vividly enacted by a preceptor who dangles from the ceiling of the initiation house.

Mutu Nyabeidilwa, a woman who lingers wherever she goes and must always be summoned back. She is represented in a kongabulumbu rite by a hornbill beak (*mutu*) in reference to one of the bird's habits: the female is imprisoned in her nest hole and must be freed by the male when the young are ready to fly out. In another dance the candidate is constantly taken in and out of the initiation house between sequences and is compared with Mutunia (a capricious person; a pun on the name Mutu) Nyabeidilwa, who must always be called to return.

Nyabilimbio, the woman whose once large buttocks are now flat because of age and work. In one dramatization the character is indicated by a flat polished shell used by men in the game of dice. It is also implied that the woman has been "flattened" by sleeping with too many men.

Nyabisabusabu, a female of bad disposition who does everything wrong. In a bulonda rite she is represented by a woman wearing a man's hat and sitting on a stool. A group of dancers crowd around her and start a quarrel. In another sequence, however, Nyabisabusabu is the well-dressed initiate and is contrasted with Wabulema (lit., a destitute person), the candidate who is not allowed to wear any paraphernalia during the initiations.

Nyamulengelenge or Nyamilenge (lit., the screaming of piglets). "The daughter of Pig who does not die on one spear thrust" is presented in a kongabulumbu rite by a warthog tusk.

Nyajinjinji, the ugly woman who is good-natured. She is suggested in a yananio rite by a hardened *busisi* mud nest of the stinging wasp. In this context the emphasis is on the secret *kasisi* rite: the candidate was filled with fear before he entered the rite, but now he finds that there is no danger or threat of death.

Nyankinkende (lit., a species of large crab), a troublesome senior wife who chases away her husband's other spouses. She is pictured in a yananio rite by two crab pincers glued together and decorated with cowries.

Nyatulondo, the woman wearing a small cloth and going to the initiations with seductive intentions. She is danced in a bombwa rite by a woman who swings a ragged piece of bark cloth hanging in front of her pubic area while other dancers try to grab it.

Sakakuliso or Sakuliso, a telltale and a denunciator who has something stuck in his eye. In kongabulumbu he is enacted simply by a dancer holding his hand before one eye.

Sakimatwematwe, the multifaced character of the wise and well-informed initiate. He is occasionally represented in yananio by two wooden masks held back to back. Two women carrying the initiation baskets in the ceremonial procession in kindi walk back to back, the baskets hanging from straps worn over the forehead. Sakimatwematwe is depicted most graphically in times of crisis or warfare; two kindi stand back to back and shake their rattles in a symbolic effort to avert violence.

Sawamazembe, one who "does not hear well" and does not listen to admonitions. The character is danced in yananio by a preceptor who covers his head with a large fiber collaret.

Wabalenga, a person who acts as if he were going to become sick and fails to perform his duties of hospitality. He is enacted in yananio by a dancer pulling away his stool whenever someone wants to sit on it: "The stool of Wabalenga, on it does not sit he who has the beginnings of leprosy."

Wasakwa nyona, who illustrates the transience of youth and beauty. In yananio he is portrayed by a leaf that grows on a tree whose bark has white stripes similar to tattoos (*nyona*). In a kongabulumbu sequence, the character is evoked by dancers showing the plaits of a mat: "Everyone who has the tattoos engraved on the forehead was [in a place] where [other nice people] now are." This idea of decrepitude and old age following beauty and youth is also rendered by a dancer showing the vulva of a figurine: the woman is old now but she must not be rejected, for she will teach the young; the initiate is old now, but he is still a fine exegete.

Wayinda, a pregnant, adulterous woman to whom an enema is administered in vain, is danced in a kanyamwa rite by women. One dancer bending forward holds a small fish trap upright against her anus, while a second dancer throws green leaves into the trap.

Virtually all invented characters symbolized by figurines are dramatically represented, with or without the use of objects, in rites that rank lower than those in which figurines are displayed. The owners consider the figurines to be abstractions of ideas that are rendered in a dramatic and explicit manner at lower levels of initiation.

The figurines thus are permanent reminders of the important lessons emphasized throughout the initiations. In their teachings the initiates do not simply glorify exemplary persons and actions, but they also stress the weakness and fallibility of humans and point to the attitudes and modes of conduct that detract from *busoga,* the good and beautiful life. The sources of evil and disruption must be kept in mind as clearly as the expressions of goodness. In their diversity the figurines thus portray the quintessential virtues of the great initiate and castigate those who do not measure up to the high standards. The threat of self-annihilation for the nonvirtuous is implied in these contrasts.

Apart from their specific meanings, all figurines reflect cross-generational continuity. These objects are inherited from well-defined predecessors through the initiation process and with the consent of the other high initiates of the group. Owners trace the origins of the figurines to the four to seven initiates to whom they are bound by kinship links. Even if they know that a particular piece (lost or abandoned) was not inherited directly but rather was carved especially for its current owner or his immediate predecessor, initiates still consider it an heirloom. The focus then is mainly on the right to inherit an object—a right acquired through consensus and initiation—and also on the privilege of inheriting the name of that piece.

All figurines owned by individuals of an autonomous group are thought to be related. They are the "children" of a single collectively held figurine that symbolizes the introduction into the group of a particular grade level associated with ownership of figurines. The images thus signify indissoluble linkages among the living and between living and dead precursors. The connection is enhanced because the images left by the deceased are not immediately transferred to a kinsman but are kept in trust by a colleague until the kinsman achieves a higher grade and is considered worthy of them. The figurines hold an intrinsic power as secret and exclusive objects that are owned by high initiates and transferred across generations after temporary exposure on the tomb. They are charged with an undefined force that can act favorably for the living. It is as if possession of the figurines ensures the permanent presence of the deceased Big-Ones and serves as storage for their power. This notion is also reflected in the occasional use of fortifying medicine made of dust scratched from the surfaces of statues. To outsiders the figurines are secret and awesome objects. Illicitly touching, manipulating, or destroying them exposes the guilty party to *kitampo,* severe physical and ritual retaliation.

Meanings of the Rites in Which Figurines Are Used

All these rites begin with an episode of variable length during which the initiates dance with the baskets or bags containing the figurines. The accompanying songs illustrate several ideas. The initiate receiving the message feels an irrepressible urge to go to the initiations: "Give me my large bag [to go]; Idungu [Distance] calls me"; "Give me my large bag that I may enter the forest [i.e., go to the dances]." The contents are heavy and as dangerous as a scorpion; there is an overwhelming desire to "get rid" of them because "they stick to the back" like *babumbu* insects, which plague elephants. Each participant is obliged to exhibit his possessions; he wants to show them to peers and to the new colleague, but he cannot do so haphazardly; "to show things does not mean to give them away." The joint display is a supreme act of solidarity and oneness. In daily life ("when they [the objects] are on the ground") the possessions of the kindi are dispersed like the seeds from *mbala* pods after they have dropped to the ground; in the rites ("when they are in the sky, on the slopes, on the heights"), they are solidly united like *mbala* seeds when the pods are still on the tree.

During the *kingili* rite the sculptures are oiled and, if made of wood, are whitened. In this secret ritual no reference is made to the figurines. The emphasis is on the process of oiling, which gives beauty to the objects, and to the gathering of high initiates from their villages and hamlets. Kingili is the kindi name for Kimbilikiti, the secret kazoo player who performs in the circumcision rite. This mysterious player is featured under other names, *zamwisengo, lutala,* and *mwimbi,* respectively, in the kongabulumbu and kansilembo rites and at the death of a yananio or a kindi. Singing in a low-pitched, loud voice, Kingili represents the male element, in contrast with Kabile, the female kazoo player who produces a strident but weaker sound. (Kabile does not perform during the initiations.) In the circumcision rites Kimbilikiti, accompanied by other secret musical characters (e.g., the *sabikangwa* talking sticks and the *twamba* bull-roarer), symbolizes absolute power and authority. In kindi, the awesome Kingili praises himself as the "Famed-One who watches over the Big-Ones on whom all affairs, good and bad, rest." His presence stresses the exclusiveness of the ceremonies, which noninitiates and persons of low rank are not allowed to attend. Before the sculptures are shown to the new initiate, they must be oiled so that they will have force and be beautiful and shiny like the initiates themselves. They must impress; they must be "in harmony, good and beautiful," just like the actors.

During the *kunanuna masengo* rite figurines contained in baskets are displayed as an "opening up" of what has been hidden. Regardless of the specific symbolic meaning of each object, together they reveal a bond of solidarity which unites the living initiates of an autonomous group and also links them with their dead predecessors. The interdependence of individuals and the non-exclusive possession of the figurines are also revealed: no single member of the group can claim them to be his personal or permanent possession; they "pass and pass like great owls" from one initiate to the other as new members are inducted.

Bele muno, one of the most secret rites, takes place outside the village or in the initiation house of a deserted village. In it the initiates attain the highest level of mystic communication with their dead predecessors. They interpret the term *bele muno* to mean a wish, a longing for those who are no longer alive: "Oh! would that they were still here!" The rite is intended to reaffirm continuity, oneness, and autonomy. The "presence" of many dead initiates is ensured by "the works they left" and by their succeeding kinsmen. In at least one area it was implied that the great initiate, even when dead, continues to watch over his children. The display of a large collectively held figurine is proof of the unity and the autonomy of a particular group. Its presence indicates that the group possesses the right to organize its own kindi initiations. Each of these figurines has its own distinct tradition: the kindi know who first obtained it and are aware of its initial location and circumstances. The figurine has various names, which are also given to some of the smaller figurines. It is a *nina,* a mother, whose presence in the group "gave birth" to other figurines; that is, its acquisition authorized the group to initiate its own members and to obtain figurines for them. Displayed in the center of the figurines, it represents the master of the land surrounded by his guardians, or Kimini, the great dancer (i.e., the great initiate) encircled by his "children." The kindi is reminded that this figurine is the *kyegamino kya kindi,* the support of kindi. The exclusiveness and awesomeness of the rite are marked by references to *lugumbo lwa kindi* (lit., the wild pigs' lair) and by the song, "I climb over the back of Ndezi [Big Leopard], I die of fear."

Finally, the *kinsamba* rite features a massive display of artworks individually owned by the kindi and their initiated wives. It is a private occasion, marked by great joy and splendor, from which lower initiates and noninitiates are excluded. "Porcupine does not eat fallen bananas in the clearing [or during the day]" means that initiates cannot make public the revelations they have received during the rite. The participants display not only anthropomorphic but also zoomorphic figurines, as well as ivory spoons, phalli, billhooks, hammers, and giant snail shells. Ivory masks, however, seldom appear. Unusual articles acquired in recent times from outside groups are also exhibited: a white china plate, a madonna, a perfume bottle, a commercial statue from a trader. The initiates use the term *kinsamba* for a mushroom species that grows in large quantities only in proximity to a *limbondi* termitary. The numerous mushrooms and the way in which they grow in the forest symbolize not only the multitude of people settling in the vicinity of a great kindi but also the solidarity that unites the kindi. Each participant in the rite is a *mukota wa kabilundu,* a leader, a son of Kabilundu (large otter; a tree; also praise name for the preceptor who makes abundant distributions).

The presentation of *kalimbangoma* images to the kanyamwa women focuses on the bond between a kindi and his initiated wife and on the nature of these women. Kindi and kanyamwa are inseparably bound; like Kasimba the preceptor-dancer and Kasele the singer, "they were born twins." The kanyamwa is a strong woman not easily disturbed by outside events, "like the stems of phrynium leaves that move with the wind, but are not cut off by it." She must be treated well, and in turn she will be favorably inclined toward those who respect her. She is markedly different from other women, and in fact "she hates uninitiated women." During the rite a kanyamwa is taught that she cannot go to the initiations without taking along her figurine. She must show the *kalimbangoma* in the *kasumba* rite, which is likened to a "gathering of birds on the *mulungu* tree; each little bird has its [own] song."

Other *kalimbangoma* presented at the yananio grade pertain to female characters who exhibit modes of conduct opposite to those expected from the wife of an initiate. The emphasis is almost exclusively on seduction and adultery: the adulterous wife of the initiate seeking "the joy of the dance" destroys herself and her children. The explanation of another set of *kalimbangoma* is directed to the men: initiates must not be seducers for they have their own wives. They must also show particular respect for old initiates, listening to their advice and giving generously to those who are hungry and weak.

PART THREE

Zoomorphic Figurines

Introduction

Animals are frequently and variously depicted in bwami as personified characters, mainly with overt reference to their habits and physical features. The importance of animals in the exegesis of bwami is easily understood. Living in a rich and largely intact forest environment, the Lega are passionate hunters and trappers. Like other great forest hunters—the Nyanga or the Komo, for example—they have a profound knowledge of animal behavior. Game meat constitutes a substantial part of their diet and is also of vital significance in the food distributions that accompany the rites.

In certain contexts, initiates as a group call themselves after a particular animal or part of an animal. These designations include Bananzogu, Children-of-Elephant or the Elephant-Folk, because of their restrained but potentially destructive power; Bakinsamba, the Elephant-Tail-Folk, because of the elephant tails the kindi display on their hats to signify status and power; Bamibinga, the Dendrohyrax-Folk, because of the dendrohyrax outer teeth the yananio wear on the front of their hats to denote status and solidarity; Binyange, Ox-Pecker-Folk, because of the bird's white beauty and its light movements, which suggest its similarity to the "children of bwami."

Virtually all types of animals interest the initiates: from aquatic and terrestrial snails to frogs, lizards, varans, and forest crocodiles; from many species of antelopes to wild pigs and elephants; from civets and genets to leopards; from galago, potto, and dendrohyrax to rodents and insectivora; from chimpanzees to gorillas (where they occur) and species of monkeys; from pigeon, guinea fowl, parrot, and hornbill to many other birds; from butterflies, termites, and red ants to centipedes; from crabs to various species of fish. All these animals and birds are mentioned in texts sung during the rites; some are frequently represented as characters in actions and as objects.

Animals are occasionally portrayed without the use of objects. In a hunting scene, for example, one preceptor posing as a *musege* antelope (*Cephalophus nigrifons nigrifons*) is chased by an aide characterizing a dog, while other initiates act as hunters. In another setting a naked preceptor imitates a duiker antelope by crawling on his hands and knees, his buttocks high in the air, until he is caught in an imaginary net. Sometimes a dramatic performance makes use of an object that has no immediate connection with the animal in question. For example, a group of male and female initiates sitting on the roof of a house wave green banana leaves or the median stems of those leaves to imitate elephants moving their trunks. In another instance a reed swatter divided into four sections is held between the fingers of one hand to suggest the small *kikuta* bird spreading its tail. Two preceptors face each other, each closely holding one hand against his chest, and press chest to chest to evoke "Pigeon Isawasalama, that inflates the chest." A butterfly (*kibebeli*) character is portrayed by opening and closing a wide bark cloth, which a preceptor has wrapped around his back, holding the rims in his hands. By rolling up and then unrolling a mat, a preceptor imitates the habits of a *kabanga* pangolin (*Manis tricuspis*): "The heart of an initiate [is] a *kabanga:* in the early morning it rolls up and in the evening it unrolls," showing that a great initiate does not endlessly foment hatred and wrath. Another example shows dancers lifting their *kisaba* aprons and singing, "Kamukumbi [lit., Golden Mole] open up for me the passage; I am being met [with danger]; I close it [the passage] with no access left." When chased by smoke the golden mole closes off the passages to its lair. The episode refers metaphorically to an initiate who hears about a place where trouble is planned and so avoids going there.

Animal characters may be suggested in rites by minimal action with elementary objects. For example, two preceptors, each holding a small piece of *musagi* wood in his mouth, face each other in a squatting position to imitate a *kankwese* fly in pursuit of rotten meat and *kinkenge,* a large black ant: "Kinkenge does not sting a child; in the mouth there is fear." Although children are scared of the insect, it does not sting. In the same sense, one who has not passed through the initiations expresses his apprehension, but there is actually nothing to fear.

Exuviae, serving as *pars pro toto* and found mostly in collectively owned initiation baskets, evoke animal characters illustrative of social and moral behavior. Among the most frequently recurring exuviae are skulls of chimpanzee, forest crocodile, *kagelia* monkey, leopard, and *nsamba* fish (*Clarias lazera*); jawbones of *nkomo* fish (*Barbus tropidolepus*) and genet; crab pincers; beaks of hornbill and *kakulikuli* birds; turtle carapaces; scales of pangolin; claws of pangolin, aardvark, and eagle; paws of duiker antelope; fangs, teeth, and tusks of *mpoma* snake (*Bitis lachesis*), dendrohyrax, wild pig, and warthog, and occasionally a small elephant tusk; molars of elephant; tibia of *kagelia* monkey; feathers of chicken and parrot; snakeskins trimmed with feathers; shells of terrestrial and aquatic giant snails and mussels; porcupine quills; and hides of *kabungulu* and *musimba* genets, bush baby, potto, wildcat, and duiker antelope. Animal horns of billy goats and *ntundu* antelopes are strikingly absent from the exuviae in most communities. Although billy goat horns (*mega*) are regularly mentioned in the texts, they are usually replaced in action contexts by small gaffs (*igobo*).

Animal characters are also often symbolized by manufactured objects: a few light wood sticks tied together; an animal hide (of a *Potamogale velox,* an arboreal pangolin, a potto, or a snake) stuffed with raffia, leaves, mosses, or a piece of banana stipe; assemblages; and zoomorphic figurines. Anthropomorphic masks in a dance and action context (see Part 4) also suggest animal characters. In rare instances an anthropomorphic figurine hanging upside down from a string represents a bat (*mulima, kakutu*). A single animal character viewed from different perspectives may be depicted in several ways, either at separate grade levels or in different communities. Ikaga (terrestrial pangolin; called by his drum name Kilinkumbi), for example, is introduced by his scales or his claws, a stuffed skin (with scales) of the smaller but related arboreal pangolin, a crude animal figurine, small or large, with four legs and one or two heads, or a similar figurine with real pangolin scales added.

Figurines, even when carved in the same way, can be identified as distinctive characters. A single figure in a ritual context may stand for as many as three different animals, but only if the sculpture is a generalized four-legged figurine with a tail. On one occasion such a sculpture was described consecutively as "My little dog Mugugundu, Chaser goes chasing," "Chameleon has arrived far going slowly," and "Varan dies in the river because of him who has placed the fish trap." The underlying ideas conveyed by the three characters converge: all things pertaining to the initiation will be shown systematically; slow, well-organized progression is the rule of bwami; interruptions and delays result from errors made by the candidate and his tutors.

The range of animals depicted by manufactured objects, however, is limited. Hornbill, dendrohyrax, and warthog, for example, are suggested only by specific exuviae (respectively, skull and beak, outer teeth, tusks). On the other hand, some animal characters are evoked only by manufactured objects (e.g., frogs by evenly cut pieces of wood attached to a string or by sculptures), and others (e.g., hunting dogs) solely by sculptures or by action without objects.

Zoomorphic sculptures occur in diverse materials, sizes, and forms. They are made of wood, bone, ivory, or *ntutu*. Some small ones (a few cm long) are individually owned by members of the two highest grades; other larger ones (up to 35 cm long) belong to individual preceptors or are part of baskets collectively owned within certain communities by members of the two top grades. There are two major morphological categories of animal figurines. The first comprises those that are small in size, are made of wood or ivory, and represent specific animals (frog, snake, myriopod, turtle, elephant, crocodile, pangolin, aardvark, or giant snail) or a particular animal type (birds, fish). These sculptures, although stylized in varying degree, nevertheless realistically portray distinct types of animals. Out of context, the carvings are easily, and with a high degree of certainty, identified as specific animals. Some highly stylized bird figurines, however, are reduced to a carved head and neck and look almost like a small gaff; some snakes may have stump legs.

Generalized quadrupeds, with two subtypes, make up the second category of sculptures. The first subtype includes fairly large, crudely carved quadrupeds in wood coated with white or red clay. Some are partly covered with scales; others have a rather long tubular tail in horizontal position, but in some specimens the tail is replaced by a second head. The second subtype, comprising smaller quadrupeds in wood, bone, or ivory, shows varying degrees of finish, smoothness, and polish. The typical elongated quadrupeds in ivory and bone stand on four short legs (from 7 to 17.5 cm long; from 2.2 to 4 cm high). The long oval head is clearly separated from the body by indentation. Circular or circle-dot eyes and an open mouth may be indicated, and the snout is flattened or sharp. The body is oblong or angular. In most specimens the back is curved or bent; in some it is flat and almost straight, in others it is notched. A long, pointed tail bends slightly up or down. The sculptures are frequently adorned with circle-dot or striated designs, mostly on the body and the tail. Some ivory and bone quadrupeds are unusual because of the angularity and downward bent position of the head.

The widest formal differences are seen among the wooden, black or dark-brown, patinated quadrupeds. These are elongated figurines of various lengths. Classic examples fall between 11 and 21 cm, with heights between 3 and 6 cm; the back is straight or bent, and there are four outward-spread short legs. The large, fairly realistic animal head either is horizontal or looks down or upward. It is explicitly detached from the body by a short or long cylindrical neck. Some specimens lack facial features; others show an open slit mouth, sometimes with teeth, and nostrils. Some figurines have ears; others have short horns. The long, horizontal tail is placed upright or curls. Some sculptures are completely covered with hide, or they may have quills, seeds, or pangolin scales on the back. Zoomorphic figurines that represent generalized quadrupeds have complex meanings because they depict diverse and unrelated animal characters.

The small, carefully carved, zoomorphic figurines in wood, ivory, and bone, realistic pieces or conventionalized quadrupeds, are fairly well represented in collections and illustrated in the recent literature (Bassani, 1977, pl. 470; Biebuyck, 1973a, pls. 25, 88–94, and 1979, pls. 1–3, 7, 9–10; Claerhout, 1968, no. 55.4.1; de Kun, 1966, pls. 28–29; Fagg, 1968, pl. 276; Golovanova, 1969, p. 225; Krieger, 1969, pl. 354; Olderogge, 1969, pl. 135; Sotheby, Parke Bernet, 1978, pl. 291). Sculptures with anthropomorphic and zoomorphic traits are rarely shown (Delange, 1967, pl. 166; Krieger, 1969, pl. 326). These zoomorphic sculptures are scarce or nonexistent in some parts of Legaland; in other areas they must be owned by yananio and kindi initiates as part of their insignia. Preceptors of high grade may possess additional animal sculptures which they display in rites as one of their specializations. The large, crudely carved zoomorphic figurines in wood and the small ones in *ntutu*, which are contained in baskets or are kept by preceptors on behalf of the ritual community, are virtually undocumented in collections and publications (Biebuyck, 1973a, pls. 23, 26; 1979, pls. 4–6, 8).

Ikaga (Pangolin)

Of all the animals celebrated in the bwami rites, the most varied action and exegesis center on Ikaga, the giant pangolin (*Manis gigantea*). The sculpture is often crudely carved as a large four-legged animal figurine with a tail (sometimes 35 cm long), but it may be enhanced by the addition of pangolin scales and red color (Biebuyck, 1979, pl. 7). Normally, each clan group has only one such object, usually owned by a preceptor of kindi grade. Related preceptors inherit the figurines from one another. In one instance the present owner had received the figurine from a classificatory sororal nephew when he succeeded him as preceptor; the latter had obtained it from a matrilateral cross-cousin whom he replaced. Among the zoomorphic figurines in ivory and bone, those held individually by kindi are refined and more realistically carved replicas of the great pangolin figure (pl. 54; Biebuyck, 1973*a*, pl. 91). In some areas these sculptures are part of a kindi's insignia, but they are not the subject of the elaborate exegesis as discussed here.

As the giant pangolin is a sacred animal, it is not hunted or trapped. When it is found dead in the forest (e.g., in a trap set for other animals), strict rules govern its distribution among initiates at all levels in a specified village (Biebuyck, 1953*b*). The death of a smaller species of arboreal pangolin (*kabanga*) demands less elaborate ceremonies. The initiation songs sometimes contrast the two species of pangolin in their habits and socioritual significance, and, as already noted, in some communities the pangolin figurine is replaced by the stuffed hide (all scales still attached) of *kabanga*. As the giant pangolin, like the aardvark (*ntumba; Orycteropus*), is a nocturnal termite eater living in burrows, the symbolism may shift back and forth from pangolin to aardvark.

Although the pangolin is mentioned at other ritual levels when its scales or claws are presented, it is used principally in a lutumbo lwa kindi rite called *kilinkumbi* (drum name of the pangolin). In most communities this rite also includes the display of ivory masks hanging from a small fence erected on the dance ground near the initiation house. Action and exegesis relating to the pangolin in *kilinkumbi* may either precede or follow the showing of the masks. At the beginning of the rite, the figurine may stand on the fence or near it; it subsequently may be moved up and down along the fence, placed upside down, or simply danced with by a preceptor who holds it in both hands. He also moves it along the doorjamb of the initiation house and runs with it in and out of the house.

Standard aphorisms accompany the appearance of the figurine. When it is handled near the fence, "Ikaga climbs up because of intelligence" is recited. Pangolin represents a junior whose seniors did not want him to be initiated to the highest levels, despite his efforts, his character, and his intelligence. This aphorism is sometimes stated in another manner as the initiates place the figurine on top of the fence and then express amazement: "Ikaga climbs up with [because of] shrewdness, he is no longer [there where he usually is]," a critique of a son who fails to follow his father's example. He is like a giant terrestrial pangolin that attempts to climb a tree.

Moving the sculpture down the fence, and then slowly back up, is accompanied by the aphorism: "Ikaga cannot arrive upward [in the sky; i.e., cannot climb]; [however] he cannot forget the place where [the moment when] the sun rises [or when the sun sets]." The reference is to the terrestrial and nocturnal habits of the pangolin, and the interpretation has sexual overtones: nobody has to be taught how to have sex; one who no longer has an erection when lying on his bed is close to dying.

The figurine is placed down against the fence: "Ikaga, the big animal, climbs down from above." This aphorism bears on earlier ones about seniors who were initially ill disposed toward the candidate but have now had a change of heart.

The largest number of aphorisms (as many as ten in some communities) are sung as a preceptor dances while leading a line of initiates and holding the figurine in his hands:

"Kilinkumbi [drum name for pangolin], the animal for which the Bakota [the most senior initiates; the masters of the land] danced." When a pangolin dies, the attendant ceremonies require large-scale participation. A kindi initiate is compared with the pangolin: Big-Ones who otherwise do not perform join in the initiation dances.

"Ikaga, greater than elephant, the animal that is being skinned on green banana leaves." The aphorism glorifies the greatness of the pangolin that is brought to the village, displayed on banana tree stipes, singed (to remove the scales), and cut up and distributed in small portions according to strict rules.

"Ikaga rejoices and rejoices because of the greatness [leadership, *bukota*] which he has taken." This further praise for the pangolin implies criticism of a person who achieved the kindi grade but has too much to say for himself and ignores the words of his colleagues.

"He who has no kalonda [initiated wife] does not eat [from] the tail of the pangolin." The people who are entitled to receive parts of the pangolin's tail are strictly defined in terms of kinship position and grade level. The aphorism also indicates that the higher initiations are forbidden to a man who has no wife capable of achieving the complementary female grade.

"Pangolin [meat] that I have eaten! Even if I go far, I cannot leave the [strong] odor [of the meat] behind"; "Pangolin that I have eaten, the putrid odor does not destroy the smell." The meat of the pangolin has a strong odor, and the direct reference is to a person who found a pangolin and ate it with some cohunters—a serious transgression of a prohibition. Indirectly the aphorism points out that even if a bad person travels far and leaves his group, the evil remains with him. Also, the teachings of bwami cannot be forgotten or lost.

"Ikaga has instructed people who were beaten by rain." The pangolin is considered to be a culture hero; the disposition of phrynium leaves on the roof of a house resembles the scales on the back of a pangolin. Inspired by this model, the Lega say the hunters learned to build better waterproof roofs than those previously used for their sheds.

"Ikaga, Bad-Bad-One, the big animal that depletes the *milunda* [animals provided to pay a fine for transgressing taboos, such as keeping a pangolin for oneself]," and "Ikaga, the tail of the animal has made me separate from the children of my father." Even a supreme initiate cannot reserve a pangolin for himself.

In optional aphorisms, the giant pangolin Ikaga is contrasted with the arboreal pangolin Kabanga or with the aardvark Ntumba:

"Ikaga does not abandon the scales that Kabanga has left." A man follows in his father's footsteps.

"Kabanga, they refuse him from the patrimony [*ntiko*] that Ikaga has left behind." A junior brother succeeds in bwami instead of a man's son.

"Kabanga [is] scales and scales, he resembles Ikaga." A junior person follows the customs of the senior.

"Remove [the burden] from me, the scales rot on my back." A person in a junior line who took over the objects from one in a senior lineage, whose son has now grown up, invites the son to take charge of the things that belonged to his father.

"I am the little Child of Ikaga, I am a little animal, I am not skinned in the early morning." Kabanga is speaking here; although ritually less important, the small arboreal pangolin must also be skinned and distributed in the presence of many people.

"Ikaga does not suffice [is not big enough] for the hole in which Ntumba was." A junior son is incapable of achieving the status of his predecessor. An initiate of lower grade is not allowed to attend the rites of a higher grade.

"Ikaga and Ntumba quarrel over one hole." The Lega sometimes affirm that the pangolin does not make its own hole but "steals" that of the aardvark. Two persons from the same womb or the same house must not dispute about land or about a woman.

In some instances the pangolin's extremely long, rapierlike, sticky tongue is compared with a snake:

"The tongue of Ikaga surpasses in length a *sanda* snake." The rites of bwami are long, and they must be accomplished systematically if one hopes to achieve the summit; the advice of elders is always needed.

"Kabanga is not the junior of Ikaga, Mulinde [Snake] is not the junior of Nzoka [Snake]"; "Ikaga eats *busise* termites, the animal that resembles Kabanga." The same singing and acting may occur in different initiations in bwami, but the statuses of initiates of the various levels differ widely.

Occasionally Ikaga is synonymous with a person of lower status rather than with a high initiate: "Ikaga rolls and rolls over the ground [in anger or in sorrow]; he who has finished the initiations scorns him." The pangolin, which rolls itself into a ball in self-defense, here represents a physically strong person of low status: a small and weaker person "who has finished the initiations" can send the lower initiate wherever he wants.

In rites where only the pangolin claw is used, a few of the above aphorisms recur, sometimes in slightly modified forms (e.g., "He who does not leave odor will look for the odor of Ikaga"; "Ikaga a teacher, he has taught people how to build houses"). There are distinctive aphorisms as well: "Mr. In-Laws, Ikaga is not given as a present" stresses that bwami is not given as a present or that one person alone cannot confer the initiation upon a beloved in-law; "Ikaga is not called an animal, on every part of its body there grow scales," emphasizes that a person who has already achieved the initiations is not to be scorned by a latecomer.

Mukondekonde (Forest Crocodile) and Mumbilumbilu (Giant Otter)

In many communities large wooden rudimentarily carved quadrupeds are part of the collectively owned kindi initiation baskets (Biebuyck, 1979, pl. 8). The items in the baskets include chimpanzee skulls, carapaces, dried epiphytes, and wooden sculptures (anthropomorphic or zoomorphic, depending on the area). Several morphologically identical zoomorphic figurines in one basket may represent from two to four semantic types: *mukondekonde*, forest crocodile; *ibilundu* or *mumbilumbilu*, giant forest otter; *lungaga*, an antelope species; and *kabwa*, the dog. The first two are interchangeable; the symbolism centering on one figurine may shift, for example, from giant otter to forest crocodile. In most communities the forest crocodile is represented by its skull; when it is suggested by a carving, the crude sculpture may have two heads and waffle-shaped designs imitating the scaly hide (ibid.).

The aphorisms focusing on the forest crocodile include:

"Mukondekonde [Forest Crocodile] does not eat Catfish in their holes";
"Mukondekonde: as is the animal so is the skinner." A tutor or guardian does not take things that are entrusted to his care.

"Mukondekonde, the child whom I give birth to laughs at my scales [or, mocks me calling me Magamba, Scales]." Although the child is beautiful, it may have a callous heart.

Mumbilumbilu, drum name for the giant otter, is mentioned in only a few aphorisms:

"Mumbilumbilu, the big animal drinks water"; "Mumbilumbilu, the big animal of the water [i.e., aquatic animal] drinks water." These aphorisms symbolically state a prescription: an initiate must not get his head wet when bathing.

"I have not trapped for it; Musungu [Poisoned-Arrow] eats animals for me." A candidate protests when he observes that many initiates whom he did not invite are participating.

"Big sharp-toothed animal is not encountered with feathers in its mouth." When a man sees his wife in the evening, he does not know who slept with her during the day.

Plates

1. A mwami of yananio grade wearing a hat of black sheep's mane with buttoned strap and a beaded necklace with leopard teeth. Note that the neatly shaven skull is largely left bare by the hat. The initiate holds a wickerwork rattle.

2. A mwami of lutumbo lwa kindi wearing a wickerwork hat studded with white buttons and surmounted by an elephant's tail, a necklace of leopard teeth, a broad belt cut from the central part of a bongo antelope hide, and an apron of bongo hide.

3. Women of bunyamwa grade wearing the typical diadem, the reddened bark cloth apron, and bunches of feathers attached to a beaded belt.

4. An initiate of yananio grade rests on his walking stick. He carries a bark box containing objects for the secret *kasisi* rite.

5. Preceptors of kindi grade play the *kimbili* and *muningati* drums.

6. An initiate (left), acting as tutor, and the candidate wait near the initiation house for the ceremonial entry of the initiates.

7. A young woman (left), acting as *kigogo*, is led to a kongabulumbu rite by her tutor.

8. A plaited skullcap, called bwami, is attached to a tuft of hair and covered by a larger hat (Tervuren, no. 55.134.84, collected around 1909).

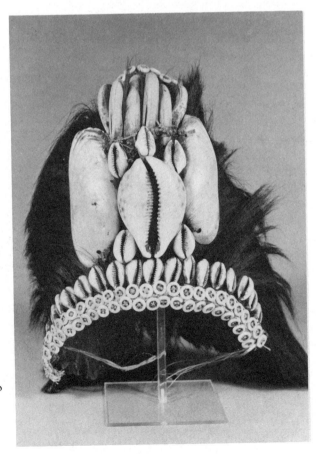

9. An impressive and rather unusual lutumbo lwa kindi hat; the black mane is adorned with buttons, cowries, a *Cypraea* shell, two polished mussel shells, and leopard teeth (Tervuren, no. 34178).

10. A coronet made of vine, feathers, cowries, and raffia worn on the head by women of bunyamwa grade during the initiations (Tervuren, no. 52.29.10, H. 28 cm).

12. Lower-level yananio initiates collect the shoulder bags at an early stage of the yananio rites.

11. Covered baskets containing collectively owned initiation objects. A ceremonial wickerwork shield and wooden spear are in the foreground.

13. A yananio initiate dances holding a polished *lubumba* shell in his mouth.

14. A kindi preceptor, flanked by a kanyamwa woman, leaves the initiation house holding a wooden figurine.

15. Bifrontal bust with arms; one
side shows male, the other side
female, genitalia (Stockholm,
no. 17.1.112, collected by Arrhenius,
stone, H. about 11.5 cm).

16. Prognathic head on a pole
(Tervuren, no. 33192, collected by
Zographakis in Shabunda area
before 1931, stone, H. 8 cm).

17. Full figurine standing on stump legs
(Tervuren, no. 71.11.1, former Lepage
collection, baked clay, H. 16.2 cm).

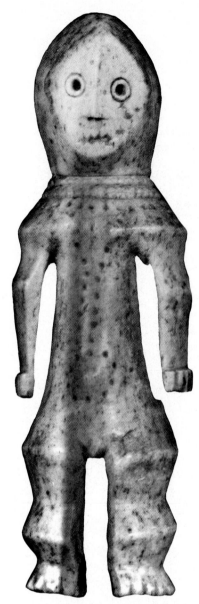

18. Quadrifrontal head on stump legs is adorned with an imitation skullcap made of resin and cowries (Tervuren, no. 56.3.19, collected by Frateur among southeastern Lega, ivory, H. 12.1 cm).

19. Full figurine with lozenge-shaped face (Tervuren, no. 19983, collected before 1917, ivory, H. 14.5 cm).

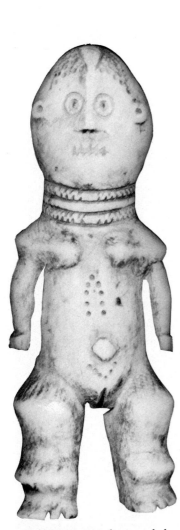  

20. Full figurine in the rounded style (Tervuren, no. 19982, collected before 1917, ivory, H. 13.6 cm).

21. Bifrontal bust (Tervuren, no. 55.3.120, ivory, H. 15.3 cm) from the Banamunwa, Kanyongolo lineage. It represents Kabukenge.

22. Peg-shaped (broken) bifrontal ivory figurine (Tervuren, no. 55.3.121, H. 7.9 cm) from the Banamunwa, Kanyongolo lineage, called Kalemba.

23. Quadrifrontal armless ivory figurine (Tervuren, no. 55.3.123, H. 18.5 cm) from the Banamunwa, Kanyongolo lineage, representing Wasakwa nyona.

24. Head on a flaring pole ending in a clublike elephant foot (Tervuren, no. 55.3.127, ivory, H. 11.3 cm) from the Banamunwa, Kyondo lineage, called Kasegasega.

25. Head on a straight, hollow pole (Tervuren, no. 55.3.128, ivory, H. 11.3 cm) from the Banamunwa, Kyondo lineage, called Mwami we Idungu.

26. Elongated bust with arms in relief on the sides of the body (Tervuren, no. 55.3.139, ivory, H. 19.6 cm) from the Banamunwa, Kyondo lineage, representing Kimbayu.

27. Slender figurine with arms akimbo in very light relief, standing on pillarlike legs (Tervuren, no. 55.3.140, ivory, H. 15.3 cm), from the Banamunwa, Kyondo lineage. It represents Kitende, a character most frequently depicted by a frog figurine.

28. Full figurine, standing on stump legs, with ajouré arms, breasts, and female genitalia (Tervuren, no. 55.3.122, ivory, H. 13.9 cm), from the Banamunwa, Katumpu lineage, called Nyanjinjinzi.

29. Trifrontal figurine without arms, standing on elongated crenellated legs, with two supplementary faces at the height of the upper arms (Tervuren, no. 55.3.125, ivory, H. ?). It belongs to the Banamunwa, Katumpu lineage, and is referred to as Myoli zakisinda.

30. Head on a tubular armless pole ending in a rounded base (Tervuren, no. 55.3.137, ivory, H. 10.8 cm) from the Banamunwa, Katumpu lineage, representing Kamukazi wazamba.

31. Armless bust on tubular base with female genitalia (Tervuren, no. 55.3.130, ivory, H. 12.8 cm) from the Banamunwa, Bulambo lineage, called Nyanjinjinji.

32. Peg-shaped, armless figurine (Tervuren, no. 55.3.132, ivory, H. 21 cm) from the Banamunwa, Bulambo lineage. It is called Kilinga, a character most frequently represented by a bird figurine.

33. Stocky bust (Tervuren, no. 55.3.133, ivory, H. 7.1 cm) from the Banamunwa, Bulambo lineage, referred to as Kakinga.

34. Head on elongated pole resting on trapezoidal base (Tervuren, no. 55.3.141, ivory, H. 9.3 cm) from the Banamunwa, Bulambo lineage, representing Sawamazembe.

35. Peg-shaped, armless
figurine (Tervuren, no. 55.3.124,
ivory, H. 14.5 cm) from the
Banamunwa, Banakatimba incorporated lineage, depicting
Nyatwiso.

36. Hexafrontal figurine, consisting of three superposed sets of
double faces, resting on a low
spherical socle (Tervuren,
no. 55.3.138, ivory, H. 18.2 cm).
From the Banamunwa,
Banalukinga incorporated
lineage, the sculpture is
referred to as Mwami.

37. Elongated head on pole-
shaped, armless body standing
on crenellated legs; female genitalia are indicated by a reversed
triangle (Tervuren, no. 55.3.7,
ivory, H. 14 cm). The sculpture
came from the Banamusiga and
was named Kakinga.

38. Round head on armless tubular body. The long neck slants on lightly curved legs and massive toeless feet; female genitalia are suggested by a slit (Tervuren, no. 55.3.27, ivory, H. 12.3 cm). The Banakimane held the sculpture, which was called Kakinga.

39. Large oval head on a short, armless bust; a large slit running vertically in the center of the bust suggests female genitalia (Tervuren, no. 55.3.28, ivory, H. 8.3 cm). From the Beiamisisi, it is known as Kakinga.

40. Elongated angular head on a short torso with one arm and long widespread legs; the female genitalia are indicated by the reversed triangle between the legs (Tervuren, no. 55.3.62, ivory, H. 13.8 cm). Held by the Baziri, it is referred to as Kakinga.

41. Large, ovoid head on a pole-shaped, armless body resting on a trapezoidal base; no sexual indications (Tervuren, no. 55.3.144, ivory, H. 11.6 cm). The object, obtained from the Banisanga, was called Kakinga.

42. Full figurine with rounded head and short, bent legs; it is decorated with linear and dotted designs, and female genitalia are indicated by a slit set in a pubic proclivity (Tervuren, no. 55.3.146, ivory, H. 10.7 cm). The figurine came from the Batoba and was named Kakinga.

43. Bust-shaped figurine standing on a base carved as an obtuse cone (Tervuren, no. 52.29.9, collected by de Limelette, wood, H. 10.5 cm).

44. Bifrontal figurine on a scepterlike body (Tervuren, no. 59.35.2, formerly in the Decerf collection, wood, H. 14.2 cm).

45. Bifrontal head on a pole-shaped body with one arm (Tervuren, no. 55.3.66, wood, H. 23.7 cm). The sculpture, from the Banalyuba, is called Sakimatwematwe.

46. Armless figurine on bent legs (Stockholm, no. 17.1.106, wood, H. 13 cm). Collected by Captain Elias Arrhenius, who ascribed it to the Bangubangu.

47. Full-standing figurine, the head covered with black monkey hide (Tervuren, no. 35409, collected by Baude in the Kunda region, wood, H. 34.9 cm). The sculpture probably represents Kakulu ka Mpito.

48. Full-standing female figurine (Tervuren, no. 55.3.96, wood, H. 33 cm) from the Baziri. Used together with the figurine in plate 49, it represents Yimbo, the mother of Keitula.

49. Full-standing male figurine (Tervuren, no. 55.3.97, wood, H. 38.4 cm) from the Baziri. It is used together with the figurine in plate 48 to portray Keitula, the son of Yimbo.

50. Quadrifrontal, pole-shaped figurine (Tervuren, no. 55.3.21, wood, H. 22.4 cm) from the Beianangi. It is called Kimbayu.

51. Figurine on a pole-shaped body ending in a pin (Tervuren, no. 32880, ivory, H. 8.5 cm), identified by the collector Baude as a *kalimbangoma*.

52. Full figurine, with two holes at shoulder height for suspension (Tervuren, no. 38635, ivory, H. 8.3 cm). The figurine was not identified by the collector Van Hooren, but it may be a *kalimbangoma*.

53. Bustlike figurine with arms (Tervuren, no. 55.3.115, ivory, H. 8.2 cm) from the Babongolo-Banakalobia, identified as a *katimbitimbi*.

54. Animal figurine symbolizing *ikaga* (pangolin; Tervuren, no. 38719, collected by Van Hooren, ivory, L. 17.5 cm).

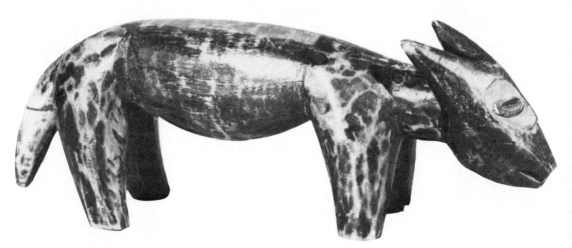

55. Animal figurine with horns representing *lungaga* (antelope; Tervuren, no. 51.35.2, collected by Hautmann among the northern Lega, wood, L. 33.4 cm).

56. Animal figurine with short ears and erect tail representing a dog (Tervuren, cliché no. 66063, Braun de Ter Meeren collection, wood, L. 13.6 cm).

57. Mugugu quadruped (Tervuren, no. 80.2.156, Walschot collection, wood with shell inlay, L. 17.4 cm).

58. Mugugu quadruped (Tervuren, no. 32499, ivory, L. 13.2 cm). The object was identified by the collectors Ledocte and Corbisier as *mugugu* and *mbwa za kindi.*

59. Faceless animal figurine on stump legs probably representing Mukumbi (Tervuren, no. 38718, collected by Van Hooren, ivory, L. 10.5 cm).

60. Snake figurine, probably *ngimbi* (Tervuren, no. 51.11.41, collected by Lemborelle, ivory, L. 14.9 cm).

61. Crocodile figurine representing Kyasula kanwa (Tervuren, no. 80.2.3, Walschot collection, ivory, L. 10.5 cm).

62. Bird figurine, probably symbolizing *kilinga,* pigeon (Tervuren, no. 51.11.40, collected by Lemborelle, ivory, L. 12.8 cm).

63. Figurine symbolizing *kitende,* the frog (Tervuren, no. 77.17.1, ivory, L. 14.8 cm).

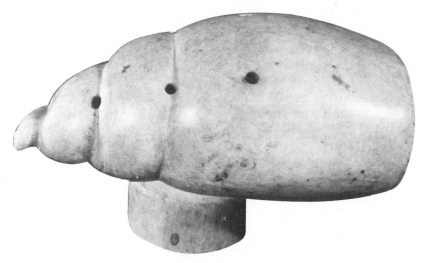

64. Figurine representing a *nkola* snail (Tervuren, no. 52.29.35, collected by de Limelette among the southeastern Lega, ivory, L. 10.6 cm).

65. Figurine probably representing the *nkomo* fish (Tervuren, no. 51.11.38, collected by Lemborelle, ivory, L. 11.1 cm).

67. *Lukwakongo* mask (Tervuren, no. 55.3.117, wood, H. 17.5 cm) from the Banamunwa. The mask was owned by a lutumbo lwa yananio initiate and had been passed down through three known generations.

66. *Lukwakongo* mask (Tervuren, no. 55.3.30, wood, H. 14.7 cm) from the Banasalu. Owned by a lutumbo lwa yananio initiate, the mask was passed down through three generations of initiates and originally came from the Beiamisisi.

68. *Lukwakongo* mask (Tervuren, no. 55.3.142, wood, H. 17.3 cm) from the Banisanga. Owned by a lutumbo lwa yananio, the mask had been passed down through four known generations.

69. *Lukungu* mask (Tervuren,
no. 32871, collected by Ledocte and
Corbisier, ivory, H. 14 cm).

70. *Lukungu* mask (Tervuren, no. 55.3.16, ivory,
H. 7.1 cm) owned by a lutumbo lwa kindi initiate
of the western Lega.

71. *Lukungu* or *kilume* mask (Tervuren, no. 55.3.85,
bone, H. 11.4 cm) owned by a lutumbo lwa kindi initiate
among the southeastern Lega.

72. *Kayamba* mask (Tervuren, no. 38753, collected by Van Hooren, wood, H. 36.5 cm).

74. *Muminia* mask (Tervuren, cliché no. 125224, former E. Beer collection, wood, H. ?). Compare Biebuyck, 1973a, pl. 39.

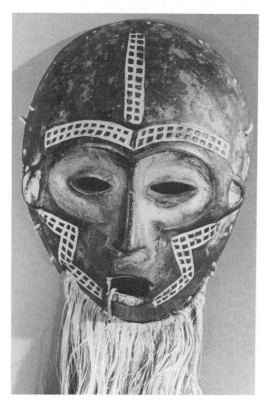

73. *Muminia* mask (Tervuren, no. 55.3.1, wood, H. 26.1 cm) from the Banamusiga. See also Biebuyck, 1973a, pls. 42, 44–45, 59.

75. *Idimu* mask (Tervuren, no. 52.29.1, collected by de Limelette among the southeastern Lega, wood, H. 24 cm). Compare Biebuyck, 1973a, pls. 38, 41, 44–45.

76. *Idimu* mask (Tervuren, no. 38752, collected by Van Hooren, wood, H. 30.3 cm).

77. *Idimu* mask (Tervuren, no. 63.50.7, collected by Prigogine, leather, H. 22.7 cm).

78. *Idimu* mask (Tervuren, no. 55.3.53, ivory, H. 22.2 cm) guarded by a lutumbo lwa kindi among the western Lega.

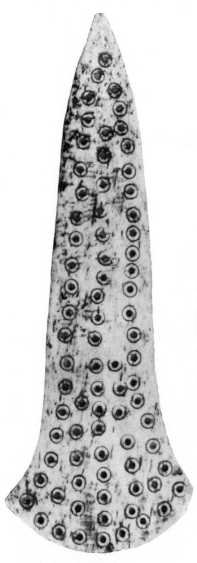

79. Ax blade in bone, adorned with circle-dot motifs (Tervuren, no. 59.7.16, Walschot collection, L. 15.2 cm).

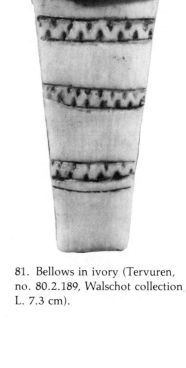

81. Bellows in ivory (Tervuren, no. 80.2.189, Walschot collection, L. 7.3 cm).

80. Exceptional ax blade in ivory, one side showing a lizard or iguana and the other a snake (Tervuren, no. 44700, collected by Lallas, L. 19.5 cm).

83. Billhook in ivory (Tervuren, no. 55.3.110, L. 30.4 cm) from the Babongolo (southern Lega).

85. Imitation leopard tooth (Tervuren, no. 38725, collected by Van Hooren, L. 7.8 cm).

84. Imitation of knife used for planting banana stipes (Tervuren, no. 60.39.66, bone, L. 20.9 cm).

82. Billhook in bone (Tervuren, no. 80.2.197, Walschot collection, L. 27 cm).

86. Representation of a vagina and phallus (Tervuren, no. 80.2, Walschot collection, 8.1 cm long and 3.8 cm wide).

87. Hammer in ivory (Tervuren, no. 52.29.18, collected by de Limelette, L. 14.7 cm).

88. Knife with iron blade and bustlike wooden handle (Tervuren, no. 51.44.2 Stillman collection; total length, 46.5 cm; length of handle, 13.4 cm).

89. Knife in ivory (Tervuren, no. 55.3.70, L. 11.9 cm) from the Bakyunga (northern Lega).

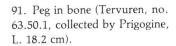

91. Peg in bone (Tervuren, no. 63.50.1, collected by Prigogine, L. 18.2 cm).

90. Mortar in ivory resting on a stool-like base (Tervuren, no. 74.21.6, collected by de Kun, H. 13 cm).

92. Phallic bone sculpture (University of California Museum of Culture, Los Angeles, no. 378–49).

93. Ivory pounder fixed in a wooden fork (Tervuren, no. 51.41.12, Walschot collection; length, 15.9 cm; diameter, 5.4 cm).

94. Ivory spoon (Tervuren, no. 35946, L. 21 cm).

95. Ivory spoon (Tervuren, no. 55.3.92, L. 16.5 cm) from the Beigala (northern Lega).

96. Ivory horn (Tervuren, no. 69.59.527, L. 33 cm).

97. Phallus-shaped whistle (Tervuren, no. 80.2.191, Walschot collection, ivory, L. 8.5 cm).

98. Full-standing figurine (Tervuren, no. 14684, ivory, H. 18.2 cm). Carved in typical Lega rounded style, the figurine was collected by Rochette before 1913 in Muvugni, a village located far to the northeast of Legaland in a region inhabited by Hunde and ancient offshoots of the Lega.

Lungaga (Antelope Species)

When depicted by a schematized quadruped figurine, the *lungaga* antelope may have short horns (pl. 55; Biebuyck, 1973*a*, pl. 89). The dramatic context is somewhat more elaborate than when preceptors simply dance with the figurines. Two similar figurines are often used: the larger one represents the antelope; the smaller one (sometimes wearing a large dog bell), a dog. As in actual hunting expeditions, the initiates loudly encourage the dog to chase the antelope: "My little dog Mugugundu, chasing animals has demolished the calves of our legs," says that a person must bear the consequences of his acts.

When the *lungaga* figurine appears alone, the following aphorisms are recited:

"The young *lungaga* antelope does not tread on a tree [fallen] on the trail." This warns against a woman who accompanies her husband to the rites but then begins to run around with others.

"Lungaga of close to the village, in the forest patch between two fields he will die"; "What has horns is hooked [in a place] where there are no vines." A person who was destined for the initiations fails because of his big mouth.

On rare occasions the horned animal figurine represents Billy-Goat, a character often enacted by dancers butting at one another with gaffs or goat horns: "Kalimba [Billy-Goat], little child of your father, even if you take care of him, he will mount you." Kalimba is the ungrateful orphan (child of another house) who scorns his guardian.

Kabwa (Little-Dog)

The dog character is frequently danced without objects by a preceptor in a hunting scene involving several actors: one is the *lungaga* or the *musege* antelope, another the dog, and the others are hunters. The hunters urge the dog on while the mock hunting net is still lying on the ground. "Little Musege, little male animal, encounters me, I have not yet set up the nets," indicates one who is not yet ready for the initiations. The dancers, as they move around, manage to set up a net in which the antelope is finally caught: "Male Lungaga that loves to run around the nets [without jumping into them] dies in the very last net."

Dogs are also portrayed in the action context by generalized, often crudely carved, quadrupeds. A dog bell attached to the neck of a sculpture may be the sole criterion for visual identification. Smaller, carefully carved figurines (pl.

56), with perked ears and a tail, more directly suggest a dog. The dog figurine is sometimes used in conjunction with a sculpture identified as a *lungaga* ante-lope (see above) or with porcupine quills (Kiko). In the latter instance a little story about Kiko and Kafyondo (the dog) is danced out. The quills are placed against the roof of the initiation house, while Kafyondo, activated by a precep-tor, runs around the pit in which Mukumbi is buried (see Part 4). Kafyondo is then moved around on the ground; he falls, stands up, and moves again: "Kiko climbs up because of shrewdness"; "Call the dog, Kiko climbs up with shrewd-ness." A high initiate (symbolized by Kiko) in the group wants to obstruct a person who desires the initiations. The maternal uncles intervene and quote this text to say: "No tricks, we want our nephew to become a yananio." The preceptor then makes the image hop around the pit, walk over the backs of the seated initiates, and climb over the walls and roof until Kafyondo finally gets Kiko: "Who-Does-Not-Chase-Well brings forth Abrupt-Chaser." Although the grandfathers did not achieve yananio, their grandchild has accomplished it.

The generalized quadruped figurine may also suggest specific dog charac-ters: Kafyondo (Good-Chaser), symbol of the leader who settles all problems in his group; Ibinga (Good-Chaser), the son of Itabingi (Who-Does-Not-Chase-Well), or, vice versa, Lwazanza (Bad-Chaser because of his abruptness), the son of Mugugundu (Smart-Dog); Kabwa ka lupembe (Little-White-Dog); Mangala (Spotted-Dog), who flatters his master; and Mupimbi, whose bell is broken.

Mugugu (Chameleon)

The term Mugugu is ambiguous. It is sometimes deliberately confused with Mugugundu (Smart-Dog), as in the aphorism: "My little dog Mugugundu, the big animals destroy our legs!" The text is sung during the display of the small conventionalized quadrupeds, while preceptors move one of the figurines over the feet, legs, arms, and shoulders of a seated kanyamwa woman. Mugugundu here refers to the kanyamwa who must not show inconstancy in her marital relationships; even after her husband's death she must remain in his group. Mugugu is represented in two ways: a crude wooden quadruped figurine simi-lar in form to those previously mentioned and collectively owned, or by a small carefully carved individually owned wooden or ivory generalized quadruped (pls. 57–58). Mugugu is simply held during a dance.

> "Mugugu, I sing during the rainy season, I have no billhook." This aphorism criticizes laziness and lack of initiative. The planting season has come but one does not prepare for the work; one desires bwami but is too unenter-prising to accumulate the necessary goods.

"Kakungukia [a species of chameleon] has finished [covered] the distances slowly, slowly." This reflects an old person who lacks strength but still achieves much because of circumspection, or an intelligent person who acquires things not readily available.

Wrapped in a genet hide, a wooden figurine adorned with resin and *bazizi* (red seeds of a vine) is held by two sitting preceptors facing each other: "Mugugu, put down the wood, you have no back." Respect is expressed for an old person who is unable to perform heavy work. Attention is often drawn to old initiates in other contexts. Although they do not actively participate in the dances, their presence is greatly desired and they passively share in the distributions of goods.

The smaller ivory *mugugu* sometimes are part of a display of figurines placed within a feather rope fence. One aphorism simply states, "Mugugu, give me things for a fire," to criticize a person who demands valuables from an old person who has "no back" (i.e., no strength) to collect firewood.

In another instance a similar presentation is preceded by a superbly enacted mock fight between two persons (throwing hats, pulling at their clothes, making faces, pulling down their lower eyelids). The fighters are separated. A group of initiates then sit around the configuration, back to back (expressing scorn), and then change to a face-to-face position (showing acceptance). Attention is directed to the zoomorphic figurine: "Do not despise Mugugu, Mugugu has no cheeks, his call goes far." When a big initiate sends a messenger with news, one must listen and follow the required course of action. Couriers are dispatched between initiates to transmit secret messages codified in various arrangements of objects.

Mukumbi (Golden Mole)

Mukumbi is suggested by the hide of a golden mole or of a *Potamogale velox* stuffed with moss, raffia, or a piece of stipe, by a small wooden or ivory conventionalized quadruped wrapped in a piece of *nsongi* hide, or by a plump, faceless, ivory figurine (pl. 59). *Mukumbi,* an insectivore, lives in the forest under vegetal debris. At one extremity of his network of galleries, he builds his nest, a round room covered with dry leaves.

In an elaborate yananio rite called *mukumbi,* a zoomorphic assemblage is hidden on a bed of sticks, bark, raffia, and vine at the bottom of a pit covered with leaves. Near the end of the rite initiates squat around the pit, which they have uncovered with great difficulty, and act as if they were being incessantly attacked by fierce bees.

"I arrive [at the place] where Mukumbi sleeps, I see the covered entrance to the hole." The candidate is close to knowing everything; nobody can fool him now.

"I arrive [at the place] where Mukumbi dies, I have not spoken mine [i.e., not said a word]." When one arrives in a village where a dead colleague is being buried, one must not start talking foolishly lest one be accused of having killed him. The entire *mukumbi* configuration is meant to illustrate the arrangements made around the grave of a dead initiate, who is represented by Mukumbi.

The preceptors, holding leaves near the hole to smoke out the animal, pull him out very slowly with a string: "Death: spasmodically Mukumbi comes out with the fire [smoke]." The preceptors may stage a mock quarrel that erupts over and over again: "Mukumbi [son] of Kalumangia does not arrive"; "Mukumbi of Kalumangia, [a place] filled with stamping of feet." In the first statement Kalumangia is seen as a smart person who always loiters on the road. He represents the high initiate who deliberately lingers before going to the place to which he has been called. In the second, Kalumangia is a place that people pass all the time; the reference is to initiates who come and go before the rites have started. They inspect the accumulated goods and make a lot of fuss.

In another *mukumbi* rite an animal figurine rather than an assemblage is used, and the interpretations are somewhat different. Waving their hands above the pit in which the *mukumbi* figurine is hidden, the initiates sing two aphorisms: "He who is stubborn, Mukumbi Musumba [another name for Mukumbi] exceeds in evil thoughts," means that an arrogant, excessively bad person will be revealed for what he really is before everybody; "I was a *kilimu* [a spiritual or mysterious being] from under the ground, fire has understood [how I am]," says that what had been hidden is now uncovered.

The preceptors then push the candidate forward: "Ignorant-One calls me Mbagu [Rat]; I am Mukumbi, I am the junior of Aardvark." The arrogant candidate calls his tutor names, but the tutor is a person who must be deeply respected. "Near the burrow [of Mukumbi] people are whispering there is no Musumba [Mukumbi] in it" means that ignorant people fail to see the meaning of things. The aphorism also alludes to the fact that the candidate has no valuables.

The initiates dance around the pit: "There comes an odor from in there, from Mukumbi, whom we chase with smoke." Initiates may receive bad news at the initiation in which they participate. The initiates pass around pieces of banana leaves taken from the pit. "I arrive at the place where Mukumbi sleeps, I arrive at Ikisa [the nest and supplies of Mukumbi]," signifies that the time for full revelation is approaching. Preceptors then search the pit and the debris: "Wakalumangia [he who lives in, is master of, a noisy place where people always pass] does not come out." The figurine is finally pulled out and shown to the candidate.

Kimpumbi (Potto)

The character Kimpumbi (Potto) seems to be symbolized only by his stuffed hide with four wooden sticks attached as legs. The assemblage is part of the contents of a lutumbo lwa yananio basket. While the initiates dance holding the objects, the following aphorisms are sung:

"The Big-Ones who have seen the initiation objects are bent under them." An initiate refuses to support a candidate and also persuades everybody else to reject him.

"Kimpumbi remains in the epiphytic growth in which Mubinga [Dendrohyrax] was." The true master of the land (Mubinga), who was a great spokesman, died and is now replaced by a nobody (Kimpumbi). The text sometimes is made more explicit by the addition of a second aphorism: "Kigilwa [Scorned-Wife] remains with the house [in the family group] in which Kilanga [Beloved-Wife] was."

"Kimpumbi, very strong, very strong; he does not let go." Unlike Mubinga, Potto does not make strident nocturnal calls; although small, he has a very powerful grip.

Nzoka (Snake)

Mpoma, a snake character, is typified by its fangs. Snakes in general and some specific species, however, are represented by a stuffed snakeskin, by a large wooden sculpture with a long straight body and an elongated flat head, or by a smaller zigzag-shaped realistic snake carving in ivory (pl. 60; Biebuyck, 1973a, pl. 94; Sotheby, Parke Bernet, 1978, pl. 29).

In one context a preceptor has made three puddles on the dance floor and sneaks around them while holding a snake figure.

"The small child plays in the shallow water, Ngimbi [deadly aquatic snake is] war"; "The small child plays at the waterfall, Ngimbi [is] death." These aphorisms criticize young people who behave foolishly toward an initiate (Ngimbi).

"I have my true [effective] funnel to administer an eye medicine with which I can remove Snake." A Big-One calls the initiations, which have a purifying effect.

On another occasion two initiates lie on a mat holding onto each other; a preceptor moves a snake figurine along their feet.

"I do not dance [play] with Nzoka, I have seen [experienced] that Mulinde [a nondeadly snake] bites." Even a lower-level initiation will absorb a large part of the goods you have accumulated.

"I thought I was bitten by Ngimbi; I do not die; lo! it is Mulinde." If the lower initiations did not kill the initiate, how could kindi?

"Igilima [a deadly snake], child of Ikuka; in the fallen tree it has built its dwelling." If a man is initiated during the lifetime of his father, who is also a high initiate, he surely will not be fooled.

"Snake has bitten me in the evening; I do not know its name." This aphorism voices the complaint of a candidate who has all the necessary goods. The initiates have inspected and accepted them, but now for reasons unknown to him the ceremony does not proceed.

Kyasula kanwa (Crocodile)

Kyasula kanwa (What-Has-the-Mouth-Wide-Open) refers to a crocodile (*kimena, kinyenge*) which is represented in several different ways: the open mouth of a basket or of a rolled-up mat; a crudely carved piece of wood, sometimes resembling a bird's distended beak or the open mouth of a crocodile; a highly realistic ivory sculpture; or a naturalistic crocodile head with open mouth (pl. 61; Biebuyck, 1973*a*, pl. 90; Claerhout, 1968, no. 55.4.1; Golovanova, 1969, p. 225; Olderogge, 1969, pl. 135). Only one aphorism is applicable: "He who does not stop quarreling will quarrel with What-Has-the-Mouth-Wide-Open." It is intended to warn a quarrelsome person who argues with someone without knowing that person's strength.

Kitende (Frog)

Frogs are mentioned in the texts not only by their generic name but also by species identification (*mutuku, nkelo, kanke, nyangulanga, nyangunu, isilia*). A frog may be represented by a realistically carved wooden or ivory figurine (pl. 63), sometimes anthropomorphized, by an anthropomorphic figurine, or by seven small sticks from a raffia palm. In some communities these sticks, all of the same length, are part of the contents of collectively held baskets of *kasisi* (yananio grade) and of kindi. They are held in the hand and rhythmically struck on the ground; or, hanging in two bundles from a raffia fiber, they are beaten on the ground, suspended from the ceiling of the initiation house, and thrown up and down. The sticks are used in rites like *kasisi* which have no music and during the oiling of the kindi sculptures when the sacred mirliton sings. In the rites, two preceptors beat the sticks on the ground, moving them back and forth from left to right as if the sticks were jumping.

"Nkelo [small frog] weep in the hunting grounds of Nyabukaba [lit., Who-Will-Be-Like-That, i.e., empty, dead]"; "Nkelo weeps, in the hunting grounds there Nkelo weeps." When no Big-One remains in the land, all weep because they are destitute.

"Kanke [Little-Frog] of Banana-Tree is the reason that Kelekwidambo [What-Is-in-the-Hunting-Grounds] was killed." A youth fights a Big-One and kills him. The kin of the victim will take revenge against the Big-One of the assassin's village.

"Kanke, even if you speak, Kilanga [Preferred-Wife] is the master of Mugio [lit., the harmony of the song; doing well]." A small person says many things but has no power; in the eyes of a husband, the preferred wife can do no wrong.

Later on, the preceptors hang the two bunches of sticks from the ceiling and swing them, throw them up and down, place them on the ground, shake them, and hold them together in a bundle on the back of the candidate. As frequently happens in initiations, the focus has shifted from the frogs to other symbolic references: "Bambala [Group-of-Mbala-Nuts] hang dangling like that; Those-of-the-Dry-Season, the maternal uncles do not come," warns that a person with a bad heart will not receive assistance in bwami even if he has all the necessary goods; "We were many in Bubala [tree that bears *mbala* nuts], the dry season disperses us," means that death comes in clusters and disperses everyone.

Rare wooden or ivory frog figurines appear as individually owned objects in the general display (*kinsamba*) of figurines in kindi. No dramatic action marks this rite; the objects are simply viewed. All the sculptures displayed, however, have individual meanings which are formulated in aphorisms.

"Kitende [Frog] sees Stupid-One, finally he goes [jumps] into the river." When initiations are held, only those who are invited may attend. In an intricate and secret system of communication, giant snail shells, wicker-work rattles, reed swatters, knotted raffia fibers, and other items are sent as messages.

"Isilia [frog species], Big-One, I shall look [let me look] at those who are in the river." When kindi is held one must keep one's eyes wide open and be attentive and cautious. It is impossible to achieve the initiations simply by flattering a prominent kindi.

"Nyangulanga [frog species] does not see [experience] the swelling [inflation of the body] on account of which Nyangunu [frog species] died." The text refers to two women, one of whom died of ritual pollution during pregnancy. The deeper interpretation signifies that if an experienced tutor in the lineage dies without being replaced, a junior has little hope of rising rapidly in the grade hierarchy.

Nzogu (Elephant)

The elephant (*nzogu*) is often mentioned in the texts. At one of the final kindi rites, the elephant, identified with the large initiation house in which most of the ceremonies take place, is "ritually skinned" with ivory knives and spoons. At other levels Nzogu is enacted by men and women who sit on housetops and wave banana leaf stems to imitate elephants waving their trunks. Elephants and kindi initiates are equated; the kindi often speak of themselves as Banananzogu, Elephant-Folk: "The place where they slept [or stampeded] cannot be forgotten"; "Where male Nzogu passed the trace does not obliterate." Ivory sculptures belong to the kindi; old patinated small tusks and whitened molars may be used in the rites. Some kindi have among their assortment of hats one made of elephant's ear; rare masks are carved in elephant hide; sculptured elephant ribs and bones are also used in the rites. Realistic sculptured representations of elephants in ivory or *ntutu* are extremely rare (de Kun, 1966, pl. 29); sometimes they are simply imported commercial pieces.

The few songs I have heard directly relating to elephant figurines speak, not about the elephant in general, but about Kalupepe (Small-Elephant), Mwepa (Big-Elephant), and Kabukutu (Strong-Elephant).

"The stampeding of buffaloes does not equal that of elephants." Juniors are not equal to seniors.

"Let Elephant, the Strong-One, break the trees." A father tells his son to do something worthy of a man.

"Baki [i.e., persons not initiated to kindi], miserable ones, come and see the herd of kindi." Noninitiates are invited to view the mass of goods accumulated for the kindi rites.

"The pregnancy of Elephant is not like that of any other animal." The master of the land is not like any other person.

"Kalupepe [Small-Elephant] calls for Mwepa [or Mwenda, Big-Elephant], and Mwepa [is] a destroyer of fields."

"Lion stronger [tougher] than Elephant, [but] Elephant surpasses him in bigness." This aphorism relates to an imported sculpture showing an elephant trampling another animal. A new initiate must not imagine himself to be stronger than his tutor.

Lions are found in savannas adjoining southern and eastern Legaland; although some initiates wear imported necklaces of lion teeth interspersed with leopard teeth, lions are never mentioned in other texts.

Kinsuluka (Centipede)

The minor character Centipede is represented by an individually owned, fairly realistic, wooden figurine at a low level of kindi. It is also celebrated during the *kamondo* dances that are preliminary to the actual initiations.

"A mwami [is] a Centipede; he does not return blank [i.e., without anything] from the journey." The reference is to gifts brought home by initiates.

"Centipede, if you want to flee the fire, flee the sound [of iron axes] in the new field [that is being made]." A person seeking high grade is encouraged to follow the advice of established initiates.

In a *kasisi* rite the centipede was carved from a wild pig's tooth: "Kinsuluka is not big, Magamba [Scales] gives him bigness." A man owes his status to bwami and to the support of his tutor.

Nkulu or Kikulu (Turtle)

Nkulu (Turtle) is most often symbolized by a turtle carapace which is part of the basket. (Different species of turtle are used, but frequently it is the *izezekumbe* turtle.) A wooden turtle head may be inserted into the carapace; often the carapace is wrapped in a feather rope. In a few instances a masked preceptor handles the carapace (see Part 4). The aphorisms point to Turtle's smallness, slowness, and intelligence: "Kikulu crosses the fallen tree, he has no calves"; "Kikulu crosses the fallen tree because of his smartness"; "Do not despise Nkulu [because of] his shortness, he speaks for Lugendo [journey; i.e., he decides how the journey will be undertaken]." Deliberate slowness in everything a high initiate undertakes is warmly praised; the old or the great initiate is frequently identified with the turtle.

On rare occasions a realistically carved ivory or wooden turtle is used in a presentation during which two elders engage in a mock fight. (Smithsonian Collection, no. 378.700, is a double-headed wooden turtle.) The action stresses the idea that elders should not fight and points out the serious consequences of quarreling. If a Little-One makes trouble with a Big-One he is sure to be defeated: "Nkulongo [Bird] and Nkulu are in trouble [with each other], they go with [i.e., are involved in] argumentation."

Nkola (Giant Snail)

Shells of giant aquatic and terrestrial snails are often seen in the rites: squatting dancers remove the shells from underneath their loincloths as if they were laying eggs ("In the village of mwami, the Parrot-Folk lay their eggs on the ground," a metaphor for wealth); female dancers emerge from the initiation house blowing into the shells ("Women of bulonda, what are you scorning Shell for?" refers to a junior wife who despises the senior wife); preceptors move a shell from the candidate's leg to his neck to signify that only a person who possesses many valuables can rise in the bwami hierarchy. One type of shell (*kikoku*) is part of the insignia of high initiates. In yananio's highly secret *kasisi* rite, during which unusual things such as quartz stones are displayed, the shell is carved from *ntutu:* "The circles [rings] of Nkola turn around his anus" warns the candidate not to oppose or contradict those who earlier gave him the initiation. A snail shell carved of ivory (pl. 64) was collected among the Bakabango-Babongolo; it may possibly have belonged to a preceptor who used it in the *byanda* ceremony of kindi. In this secret rite the kindi placed the shell between a circle of wickerwork rattles and put special emphasis on its spirals. The term *lubingo* (designating the spirals) resembles the verb *kubinga* (to circumvent someone imprudently); the spirals, equated with wrinkles, also suggest old age. The kindi then view themselves as Binankola, the *nkola* breed: "When it dies out then the youth destroy one another."

Birds

Many birds are mentioned in the texts without being embodied in objects. Others are symbolized in various ways: the hornbill (*mutu*), for example, by its beak; the parrot (*nkusu*), by its red tail feathers.

Kantamba (Glider, Sparrow-Hawk) is concretized by hand movements or by three simple pieces of light wood (kept with other objects in the collectively held baskets), accompanied by the following texts:

"Let me glide as Kantamba glides! [This outcry] has killed Kinkuba [bird] losing his trail in the forest." Kinkuba wanted to imitate Kantamba but failed to do so. One who tries to measure up to wealthy initiates and thinks that he can do as much as they do will fail.

"Kantamba, Forgetful-One, the Master-of-the-Sky, dies [is killed] with a pipestem [made of the long perforated midrib of a banana leaf]." One who quarrels with his wife and chases her into her house is severely beaten by her with a stick.

"Kantamba glides on earth [low], glides in the sky [high]." An initiate has a wealth of knowledge; he is informed about matters that concern him, both directly and indirectly.

Kantamba is frequently represented in other ways. Dancing with a long slit piece of vine called *kasala* (used to perforate the banana leaf midrib from which a pipestem is made), two preceptors bend it like an arch above their heads. An aide points to it with a stick.

"Kantamba dies because of a pipestem; a liar is known, is talked about [pin-pointed]." A liar in general is indicated, but the text relates particularly to a person who claims to be an initiate in another group; the initiates quickly realize that he speaks nonsense.

"Kantamba Mulumbu [Stupid, Forgetful], Master-of-the-Sky, is beaten by rain." The expression "to be beaten by rain" is applied frequently to a serious or dangerous situation. It refers to a high initiate's son who fails in his attempts to be initiated.

"The things Kantamba has done make Kinkuba [bird] return on the road." The continual lying of a member of one's group may cause trouble for the seniors.

Kantamba is also suggested by moving a mat horizontally up and down in the air: "Kantamba has pursued and pursued Sky; he will not meet him." The same action is used with a small door made of wooden laths and decorated with black dots: "The Great Initiate [is] Kantamba gliding near the earth, gliding in the sky."

The *kakulikuli* (or *kwangwakwa*) bird is illustrated by its beak (with wicker-work around the skull), by a spiral-shaped piece of vine, by a rudimentary wooden neck and beak sculpture often resembling a gaff, or by imported ivory bird sculptures. The beak or wooden sculpture is part of the lutumbo lwa yana-nio basket; in some areas such beaks are individually owned by a yananio as a *kalimbangoma* (see Part 1). The beaks or the sculptures are danced with and explained in the following aphorisms.

"Kakulikuli, the little bird loves to talk much," or "Kakulikuli, the little bird, begs for words." This warning against back-talking criticizes a candidate who likes to make objections when told to perform a task.

"Kwangwakwa [Tattler], I am tired singing for the termitaria; there are no termites in here." A high initiate is tired of admonishing younger people who do not listen.

"Kwangwakwa does not sing for the termitaria; [he does] singing for the termites, only for them"; "Kongwakwa, the little bird that sings for the termites." The bird sings when the termites swarm. Kongwakwa is the master of the land who is lonely in his group and the older kindi who must be present before an initiation can be held.

"What-Lacks-Water has placed the lip [the beak] near the puddle [of water stagnating in a fallen tree]." A powerful initiate speaks about his protégé whom he proposes for initiation even though the protégé has few goods. If an initiate is refused by his own group, he goes to his maternal uncles.

The *ngati* bird is represented in *kasisi* by a large head and a zigzag-shaped body made of *ntutu*. It is accompanied by the aphorism: "Kakumba [Secret-Council] provides sick care to Mwangu; [this] is the manner by which the Big-Ones die."

Kilinga (Pigeon) is sometimes portrayed by a rudimentary carving in *ntutu* or a more realistic one in ivory or wood depicting an erect bird with a big belly (with or without legs and tail; pl. 62): "Kilinga inflates the chest, in the [village] enclosure comes yours [i.e., your death or your problems]"; "Kilinga, Mr. Infla-tor-of-the-Chest, in the enclosure will come yours." One who constantly en-gages in quarrels and extends them to other households and villages will surely be overcome by them. Kilinga may also be evoked by a dancing preceptor who holds a reed swatter or a stick with feather bunches against his chest, moving it up and down.

In one area an ivory figurine represented Nyandende, a stork "whose tongue surpasses its lips," a person who causes trouble because of excessive talking. In several instances new types of bird sculptures imported from the outside and made of ivory or cow's horn were identified: "Kokonyange [Ox-Pecker] nests in Itilangwa [tree]; each little bird, each one enjoys the sun." The person succeed-ing in the initiations is like Kokonyange enjoying the sun.

Fish

Certain fish (*nkamba, nsamba, nkomo*) are frequently mentioned in initiations, sometimes in conjunction with their exuviae (skulls and jaws). The exuviae are among the contents of the collectively held kongabulumbu bags and yananio and kindi baskets, but they are never replaced by sculptures.

Fish are only rarely represented by ivory or bone carvings, which are owned individually by kindi (pl. 65; Biebuyck, 1979, pl. 3). These fish miniatures (known specimens are about 11 cm long) may represent any of the above three fish. Nkomo (*Hydrocyon goliath*), whose voracity increases its vulnerability to traps, symbolizes an old man who is ridiculed because he is constantly begging for something, or a talkative young man who haphazardly asks for advice and runs into trouble. Nkamba (*Chrysichthys cranchii*) illustrates the exclusivity of bwami ("The Nkamba-Folks do not carry those who are not of their group") and the depth of knowledge of the initiates ("Little-Child of the Master of the Land, in deep waters it is that Nkamba swims"). Nsamba (*Clarias lasera*) depicts the tutor who enjoys fame and prestige when he adequately carries out the responsibilities he has assumed for the candidate ("Nsamba is honored by every fish that is in the river"). Nsamba may be the master of the land; when he is angry, all the little people die of fear: "Nsamba rages in the pools in which died a big thing." Nsamba is also the deceased high initiate whose works survive: "I know Nsamba because of his barbels, and lo! Nsamba is dead."

Conclusion

The uses and functions of animal figurines in the bwami association, mostly linked with high-level initiations of yananio and kindi, are similar to those of anthropomorphic figurines. Some animal figurines are owned individually and obligatorily by all male members of a certain status; others belong to high-ranking preceptors for use in performance of their specialties; still others are placed under collective control in the initiation baskets. Crudely carved figurines in the last category are distributed in nearly all communities. The small, individually owned, and usually more refined animal sculptures, however, are highly developed in some groups but occur only sporadically in others.

Animal figurines do not represent theriomorphic spirits or divinities. They are not totemic ancestors and are not used in hunting magic or divination. They are not restricted to ritually significant animals. Although there are regional differences, animals that require special rites and distributions organized by bwami include the pangolin, the aardvark, the bongo antelope, the genet, the leopard, the python (*kitemutemu*), the *mpoma* (*Bitis lachesis*), *kibukusa*, and *kamitende* snakes, the *izezekumbe* turtle (*Kinyxis bellicosa*), the eagle, the *nkamba* fish, the *Potamogale velox*, the dendrohyrax, and the *Felis aurata*. Among them only the pangolin is frequently symbolized in sculptures. There are rare sculptured renditions of the aardvark, but images of turtles and snakes are not explicitly identified with the species noted above.

The animals selected for iconic representation have striking physical or behavioral attributes. Some, like the pangolin, are also considered to be culture heroes; others, such as the frog, play a role in etiological tales (Frog argued with Lizard about man's destiny; Frog was going to ask the Creator to make men immortal, but when he arrived Lizard, who wanted men to be mortal, had already won the Creator to his cause). Anthropomorphized animals provide initiates with many additional characters that are known exclusively by their animal names.

PART FOUR

Masks

Introduction

Masks are most highly developed in central and southern Legaland. They fall into five semantic groups, determined to some extent by size, material, and formal features, which overlap functional categories. The following types of masks are discussed in detail in this chapter:

1. *Lukwakongo,* associated with lutumbo lwa yananio, are small masks made of wood which have fiber beards and whitened faces. In areas where masks are less highly developed, unusual small wooden ones called *kungu, koungu, kilume,* or *kikungula,* sometimes reddened, may be used. I saw some of these masks among the northern Lega. In one rite a group of kanyamwa women emerged from the forest and encircled a woman who wore an ovoid wooden mask on her face which was whitened around the eyes. It was so narrow that the woman could see on both sides of it. The mask had a long, wedged, wooden beard extension that reached from the top of the woman's forehead to below her chin. I have seen no masks of this kind in collections; the mask reproduced in Goldwater (1968, p. 37) is a larger variation, but it lacks the chin extension.

2. *Lukungu,* small ivory or bone masks, are linked with lutumbo lwa kindi. They may be molded in copal or carved from highly polished wood. Fiber beards are sometimes attached to them.

3. *Kayamba,* large, whitened masks with fiber beards and horns, are worn in front of the face by dancers wrapped in white bark cloth. Linked with the yananio and kindi rites, they belong to preceptors or are part of collectively held baskets.

4. *Idimu* are large face masks made of wood (adorned with fiber beards) or ivory. The wooden ones, associated with yananio and kindi, are kept with other initiation objects in collectively owned baskets. These wooden *idimu,* usually whitened, are sometimes worn on the face or at the back of the head; they are also affixed to fences in the middle of a display of maskettes or are placed on symbolic graves. In unique rites they are part of the attire of women of high initiatory status. The rare ivory *idimu,* associated with kindi, are held by the most senior initiates for a group of interacting ritual communities. These large ivory masks are not worn but are displayed with others on a fence.

5. *Muminia* form a subcategory of *idimu* masks. I have found only wooden *muminia* belonging to specific lineages and transferable in a close agnatic line. *Muminia* masks are worn on the face or on the skull or are attached to fences. Of all the Lega masks, they are the most flexible in usage, occurring even in the lower rites.

All Lega masks are primarily symbols of status; as such they are part of the hidden insignia belonging to individuals or groups. Only men of lutumbo lwa yananio and lutumbo lwa kindi may individually own the wooden and ivory (bone, copal) maskettes (*lukwakongo, lukungu*), together with other sculptures, as emblems of rank. The designation of status is so important that a person who moves from yananio up to kindi replaces his wooden mask with an ivory one. Initiates at the two highest levels of the two supreme grades, having had considerable experience, are considered to be the wisest and morally most outstanding persons. They are the pillars on which the bwami structure rests.

The maskettes are compared with hammers left by dead ancestors and predecessors. Hammers symbolize the creative energy of high initiates, living and dead, through whose precepts bwami maintains its purpose and integrity. When hammers resound in the smithing place, everyone knows where it is and what is happening there; everyone understands the sacredness of that place. The maskettes likewise remind their owners of the "words," or the principles established by their predecessors; they permanently alert initiates to their duties.

Maskettes represent, not particular individuals, but generalized human faces, such as that of a father, a giver of life and a person in authority. When used in dance contexts they serve as reminders of the great virtues the fathers strove for and of the vices they rejected. The virtues must be cultivated generation after generation to maintain bwami and preserve the social order. The cold, stern, immovable, passionless faces of the masks signify the ever-present ancestral sanctions of the virtues.

The skulls of high-level initiates traditionally were preserved by their descendants in village shrines. The maskettes, constantly referred to as skulls or "gills," are symbolic replicas and extensions of the skulls. The skulls remain in their shrines, but the masks can be taken to the initiations. When initiates display their maskettes in prescribed rites, they view them as embodiments of their forebears—that is, as living ancestors. Man and mask form an entity that reflects permanence and continuity; ancestor and living elder are as one, since living and dead elders maintain identical goals and values. Showing disrespect for initiates is just the same as displeasing ancestors.

Maskettes present a rich iconic field for semantic elaboration. Their formal details become the focus for positive and negative formulations about values. The mask has a large forehead (*malanga*) but no hair (*luzwili*); it has eyes (*meiso*) and eyebrows (*nkige*) but no pupils (*kamoni*), irises (*mutimbu*), or lashes (*mikeido*); it has a long straight narrow-ridged nose and a mouth (*kanua*) with marked front teeth (*mantalabusio*); it has cheeks (*itama*) and a beard (*lunzelu*); it is shiny (the polished surface of the ivory masks; the white on the wooden ones). These features are identified and interpreted during ritual action, which serves to enhance the formal details (e.g., moving or shaking the beards, placing a leaf in the eye of the mask or a stick in its mouth) and also provides additional meanings. For example, maskettes may be displayed, held in the hand or against the chin, worn against the forehead or the cheek, worn on the front or the back of the head, swung around in the air or pulled over the ground, placed upside down or viewed a tergo, piled in heaps, or hung in a certain order from a pole or a fence.

When the larger masks (*kayamba, idimu, muminia*) are manipulated in dance contexts, interpretation focuses on details of form and action. All these masks are held in trust by specific individuals on behalf of a collectivity of initiates. Some of them are kept in baskets that are transferred from a recent initiate to the newest one, according to the cycle of initiations within autonomous groups. Others are owned by senior initiates who represent lineages that first received certain rites from elsewhere and then introduced them into the local community. These larger masks, which are inherited by men who belong to close-knit agnatic descent lines, signify the sense of unity and solidarity in groups of initiates. In addition, rare masks exclusively held by lineages bring immense prestige to their owners. They validate the seniority claims of specific persons and lineages.

Lega masks in general, and maskettes in particular, are unique; they differ from masks made by some of their neighbors and are similar to those of other groups. Nyanga dignitaries wear large hide masks, adorned with hornbill beaks and feathers, as hoods in circumcision rites (Biebuyck, 1973b). The Komo have only one functional category of wooden face masks (*nsembu*) used as a male and female pair in the initiations of diviners (*abankunda*). In my opinion, some large wooden Lega masks, mainly the *muminia*, represent a very ancient tradition and have their closest morphological equivalents among the Komo. Among the Bembe, large monoxyle polychrome masks are used by the *alunga* association; polychrome plank board masks, in circumcision rites and by the *bugabo* association; beaded cloth or hide masks, by the *elanda* association; and rare wooden masks with horns, in the higher rites of bwami (Biebuyck, 1972a). The latter are the closest parallel to the Lega *kayamba* masks. The Lega and the Bembe share a common tradition, as the Bembe who make the horned masks are related to the eastern Lega, and they reserve these masks for the bwami initiations, which were derived from Lega rites. The Hemba (particularly the Mambwe), to the south of the Lega, carve wooden "masques singe" with curiously protruding wide-open mouths for use as house protectors and providers of fertility (Cornet, 1975, pls. 92–93; Neyt and de Strycker, 1975, pls. 59–61). These small masks (examples noted measure 16.5 cm and 19.3 cm) are not utilized as face masks, and from certain points of view they have functions that overlap those of the Lega maskettes. Some of them have ovoid outlines, and some faces are heart-shaped with oval slit eyes placed horizontally or slanting in bulging or protuberant eyelids. In formal respects, then, they also have certain morphological characteristics in common with Lega maskettes.

Lukwakongo Masks

Forms

The Lega classify wooden maskettes under the general term *lukwakongo,* even though their functions differ. These masks vary widely in artistic quality, degree of finish, and representation of features, yet they show common morphological characteristics (pls. 66–68).

The typical mask is carved from light wood, preferably *muntonko* (also used for stools and figurines). Its beard (*lunzelu*), sometimes long and dense, is made of various materials (fibers of banana tree bark or, more rarely, raffia or the inner bark of other trees), which are replaced as needed. The beard is fastened to a number of holes in the chin and the jaws of the mask. Initiates sometimes dance with only the beards, holding them against their chins or using them as collarets. Through holes near the edge of the mask, at eye level and above, a string may be attached so that the mask can be carried or fastened to some object. The string may be replaced by a horizontal or vertical wooden handle carved with the mask from a single piece of wood. The entire facial concave area is whitened, but collected specimens show only traces of kaolin. Renewed application of the white clay is part of the rites. The white color is sometimes restricted to the area around the eyes, nose, and mouth of the mask. The forehead and the contours are usually polished dark or light brown, but the entire front part of some masks is whitened or shows traces of kaolin. The back of the mask, usually concave and unpolished, shows adz marks, but occasionally it is almost flat. The height of the average *lukwakongo* maskette is less than the length of a Lega hand; examples I collected range from 13.8 to 18.9 cm. Genuine *lukwakongo* masks illustrated in museum catalogs and in African art books measure about 10 to 23 cm, but most of them fall between 13 and 19 cm (e.g., Altman, 1963, pls. 3, 7; Bassani, 1977, pls. 51–57, 60–63, 471–476; Biebuyck, 1973a, pls. 34–36, 43, 60–62; Cornet, 1972, pls. 256, 260, 263, 265–266, 269; 1978a, pls. 333, 339; Fagg, 1970, p. 151; Krieger and Kutscher, 1967, pl. 76; Leuzinger, 1972, pl. X-2; Museum of Primitive Art, 1966a, pl. 32; 1967, p. 8; Parke-Bernet Galleries, 1967, pl. 108; Plass, n.d., pl. 40C–D; Sotheby and Co., 1960, pls. 126, 128, 129; Sweeney, 1935, no. 462; Van Geluwe, 1967, pl. 44).

Overall, most masks are ovoid, but some are wider than others at eye level and at the temples. (Examples I collected have the following measurements: 13.8 cm × 8.4 cm, 14.7 cm × 9.5 cm, 15.5 cm × 8.9 cm, 17.3 cm × 10.9 cm, 17.5 cm × 9.2 cm, 17.8 cm × 12.0 cm, 17.9 cm × 10.2 cm, 18.6 cm × 12.4 cm, 18.9 cm × 10.1 cm.) Some masks thus look elongated while others are rounded. The contours of the forehead and the chin are often rounded, but some masks have straight contours and look almost rectangular.

The face is usually divided into two or three distinct areas: the high bulging forehead (bare, with no indication of hair or headdress, though in rare instances a skullcap is suggested) is set off from the face by a sharp ridge that joins the eyebrows at the base of the nose and runs to the corners of the mouth, forming a heart-shaped, concave plane; the chin and the rim of the mask then form convex planes. In other instances, however, from the eyebrows down, the ridge forms a concave plane that coincides with the outer edge of the mask. There are also examples of faces with rather flat or convex forms.

The pierced eyes are carved as ovoid slits or circles in either light or high relief, with eyelids indicated. Eyes that are not perforated are marked by an oblong groove that may be filled with white clay. Eyes, set in a horizontal or slanting position, are sometimes unevenly placed. The fine, long nose flares toward the top in a reversed triangle or lozenge; sometimes the nosewings are realistically carved. Some of the elongated masks have considerable space between the nose and the upper lip; in other types the tip of the nose almost touches the upper lip. The mouth is formed by a small or large rectangle or by an ovoid, spherical, or crescentic opening; sometimes it is slightly protuberant. The mouth is usually open and front teeth are frequently indicated by indentations on both upper and lower lips. There is no attempt at a realistic presentation of the lips. The mouth may be so low in the face that the chin is almost nonexistent. On most masks the only surface decoration is the white kaolin applied to the face. Sometimes several white parallel lines run across the forehead and a vertical line reaches the base of the nose. Ornamental designs include small holes arranged in lozenge shape on the forehead, or linear parallel striations on the edge of the mask, the eyelids, and the forehead. Triangular striations on the foreheads of some masks resemble Lega facial tattoo patterns.

In morphological details, *lukwakongo* are similar to the other ivory, bone, and wooden masks of the Lega. As a group they have much more unity than the ivory, bone, and wooden anthropomorphic figurines. *Lukwakongo* masks are "the semblance of a man"; they are conventionalized and stylized renditions of Lega faces and Lega concepts, but they are not individual portraits. In action contexts these masks represent innumerable characters and are sometimes referred to as "skull of my father" (i.e., an object that belonged to a person in the position of father, predecessor, or progenitor), but they are never considered to be the likeness of a particular person or the materialized representation of a spirit.

Terminology

The generic denomination for these wooden masks is *lukwakongo* (rarely *lukongo*), although the term also designates the polished mussel shell (*lubumba*). A *lubumba* shell fastened to a hat near its rim is one of the insignia of yananio initiates. The folk etymology recorded in various Lega communities gives slightly different interpretations of *lukwakongo*. The term *lukwo* means death, and *-kongo* is derived either from *ikongo*, a herd of animals or a group of humans, or from the verb *konga*, to track (as a dog or a hunter does). Some Lega see a connection with *kongola*, to pluck or to harvest (e.g., mushrooms). The etymologies emphasize linkages between the mask and death and, by extension, the dead. The inference is that death tracks down everybody, gathers all, and breaks up everyone. Death, however, also brings people together, causing them to follow one another in the right way.

In song and action contexts (see below), masks displayed in groups are referred to as "skulls of those who died" (*bakule*), "hammers that were left by the ancestors [*basumbu* or *balimu*] and by those who were," or as "graves" (*malumba*). A single mask may be spoken of as the "skull of my father" (as ivory masks may be), but masks are not called "the dead" or "the ancestors" as such. Although later discussions will help to clarify these denominations, it may be said here that masks, like skulls, are among the permanent remainders of a dead person, and they stay for some time on his grave. The dead do not return, but they are always remembered by the lasting signs they left behind. Masks passed on to successive generations of initiates are a sign of creativity, survival, and continuity. The small hammer (*nondo*) is a precious tool owned not only by blacksmiths but also by the heads of autonomous lineages to enable them to perform minor tasks (e.g., smoothing the dents in a blade). Like the adz (*nkondo*), the hammer is a "creator"; it makes things that last. Direct identifications are made with the phallus, the life-making organ: as *muntonko* wood rots but is transformed into a durable object when shaped into a mask or stool, so a mortal man lives on in his children. The mask is a reminder of the universality of death as well as of the triumph over death.

Lukwakongo masks, unlike ivory and wooden figurines, do not have specific names. They are never called the "hammer left by so and so" or the skull of A or B. A mask comes closest to individualization when it is called "skull of my father," but even this is a generalization because a Lega knows perfectly well that the mask he acquires did not necessarily belong to his father; "father" here means progenitor, creative force, a person in a position of authority vis-à-vis the speaker. Numerous stereotyped characters identified as individuals or as groups are, however, suggested by the masks in dance and song contexts.

Ownership and Acquisition

Lukwakongo masks are the privileged possessions and one of the essential insignia of lutumbo lwa yananio initiates. Every male member of that grade normally owns one *lukwakongo,* but at a given time all lutumbo lwa yananio do not actually possess masks. In one large community, forty lutumbo lwa yananio participated in the rites, but only twenty-four of them had masks. Among those who did not have masks were four recent initiates still in possession of the collectively held baskets; their masks were kept in trust by tutors until it was time to surrender the baskets to new initiates. The four keepers of the *kasisi* baskets also had no masks. One person whose initiated wife had died had temporarily given his mask in trust to an initiated relative. Normally each of the remaining seven would have had a mask, but under colonial pressures they had, as the Lega put it, "thrown it away" (i.e., sold it to a white man, lost it in a raid, or simply discarded it for fear of sanctions). In some communities all incumbents of lutumbo lwa yananio belonging to a single minimal lineage shared one mask, which was entrusted to the most junior initiate.

Like other insignia, the mask is acquired through the yananio initiations. It generally passes from initiate to initiate within a fairly restricted agnatic group, either when its user advances to the lower levels of kindi and a kinsman moves up to lutumbo lwa yananio, or when a person of yananio grade dies and a kinsman is initiated as his replacement. Masks thus have often been transmitted from person to person over a number of generations. The patterns of transfer within major agnatic lineages may be illustrated by examples. In one instance, A received a mask when he replaced a senior brother B who had died; B had acquired it when his senior brother C had moved up to kindi; C had got it from his senior brother D; D, from his senior brother E; E, from his little father F; F, from his senior brother G; G, from his own father H; H, from his father I; I, from his father J. In another example, A got his mask from his senior brother B when he moved up to kindi; B, from his father C when he moved up to kindi; C, from his father D when he died; D, from his father E when he moved up to kindi; E, from his father F when he died.

Most patterns of transfer are similar: from real or classificatory senior brother to junior brother, from real or classificatory father to son. Rarely the present owner has acquired a mask from a classificatory junior brother or a classificatory grandfather (i.e., senior brother of his father). In some instances a man who had originally acquired his mask from another agnatically related lineage or from a group of maternal uncles had subsequently passed it on in his own lineage according to one of the above-mentioned patterns. It is noteworthy that a man does not know which mask will be his until he reaches the particular lutumbo lwa yananio rite in which masks are transferred. In fact, he may never have seen any of the masks before, and hence the frequently repeated song: "Reveal to me the things father has left."

Manner of Keeping and Functions

The individual *lukwakongo* mask is kept with other insignia in a shoulder bag (*nsago*) made of antelope or goat hide or plaited in raffia or vines. Guardianship of the bag is entrusted to a man's senior initiated wife of bulonda grade (called kalonda or kalia), who keeps it in her house. She carries the shoulder bag on her back (hanging from a headband) when she and her husband go to the initiations, for an initiate must bring the tokens of his rank to the rites he attends. When an initiate dies, the mask, with other insignia, is temporarily displayed on his tomb (in the house of his kalia wife) in care of the guardian of the tomb. At the end of the funerary ceremonies (some weeks after a person's death), the guardian takes the mask and insignia home to transfer them to the new candidate's principal initiator or tutor.

The mask is part of the essential set of secret insignia owned by a lutumbo lwa yananio, who has also acquired other visible paraphernalia, such as the reed swatter and the distinctive hats and belts. The insignia function as a badge or an identification card and must be displayed during the closed rites of yananio. In the dramatic context of the initiations the masks also serve as iconic devices that help to illustrate and reaffirm the value code of the association. In dances, songs, and actions they are used to depict characters and situations. In addition, as linkages with past initiates, the masks function as symbols of continuity, as a way of maintaining the presence of deceased initiates and of allowing the living to identify with them.

Uses and Meanings in Lutumbo lwa Yananio Initiations

Lukwakongo masks are used in several rites of lutumbo lwa yananio, singly or as a group (i.e., each yananio exhibits his personal mask). In some ritual communities they may be used, singly or in a group of two or three, in a lower-level initiation, but they are always manipulated by initiates of higher rank. In yananio, *lukwakongo* appear in rites that utilize only masks, or they may be part of configurations that include other sculptures, natural items, and assemblages. The masks are owned and handled by men, but in some communities the senior initiated wives of the yananio may manipulate their husbands' masks in the presence of the men. The men with the masks wear only their regular dance paraphernalia (hats, necklaces, belts, loincloths, bunches of feathers, hides). When women use the masks, they are completely dressed in sheets of white bark cloth, which hang from the head to the legs.

In a series of performances the masks are handled in a variety of ways. A mask is attached frontally to the side of the hat in such a way that its beard, rather than the mask itself, covers the face. It is held under the chin vertically or horizontally and moved so that the beard dangles left and right; it is carried in the hand or held by the beard with the mask hanging downward. Masks are placed on the ground in a circular pile with the beards touching, or on top of a pit filled with leaves and other objects. The masks displayed on the ground are pointed at or protected by the hands, or they are kicked. In some rites one or more are pulled away with the hands or with the toes; they are then hidden behind someone's back. Or a dancer with a mask in each hand swings and crosses his arms so that the beards float around or are thrown across his shoulders. Sometimes masks hanging from heads are turned so that the backs of the masks become visible; a leaf is placed in the eye of one mask; one mask is tied high on a pole; or two masks are held back to back, Janus-like.

Most of these manipulations occur in dance contexts, but sometimes the initiates simply sit on stools, run around, or move in crouching, bending, and jumping positions. When a performance focuses on a single mask or on a group of two, the action is undertaken by a preceptor and his aides.

The sung proverbs, which are part of the exegesis, center alternately on such aspects as the mask as a legacy, a permanent object, and a symbol of continuity, and its general role and purpose; the beard as a symbol of the elders; morphological features of the mask (the skull without hair or hat; the eyes that do not see; the absence of eyelashes; the well-formed nose; the silent mouth; the front teeth engraved on some masks; the cheeks); the particular action with or around the mask (e.g., hanging it high on a pole; holding it by the beard, the skull down; turning it so that the back is visible; displaying masks in a group; furtively taking away a mask; placing a leaf in the mask's eye). The elements of form and action are frequently intermingled.

It is difficult to explain the meanings of these manipulations because piecemeal interpretations are given by preceptors in different contexts. To a large extent, every preceptor representing a ritual community has his own way of doing things. As noted repeatedly in initiations, each community has its own style of acting, partly inspired by common practices and by the models set by other groups with close historical or social ties. As a thinker the preceptor wants to excel and to be original. He adds to and subtracts from the common corpus of explanations; he emphasizes certain aspects more than others; he is inspired by methods he has observed elsewhere; he invents or on a particular occasion forgets some points, which he may later add or eliminate. He may take some meanings for granted because the initiations form a continuum. By the time the candidate reaches the lutumbo lwa yananio rites in which masks are used, he has gone through many other initiations where similar or complementary ideas have already been communicated. When masks are only a part of a larger configuration of objects and action contexts, part of their interpretation lies in the total rite. In the communities I studied, however, some fundamental types of information were always repeated, perhaps in slightly modified form. In accordance with general Lega practice, some aphoristic statements about masks apply in other contexts to different natural or manufactured objects.

The comparison of events and sequences in one community with those observed elsewhere points to the meanings conveyed by masks in action contexts. In ritual community A, for example, the first day of the rites was marked by the spectacular ceremonial entry into the candidate's village of all participating yananio, kindi, and their initiated wives. The initiates, dressed in their usual paraphernalia, were carrying reed swatters (or wickerwork rattles if they were kindi); shoulder bags and baskets contained the collectively held initiation objects. After the entrance ceremony, the initiates danced with and sang about the shoulder bags and the baskets without revealing their contents.

The masks appeared about five o'clock the next morning. A row of kalonda women emerged from behind the houses. Each woman, cloaked in white bark cloth (hung over the head like a hood but leaving the face visible), wore a small mask affixed to her cap high against the forehead, the beard falling to the lower part of the face. Moving silently and slowly, in bent or crouching position, the women reached the dance ground and sat down on stools in a line, facing a feather rope tied between two poles. Only the most senior initiated wife of each yananio present wore her husband's mask. The women were alternately identified as the Big-Ones-Who-Are-in-(the village called) Harmony, Big-Ones-Who-Are-Nice, and Big-Ones-Who-Are-Well-Prepared (for the ceremonies). They were also referred to as the "row of Nyakamuno," which in this context meant women called together for serious business. In other contexts

"Nyakamuno" is synonymous with witch or thief: "I leave my shoulder bag in the house of a witch, in the house of Nyakamuno [whose] heart is black." Still seated, the women slowly nodded their heads so that the beards dangled in front of the lower part of their faces; sometimes they held the beards in their hand as if to show them.

The initial aphorisms were presented as an imaginary dialogue between candidate and initiates. At first the songs focused on the beards. The mask wearers were called Big-Ones and Children-of-the-Beards (i.e., members of an imaginary group called the Bearded-Ones).

> Candidate: "Big-Ones do not show me [to tease me] the beards; my father died with one [a beard]," as if the initiates by their attitude had been telling him that this beard (i.e., the status represented by a mask) was not for him. The candidate maintains that his claim is fully justified because his "father" was a yananio.

> Candidate: "I hate the greatness of the Bearded-Ones, greatness that is even [i.e., of the same size]," criticizing the lack of leadership which prevails in a group and leads to controversy.

> Initiates: "When you eat with a Big-One, the toothpick is always between the teeth," warning the candidate to remain silent and reserved when confronted by the elders.

The imaginary dialogue then concentrated on the distributions of food and valuables, as if the initiates were saying: "All right, you have a legal and moral claim on this mask, but have you amassed the necessary valuables?"

> Initiates: "Gourmand knows to eat! The food morsels drip from the cheeks." This text has a double meaning: to the candidate it says that initiates require lavish distributions; the initiates are criticizing Kiliabundu (Gourmand), one who is too eager and too impatient to get his share of food and valuables.

> Candidate: "Mr. Call has mumbled against me: he is not [one of] ours this one," an expression of discontent by some initiates because of inadequate distributions of goods and also a criticism of initiates who cause obstruction.

> Initiates: "Kibunge [who has no goods] weeps and weeps for bwami, [but] on his skull there is not a single hair." A tuft of hair is left on the shaved skull of an initiate so that the skullcap, the supreme symbol of membership in the association, can be attached to it. This text cautions initiates to be wary of persons who do not have the requisite material goods.

> Initiates: "Bisindi [small animals] of in here [i.e., of this village] do not laugh [for it would be the equivalent of] laughing at the skulls of those who have died." Candidates must remain impassive during the initiations; laughing would require payment of fines and might lead to grave consequences.

> Initiates: "Everyone who has the signs of beauty on the forehead is still in the place where he used to be," a further elaboration of the preceding concept. An initiate was young and beautiful; that he is old and decrepit now is no reason to make fun of him. As he still has the status he acquired when he was more vigorous, his words must not be rejected.

Candidate: "Show me the eyes [i.e., the face], it is not on the back that I have died of bad luck." The candidate is firm in his quest; he is ready to face reality and will not turn his back on it; he wants to know how his predecessors accomplished the rites. There is an allusion to warfare: one faces the danger and does not back away from it.

Initiates: "Mr. Well-Formed-Nose is [full] with seductions surpassing his companion." The initiates are pleased with the candidate's persistent efforts to achieve yananio status.

Candidate: "Big-One rocks me asleep [in the arms], he does not see," a show of respect for the elders. Even if they are old or blind, the candidate wishes to have their advice.

After the imaginary dialogue, while the masked women were still sitting behind the feather rope, the initiates delved deeper into the moral philosophy suggested by the masks:

"Eyes of the One-Who-Does-Not-See, the fruits of Nkumbi do not see." Non-initiates are like the children of Nkumbi (a nut with a slit that is interpreted as a blind eye) because they have not learned how to see. Many of the things said and done during the initiations proceed from common knowledge, but they acquire their full range of meanings only for the initiate.

"I arrive at the place where Mugila died, every leaf is anointed with white clay." This very difficult text is also translated as "I arrive at the place where Mugila [Diviner] failed, and Lusamba [Leaf] anoints Mpemba [White-Clay]." Literally it refers to the secret burial of a high initiate. Before being placed in a grave dug in his senior wife's house, the dead man is carried by his colleagues to the center of the village and then back to the house in his last farewell to the village (*Kimini ekulaga mulungu*). During the rite, punctuated by special drumbeats (also heard when initiates make their ceremonial entry into the candidate's village), the initiates march on reddish phrynium leaves and other leaves sprinkled with white powder. As explained elsewhere in this volume, the initiates criticize and reject the *bugila* divination because it leads to false accusations, turmoil, poison ordeals, more deaths, and further strife in the group. The initiates have their own methods for detecting the person who is magically guilty of the death of his or her kin. When this person is found, the initiates look for reconciliation through blessings and formal proclamations (Lusamba anointing Mpemba). Such ceremonies take place near the dead initiate's grave, where his masks and other insignia are displayed.

"I thought that my father was asleep and lo! he is looking at me with one eye." The mask with its eyes almost closed recalls the old man who lies in a long chair and always seems to be asleep but who in fact is the guardian of village morality. In other contexts, this aphorism is often sung without the masks being present; the initiates then simply cover their eyes with their hands.

"[The leaf] that covers Bush-Baby [Moko] is the leaf that causes his death." The immediate reference is to the bush baby which builds a nest in a tree hole and betrays its presence to the hunter by letting some leaves stick out of the hole. The text indirectly concerns a person called Moko, who is wronged by those very individuals (a wife, a child) who were his support. In this and the following aphorism the preceptor who provides the songs and leads the dances is obviously elaborating on the term "leaf," mentioned in a previous aphorism, and on death, which in Lega thinking is often caused by a man's wives.

"Bush-Baby [son] of Kibezi [drum name of Bush-Baby] carries skulls, he leaves one." The skulls are the masks. Bush-Baby (an initiate) evokes the tutor who brings the masks to the ceremonies. He will leave one with the person now being initiated.

"[The mouth] that Stupid-One [Munyungu] has grown! He grew a mouth that is not for speaking." Munyungu looks on stupidly when others talk to him and thinks only about food. He is an inept speaker; he does not know how to use the correct words in the appropriate setting. Although his father was an initiate, Munyungu gets nowhere while other more capable kin achieve yananio status.

At this point the women reversed their masks so that the backs faced frontward.

"The wife of a Big-One [is] a fallen banana tree which is of no use on two sides." Acting in accordance with the laws of bwami is the only path an initiated wife should follow.

"Nkingi [Bark-Beater, often synonymous with Phallus, has] a nice sleeping place; inside the bed there is dirt." The initiate has a beautiful wife but her "heart" (mind, intentions, behavior) is evil. The aphorism further expands the idea that the initiate's wife must abide by the laws of bwami.

"Big Mutuka [drum name for Chimpanzee] rots [at] the anus [but] does not rot [at] the eyebrow." The chimpanzee is killed, but his skull is preserved in a basket as an initiation object; a man dies, but his achievements remain, and his son continues his position.

"Mutuka builds for Yende [Anus], [his own] shoulders are beaten by rain." An initiate who promotes others and fails to take care of his own people is criticized.

"He who falls from the hills [i.e., falls down from something high] recovers; he who falls from the sky does not recover." If a woman casts the evil eye on someone, that person will die because women are experienced in witchcraft. The preceptor has again returned to earlier statements about women who do not follow the laws of bwami.

The seated women now removed the masks and held them by their beards so that they hung upside down.

"Mulima [Bat] hangs upside down because of the word that Sun has told him." In other situations this text is sung in conjunction with a figurine that dangles from the ceiling of the initiation house with its head down, or the preceptor himself who hangs from a vine. The text synthesizes an etiological tale, but here it applies to the anger of an initiate who has been badly treated by someone.

"[Feathers of] bat [*mulima*] are not fixed on a feather hat [*isala*], the little animal with sharp, biting teeth." The text in its personified version reads: "For Mulima [Bat] a feather hat [*isala*, i.e., the bwami initiations in which the feather hat is an initiation object] is not assembled [because] he is Little-Animal-with-Sharp-Teeth." This text pertains to earlier expressed ideas that candidates who are verbally aggressive will fail in their efforts.

"The wife of a Big-One shines [has a beautiful body], she is not for calling." The candidate or any other person is warned against attempting to seduce an initiated wife.

The women then placed the masks on the ground in front of their feet, with the beards in front: "Let us sit on the ground, Nsagia [Fallen-Leaf] surpasses Katanda [Mat]." It is as if one initiate were saying to another, "Let us sit on the ground because the dry leaves placed under the sleeping mat for more comfort have fallen out." In reality, the text refers to a quarrel between two persons; Nsagia, who is wiser, tells Katanga not to pursue the fight.

After these aphorisms were sung, the feather rope was rolled up and removed; the sacred fence that separated the candidate from the knowledge of the masks had fallen down. The women took off their white bark cloaks. Then came another reminder that initiated women must not be seduced and that seduction leads to disorder: "Who removes the clothing is of no good; the body is bad, bad."

The mask sequence finished, the masks were stored. Later in the day, after the initiates had rested, eaten, and discussed events, two long performances centered on the stools (*kisumbi*) and the polished mussel shell (*lubumba*), both privileged possessions of high initiates. Toward evening the masks appeared again in a rite specifically called *lukwakongo*. All yananio initiates, crouching, bending, and moving up and down in a fairly compact group, arrived at the dance ground. Each held his mask lying openly in his outstretched hand. A preceptor's aide danced around the initiates with a short wooden spear and an ajouré wickerwork shield. In several other rites, manipulation of the spear and the shield depicts symbolic warfare. The maskers produced drawn-out "oooh's!" while preceptors and singers sang the aphorism: "The hammers which the ancestors [*basumbu*] left, *lukwakongo*, the hammers which the ancestors [*balimu*] left." The event was intended to encourage the children (the descendants of those who had previously done bwami) to follow in their ancestors' footsteps. The hammer, a useful object owned not only by blacksmiths but also by lineage seniors, symbolizes the "straightening out and the smoothing of the candidate." It is also a cryptic reference to phallus as a symbol for creativity and continuity.

The initiates next sat down on their stools and formed a circle. They placed the masks in front of them on the ground and then piled up some of them in the center of the circle. A preceptor ran around the seated initiates, clapping his hands and asking: "Ah! Where is father's skull?" One by one the masks in the pile were removed, as if the participants were searching for a particular one: "Bring together [assemble] the *malumba* [graves, skulls] that I may know the skull of my father." The candidate expresses impatience to know and to do what his father knew and did. This aphorism, in different variants, is often sung when a particular object destined to be given to the new adept is presented.

Two masks were then placed on the ground; a preceptor danced around them, picked them up, and swirled his arms: "I have arrived at Mutupo [place where elephants or other animals sleep and where plants are uprooted; here a village] of Nzogu [Elephant], every leaf is anointed with white clay." This apho-rism is a variant of a text sung on other occasions: "I have arrived at the place where Elephant slept; every leaf, every one, has a spot of soil." The focus is on the whiteness and the similarity of the masks, which are cryptically referred to as leaves. The resemblance was further stressed when the preceptor, holding the two masks, danced in front of the candidate: "Two Tulimu [insects]: Tumbu-kutu [insects] resemble Ndoku [insects]." The similarity of the masks recalls the oneness of the bwami association; the status of one yananio does not differ from that of another.

The same action continued with the song: "Kitindi that father danced with, I am now dancing with it." Kitindi is a dance in which a marionettelike figure several meters tall, made of bark and fibers, appears in the forest; the term is often used as an equivalent of bwami to emphasize the continuity of the associ-ation. The long bwami initiations are often likened to a tall tree that is difficult to climb; those who suffer from dizziness never reach the top.

The second phase of mask presentations closed when the preceptor held the two masks together back to back like a Janus head, swinging his arms in the air: "Sawabuzumbu [Mr. Raffia Tree; a species of raffia tree] disperses the tops [where some leaves had not yet blossomed]." The candidate has now finished most of the initiation, and he can soon begin thinking about participating in the yananio dances.

The third day began with elaborate dances and exegesis about two large pieces of bark cloth. The baskets with collectively owned initiation objects were then opened and the contents systematically interpreted. The baskets con-tained no masks, but there were two chimpanzee skulls, one forest crocodile skull, a wooden zoomorphic figurine, a small trident, a large snail shell, a pangolin scale, a large mushroomlike growth, a *mbili* nut (used as fishing poi-son), a mussel shell with perforation, and a phallus-shaped wood sculpture. At dusk the long and highly secret *mukumbi* rite took place in the initiation house. Instead of music, the seated initiates imitated the calls of chimpanzees and the trumpeting of elephants. After the candidate and his tutor entered, they were received by a preceptor who led them around a configuration of objects and then seated them near it. The assemblage was fairly simple: a row of reed swat-ters, flanked by several large snail shells, led to a small covered pit. Copper-bladed knives stuck in the ground were surmounted by tufts of porcupine quills; a feather rope was attached to the knives, which were placed in a circle around the pit. The covered pit was later revealed to contain twenty-five differ-ent specimens of leaves, a pangolin and an aardvark claw, a mussel shell, and an animal representation. On top of the pit was the heap of soil removed when the hole was dug; on the heap lay a mask, a carved piece of elephant bone, and a wooden animal figurine. One by one the swatters and snail shells leading to the pit were removed: the swatters depicted the distance between two major rivers (a concept used to designate a number of related lineages that constitute a territorially compact group), and in bwami terms the length of the initiations; the shells stood for the many abandoned village sites located in the area between the rivers. The fence built around the pit represented a group of initiates gathered to protect as well as to settle important affairs. The total configuration, however, symbolized the grave of Mukumbi (Golden Mole), a dead yananio initiate. It realistically reflected the actual practice of temporarily displaying the deceased's insignia on his tomb in the house of his senior initiated wife.

The fence was removed with the often repeated statement: "Every clan lights the hearth in its own manner," stressing that every autonomous clan makes its configurations (called hearth) according to its own customs.

The preceptor and aides then focused on the mask. Sitting around the pit, they moved their trembling hands above the mask: "Who will remain behind here [stay here for a while]? Kagalama [one who has no strength to go to the forest and lies on his back in a long wooden chair] will stay here." The reference is to the custom of selecting a guardian of the tomb who will later assume trusteeship of the insignia left there. Restlessly moving their arms, legs, and heads, they then sang: "In the men's house of Itamba [a village where many come and go] there is a guardian, it is not a place to steal from." The guardian of the tomb protects it from theft and witchcraft.

With the aides still sitting around the pit, the preceptor took the mask with shaking hands, singing: "Everyone who had the signs of beauty engraved on the forehead is still in the place where he used to be." Although his youth vanishes and his flesh decays, a man's achievements remain forever.

Still holding the mask, the preceptor now placed a leaf in one of its eyes: "Meddlesome person with one eye does not miss [let pass] a word of what is being said." The aphorism points to an evildoer who might have caused a death, and it is also a prelude to the subsequent appearance of such a wrongdoer. The mask with the leaf in the eye is placed back on the pit: "Even if one has [only] one eye, his eyelashes will still be plucked out." Initiations eliminate evil because initiates know how to handle wrongdoers.

Picking up the mask (leaf removed), shaking it, and placing it back on the pit, the preceptor sang: "I look down on the face of Zumbi [a tough person] where rain is falling." Zumbi, a big man, is angry because people are backbiting and talking wildly. The mask was then left on the pit.

"I was on the side of the trail and Mubungu [one who overhears conversations with evil intent] makes me known [reveals my words]." The text continues an idea expressed earlier about meddlesome people and again anticipates coming events. At the same time, the backbiter and the gossiper are criticized and warned that their double-talk will be revealed.

"Mantalabusio [lit., front teeth]: travelers who pass, who go." The front teeth represent the yananio and remind those of lower grade that although their kin are now incumbents of the higher grades, they will die and make place for the junior initiates.

"Mr. Cunning hides himself." This is another reference to a wrongdoer who is hiding out in their midst. Mr. Cunning indicates a person who has beaten or injured someone and then tries to hide so he will not be discovered.

"Mr. Jealousy hide yours [i.e., your wife]! Nzogu [Elephant] is wearing the dance aprons [of animal hide]." This digression (the Lega are fond of such fantasy) is inspired by the previous allusion to a person who beat another. It mockingly tells the candidate not to be jealous of his wives because they look eagerly at the well-dressed initiates.

The preceptor now fastened the mask to one side of his hat to represent Zumbi. As he ran around he touched the knees of other seated initiates: "Come and see how Zumbi is dancing with his children." He continued to pull their arms as if announcing joyful news: "Come and see how Zumbi is laughing with his children." This text alludes directly to the custom of men and women dancing in a single row with their children and grandchildren during the initiations, a practice allowed in other circumstances only with grandchildren. Now Zumbi and his children started to push and to hurt one another as if they were engaged in a brawl: "Come and see how Zumbi and his children treat one another badly." Zumbi is old; he plays with his children and instructs them to do this or that, but he himself does not remember clearly how things should be done. By his blunders he causes agitation and creates discord.

The mask was placed back on the pit; initiates held their hands close above the mask, but one of them wanted to remove it: "The grave [the mask] that has no guardian, that grave [mask] will be stolen." The direct reference is to the custom of guarding the tomb. This text, however, is really a complaint about a lineage many of whose members had achieved yananio in the past, but now there is no one left to continue the tradition.

While some initiates were still protecting the mask, one of them tried unsuccessfully to kick it: "We are guarding our tomb, do not sleep." Immediately after this text had been sung, the initiates sitting around the grave fell asleep (holding their hands in front of their faces). The wrongdoer who previously had failed now managed to steal the mask and hide it behind the candidate. When the initiates woke up, there was an uproar. A *mugila* diviner was quickly consulted. He threw the divination bones; he blamed one initiate, then another. There was turmoil; the initiates tossed their hats on the ground and acted wildly. The bones were thrown again; the wife of an initiate was accused of witchcraft, but her husband protested violently and attacked the diviner. One initiate was already symbolically preparing bark scrapings for the poison ordeal. To prove the truth of his oracle, the diviner drank the poison but did not succumb. The woman (represented by a male dancer) was urged to take the poison, but first she ran around anxiously inquiring whether or not she should drink it, and the initiates told her to do so. She took the poison and fell against the candidate, but she was saved by an initiate who placed a piece of carved elephant bone (the yananio-level equivalent of the kindi ivory spoon) in her mouth.

Although these dramatic passages contain no explicit references to the mask, the interpretation of the performance still concerned it. A man was selected by a true agnate or maternal uncle to "restore" (by means of his own initiation) the grade level that his "father" had achieved and, after hesitating, he agreed to do so. In the meantime the insignia left by "father" had passed to another initiate (frequently of another group) who had acted as guardian of the tomb; they would now be returned, provided the appropriate quantity of goods was given to the custodian. Those who would rather retain these insignia were warned that they would not be saved from the poison ordeal.

In the subsequent action, exegesis was provided for the other objects placed in the configuration (the porcupine quills, the animal figurine, the carved piece of elephant bone) and for the twenty-five leaf specimens that were taken from the pit one by one. As soon as the last leaf had been removed, Nkunda (lit., a scout bee; symbol of the preceptor) appeared on the village grounds. Two preceptors, wearing numerous feather tufts around their belts, had several small *lukwakongo* masks attached to their hats. They were followed by one preceptor carrying a basket and others (without masks) waving leaves to chase bees. The party had been on an imaginary search for honey; as they looked for it they had used their wooden axes to open holes in the ground where bees nestle. The honey harvesters, crouching and holding one another's shoulders, with the candidate squatting near them, approached the pit. The first man in the row deposited the products of the harvest (symbolized by pieces of banana bark). There was no direct reference to the masks, but the preceptor was compared with Nkunda (Scout Bee). Without the preceptor no initiation can be held; he arranges the configurations, decides on the songs and their sequences, and is the leading or solo performer. This enactment concluded the display of masks in the lutumbo lwa yananio rites.

Although this lengthy analysis of initiation rites in one community does provide fundamental information about *lukwakongo* masks, it does not fully cover the wide range of their uses, functions, and meanings. Intensive study of yananio initiations in several autonomous communities reveals not only that the sequences described above illustrate several independently recurring features, but also that they deviate from practices that prevail elsewhere. There are significant similarities in the role played by *lukwakongo* masks in yananio ceremonies everywhere. All participating male yananio dance with their individual masks. They arrive in a closed formation (compact group or crescentic row) on the village grounds; some wear the masks on their faces or sideways on their hats, whereas other participants hold them in their open hands. Groups of two crawl toward each other; they crouch, bend their backs, jump up, and slowly move up and down. This action is always accompanied by an aphorism referring to the masks as hammers left (or forged) by ancestors (*bashumbu, balimu*), those who have died (*bakule*), or those who have gone (*beinda*).

Attention is invariably drawn to the beards. The masks are held at the lower lip or under the chin (vertically or horizontally) by the dancing or sitting initiates who move them left and right so that the beards float broadly. The various aphorisms sung in different communities designate the mask-holding initiates as Bakulu (Big-Ones), sometimes as Bakulu ba Kwalanga (Big-Ones of the village Kwalanga; lit., place where it climbs), or as Bakulu ba Kwidomba (Big-Ones of the village Kwidomba; lit., place of the grave). Among the aphorisms are "Big-Ones do not scorn me [do not show to tease me] with the size [lit., bigness] of the beards; father had one also"; "The Big-Ones of Kwalanga [or of Kwidomba] move their beards [make their beards shiver], they are not eating anything." Those who hold the masks are viewed as living extensions of the dead, as guardians of order and upholders of custom.

Preceptors then have an opportunity to elaborate on the beards. The masks are held by the beards, two masks are butted against each other, or pairs of initiates touch the beards of each other's masks to depict the character Kilimba (Billy-Goat): "Kilimba does not grow a beard if it has no breeder"; "Kilimba that is caught by the beard will not shake it anymore"; "Kilimba breaks Lutambi [the vine that ties it to a pole], it goes to die"; "Kilimba that escaped from father, I hold it by this beard"; "Kilimba of my father, Kankutungwa [lit., Goat with bent horns] butts the horns." In the first three aphorisms Kilimba is the candidate: to achieve yananio status he needs the advice of his tutors and the support of many initiates, for without help he will fail, like the billy goat that broke loose and was killed by a leopard. In the fourth aphorism Kilimba relates to the mask itself and the yananio initiations as a whole; a person who achieved a higher level than his father is praised. The last text evokes strife in the group, but Kilimba, the old initiate, is called upon to separate the fighting men and to settle the problem.

The masks invariably are placed on the ground in a closed circle with the beards touching at the center. The most frequently heard aphorism was: "Two Tulimu [insects]: Tumbukutu resemble Ndoku [species of white ants]." The text has multiple meanings. These insects, like the masks, show great similarity. The stress then is placed either on the equality of yananio status or on the identity of the status that father and son have now achieved. On the other hand, the insects are not exactly the same, and thus the emphasis may shift to a group of initiates who outwardly look somewhat alike (similar paraphernalia) but whose hearts and minds may vary widely.

When the masks are placed on the ground, various actions and interpretations follow in different communities. Possible performances include the following.

The masks are displayed first on the ground, one in front of each sitting yananio, while a preceptor runs zigzag among the seated initiates: "Who will show him the teaching of Yano, it does not fit many." Caution is required during the initiation so as to avoid mistakes.

Some of the masks are then placed together in a circle, the beards touching: "Assemble the graves [i.e., the masks] that we [or I] may know the skull of father"; "The graves [i.e., the masks] meet one another, I do not know the skull [i.e., which one is my father's mask that I will receive]." Other masks are assembled in a pile: "Ikungu [lit., Big Elephant] does not lie down unless Nzogu [i.e., the other elephants] have lain down in the open space"; "In Bukindu [lit., Abandoned-Village-Site] where father was, I see Mulula [lit., distant place that can only be pointed at]." These aphorisms stress the desire of the candidate, now that he has progressed thus far in the initiations, to see and receive the mask of his predecessor. They also emphasize the impossibility of holding initiations if many participants (including tutors and preceptors) have not been called.

A preceptor may pick up one or more masks and do several things with them. Taking one mask and placing it facedown in his open hand, he stretches his arm to show it to the candidate: "It is not encountered in the mud the skull of him who spoke for the land." This text glorifies the initiate whose achievements remain long after his death.

The preceptor holds several masks upside down by their beards: "If you have intelligence [perspicacity], think how it is there where you are going"; "He who asked you will accuse you of lies you have not said"; "It is not a kinship that makes the count of skulls on the village place." These aphorisms focus on the masks that hang upside down, a position symbolizing anger, tension, and strife. The candidate is warned that unknown and unseen dangers, such as false accusations, witchcraft, transgression of taboos, and adultery, are lurking everywhere. The initiate therefore should be thoughtful and cautious in whatever he does or says to avoid not only personal harm but also violence and retaliation that may lead to the extinction of his group.

Hanging the mask on his shoulder with a string, the preceptor sings: "In Yombe there died many, Kansilembo ka Mulamba [lit., *kansilembo*, what has a good sound; Beautiful-One, Son-of-Ivory] is being wept for." Suspending the mask on the back recalls defeated warriors who place their shields on their backs while fleeing. In other contexts there are similar evocations of the defeat and wholesale destruction that befell some Lega in a war with a Komo-derived group. The aphorism repeats the often stated principle that initiates are men of peace and nonviolence.

The preceptor takes two masks from the circle and pulls them by their beards over the ground. Holding one in each hand, he swings his arms crosswise so that the beards swirl in the air and across his shoulders. He sings, "Two Ngalia [girls born after boys in the same family]; Tumbukutu [insect] resemble each other," to mark identical status, and "Kitindi [dance] which father danced, shall I not dance it?" to stress the candidate's intention to follow in his father's footsteps. The movements (opening the circle, crossing the arms, then opening them) symbolize that what had been closed to the candidate is now being opened (revealed) to him.

Poking the mouth of the mask with a stick, the preceptor munches: "When eating with a Big-One, the toothpick is always between the teeth." It is a mark of respect to eat slowly when eating with elders from the same dish, and it is also necessary to remain silent when they speak.

In some performances in which the men display *lukwakongo*, a preceptor is cloaked in bark cloth and wears a larger whitened mask of another category (see *Idimu* Masks). On this occasion he represents the evil characters Samunyamwa and Sakalangalanga.

The *mukumbi* rite, an intrinsic part of the yananio initiations, celebrates the proper burial of yananio (and kindi) and the care lavished on their graves. The degree of elaboration of the rite varies widely. Some communities place strong emphasis on it; others indicate that the rite was borrowed "more recently" from another group; still others do not perform the rite at all. There is also a wide variety in type and number of objects displayed in the *mukumbi* configuration and hidden in a pit. At least one wooden mask is always placed on a pit as part of the configuration. In some groups it is the small *lukwakongo* mask; in others, a larger whitened *idimu* type; and in one instance, a large *muminia* mask.

In the *mukumbi* rite the *lukwakongo* was often handled differently from the way it was used in the initiation described above. An aide removed the mask from the pit and held it against one of the poles supporting the initiation house. A preceptor holding a mock bow and arrow, and frequently rubbing his chest with his hand, aimed repeatedly at the mask, but each time the mask was moved to the back of the pole: "Kagelia [a small cercopithecus that is hunted with poisoned arrows] does not move in the thick of the vines; he who is searching for you does not see you." The mask was then moved slowly down the pole to the ground: "Kagelia that descends and descends, descends to the ground." The reference is to a young man to whom an elder had spoken harsh words; instead of reacting, the youth just kept quiet to prevent the elder's anger from rising. Having taken this nonprovocative attitude, he could move freely without fearing further trouble. When the mask was placed on the pit, attention shifted to other displayed objects (a small shell, a pangolin scale, a hornbill beak, a knotted vine, a chimpanzee skull, a wooden animal figurine).

The preceptor then picked up the mask and sang: "Kilimba [Billy-Goat] does not grow a beard if it has no breeder." The immediate meaning is that a man who has no close female relatives whom he can marry outside the group lacks a lucrative source of valuables for the rites. As noted earlier, this text also stresses that no candidate can be successful without tutorship. The aphorism reinforces an idea arising from the interpretation of an animal figurine in a previous sequence. The figurine represented an expert hunting dog who always chased wherever it went, indicating the superiority of higher initiates and seniors, without whom nothing could be realized. The performance then centered on a knife whose haft was surmounted by a tuft of porcupine quills.

Again the mask was placed against a pole of the initiation house: "Mulala [a species of bat] flies in Menze [a tree] because he fails to find Mpunza [a hole in the tree]"; "Nduma za Mulala [Implacable Heart, son of Bat], an endless evil; he has refused [to give to] Lusiya [Bat] an ax to cut with it the dense forest growth." Mulala finds no place to hide and no one who will support him; his quarrelsomeness and his rawness of heart have alienated those who, like his maternal uncles, could be of help to him. The aphorisms express in negative terminology the need for goodness and flexibility; they rephrase two texts sung about a porcupine (represented by its quills): "Kiko [Porcupine] that flees into its rocky lair is saved"; "Kiko that flees into a fallen tree, perishes."

I observed in only three communities a very elaborate rite in which women manipulated the masks. Although these female rites repeated many things that were said and done in other areas when men presented the masks, much additional information was provided. In two places the women handling the masks were designated as Binumbi (Nice Crowd). The setting was basically the same as already indicated: dressed in cloaks of white bark cloth, the senior initiated wives of the yananio who were present entered the dance ground and took seats behind a feather rope before manipulating the masks. In one community, however, their activities were counterbalanced by independent performances by two preceptors who wore whitened horned *kayamba* masks. Here I note only actions and words that differed from those in the rite described earlier.

When the women first appeared they were holding the masks in their hands; after they were seated they affixed the masks high on their foreheads so that the beards covered most of their faces. As they did so, they sang two aphorisms:

"Lightning appears on the forehead of Nyamisenio [Troublesome, Arrogant Woman who squints when one speaks to her]." A woman of this nature will surely encounter trouble.

"Mulangalanga [Well-Formed Nose; Bold] is [too] long, he or she becomes a licker of honey." The reference is to a person who treats his benefactor badly; his nose is so long that it reaches his mouth.

Then hanging the masks at the back of their heads, the women sang: "The ones [skulls] that are lying on the back, the skulls of the Banamuningi." Many of the Banamuningi were killed in warfare with the Tunganda (i.e., the Komo and Komo-derived groups). In the aphorism they are indirectly voicing a bitter complaint about the prohibitions placed on bwami.

Pointing to the masks, the women next sang: "The things of Musongelwa [she who is married out of her group] are lying on the back [so that they can be seen], they are broken [into pieces]." The aphorism alludes to the adulterous woman constantly criticized in the initiations.

The women then placed the masks facedown on the ground: "The ones that are lying on the back, the skulls of the Banamuningi"; "At the time we were overpowered in Tubala [a historical place; also the home village of the hero Mubila] we carried the shields on the back." The latter is another historical reminiscence. The masks on the ground were then turned over and the preceptors grasped them by their beards: "Chicken sees the sun, to open [the door] surpasses him." The candidate is like a chicken: he may have many goods and followers, but he cannot organize an initiation by himself.

One preceptor danced and disturbed the order of the masks; another one put them back in place but facedown: "Ikolo lya Kikuku [lit., Tuber of Yam] when you dig it up do not leave it outside." When a man quarrels with his senior wife, he must not chase her because reconciliation is possible.

The women now took all the masks in their hands and put them in a facedown position: "The water that Big-One holds in a piece of banana tree bark rocks, [but] does not spill." One who is well supported by a senior will not fail in his endeavor. The aphorism—"Rich and poor: from one belly they have come"—means that the faceup and facedown positions of the mask respectively symbolize wealth and poverty.

Once again the women placed the masks in front of their faces and sat down, nodding their heads. The preceptor danced along beside the feather rope, his hand outstretched toward the women.

"Let me pass into the abandoned village site, the foreheads of buffaloes are fierce [tough]."

"At the bottom of slit-drum where Adz has reached, Arms have not reached." Adz is the initiate; Arms are his noninitiated kin who help him to find game and collect other goods but will not delve into the secrets of bwami.

"The things that Adz has done make Arms famous." The entire group benefits from the initiation of one of its members.

"Slit-drum would not have spoken, Mombo [lit., slit-drum pounder] gives him a voice." The help of kinsfolk enables one to complete the initiations.

All masks were then put on the ground; the preceptor picked them up and placed them around the candidate, then pointed at them and showed them to the other initiates: "Nkwale, Mr. Restless Traveler, will encounter Kinsamba [abundance of white mushrooms] lying flat." This idea, frequently expressed in many variations, emphasizes that an initiate must not be a restless traveler who leaves the village early in the morning, because all kinds of danger await him on the road.

The women, still wearing their white cloaks, now rose from their stools and bound the masks to the backs of their heads. They passed the feather rope, placed their stools together, and stood in a group: "Those who were defeated in Tubala [symbolizes a bad village and also vulva], on the back they carried the shields." The historical reference is to defeat in war, but the underlying meaning bears on the candidate. As he has given the initiates the required gifts and payments, they may give him the insignia and leave.

The women danced in a group, widely swinging their cloaks: "Disperse Monga [tops of the oil palms], Sawabuzumbu [Mr. Buzumbu; *buzumbu* is something that bends over because of its length], and Kanyabutyege [short-statured person], dance with your mother." The women danced with their torsos bent forward, while preceptors zigzagged between them: "In the village of Waba [wealthy person], Elephant goes in it plop! plop!" These aphorisms signify the end of the mask sequence and the forthcoming end of the yananio rites. The initiates present, including some kindi, are already visualizing themselves coming to the candidate's kindi initiation.

I have observed the *bilimbi* rite as part of a lutumbo lwa yananio initiation in only one group. The full stem of a young parasol tree was planted in the village place; all the branches were removed except for four stumps near the top of the stem. The pole was anchored by four vines attached to the four stumps and to forks hammered in the ground. A small *lukwakongo* mask was fastened to the stem at the height of the stumps. The structure was called *bilimbi bya igulu,* the slopes of the sky or the high mountains. While it was being erected, the initiates sang: "I do not travel on the same trail with one who hates me [for] he might make the slopes of the sky fall upon me." The song, like so many others, stresses harmony and esprit de corps among the initiates.

Preceptors and initiates danced around the pole, accompanying each of the following actions with a song: moving the hands upward along the vines; pointing with the left, then with the right, hand upward, sliding the hand upward along the vine, and finally placing the hand on the pole; same action, but finally licking the pole; pointing upward, then placing one hand against the pole; moving the hand upward along the vine, then stroking the pole; holding hand palms together and making a chopping motion toward the pole; pulling the vines loose from the forks and moving the pole; pointing to the mask; pulling the pole out and placing it on the ground.

The first sequence of actions emphasized the total construction. The pole represented the field of kinship relationships; the four stumps symbolized the four maximal lineages that constitute the agnatic core of a clan; the mask was identified as *kidande,* a term literally referring to incorporated segments (i.e., those lineages that are related to the agnatic core through a female member of that core) but often used in contexts like this to designate all relationships traced among maternal uncles and sororal nephews. This fundamental aspect of kinship structure is often presented in the initiations by means of a four-legged stool with a central protuberance or by four cowrie shells with a nutshell placed in the center. The exegesis on the whole arrangement was condensed in four aphorisms: kinship included the agnates and the maternal uncles, and their total help was vital for a successful high initiation; despite trouble among the agnates, hope remained with the maternal uncles; the trouble arose because the candidate had found the women who were married to his agnates "too tasty"; the agnates coming from different villages were planning to leave, like bats hanging upside down because of wrongdoings. It was in vain to attempt the initiation without securing the help of some Big-Ones. Many goods would be needed because the tree of kinship was shaky (like a dried-up tree one was climbing to collect young parrots and lock them in a basket). The help of one person alone would not be sufficient, for "Bwami is the [strident] call of Dendrohyrax, one never speaks alone." All this explanation applied to Munumbu, an imaginary stupid person who had upset and provoked the initiates, and not to the candidate. He was straight like a *musoka* tree, as he had the right moral qualifications and the necessary valuables. In a final sequence attention shifted dramatically to the mask, hung high above the people as the image of death, which like the new moon may be seen by every clan group. The mask is a reminder that death is universal and strikes everybody, and that when death comes it is inappropriate to get overexcited and threaten others with retaliation.

The episode ended when the tree was placed on the ground to show that the initiates were dealing with a true candidate and not with a Munumbu. When the last song had been sung, initiates cut pieces from the vines for fishing and hunting charms because objects that have been used in this ritual manner have an intrinsic force.

Uses and Meanings outside Lutumbo lwa Yananio

In certain communities single *lukwakongo* masks are used in rites other than those of lutumbo lwa yananio. In the *itungilo* performance of kongabulumbu, a *kigogo* girl (a young virgin, close agnate of the candidate) wore a mask with a genet hide attached to the chin and carried a feather tuft in each hand. When the candidate arrived at the initiation house and was asked by the preceptors if he had seen an elephant (i.e., the young woman), he promptly replied: "Yes, but it is not yours." A hunter's killing of an elephant is not something to hide or argue about; rather, it is a joyful event that must be widely proclaimed.

In the *mumpanda* rite that followed the kongabulumbu initiation in one community, two initiates wearing whitened masks sat hidden behind a fence. They showed their faces intermittently and then placed the masks on the fence. They represented the Beyamungu, the senior initiates on whom all others lean for protection and counsel. The seniors were compared with a tree that fell into the river, to which a drowning person clings for survival.

In one community a *lukwakongo* mask was used in the *ndinde* rite connected with the *muzigi* initiation of the wives of a ngandu initiate. A woman lying on a mat was covered with a large sheet of bark cloth; the preceptors had placed a small wooden mask on the cloth near her face. Hidden under the bark cloth were two knives, one with a wooden blade and the other with a copper blade. As the woman represented Ikaga (Pangolin), they were called "knives of the pangolin," and in this area they were the privileged possessions of a ngandu initiate. The songs, however, did not explicitly mention the pangolin.

The preceptors first took the knives and danced with them above the woman, who began to shake: "When you hide civet under the fallen *nkungu* tree, do not go fleeing him." The interpretation is that anyone who is in trouble with a senior must not flee from him; when one's wife leaves because of a quarrel, one must go find her.

The preceptors next simulated a haphazard cutting of the animal: "Give me my knife, let the hide be removed from Elephant." They were referring to a person who makes trouble with the master of the land, of whom, in this event, strangers will not be in awe.

The bark cloth was now removed; the woman had bunches of feathers around her ankles and a pangolin scale in her mouth. She got up, cloaked herself in the bark cloth, and placed the mask in front of her face. The preceptors sang, "Give me my little knife, in Kilinda, Elephant is being skinned, in the village of Mugumi," and proceeded to pull and cut randomly at the cloth. Their behavior meant that if everybody takes the things he believes are his due, conflict and destruction will ensue. The mood changed when the masked woman danced around and received gifts. She no longer represented the pangolin but rather a villager or a stranger who had found the animal in a trap and was bringing the news to the elders, which is the proper thing to do.

In one bombwa initiation, a preceptor wore one mask on his temple and another on the back of his head. He had a collaret of dried banana leaves around his neck and a feather hat on his head. Walking around with a plate, he represented Kingungungu, a poor old fellow begging for food; initiates obligatorily threw shell money onto his plate. The scene emphasized hospitality and generosity in giving: nobody may refuse to share food with a person who asks for it or who arrives as a guest. By requesting gifts that could not be denied, Kingungungu was also depicting a village headman or a lineage head whose demands may not be rejected by subordinates.

In another bombwa rite a group of initiated women entered the village carrying leaves. One woman danced in the middle of the group. She was wearing many necklaces, and a *lukwakongo* mask was attached to the front of a cowrie-studded hat so that the beard floated down over her face. She was portraying Nsamba, the child of Nyaninki. The women were returning from a symbolic fishing party in which they had used fish poison (represented by leaves that are actually used to poison fish) and singing: "Nothing passes in the place where the fish poison of Balumbu is being pounded." Nsamba was their big catch.

Another group used two *lukwakongo* masks (called *kilume*), the faces rubbed with red grit and decorated with white lines, in a kindi rite. The masks, together with a wickerwork rattle, were placed in a small configuration to signify elders who come to the village. The initiates next planted a banana stipe in front of the initiation house and placed one mask on a heap of dirt around the stipe. A preceptor pulling a turtle carapace with a feather rope emerged from the house, approached the stipe, squatted, and picked up the mask with his teeth. After scattering the dirt he set the mask back in its place near the banana stipe. Mpoko, the banana stipe, represented the village; the preceptor with the turtle shell embodied a master of the land who arrived in the village to settle all differences between people. Picking up the mask, smoothing the dirt, and placing the mask back symbolized the achievement of a lonely person: his seniors were dead, but he was nonetheless able to achieve a high grade through his own strength.

For a full understanding of the texts relating to *lukwakongo* masks it is important to realize that some aphorisms occur in variants and that some are also sung in conjunction with other objects and in different action contexts. The classic texts sung about the masks ("I know my father from [his] skull and lo! father is dead"; "I know my father from [his] skull; I have not seen [the place] where he died") are quoted with slight variations during the presentation and transfer of other insignia and paraphernalia. I have heard the following texts quoted in connection with reed swatters, mussel shells, belts of raffia or bongo hide, *nsamba* fish skulls, and warthog tusks: "I know Big-Initiate from his reed swatter; I have not seen [the place] where he died"; "I know Nzali za Kibondo

[Nzali, son of Raffia] from his belt; lo! Nzali is dead"; "I know Nsamba [fish] from his gills; lo! Nsamba is dead." In each instance the text is meant to present the material object as a permanent linkage between the living and the dead. One receives and keeps objects that belonged to persons who have been dead for a long time; one hears others talking about dead initiates when they show the objects that once belonged to them.

The meanings of other texts sung about the masks are more clearly illustrated in different contexts. As an example, "The Big-Ones of [the village called] Harmony shake the beards; they have eaten nothing," is sung while a preceptor dances with a collaret (made of strips of dried banana or palm leaves) hanging under his chin which he moves left and right. The text warns that one must not approach elders who are sitting together in secret council or infer that they are plotting or backbiting, for it is likely that they are quietly dealing with the country's serious problems.

The complex text, "[The water] that Big-One carries does not spill," is vividly illustrated in dances with a *lubumba* shell. In one performance a dancing preceptor sings while holding water in the shell: "[The water] that Big-One carries does not spill; it rocks and rocks; [the sap of] *kikuba* [tusk of a banana flower] cannot spill." This text, sung during the female bulonda rites, has sexual overtones and stresses the bonds of fidelity that link an initiated wife with her husband. In another dance the shell is held in cupped hands: "[The water] of Kikinda [a river]: if you tie it [i.e., draw water from the river with a banana leaf], it will break the green banana leaf." The reference is to the candidate's readiness for the rites; delegates come to inspect and count the goods he has stored in packages and baskets. Finding them adequate, they invited him to go ahead with his final preparations ("break the green banana leaf," i.e., open the packages for distribution of their contents).

The sequence in which initiates hanging their masks on their backs are compared with retreating warriors may be dramatically enacted with an actual miniature shield or a shieldlike door: "They fought in Kabala [a village; also a man or woman with small genitalia]; on the back they carried the shields." The interpretation clearly refers not only to actual retreat in warfare but also to the symbolic warfare that occurs when men and women have sexual intercourse, with the men being beaten by the women ("the penis is the first to fall").

The aphorism, "[The words] of Samusongelwa [Mr. To-Whom-I-Am-Married] call me a witch, they are unfolded," sung about masks lying upside down, also refers to a *lubumba* shell. The shell is turned so that its concave side is visible: "Big-One who hates you [is like] a snail lying upside down on its shell." The initiates, their arms and legs spread wide, dance toward the shell and sing the first text. The dancing elucidates the meaning of the text: initiates are criticizing a woman who is too ready for seduction.

Lukungu Masks

Forms

The Lega produce maskettes called *lukungu* (skull) in ivory and bone (pls. 69–71) and occasionally in copal (Bonew, 1974, p. xiii) or highly polished wood (Biebuyck, 1973*a*, pl. 58). These small masks belong to individual lutumbo lwa kindi initiates. As there are obviously fewer kindi than yananio, the number of *lukungu* masks is smaller than the number of *lukwakongo* masks. The exegesis provided for the ivory masks to some extent overlaps that given for the *lukwakongo*. Usually, however, much less information is conveyed about the ivory masks than about the *lukwakongo*. The implication is that persons achieving the highest kindi levels no longer need the detailed instructions given at the lower stages because, by completing all the grades, they have gained information and understanding. Individual kindi also possess many sculptures and other insignia that enhance their knowledge.

The maskettes closely follow the general form of the wooden *lukwakongo*. Most of them are ovoid and convex with a concave facial plane, but some are flat, and in rare examples the top and bottom (chin) of the mask are not rounded but straight. In others the face is concave only around the eyes. On the average, the ivory and bone masks I collected ranged from 7.1 to 12.3 cm in height (with many in the 9- to 11-cm range) and from 4.4 to 6.6 cm in width. Ivory and bone *lukungu* masks at Tervuren (excluding those above) measure from 6.0 to 17.4 cm, but many fall in the size range of those I collected. *Lukungu* masks illustrated in the literature range from 5.0 to 19.5 cm in height (e.g., Sweeney, 1935, no. 455, and the score of authors who have reproduced this famed mask; Biebuyck, 1973*a*, pls. 38–39, 56–57; Dorsingfang-Smets and Claerhout, 1974, pl. 88; Elisofon and Fagg, 1958, p. 240; Frobenius, 1933, p. 538; Gaffé, 1945, no plate numbers; Laude, 1956, p. 38; Leuzinger, 1972, pl. X-12; Lunsford, 1969, pl. 126; Maesen, 1950, pl. 53; Noll et al., 1972, p. 104).

The eyes of the *lukungu* masks may be oval, round, cowrielike, or shaped like coffee beans; some have protuberant rims and others are perforated; in some specimens the eyes are placed horizontally but are uneven, while in others they slant. Noses are mostly long and narrow but flare toward the top in triangles and lozenges; some are very short, others are broad and form a straight line. The oval or round mouths may be perforated, and teeth may be indicated on the lips. Some masks have *nkembe* dots or shell incrustations on the forehead and circle-dot, dot, or linear designs on rims, forehead, and cheeks. The rims of the masks have several holes: two in the upper middle for a string so the masks can be hung from a fence, and several around the chin by which a fiber beard may be attached. The patinas of the masks are yellow, grayish yellow, and deep red. The quality of workmanship and the finish of the masks show wide diversity.

Uses and Meanings

The ivory and bone sculptures (masks, figurines, and other carvings) every participant kindi brings to the initiations are oiled at an early stage in the rites. During this secret ritual Kingili, an initiate, sings through a mirliton that is made of ivory for kindi, at least in some communities. Kingili is a mysterious singer, an extraordinary being whose awesome presence creates a feeling of terror. The oiling of the initiation objects is called *kubongia masengo,* to anoint, to harmonize, to bring into unison, to give force to "heavy objects." The rite is required when such objects are "moved from one place to another," from their "dormant" state in the shoulder bags to an "active" state in the rites. A mat is placed in the initiation house; the tutors bring oil, salt, peanuts, and bananas. The oil (*mombo*), which is extracted from various species of nuts, such as *busezi, bunzeke,* and *kilanda,* beautifies and also protects the skin against scratches and scabies. The oiling is done by kindi aides called *kalombola* or *kalia* (traditionally each kindi had such an aide-de-camp), who are close kinsmen of ngandu grade. The tutor and his helpers place handfuls of shell money before each object displayed and oiled.

Kingili sings throughout the rite, which takes a lot of time because it includes dinner for the initiates. Kingili, "who has now gone on his journey," encourages the initiates to "let their new colleague taste the sweet taste" of the objects he has coveted so much. He orders everyone to remove the objects from their shoulder bags and show them. The oiling begins with Kingili's song: "Kabongi [who likes to anoint with oil] of Malinga [the lowlands], Kabongelo [lit., small calabash with oil] does not sleep without oiling himself." While the oiling takes place Kingili sings a variety of songs. Just as the objects will shine after oiling, so will the new initiate; formerly he was like an orphan whose legs were dirty because no one had fetched water with which he could wash himself. The impatient candidate, who is now on the threshold of the revelations, is likened to a "frog croaking [the Lega say weeping] in Malambo [the game-rich hunting grounds]." He rejoices at the thought of his imminent blessings; he is reminded, however, that, like "a rat running and running around in a conceited manner on the back of a snake," he is still in an ambiguous and even dangerous situation.

Kingili also talks about the initiates: "The Banambala [Breed-of-Mbala-Pods]: on the ground they disperse; above [in the sky, in the heights, on the tree] they form one group." The initiates attending the rites are repeatedly said to be up "high," "in a place where it climbs," or "on the tops of the mountains." Initiates, as members of different kinship groups dispersed in hamlets and villages, join together for the ceremonies. The text also emphasizes the often formulated concept that bwami ("the fruit that came from above"), although it has a single origin and is basically uniform in structure and ideology, has developed into many strains that reflect different ways of doing things and different organizational patterns. When the oiling is finished, the sculptures are put back into the individual shoulder bags: "The initiates are shrewd, they show you [things], they do not give [them] to you." This rite is followed by a long sequence centering on the mat.

The contexts in which the ivory and bone masks are displayed vary in detail from community to community, although there are recurring patterns. In some groups the masks are used only once during the lutumbo lwa kindi initiations, to conform with the appearance of the wooden masks in lutumbo lwa yananio. In one variant the participant kindi initiates danced in one line; holding the masks low in their hands and murmuring "koookooo," they executed brisk movements. The choir sang, "Lukwakongo the hammer that the Dead-Ones have left behind [for us]," a song identical with the one used when the wooden masks are exhibited. The initiates then placed the masks facedown on the ground: "Big-One who hates you, places Mugamba [Snail Shell] on the belly [i.e., on its front part]." The masks were turned faceup: "Big-One who loves you places Mugamba [Snail Shell] on its back [i.e., on its back part]." Both songs refer alternately to a tutor who is ill-disposed and to one with good intentions; the first tutor ruins the candidate's chances for initiation, but the second one wants his protégé to know everything. A preceptor then danced holding two masks in his hands and alluded to old initiates who are no longer forceful yet deserve the deepest respect. Continuing the same dance, "The water in the plantain leaf that Big-One carries does not spill" stresses the careful guardianship of those charged with preserving the sacred legacies. All masks were then removed as the initiates sang: "The initiates are [full of] shrewdness; they show you, they do not give you."

In a second variant the action was even simpler. The kindi emerged, moving in a crescentic line through the village; their initiated kanyamwa wives ran away from them in a group at the encounter. This unexpected action developed during the interpretation of the contents of the collectively held basket. Immediately preceding the appearance of the masks, the preceptors danced with the skull of a *nsamba* fish and sang: "Nsamba [son] of Nyamakolo [seed of *kihama*], we know him from the gills." This text emphasizes that a man is known for his achievements and for the sacred objects he leaves behind him when he dies. The arrival of Nsamba announced the emergence of the mask carriers with a variation of the familiar song: "Lukwakongo, the hammers that the Dead-Ones and the [living] people have forged." The kindi then hung the masks from their shoulders on strings: "Mulambu [lit., a net hunt that lasts many days] of Kwidombe [lit., Place-of-Polygamy; here, name of a village], wherever he goes he has his Kalemba [lit., hunting net wound in large circles hanging from the shoulders], it does not remain behind." This text notes that the masks, as essential insignia of kindi rank, must be brought to the initiations for display. Kalembe also refers to the initiated kanyamwa wife who must accompany her husband to participate in the rites. After this short episode the masks were removed and the interpretation of the collectively owned objects continued.

In communities that do not perform this simple ceremony the masks appear as part of an elaborate configuration in a rite called *kilinkumbi* (drum name for the pangolin). It has four variants. In the first, the masks were attached with strings to a small fence (made of latticework), and an animal figurine representing Kilinkumbi was placed close to the fence. Immediately before construction of the fence, the initiates sang of their exclusiveness and compared themselves with the Banankamba (Chimpanzee-Folk) who "do not carry one who is not theirs [i.e., who does not belong to their breed]." When all objects had been displayed, the songs centered first on the animal figurine. The initiates later danced in front of the fence, designating the masks: "Kabiya [a village] is [filled with] pits and pits, the skulls of the Banamuningi." This text is a historical reference to the total defeat of the Banamuningi clan in battle, but indirectly it praises a group many of whose members have achieved the high grade of kindi. Continuing the same dance, the initiates sang: "The kinship group [whose members] accuse one another of skulls [i.e., of killing one another] is dead [i.e., falls apart]."

Dancing around the fence, the initiates then sang several aphorisms:

"An initiate is not laughed at [ridiculed] because of his big head and a ka-londa woman is not told [look at your] long [or flat] buttocks." The seniors deserve respect.

"In our village, in Lununatondo, there remained countless skulls." An elder complains that he remains lonely because his group dispersed and died out after too many accusations and curses were made against it.

"Even if you build [a village] for many, the corpse is what you will remain with." The indirect reference is to a young man whose father was a kindi; the teachings of bwami remain in his heart and he cannot reject them.

"In the same manner that the glowing charcoals remain [in the hearth] so the corpse remains in the village." This bears directly on the custom of burying high initiates in the village; the text indirectly points to the initiations, which are strenuous, secret, and indestructible.

"It will not be heard again, the corpse; they say farewell to him with the drum"; "He who died does not return again, he goes and throws the neck rest away." The dead do not return.

"Show me the place where he used to sleep, he who died did not go with the bed supports." The dead survive in their works.

"The noninitiates rejoice and rejoice, the Lwalaba River is visible at its sandy shore"; "Noninitiates, even though you see our loincloth, you do not see our testicle." Both songs originated when early colonial prohibitions began to interfere with the bwami association. These songs criticize the new arrogance of noninitiates, referring essentially to all those who wanted to reject the customs through religious conversion, Western education, and emigration. The kindi complained about the loss of respect, but at the same time they warned that their secrets would be preserved.

The masks and the fence were then removed, and each initiate put his mask back in his shoulder bag: "We remove the traps if we fail to catch animals, we will trap in another place." The same thing is said about a woman who rejects her husband; he tells her to go and to have her family return the marriage goods.

In the second variant, the *kilinkumbi* rite immediately followed the ceremonial entry of the initiates. A small latticework fence was built; the ivory masks were fastened to it around a large, unusual *muminia* mask (see below). Behind the fence stood a wooden animal figurine covered with pangolin scales to represent Kilinkumbi (Pangolin). A feather rope led from the large mask to an ivory scepter fixed in the ground a few meters from the fence; pieces of the thigh bones of turtles were hanging from the rope. Preceptors and initiates in turn, holding the feather rope, ran twice along it from the scepter to the large mask; the first three aphorisms referred to that mask. They then danced toward the fence, singing: "Assemble the graves [skulls] that I may know the skull of my father." This often heard text expresses the candidate's desire to see and obtain "father's" mask. Then the focus again shifted to the large mask, which symbolized the sole survivor of the battle of Ikonge.

The big mask and all the ivory ones were then turned facedown against the fence: "The Ones-Lying-on-the-Back, the skulls of the Banamuningi," a reminiscence of war and destruction at the battle of Atondo. Again the faces of the masks were turned frontward, and the initiates danced in wide circles around the village place. A preceptor picked up a mask and began rubbing his forehead as if he were brushing insects away. One by one the other masks were removed by the preceptor and passed along to an aide, who placed them on the ground. Each initiate took his mask and put it back in his shoulder bag: "Owl, Bad-Bad-One, disperses the wasps." This is critical of a person who has leadership qualities, wives, children, and wealth but is unfit for responsibility. People have lost their respect for him and abandoned him.

In the third variant of the *kilinkumbi* rite, the ivory masks were fastened to a fence around a large whitened *idimu* mask (see below). An animal figurine with scales to represent Kilinkumbi was placed on top of the fence. A feather rope ran from the large mask to a *matakale* stick (a walking cane surmounted by an ivory figurine) stuck in the ground a few meters away. The initiates first danced one by one along the feather rope, holding it with both hands and moving from the stick to the mask. They said that they came here as one group and that the trail leading to the place where animals gather to lick food was very long. The exegesis centered briefly on the animal figurine. Then the dancers, proceeding to the fence, pointed first to the large mask symbolic of the master of the land who attracts many people to him, then to the other masks: "Bring together the graves, that I may know the skull of my father." This text was intended to draw the candidate's attention to the mask that belonged to his "father," which he would now see for the first time. The dance around the fence continued with the following aphorisms:

"On the parasol tree there blossom many flowers; a stultifying spectacle."
The beauty of the masks is praised.
"The kinship group that takes count of the skulls is dead [finished]." This criticizes the members of a group who quarrel and make accusations too often.
"Nkulu [Turtle], heavy rain with thunder does not fall on me [wet me]."
Kinsmen cooperate when one of them is in trouble.

The initiates then danced around the fence again, pulled it out, and placed it with the masks flat on the ground: "I am weary of putting its supporting poles straight, the fence does not stay straight." This criticizes a woman or a child who does not listen to advice.

Everything was then removed: "Everyone who came goes home, the Anointed-Ones go to Itima [lit., the place of no return; here synonymous with initiation house, where the initiation objects are placed]." This text is frequently sung in other contexts when a cycle is finished or during the burial ceremonies for high initiates.

In the fourth variation of the rite, a small fence was erected and behind it stood a *kilinkumbi* animal figurine. A feather rope was tied from both poles of the fence to a gaff fixed in the ground a short distance away. Ivory masks were placed on the ground inside and outside the triangle formed by the rope. The interpretations began with the animal figurine and then shifted to the masks.

Approaching the configuration one by one, the initiates each attempted to take a mask, but a preceptor sitting near the fence held them back: "In the initiation house of Itamba [place where many people pass] there is Kilangi [a guardian]; it is not a place to steal from there." The reference is to the guardian of the tomb, the protector of the insignia that will be transferred to the successor. It also relates to a big man in a kinship group; if there is such a man, no one will try to fool the young men in the group.

A preceptor then stepped on the rope and pretended to have injured himself: "I am Kitanga [Swamp], I make Migogo [Fallen Trees] rot, I do not make Mikele [Thorns] rot." If a kindi who has male descendants dies, they will revivify his name and deeds.

The initiates picked up all the masks and danced with them:

"Assemble the graves that I may know the skull of my father"; "I now know father from the skull, I have not seen [witnessed] the time he died."

"[The skull] rots in Kitanga [Swamp], the skull of the late Mungema [lit., he who took up the ceremonial spear and shield]." This complaint concerns a family whose dead kindi has no successor.

"Moko [Bush-Baby], Stupid-One, carries skulls, he leaves one behind." The initiates address the candidate and tell him not to expect to get all the masks; only one will be provided by his tutor.

In some communities ivory masks are used in yet another rite, called *ibugebuge* (lit., danger; to tackle in fighting; to jump at each other's throats). In two instances the masks were fastened, at the same height and at fairly equal distances apart, to a *mukolo* fence made of several standing poles with one transversal beam. In a third instance, however, no ivory masks were used because the kindi initiates in this group did not own any. Instead, the kanyamwa wives, wearing their husbands' hats, stood silently behind a fence; they placed their hats against the fence, moved them slowly left and right, and later deposited them on the ground.

In the first variant of the *ibugebuge* rite, the kindi and their kanyamwa wives emerged from the initiation house and circled the fence. The kindi talked behind the fence, fixed their masks onto it, and rested their elbows on it. Two initiates, wearing lavish dance paraphernalia and holding feather hats in their mouths, twice emerged from the initiation house and disappeared again. When they came out the third time, they ran around the fence and then behind the women, who were facing the fence from a short distance away, and vanished again. After repeating this sequence, they appeared again and zigzagged among the initiates and then among the women, and each time they stopped and nodded their heads. In the course of this dance they executed many movements: holding the thigh, stretching a leg, squatting and resting on their hands and feet, shaking their backs, stretching their arms in the air, drawing circles on the ground, and holding each other's shoulders while moving the torso left and right. All this action was accompanied by only one song: "Ibugebuge is ready; I climb on a very slippery tree."

The action in the second *ibugebuge* variation was somewhat similar and the same song was used. The two preceptors, however, wore masks (a *muminia* and an *idimu;* see below) and an abundance of dance paraphernalia. They also appeared and disappeared with many movements: zigzagging between the standing kindi and the women, halting and shivering, crouching and holding each other face to back and then face to face, crawling under each other's legs, and flooring each other. The preceptors were depicting two persons who had committed a dangerous deed (*ibugebuge*) by transgressing a major prescription (e.g., failure to bring to the village a pangolin found dead in the forest; seduction of a father's wife or of a kanyamwa woman; boasting that they were ready for the initiation but showing that they were unprepared). All the meanings are expressed in the dance action. In the beginning the dancers hesitate to come out, they shiver, and they constantly move back into the initiation house to signify that they have committed a dangerous act. They later engage in activities that are the precise causes of *ibugebuge:* running around the kanyamwa to seduce them, fighting, quarreling, and particularly flooring someone. The entire episode informs the candidate that to attain high status he must avoid all sources of self-inflicted danger. The kindi is immune to war (in wartime, nobody may kill a kindi who holds the wickerwork rattle), and he is a peacemaker (during the fighting, two kindi stood back to back shaking their rattles to stop the quarrel). The kindi is merciful, and he forgives those who wronged him (symbolized by the two dancers passing under each other's legs; the action is called "remove your companion from between the legs").

The *ibugebuge* rite also warns the candidate, whose situation is dangerous, that nothing must go wrong, now that the initiation is rapidly drawing to a close. The sacred mirliton Kingili (Manly-Stride) had sung immediately before *ibugebuge.* Asking who had called him, he was told that it was "Idumba [lit., grave], a great mwami," signifying that the affair was very important. Kingili's reply, "Kindi will not sleep any longer," means that the biggest initiate of all, Kingili, had arrived and that no delay in the proceedings would be allowed. Then Kingili, mentioning the drum names of all the kindi present, had instructed them that no one should go to sleep until the initiation had been completed. Nobody may ignore so explicit an order. Thus the candidate, his tutor, and all kindi face potential trouble and must proceed with caution. The *ibugebuge* rite vividly portrays their difficult situation.

In some groups an ivory mask is also used as part of an assemblage. On one occasion I observed such a ceremony. A banana stipe (about 50 cm high) was dressed in hides and a raffia loincloth; feather bunches and cowrie-studded disks, otherwise worn by women, hung from two sticks serving as arms. The stipe was surmounted by a kindi hat from which the mask was hanging. When the candidate entered the initiation house, the assemblage area was closed off with a collaret of fibers and a shieldlike lattice door: "Open the door for me, Masters-of-the-Initiation-House, that I may see how it is adorned there." The screen was removed: "Come and behold Kitunda [lit., a harvest or storage of all kinds of things], Kitunda of kindi." All objects described above are also worn as paraphernalia by kindi and kanyamwa. While the assemblage was being displayed, the following aphorisms were sung:

"In the men's house of Mitamba there is a Kilangi [guardian]; it is not a place to steal from." When the kindi initiation house is ready and the initiation objects have been brought there, it will never be left unguarded.

"Children of the men's house: I encounter those who carry corpses"; "Come and see: the Balega tie me with strife [arguments, disagreements]." A person can find asylum in the men's house.

While the initiates were removing the assemblage they sang: "The Dead-Ones do not give me animals; let me inspect the traps." If a candidate has not provided adequately for the initiations, the bami will not soon return to help him.

Ivory masks are sometimes part of the display of artworks in *bele muno,* a final kindi rite requiring initiation objects. Usually all pieces individually owned by participating kindi and kanyamwa are placed on the ground in front of their seated owners, but some groups put them behind a fence covered with hides. There is no music or dance because *bele muno* represents a moment of contemplation and admiration. Led by tutors and preceptors, the candidate is shown the pieces and selectively learns their aphoristic interpretations. The texts, which do not specifically relate to the masks, allude to the wonders of bwami: "Mr. Cutter of Mbala fruits; in the sky there are many ways [of doing things]"; "I have not said mine [i.e., my words]; I have clasped the back of my head"; "What Elephant has built for himself is not beaten by rain." The rites produce unusual and unique things, whose meanings and power awe the candidate.

Kayamba Masks

The wooden *kayamba* mask, largest of all Lega masks, is horned, completely whitened, and elongated. The chin, to which a fiber beard is attached, and the top of the forehead are squared (pl. 72). Few *kayamba* masks are illustrated in the literature (Bassani, 1977, pl. 62; Biebuyck, 1973*a*, pl. 37; Claerhout, 1956, p. 32; Cornet, 1978*a*, p. 338; Leuzinger, 1963, p. 200; Sotheby and Co., 1960, p. 33 no. 127); those that are vary in height from 14.0 to 29.36 cm and 41.2 cm. Delhaise (1909*b*, no. 133) reproduced without explanation an unusual *kayamba* with short horns jutting forward from the middle of a large forehead. Three interesting masks (classified in Tervuren as R.G. 2465) were collected by Dargent (Tervuren, Dossier 148) and received at Tervuren in 1910. Dargent, who was a *chef de zone* in Ponthierville, *secteur* Lubutu, *poste* Walikale, sent a number of objects attributed to the Batembo, the Baleka, and the so-called Kusu to Tervuren. He called the three masks *kongo* and ascribed them to the Baleka; he said they were worn on the face by the "opérateur circonciseur." The crudely carved masks, probably made in the transition area among Komo, Lega, Nyanga, Hunde, and Havu, either by the Leka riverain groups incorporated with the Komo or by the Bakwame, who form a boundary between the Komo and the Lega, might be classified as *kayamba*.

Kayamba masks were observed in only a few communities, where they were linked with the lutumbo lwa yananio initiations. They usually belong to the preceptors, who often own specific objects as hallmarks of their specializations, but sometimes they are among the initiation objects in the collectively held baskets.

After a performance with genet hides, two preceptors dressed in white bark cloth and wearing *kayamba* masks suddenly appeared. Dancing and brandishing mock spears, they attacked each other in a representation of Kilimu kya yano, people who, though familiar with bwami ideology, whisper behind the backs of others and divulge secrets. The maskers were also referred to as Mankolobo (Expert Swimmers, Masters-of-the-Water, who were drowning in their own water). After a brief performance they disappeared into the initiation house, but soon they returned holding a sleeping mat in a vertical position. Behind the mat a preceptor wearing a white cloak and a horned mask squatted, occasionally moving around and showing his masked face above the mat. The preceptors sang: "Kayamba [Shrewd-One] who comes from a remote place cannot be bad"; or "Kayamba is smooth [*kolokolo*, a term signifying a body without scabies and coated heavily with red color and oil]; he who comes from far is not dirty [i.e., knows how to take care of himself]." Kayamba represents a person (here a preceptor) who brings news from a remote place; people were willing to listen to him, but it soon turned out that he was lying and gossiping. The point was emphasized when the preceptors went back to the initiation house. Two of them emerged, each wearing a horned mask but jointly holding a cloak above their heads: "They come, they go, they follow each other, Kambimbi [Arch-Shrewd-One] and Kalulungula [Who-Turns-News-into-Lies]." This short dramatic episode formed an interlude between presentations of the genet hides and of the polished mussel shell. The action suggested criticism of people who come to the ceremonies with evil intentions. Indirectly it emphasized that such people were not present at this initiation and that they would not be tolerated. The latter point was vividly illustrated by an initiate who ran around the maskers with his wickerwork shield and mock spear to keep unwelcome visitors at a distance.

In another community two *kayamba* maskers appeared in conjunction with the *binumbi* rite, in which initiated women manipulate the masks (Biebuyck, 1973a, pl. 37). As soon as the women (described as the Nice Crowd) had arrived and were seated, two preceptors sneaked into the village from behind the houses. Cloaked in Western-made jackets, wearing the horned masks on their faces, and shaking wickerwork rattles, they represented evil characters. On their arrival the choir sang: "The little trail that came from Musuku [a village; lit., a tree that produces resin] will set the village aflame." The two maskers who came from nowhere (i.e., from the side of the village and not from the main trail) symbolized the advent of unwelcome troublemakers. The preceptors now squatted behind a mat held in a vertical position by two aides: "Kayamba is shining, who comes from a remote place cannot be bad." They then hid behind the candidate: "The Big-Ones, Masters-of-Mbungu [wading place], in Mikula [Trees-Fallen-in-the-River; here on the side, away from the beaten track] there they go to sleep."

In another performance two maskers ran behind the houses but soon reappeared and raced wildly through the village: "They go, they follow each other, Kambimbi and Kalulungula." Later they removed the masks and placed them in the initiation house. Dancing along the feather rope behind which women holding *lukwakongo* masks were seated, the two begged for food with outstretched hands. Attention then shifted to the women and the small masks. As in the first example, the action illustrated the unacceptability of intruders and troublemakers, who have no place among the Nice Crowd. The candidate had already seen these *kayamba* masks in the *mukumbi* rites of yananio, but he had received no explanation. In this elaborate rite the contents of two baskets, collectively owned by yananio of two maximal lineages, were displayed separately on the left and right sides of a pit. Among the objects in each basket were a *kayamba* mask, several *idimu* masks, and other items such as forest crocodile skulls, elephant molars, pangolin scales, and hornbill beaks. The *kayamba* masks thus were part of a group of initiation objects which expressed the autonomy and solidarity of kinship groups.

Muminia Masks

Few wooden *muminia* masks have been reproduced in published sources (Biebuyck, 1973*a*, pl. 39, the large wooden mask, and pl. 59; Dorsingfang-Smets and Claerhout, 1974, pl. 85; possibly Von Sydow, 1954, no. 121B; and Krieger and Kutscher, 1967, p. 84). The masks illustrated in Biebuyck and in Dorsingfang-Smets and Claerhout measure 26.1 cm and 25 cm, respectively. The large convex masks are blackened, but the concave oval eye sockets around open ovoid eyes are whitened. The large forehead is adorned with a band of waffle-shaped designs, which in one specimen are repeated on the cheeks. The open rectangular mouth, the small flap ears, and the sharp-ridged nose that flares upward occur in other masks and figurines. A large fiber beard is attached to the mask (pls. 73 – 74).

The *muminia* I observed in the field had a very special meaning. Each one belonged to a small incorporated lineage that had historical antecedents among the Babongolo, a group of southern Lega who were important in the early dissemination of the higher bwami grades. The mask was held by a lutumbo lwa yananio initiate on behalf of his lineage; he considered himself to be the custodian (*mukumbilizi*) of the mask. According to the oral tradition, the mask had always been kept by and transferred in a close agnatic descent line within the lineage. There was only one mask of this type, and when initiations were held among eight different but ritually linked clan communities spread over a large area, the keeper of the mask would be invited to participate—hence the bwami interpretation of *muminia* as "indispensable for initiations" and "used in many initiations." In contrast with other masks, the *muminia* was used in both lower and higher initiations. The pertinent contexts of usage in kongabulumbu, lutumbo lwa yananio, and lutumbo lwa kindi rites are examined below.

1. *Kongabulumbu.* Through initiation to kongabulumbu, the lowest grade, an individual becomes mwami, a member of the bwami association. This initial rite, a prerequisite for achieving the more advanced grades, is considered an extension of the circumcision ceremonies. Kongabulumbu is essentially the process of learning etiquette, morals, and legal and social principles. The teachings formulated in aphorisms are visually demonstrated by the use of simple objects (most of them derived from nature) in a context of dramatic action. The extremely secret ceremonies are held at night in a closed initiation house in the village or hamlet. Initiated women are excluded, although in one phase a young virgin, a close agnatic relative of the candidate, does participate. The songs and dances are accompanied, not by the usual membranophones and slit-drums, but by secret instruments (large percussion sticks, mirliton, bullroarer, and a bamboo tube blown in an empty pot) normally used in the circumcision lodge, by anklet bells (made of pods), and by small percussion devices (scepters or ax blades in elephant bone). Kongabulumbu is a closed in-group

affair organized by a village group or a major lineage, although initiates of other groups may attend.

Throughout the rite the candidate must show restraint, self-discipline, and humility. He is helped by a tutor, a close initiated relative, who advises him on all matters (e.g., correct attitude, distributions of food and other goods). The symbolic weakness of the candidate is vividly emphasized in the beginning phases of the rite by his tutor's guiding and physically supporting him. In later phases the candidate passively undergoes whatever physical treatment is imposed by the preceptors. Throughout the rite he is made aware of the superior intellectual and moral force of the initiates and of the power of their association. The candidate is continually confronted with objects, mostly derived from his familiar environment, which acquire multiple, unusual, and mysterious new meanings in the setting of bwami.

In this context the large *muminia* mask is used twice. It appears first in the *musutwa* cycle when the objects contained in a collectively owned bag are displayed and interpreted. Dressed simply in a new loincloth and a belt of vine or banana tree bark, the candidate accompanied by his tutor arrives near the closed door of the initiation house. He cannot immediately get to the door because it is barred by two initiates sitting cross-legged outside. This procedure warns the candidate to use caution in approaching a place where he does not yet belong. The two initiates withdraw after each receives a gift, and the tutor rattles the door. The initiates inside the house interpret this as a good sign; it reminds them of a pious son who at any time of the day knocks at his father's door to bring him something from the hunt or the harvest. The door is opened by a preceptor. Upon entering the house, the candidate and his tutor are faced once more by two cross-legged initiates sitting between the threshold and the "hearth," a covered configuration of objects placed in the center of the house. As the crossed legs of the initiates signify anger, the candidate is warned that he must be very cautious. The preceptor who has welcomed the entrants and received a gift now steps across the legs of the seated initiates (as if he were traversing a thorny vine) to indicate that all is well. The preceptor leads the candidate and his tutor around the hearth, while the accompanying song invites the initiates to show hospitality. Although a stranger is normally welcomed by being provided with a stool, the candidate is simply invited to sit on the ground.

The candidate has barely seated himself when his attention is drawn to a corner in the back of the house. Sitting in the dim light of the resin torches is a preceptor wearing on his face the *muminia* mask, the long fiber beard hanging down over his bare chest. Two songs are sung while the masker sits, nodding his head: "Little-Eyes let us fly; wherever one goes, one must send the eyes out far ahead"; "Kitumbilwa [Boaster] sees a man; it is bad to boast, to brag about one's self [or about things one has not done or is not fit to do]." Both aphorisms elaborate on the concepts of caution and restraint.

A preceptor now removes from the hearth a mock bow and arrow (made of vine) and simulates shooting at the masker:

"I thought I was going to hit Mbezi [a monkey], the arrow of Kalenganya [Who-Aims] misses [its target]." This aphorism once again reminds the candidate that his aim to achieve the good and the beautiful will fail unless he fulfills all prerequisites.

"[The arrow] which Sulukutu [Owl] has shot has broken Wandio's [Eagle's] eye." The text advises against looking for trouble, which ultimately affects the elders, and warns against interference in matters about which one has no knowledge.

"The poison ordeal that Nzogu [Elephant] has drunk has turned our village upside down." This song elaborates on the consequences of troublemaking, which breeds dissension; accusations lead to the poison ordeal that causes even more turmoil. In dramatic performances the initiates often decry the inadequacy of poison ordeals, which do not solve problems but only lead to more violence and to death.

The preceptor then rubs one of the mask's eyes with a leaf: "Mutwa [Pygmy; Man-of-the-Forest], [child] of Makese [honey], [child] of Masambo [honey], they bewitch him with an eye sickness." The action depicts the treatment of the eye with herbs. It points symbolically to the cathartic power of bwami: the initiations eradicate bad manners and attitudes and also counteract witchcraft.

The preceptor now places the mask on his skull so that the beard covers his face; he holds the beard and nods his head: "He who does not get tired of shaving, will shave [the hair or beard] of Mungaminwa [Bumps-on-the-Head]." One who likes quarrels will run into trouble with the elders.

After this episode the mask is placed in a shoulder bag, and attention shifts to the interpretation of the natural objects displayed in the hearth. After the initiates leave the house, there follows a long interlude of songs and dances in the village place. This segment ends with the statement: "Kasele [Who-Knows; i.e., the preceptor] wants to find out [to explore] whether the village place is white." The initiates want to test the candidate to determine if he is fit to finish the initiation cycle.

The initiates reenter the initiation house, prepare the *kagole* configuration, and explain the objects in song and action. Immediately preceding the second appearance of the *muminia* mask, the songs focus on death and evil: children cause trouble, but the elders are accused of teaching them bad manners and then becoming victims of the children's evil deeds; a mwami among the Batoba committed suicide by hanging (a method used by women but not by men).

The masked preceptor now appears; he moves around in a crouching position, gesticulating and speaking to the seated initiates in a hoarse voice: "Sakibigabiga [Mr. Evil-Deeds], Mukandama [Confusion-Maker], junior brother of Ntonge [a fish, referred to as the leopard of the water]." The direct reference is to Mukandama, a historical personage famous for his feats in warfare; he used to tease young men and boast that he had killed one of their grandfathers, and the young men finally conceived a plan to kill him. The aphorism means that one must not brag about one's actions, for they might be insulting or evoke bad memories.

The preceptor next changes the position of the mask so that it rests against his temple, the beard hanging over his shoulder and partly covering his face. He pretends to feed himself with an ivory spoon, eating slowly and with difficulty: "Kisabulunda [Glutton], see how he [the old man] eats roasted bananas." This text emphasizes the respect an old man deserves; when he arrives, one should give him hospitality in one's house so that he can eat there quietly, away from children who make fun of him and laugh at his eating habits.

The masker now sits close to and behind the candidate and, sliding down, pulls the candidate with him: "Kabuluta [Little-Puller] pulls me, my father, splitter of hatred." It is wrong to dig up old rancor that prevailed among the fathers; one who constantly brings past difficulties back into a discussion is seeking trouble. The masker mock fights and wrestles with the candidate, then floors him: "Many a thing upon many a thing is done on the other side [of a village, of a river]." Disputes and violence between two seniors or two interrelated groups destroy the village and disperse the people. Crouching behind the masker, the candidate takes hold of his penis; squatting, both move along the row of seated initiates, the masker loudly protesting: "It is not a child that causes in me the pleasure of ejaculation, it is not a child." The text criticizes a person who seduces the wife of a father or a senior brother, or who fights with his senior and grabs him by the penis, the neck, or the belt. The masker, followed by the candidate, moves around in a crouching position, producing sounds like "brrbrr" and "yiiyii." "Mutubu [Monkey], Mbezi [Monkey] of the fallow land, tardily and cautiously [he walks]." Nothing done too rapidly is good; in every enterprise slowness and caution are the hallmarks of the initiate.

The mask is put back into the shoulder bag, but some actions begun by the masker are continued by the unmasked preceptor: he grasps both arms of the candidate but fails to floor him; two preceptors push him toward each other; the candidate is floored; the preceptor sits above him and pretends to pull hairs from his chest, but instead he spits out chicken feathers; finally, standing with spread legs above the prone candidate, the preceptor points at him as if he were talking to him. These actions stress that the candidate, who is close to finishing kongabulumbu, is now a strong person, one who is protected by kinsfolk on both mother's and father's sides. Even if he is powerful, however, he is still weak if he has no following. The candidate is a mwami now; he no longer has "a heart of chicken feathers" but "a heart of reflection." The new initiate must continue to listen to advice if he wants to succeed fully and to rise in the bwami hierarchy.

The masker assumes various roles in these rites. In opposition to the candidate, in his first appearance the preceptor represents the know-how, the power, and the threat of bwami. The initiate is a cautious person; he is not a troublemaker, a braggart, or a meddlesome man, but rather a slow-acting elder. The candidate (i.e., the noninitiate) is depicted as an unwise, impetuous, and troublesome person; he is an archer who misses the target, an owl who seeks trouble with an eagle; his precipitous actions lead to his own demise (Elephant in poison ordeal). In the second rite the masker temporarily assumes the role of troublemaker; in contrast with the candidate's failings, he again underscores the initiate's positive values, such as discretion, caution, and slowness. The mask gives the preceptor a certain immunity so he may engage in actions that otherwise would not be tolerated. The presence of the mask, as a symbol of solidarity between kinship groups, acts as the supreme sanction of the high values of bwami.

2. *Lutumbo lwa yananio.* The *muminia* mask appears once during the rites for the second-highest grade, lutumbo lwa yananio. After the long and secret *mukumbi* episode symbolically explaining burial practices, two maskers appear from behind the dwellings in the *nkunda* rite. The first one has feather bunches around his waist, his chest and back are covered with two *mpaga* (*Felis aurata*) hides, and he wears four masks: a *muminia* on his face, a whitened *idimu* mask (used during the preceding grave rite) on the back of his head, and two smaller wooden *lukwakongo* masks, one against each temple (Biebuyck, 1973a, pls. 41–43). Below the face mask he holds a genet hide and a wooden ax. The second dancer, also with feather bunches around his waist, wears a snakeskin trimmed with chicken feathers and carries a bundle of dried leaves. Two *lukwakongo* masks are attached to his hat, one on each side. Each masked preceptor is followed by an unmasked aide carrying a small basket. The principal masker is identified both as a scout bee (*nkunda*) and as a honey gatherer (*mutagi wa buki*). He and his aides are equipped to collect honey: an ax to enlarge holes in the tree or in the ground, burning sticks and leaves with which to chase the bees, and a basket for the honeycombs. Quickly and noiselessly, unaccompanied by song or music, the party runs around, stopping here and there. The group finally enters the initiation house and halts in front of the pit of Mukumbi. Only one aphorism is sung: "Scout-Bee comes; Lupapula [lit., who chases with smoke] gathers honey." This text is sometimes sung without masks in the kongabu-lumbu rites when the candidate places his hands on the forehead of every initiate ("Scout-Bee, wherever he goes, looks for Holes-in-Tree"). Just as the scout bee searches for sources of pollen, so the honey harvesters have now found a source of honey; they symbolically cut around the pit with an ax, chase bees with smoke, and collect pieces of wood (representing the honeycombs). As the mask episode ends, the preceptors in the initiation house stage a vivid performance of a divination scene and a poison ordeal.

The total action has several meanings. The *mukumbi* rite explains the death and burial of a high initiate and the guardianship of the grave. In the *nkunda* performance an older initiate of high prestige and profound knowledge is already making a reconnaissance of possible candidates to replace a dead colleague and kinsman. At the same time, the demise of a prominent initiate is also the occasion for designating the persons magically guilty of his death. The conventional methods of divination and poison ordeal are implicitly criticized. In the honey-gathering scene, the scout bee represents the tutor (*kakusa*) as a good and noble person who looks for candidates to replace a dead colleague and to ensure the continuity of bwami. When the dancer wears three other masks on the back and sides of his head, he is symbolizing a tutor who searches in all directions for a successor to the dead kinsman.

In another community the *nkunda* performance was more spectacular. Wearing many feather bunches, one preceptor has a *muminia* mask lying almost flat on his skull; a white *idimu* mask is attached to the back of his head; in his mouth he holds a tuft of feathers and quills. He is followed by a second dancer with a *lukwakongo* mask on the side of his hat and by several unmasked aides, one carrying a basket and the others bringing bunches of leaves. Coming from behind the houses, the two maskers face each other in a crouching position, moving their bodies and heads up and down and sideways. The head of the principal dancer is so close to the ground that his mask is almost vertical. Always in a bent position, the group zigzags among kanyamwa women standing in a row, frequently halting, squatting, and moving heads and torsos up and down and sideways. They continue their searching movements, halt, and simulate cutting the ground with a wooden ax (as if they had found honey), while the aides wave bunches of leaves to chase the bees. The dancers move toward the initiation house, halt, repeat the nodding and rising and falling movements, and enter. The dance performance is punctuated with songs: "Let Scout-Bee come, hovering, removing honey"; "Scout-Bee, wherever he goes he examines the holes [to determine] if they are good." Several aphorisms are sung as soon as the dancers have entered the initiation house and stopped at the *mukumbi* pit. The maskers and aides, crouching in a row, hold one another's shoulders, while the principal masker simulates placing the products of the harvest in the pit: "At the time Nkunda went to Kabala [a region]: whenever he is called, each time he goes." The preceptor is indispensable for the initiations. Moving his hands above the pit: "I have arrived in the place where Mukumbi sleeps, I arrive at the nest of leaves"; "They put together clever things in the same manner that Mukumbi has put them together in his hole." The latter aphorism reflects the candidate's newly acquired knowledge; he has witnessed the secrets of *mukumbi*. Removing *mukumbi* (a piece of *Potamogale velox* hide stuffed with raffia) from the pit: "Death, convulsively kicking Mukumbi emerges from the hole." Thus the end of the performance is signified. The aphorism also encourages the new initiate who hopes to move ahead in bwami to look around and search everywhere for tutors and persons who can help him.

3. *Lutumbo lwa kindi*. The *muminia* mask appears twice near the end of lutumbo lwa kindi, the highest initiation. A preceptor wears it flat on his skull so that the beard covers his face. Inside the entrance to the initiation house, he rests close to the ground on hands and knees behind a cloth. His face is so low that the mask is almost vertical. A pole forms a threshold before him. In both hands the masker holds a carapace, which is partly covered by the long beard. He moves his head slowly forward and backward, as a turtle does. A preceptor and the tutor are seated by the entrance, one on each side. Singers and drummers outside the initiation house intone: "Big-One of Turtle sets out [on a journey] to kindi." The masker represents an old high initiate who visits a junior;

the latter rejoices at the prospect of advancing to the kindi grade. The masker, moving the carapace close to the pole, raises it against the pole to imitate a turtle trying to crawl over an obstacle: "Big-One [son] of Turtle crosses the fallen tree." This and the preceding text allude to the custom of allowing a powerful kindi, who is tired of seeing his protégé's initiations being delayed, to settle in the candidate's village and decree that he will not leave there until the rites are completed.

The mask is now placed high on the forehead so that the beard does not cover the mouth; the masker is symbolically fed some banana paste with an ivory spoon. He nods his head like a turtle: "The Big-Ones [sons] of Turtle, I leave [them], they are eating a banana paste." This aphorism reminds the candidate that to be truly hospitable he must offer only well-prepared food to a kindi.

The masker, resting on elbows and knees with his head very close to the ground, crawls forward and backward behind the cloth. He shakes wickerwork rattles hidden under the beard; initiates outside wave leaves: "I surmised that Mukumbi [Golden Mole] was in [the hole], and lo! [it is] Ntumba [Aardvark]." The initiates are telling the candidate that the rites are more important and more demanding than he might have anticipated.

While the masker holds his head near the threshold pole as if he were stuck, preceptors bring sticks and place them near the entrance: "Ntumba [Aardvark] is not chased with [the smoke of] dried leaves; cut firewood." The action and the text explain how an aardvark is smoked out of its hole; as it is a large, tough animal, abundant smoke must be produced with wood and bellows. The text fits logically with the preceding one: the trappers thought they were dealing with a small animal and instead they are facing a large one. An allusion is made to the large quantity of shell money needed for the rite.

Two initiates now slowly pull on a vine placed under the mask as if they were bringing out the dead animal; the mask sticks out beyond the threshold: "Go and cut *mbubi* vines, Ntumba sits stuck in the hole." This text reminds the candidate that if his agnatic group does not have enough goods to give him, many other sources are available, such as maternal uncles and in-laws. The two initiates continue to pull on the vine, while the masker slowly crawls out of the initiation house. The initiates seize him (it now becomes evident that aardvark claws were attached to the end of the vine): "Ntumba emerges from the lair." The initiation is successful, and masker, preceptor, and tutor are given large quantities of shell money.

The mask is removed. Led by a preceptor, a row of men and women, sitting on the ground close together with arms clasped around one another's abdomens, slowly serpentines from the initiation house to the end of the village. Under their buttocks they drag garbage (leaves, vines, fibers, ashes) that had accumulated in the initiation house since the last rites had been held. This action symbolizes the change of heart in and the complete transformation of the new kindi, from whom all "dirt" (evil) has been removed. This "garbage" has a sacred power: it is subsequently burned and the ashes are collected by all initiates present and used as hunting or fishing charms.

After this episode two preceptors reappear. The first wears a *muminia* and the second an *idimu* mask during a rite in which all kindi hang their ivory masks from a fence (see *Lukungu* Masks, above). During the *kilinkumbi* rite in one community, however, a *muminia* mask was fastened to the middle of a fence to which each kindi had attached his own ivory mask. A feather rope led from the large mask to an ivory peg set in the ground a few meters away. Each kindi danced twice along the feather rope toward the fence: "In the place where a mwami has been killed, in Musinge [lit., a vine of which hunting nets are made] there has arrived a crowd." The direct reference is to the gathering of the masks and the initiates, but the text also alludes to the dangers inherent in serious quarrels: if a person with whom you have quarreled dies, you will be accused of having caused his death.

After the preceptor removed the rope and the peg, all initiates and their wives danced in a wide circle around the fence. The women then broke the circle and danced separately, while the men danced consecutively in groups of four: "Nkenge [Bongo Antelope] lingers [morning comes and he is still there] in Malambo [lit., places where many animals gather to lick salt; Hunting Grounds]; for what [how is it possible]?" Nkenge is the candidate who, with his tutor, is supposed to call the initiates together; the kindi wonder why he has not done so.

The circle of men and women danced around the fence while the leading preceptor moved toward it: "I go hungry to [the village of] Ngeze [small animal that eats bananas and palm nuts]; I shall not eat a ripe banana." Ngeze symbolizes a person who does not like to work; he has no banana groves of his own. Initiates cannot go to a place where no food is available.

Attention shifted for a moment to the ivory masks ("Assemble the graves that I may know the skull of my father"), as small groups of initiates left the row of dancers and moved toward the fence. The same action continued and the next song centered on both the *muminia* and the ivory masks: "In Ikonge [place where things have been pulled out, extracted] we are exterminated, all of us, completely." This text evokes a war in which the Banamuningi were destroyed. It is implied, however, that one of the group survived (represented by the large mask); he had sons who revivified the group. It is noteworthy that the mask used belonged to a lineage of the Banamuningi mentioned here. First the large mask, and then all the others, were turned facedown against the fence: "The ones lying on the back, the big skulls of the Banamuningi." The Banamumingi and many others perished in the battle of Atondo. The masks were placed faceup, and the initiates danced in a large circle. A preceptor removed one mask, rubbing his forehead as if he were brushing away insects; one by one all the masks were removed from the fence and passed to an aide, who placed them on the ground. Each initiate subsequently took his own mask and put it into his bag: "Sulukutu [Owl], Bad-Bad-One disperses Lusungu [Wasp]." A bad person possesses seniority, women, and goods, yet he is not respected or followed by others; people flee from him and disperse. Indirectly the text warns persons not to take things that do not belong to them.

In another community a *muminia* mask with large whitened eye sockets was affixed to the lower center of a fence and surrounded by ivory masks. The preceptor moved toward the fence along a feather rope, removed the mask, and disappeared into the initiation house. When he reappeared he was lavishly adorned with feather bunches, and he was wearing the mask horizontally on his skull. He was accompanied by another dancer clothed only in feather bunches. Both dancers held feather tufts and quills in their mouths. They soon halted, squatted, and faced each other, moving their bodies and heads up and down; the masker's head was sometimes so close to the ground that the mask was in a vertical position. The two dancers, in a bending, then squatting, position and still moving their heads up and down, zigzagged among the standing kanyamwa women. They squatted again facing each other, the feathers and quills in their mouths touching. They disappeared into the initiation house and reemerged, the preceptor now wearing the *muminia* mask on his face and an *idimu* mask on the back of his head; the second dancer had a *lukwakongo* mask fastened to the side of his hat. They moved in a bent dance position, followed by a third initiate carrying a basket and by several others waving leaves. They reenacted the honey search, frequently halting and symbolically cutting holes in the ground, and then slowly disappeared into the initiation house.

Idimu Masks

The term *idimu*, related to concepts such as *balimu*, *kilimu*, *malimu*, and *mulimu*, is difficult to translate. *Balimu* is often used synonymously with *basumbu* (ancestors), *bakule* (the dead), and *bein(d)a* (those who were) in statements like "Lukwakongo: the hammer that the Basumbu/Balimu/Bakule/Beina left." A text such as "Balimu you do not give me animals, I am removing the nets, I am going," explicitly refers to the "dead fathers" who refuse to help protect their descendants. Implicitly, however, the term *balimu* stands for high initiates who are, so to speak, extensions of the dead. The above text is interpreted as a complaint by an initiate who is not well received in the village of his colleagues. In an aphorism that frequently concludes a rite, the initiates sing: "The Anointed-Ones go to give a final farewell" (Anointed-Ones is sometimes replaced by *balimu*). In a few texts *mulimu* is used as the equivalent of *mpala* (initiation), which might be a vague reminder of *molimo* among the Pygmies. *Kilimu* may be applied to skillful preceptors as well as to well-prepared configurations, dance actions, and assemblages. As an example, two initiates dancing face to face while hiding under a large bark cloth sing: "You who do not understand, come and see *kilimu kya yano*; it does not fit many." *Kilimu* here has an ambiguous meaning. On the one hand it seems to imply the wonderful preparation underlying the teachings (*yano*). On the other hand, when sung in the above circumstances with a third person making a mock attack on the other two with a wooden spear, *kilimu* is a person who betrays secrets. After being in a private council with two others (symbolized by the two dancers hidden by a cloth), he informed a third party about their plans and decisions. In another performance, called *malimu*, initiates run around grimacing and making ridiculous gestures to test the self-control of the candidate, who must remain impassive before the amusing spectacle.

For these reasons it seems unwise to translate *idimu* simply as ancestor, as if the mask represented a specific ancestor. The term evokes two images: the high initiate, who as an elder is also a living ancestor; and the mysterious and secret object, whose meaning is privileged information. A dead person is *kiligiza*, that which disappears and does not return, but the great initiate survives in the objects transferred to his successors: "Kiligiza leaves to Mbulu [Varan] Mitengyo [Rustling-of-Leaves]"; "Lukubi [vine used for basketry and tying] died on earth, and in the sky [i.e., high in the tree] he placed the grave." If an initiate dies in a foreign place, his hat and other belongings must be returned to his home village, where some of them are buried in lieu of his corpse.

The whitened wooden *idimu* masks with beards are enlarged replicas of the *lukwakongo* (pls. 75–76; Olbrechts et al., 1958, no. 16, 28.5 cm; Maesen, 1959, no. 300, 24 cm; Leiris and Delange, 1967, p. 360; Leuzinger, 1972, pl. X-9, 23 cm). They are part of the collectively owned baskets linked either with yananio or with kindi. In areas where the large *idimu* is used in yananio initiations, it appears mostly in the *mukumbi* rite, replacing the smaller *lukwakongo* mask. When the candidate led by his tutor arrived at the initiation house, he was greeted by initiates imitating sounds produced by chimpanzees, elephants, and aardvarks. This action criticized youngsters who, seeing a big man arrive in the village, began to groan in derision and contempt. The candidate was led by a preceptor around objects covered with a goat's hide and then was seated. When the hide was removed (a gesture telling the candidate that nothing would be hidden from him), a configuration of objects was revealed: a feather rope was tied around four knives stuck in the ground, two of them adorned with feather tufts. Inside the fence a few snail and mussel shells and pangolin claws were placed around a covered pit on which the *idimu* rested. After the fence had been removed, attention was immediately concentrated on the mask. The principal actors were several preceptors, including one who sat on a stool near the pit to represent the guardian of the tomb. The following sequence of dramatic performances occurred in the *mukumbi* rite.

A preceptor came, dancing with open hands and pointing toward the guardian as if asking something: "When the village is aflame [it is befitting that] you ask those who remained behind [in the village]." When one returns from a journey and finds trouble in the village, before engaging in quarrels one must ask those who stayed behind about it.

One by one the initiates left a row of dancers, came to the pit, and motioned to it as if asking a question. The guardian answered them symbolically: "Tindikiti [an insect] whom Lulue [hole of burrowing animal] has seen, do not scorn him." It is good to show respect for a senior and to request information from him.

A preceptor designated the mask with his hand: "Nyambi, my child, has eyelids, he has no iris." This characterization is elicited by the form of the mask: it has eyelids but its eyes do not see. Nyambi represents a young man who is physically beautiful but morally ugly (a fighter, a thief, a seducer).

The preceptor moved his hand toward the mask, as did the guardian: "He who falls on the eyebrow of Zumbi sees [experiences] war." One who mistreats the village senior (Zumbi) runs into trouble. The guardian now held the mask sideways against his temple and pulled its beard; two preceptors came to observe: "On the face of Zumbi there falls rain." The senior who was wronged is angry. The two preceptors furtively approached the seated masker and pulled his toe, startling him: "I thought that my father was asleep, and lo! he is looking at me with one eye." The aphorism, often recited in other contexts, refers to the old man who watches over the village; he seems always to be asleep but nevertheless hears everything that is said and sees everything that is happening.

The mask was again placed on the pit; the guardian circled his hand around it and touched the heap of soil on which it rested. Two preceptors acted as if they wanted to grab his hand: "In the men's house of Ibonga [lit., Harmony, Niceness; Ibonga is the senior of this house] there is a guardian; it is not a place to steal there." The aphorisms shift back and forth from the old village guardian to the guardian of the tomb; both protect against thieves and witches.

The guardian next tied the mask to the face of one preceptor who, crouching, walked around holding the mask's beard in his mouth; he pulled at the seated initiates and rubbed their arms: "Come and see how Zumbi plays with his children." This play is dangerous because the senior Zumbi is starting trouble.

The guardian now placed the mask on his skull; two preceptors danced toward the candidate, miming anger (by puckering their mouths); the candidate was floored on his back: "The call which Zumbi calls against me! lo! he comes to kill me." The aphorism, interpreted as a call and answer, stresses the need for reconciliation: a young man did something wrong; a village elder shouts, "Beat him up"; the young man's protector replies, "Do you want to kill me?" The guardian again placed the mask on the face of a preceptor who then started to jump around wildly; powerless, he fell down and was helped up; the candidate was floored: "See how he splits his village and his children." The initiates are reminded that a senior should not be a bellicose person; instead, he must always look for reconciliation.

The masked preceptor, in a crouching position, jumped around to imitate a *kulungu* monkey; he seized the candidate and floored him: "Nkulu [Turtle] and Mbezi [Monkey]: Kulungu [Monkey] plays in the *busezi* tree [whose fruits he eats]." People of different kinds and various kinship groups perform together in the initiations; fathers dance with their sons, although outside the initiations a man dances only with his grandsons. Elders, even when they are junior to one's father, demand respect.

The masked preceptor, still hopping and jumping unrestrainedly, again floored the candidate: "The Ones-Who-Boast-about-Big-Things shake the house poles, but others will shake them." A youth bragged that he was very strong, but younger ones can now beat him; one who scorns an elder will later be scorned by his juniors. As the mask sequence ended, the guardian and preceptors proceeded to open the pit and to interpret its contents.

In the *mukumbi* rite of another community, eight *idimu*, together with horned masks and other objects, were displayed around the pit. The *idimu* were arranged in groups of three and two. Because they are contained in the collectively held yananio baskets, their number reflects the internal kinship structure of six participating maximal lineages; in two of those lineages two subdivisions (major lineages) had acquired their own baskets because of their numerical size and their internal tensions.

Very little action centered directly on the masks. The preceptor pointed at one of them and then caressed its beard:

"Kagelia [Monkey] you show my strangers [guests] and I do not show yours."
This text implies a dialogue between two initiates. One of them received his guests properly, but his colleague caused them trouble; the first asked the second how he could act in that way, inasmuch as the first one behaved properly when the second one was receiving guests.

"Bigness of the beards, bigness that is even." An initiate tells another that since they are of equal grade they have the same status. Even if everyone has reached the same level, however, there are still seniors and juniors, expert preceptors and followers, experienced tutors and initiates, who precede others in achieving the grade.

Another mask was then singled out: "What remains from the Deceased-One [is] the bone [lit., the limb] of the arm." This powerful statement, repeated in other forms in different contexts, points to the permanence of art forms as symbols of the achievements of those who died long ago and as material representations of their continuing existence.

In a ritual community geographically and socially close to the group just analyzed, the sequence in which the *idimu* mask was placed on the *mukumbi* pit was somewhat different, although many similar ideas were expressed. A group of initiates sat on stools around the pit; they moved their hands above it and then turned around on their stools. Trembling, a preceptor picked up the mask. He placed a leaf in the mask's eye and put the mask back on the pit, picked it up again, trembled, and returned it to the pit. The preceptor then tied the mask to the side of his hat, ran around and touched the knees of other initiates, then pulled at their arms to express joy. The initiates, however, started to push one another. The mask was placed back on the pit, and a group of initiates held their hands close together above it in a protective gesture. One dancer attempted to seize the mask; another, to kick it. The initiates then covered their faces as if they were sleeping; a preceptor came, stole the mask, and hid it near the candidate. When the initiates woke up, they searched for the mask; as they failed to find it, they ordered a divination to discover who had stolen it. The diviner designated one person and then another as the thief. In the brawl that followed, hats were thrown on the ground. The diviner now accused a woman (enacted by a male dancer) and was attacked by her husband. Other initiates were already preparing bark scrapings for the poison ordeal, because the diviner's verdict was not trusted. The accused woman ran around anxiously, inquiring if she should drink the poison; the others shouted that she should. The woman drank it and soon succumbed, falling down against the candidate, but a spoon was placed in her mouth as a sign that she should be saved. A preceptor started a new search procedure by placing leaves in a long row and following the trail—it led to the real culprit, the candidate.

As the actual mask sequence had ended by the time the divination session began, attention shifted from the mask to the actors and the action. References were made to various characters: Kagalama, the weak old man who lies in his chair and remains as guardian of the village; an old person, beautiful in his youth but now decrepit, who yet continues to deserve the deepest respect; Munyungu with one eye, a meddlesome person looking for trouble; One-Eye, a bad character but one who can still be redirected toward better habits; Zumbi, a tough man who is angry because others quarrel with him; Mubungu, who overhears and reports conversations; Mantalabusio (lit., front teeth), those who were initiated first and who steadfastly look for successors; Kamanwa, the Cunning-One, who tries to hide evil deeds by flattery; Salugi, who is jealous because his wife admires the well-dressed initiates; Zumbi again, who enjoys playing with his grandchildren but gets angry when they cause trouble.

In the *mukumbi* rite of yet another group, only one large whitened mask was placed on a pit surrounded by a fence of four knives and a feather rope. The action relating to the mask focused on a preceptor who behaved like a sorcerer. Crawling toward the pit, he cautiously touched the mask: "In the place [in the house] where a sorcerer enters, do not sleep"; "At the grave where a sorcerer rambles during the night, do not sleep." The preceptor, seizing the mask's beard with his toes, pulled it away from the grave: "The grave that has no guardian will be forgotten." The episode had been immediately preceded by a performance in which a preceptor had consecutively placed a pangolin scale against the forehead of every initiate present and identified them as "Masters of Sunrise," to signify that none of them were sorcerers, who work at night. This performance was quickly followed by a divination scene, disputes about the verdict, the diviner drinking the poison, and the accused succumbing against the candidate.

In one community, *idimu* masks accompanied the appearance of the small *lukwakongo*. Two preceptors dressed in bark cloth and wearing large whitened masks danced around two closed circles of initiates who held the *lukwakongo* in front of their faces. The aphorism, "They are not ours these ancestors here who come from the inextricable forest," contrasts the small *lukwakongo* masks identified as the "hammers of the dead ones" with the large masks that as strangers ("they are not ours . . . ") represent the arrogant character Samunyamwa. The action returned to the smaller masks and then shifted back to the large one: "Mr. Bold [who quickly stands up] goes off with the woman with fallen breasts with whom I was." The presentation of this boisterous character warns a candidate or other person about the consequences of seducing an initiate's wife.

Wooden *idimu* masks are also used in the kindi rites. They may be part of the collectively held basket, or a kindi may keep them in trust on behalf of all the colleagues who belong to ritually linked maximal lineages. One large close-knit clan group had three *idimu* masks, each kept by a kindi for the three sets of two linked maximal lineages which constituted the clan community. The masks were transferred within close agnatic descent lines, but if no kindi was available, the mask temporarily passed to a maternal uncle or sororal nephew of another lineage in the clan. These large *idimu* masks entrusted to a particular lineage were rarely made of ivory, but I did collect one specimen (pl. 78; Maesen, 1960*b*, pl. 105; Biebuyck, 1973*a*, frontispiece). Such ivory masks had become extremely scarce by the 1950s, although in earlier times kindi of other groups has possessed similar ones. It is possible that some large ivory masks in collections could be *idimu* (e.g., the Stoclet mask, 20.5 cm, illustrated in numerous publications since Sweeney, 1935; Himmelheber, 1960, p. 408; Museum of Primitive Art, 1962; Newton, 1978, p. 66). Some leather masks (pl. 77) may also be *idimu*.

In some areas the wooden *idimu* masks are presented during the "opening of the basket" rites of kindi. After the display of a carapace and a hornbill beak, the preceptor danced with the mask, singing: "The Big-Ones are turning around, they show you the legs [and] hide you the arms." This aphorism refers to initiates who assert that they will cooperate in a candidate's initiation, but who in fact are ill-disposed toward him. The preceptor held two masks together by their chins and sang: "Mbulu [Varan] died in the river because of Who-Has-Set-Up-the-Fish-Trap." Since the initiate went to the rites of his own accord, the candidate cannot be inculpated and the initiations must not be suspended because a visiting initiate had a bad experience.

Very old wooden *idimu* masks were part of another group's lutumbo lwa kindi baskets, which contained numerous natural objects and a phallus-shaped *yango* pole but no figurines. During the display and interpretation of the basket, almost no attention was paid to the *idimu* masks; instead, the small ivory masks appeared once during the rite. One text in the basket sequence, however, alluded to the mask, which suggested the teacher: "I have my teacher-adviser against whom I lean [whom I can trust], he is used to my manner [of doing], he does not leave [me]."

During the *kilinkumbi* rite of kindi in one community, a white wooden *idimu* mask was fastened to a fence and surrounded by eight ivory masks. A feather rope led from the fence to a *matakale* stick. One by one the kindi danced from the stick toward the fence; holding the rope in both hands, they sang, "Here we are descending in one group, here in Kasinge [lit., a vine of which nets are made]," to illustrate their esprit de corps. All kindi then danced in a row around the fence, stopped near the stick, and one by one moved along the rope, pointing at it and then at the *idimu* mask: "The animal trail is big and very, very long, it arrives at Idambo [lit., place where many animals gather to lick salt or to drink]." Here the mask represents the Beautiful-One (Kikuni), the master of the land; he is the center of all attention, the place where all trails converge. The initiates danced around the fence, indicating first the big mask and then the others: "Come and see Kikuni of kindi." All come to see the master of the land because he is a giver.

The *kampumba* rite is part of the lutumbo lwa kindi initiations, but it concerns particularly the women of kanyamwa grade. When the candidate and his initiated wife enter the initiation house, they find a number of seated kanyamwa women who shake their feather paraphernalia. Four of them beat the membranophones and the slit-drums, and behind a cloth are seated two kanyamwa, masked and dressed in white or red bark cloth. The *idimu* masks they wear belong to the men and are kept in trust by senior kindi for the members of linked maximal lineages. The candidate places his hands on the knee, shoulder, and heart of the maskers, while the following aphorisms are sung:

"We are exchanging greetings with the Dead-Ones. Samba! [verbal greeting]." For the candidate who does not participate in singing, the touching is a mark of greeting.

"Kisina kya Magungu [lit., Root-of-Phrynium] rocks and rocks [in the wind] without being cut [by it]." This aphorism refers to a kanyamwa who may want to leave her husband but cannot, as their bond cannot be broken.

"Kasimba [Preceptor] and Kasele [Singer] were born twins who run together." Even if there is trouble, a kindi and his kanyamwa cannot separate because they are bound by too many ritual sanctions.

"We go peeling off bark [to make bark cloth] in a place where the hills rise and rise." If men treat women well, the women will not leave them.

"The maiden who has not learned *lwila* [lit., the chattering of women when they leave for the fields; symbolic for initiation] is a Kambalu [tree] ka Mutandamo [a somewhat elevated place situated between two brooks, a good location for building a village; trees growing there will be cut to clear the space]." A noninitiated woman is nothing.

"Mulobo [lit., who moves the penis in and out in intercourse] ambushes me; those who are in the village simply look on." A woman complains about her husband because he beats her, and criticizes his fathers and brothers because they do not help her. Reference is also to seduction.

"Mondo [Emaciation], [child] of Mma [mother], sift! Mondo of Mma is not left to die of hunger." A diligent senior wife tells her junior wives to prepare food quickly for their hungry husband.

"Kampumba [Little-Old-Person] eats ripe bananas, he or she dies of hunger." The song demands that the candidate bring a large bunch of ripe bananas.

"They greet each other, Kampumba [and] Musombo-idima [lit., who hates reflection, thought]." The female candidate is fully accepted; she has successfully passed through the strenuous kindi initiations.

"Go and remove the burden, the Balimu [great initiates] eat [abundantly]." While the masks are being removed, the song requests that goods be distributed to the group as a whole and separately to each of the maskers and drummers.

PART FIVE

Other Sculptures

Besides masks and figurines, bwami members introduce into the rites an impressive array of small sculptures in wood, ivory, or bone (miniature tools and weapons, musical instruments, pendants), and phalli, spoons, staffs, stools, tusks, and other objects. One might be tempted to call them minor sculptures, but they are functionally as essential as the major carvings. Conceptually, they illustrate some of the great themes of bwami ideology and complement or expand on ideas conveyed by other objects. Aesthetically, they include exquisite examples of Lega art. The simplicity of form and the beauty of their patinas make them very appealing. These sculptures are widely distributed throughout Legaland, and some are used at initiation levels below yananio and kindi; some are also used by the Bembe and the Nyindu. Depending on function, the sculptures are owned individually by initiated men and women of different grades or are placed under collective control in initiation baskets and bags.

Arms

The crudely carved wooden arm called *kuboko, ikoko,* or *mugombo,* sometimes with an indication of three fingers resembling a pronged or trident-shaped stick, is used mostly at the yananio level but occasionally in kindi. It is not found in all communities, but where it is used it is part of the collectively held yananio basket. The composition of these baskets differs; in groups that utilize the arm, the baskets contain no anthropomorphic figurines but rather natural objects and other carvings such as a wooden phallus or wooden animal figurines.

As one of the collectively controlled insignia, the arm usually appears in rites that reveal and explain the contents of the baskets. Only two aphorisms are sung about it in each sequence. The most frequently heard text is sung while a preceptor holds the object, pointing forward, in both hands: "The arm of the sick stretches out [to ward off] the witch [that wants to kill him]." The arm symbolizes the desperate gesture of a person looking for protection against witchcraft. The aphorism also refers to one who, failing to receive help from his patrikin, appeals to his maternal uncles and in-laws. This meaning is closely connected with exegesis of a staff (*igobo*): "Where the arm cannot reach, Gaff-of-Mother can." Another often heard aphorism is conceived as the supplication of an ailing person: "Let me sleep another day; the one whom a person has married makes him live long without sickness." All women are potential witches who cause men to become sick and to die; they have power over a man's life-force (*kalamo*).

The arm is also viewed as a cut limb: "You cut your father's child an arm; did you think perhaps that retaliation [also destituteness] would not come?" Fighting is criticized constantly in bwami as a source of misery and trouble; to cut off a person's arm in a brawl or to lose an arm in violence is particularly evil. (There is also a Mr. One-Arm among the figurines.) Thus it is in a person's self-interest to avoid severing a kinsman's arm, because in the event of later difficulties that person would not be able to help.

The idea of violence leads to other proverbs associated with the arm:

"In the village of Yombo many died; Kansilembo [here, the headman] is being wept for." The seniors stay in the village when there is war. Kansilembo, the headman who remained behind, was ambushed and killed. The text also implies that all evil and sorrows attributable to juniors will ultimately affect seniors.

"Sabigombo [Mr. Big-Arms] died among the Bouse [a group of hunters incorporated with the Lega] and among the Babinza they have done the weeping for him." Sabigombo was killed by another political group; sorrow for him led to revenge.

The term *kuboko* (arm) is also used in common parlance to designate the shoulder of an animal, and one aphorism elaborates on this usage: "A woman [is like] the shoulder of an animal; he who gets it, refuses it [does not want it]." In the distribution of game or goats, the question as to who gets the shoulders, the legs, and the back inevitably leads to arguments about seniority rights and privileges. In the same sense, a man obtains a wife but then finds he does not like her.

In some contexts the arm is whirled around in the air: "Kuboko [son] of Musumbu [lit., ancestor] harvests fruits." A tutor sees to it that all the goods necessary for an initiation are available and then ensures equitable distributions. The text also suggests that the sculptured arm, as part of the legacy of objects left by predecessors, is a means of obtaining gifts and payments from the candidate. In other contexts the initiates frequently point out that initiation objects can produce wealth.

In one community, while a row of initiates danced holding one another's shoulders, a preceptor brandished the arm and simulated chopping at them. The row of dancers was likened to a *kagolomba* (hardwood tree) and the arm to an ax: "Kagolomba, Destroyer-of-Axes, that other one [i.e., ax] is broken." Kagolomba symbolizes a person who does not listen to good advice given by others.

When a simple trident replaces the wooden arm, it usually represents Kuboko Satu, Arm-Mr.-Three (Fingers) or Kati kane (My Piece-of-Wood). The character Satu (or Wesatu) in other contexts (with or without a figurine) represents an injured person who is unable to complete the initiations; he cannot assemble the necessary goods because he lacks a hand or an arm. Kati kane symbolizes an old person who can no longer work; nevertheless he must not be rejected or scorned. A stick with four prongs was used in one community to signify an outstretched arm: "The child that is not yours; [when] you ask him, do not stretch the arm out." One must not ask for things from a person who is not one's real father.

According to Lega tradition, in earlier wars the arm of a slain enemy was brought home as *bulilili,* a trophy proving that he had been killed. This practice was initiated because men boasted too often about their war feats, fooling others by dipping their spears into a reddish tree sap. Dances of joy, which also take place when a leopard is killed, were performed in the village and the arm was then thrown away in the forest. Delhaise (1909*b,* p. 165) reported a related custom. A demanding father often required his son to give multiple proofs of manhood before he would be provided with his first wife. Pushed to the extreme, the son would then ambush a person in another village group, kill him, and bring home his arm or his genitalia, thus forcing his father's group to pay heavy compensation.

Ax Blades

Ax blades in wood or elephant bone (from the ribs or a shoulder blade), found primarily in the intermediate grade of ngandu, are also used at the kongabulumbu and kindi levels. In some areas ax blades are displayed together with individually owned anthropomorphic and zoomorphic figurines and spoons in the *kinsamba* rite of kindi. Axes sometimes serve as percussion instruments to replace sticks or pegs in kongabulumbu.

The ax (*isaga*) is an important tool in a forest culture. The Lega say that the ax, the billhook, and the spear are their three most valued implements (to fell trees, to clear undergrowth, to hunt animals). Together with knives, bracelets, needles, and razors, they serve as exchange media in matrimonial and other transactions (e.g., acquisition of rights, purchases of oil from the Songola, distributions of gifts during initiations). The axes, billhooks, and spears used in initiations are never made of iron. In fact, the only metal objects so used are a sewing needle and the small double-edged knives with copper blades (often replaced by miniature knives in bone or ivory), though wooden or bone and ivory objects are occasionally referred to in the songs as *byuma,* iron tools. Ax blades and billhooks, often intermingled in the rites, serve as reminders (*kakengelezio*) that without them (i.e., without work) there will be no food. In other words, they are symbols of diligence and labor.

Ax blades made of bone are realistic replicas of iron axes: a broad blade with a crescentic or straight edge that gradually narrows into a point and sometimes with a pointed shaft. Blades may be decorated with circle-dot motifs (pl. 79; Biebuyck, 1973*a,* pl. 105). In rare specimens (pl. 80) both sides of a deep-red patinated blade are adorned with a carving in light relief: a realistic snake that bends along the rim on one side, and another reptile (varan or chameleon) on the other. Some other well-patinated, dark-brown or red, oblong or flat pieces carved from bone, though not really resembling ax blades, are so interpreted.

While dancing during the rites, initiates hold the ax blades in their hands and execute chopping movements.

"Kakuma [Big Ax], strong ax will die [perish, break] in [the process of] being borrowed." As the initiates engage in a mock fight, one of them tries to take away the ax. This most frequently sung aphorism alludes to different characters: a person who always looks for trouble and relies on violence will perish because of his behavior; women running around with other men during the initiations cause dissension; children who do not listen to their fathers' advice "die a bad death." In a positive sense, Kakuma symbolizes the wise and able tutor who served as a vital source of support and advice in a group but who is now dead.

"He who has no team [of three or four persons working together] does not clear the inextricable forest of vines." Without the cooperation of many people, nothing can be achieved; no one can be master of the land unless he has a large following.

"Give me my old haft, ax broke at the haft." The ax haft that is made from the hard buttresses or aerial roots of the *lusele* tree does not easily break. The text refers to a group that has held no initiations for some time. As there were no initiates of a high grade, the objects representative of their office have been kept in secret by initiates of other groups. A young man now ready to revivify the rites asks that the trustees initiate him and return the insignia.

Reflections about an ax that is ineffective sometimes lead to statements about an inadequate iron tool: "Katetele [lit., a bad metal implement] boasts at the beginning of the cultivating season, the masters of the dry season will refuse him altogether [saying that he asks in vain]." It is wrong to boast about things one is unable to do.

When an ax made of *musage* wood is used, the focus may be on both the form of the ax and the material of which it is made: "Musage [tree] is the highest in honor; on *musage* the ax that cuts the forest comes to an end [breaks]." A new ax is tried out on a soft tree like *musage* to see if it is sharp and strong: it is proper to start dealing with small matters before attempting to handle larger ones. Another aphorism, "On the parasol tree ripens [grows] the ax that will cut the forest," means seniors who are honored will in turn show respect. The text alludes to a poor person who should not despise a wealthy one, for the latter may help him obtain the goods necessary for an initiation.

The process of making an ax may be stressed instead of the implement itself: "Even if you are a skilled craftsman, one hammer cannot straighten [sharpen] the blade edge." The blade is placed on a heavy hammer that serves as an anvil, and it is then worked by a smaller one; a man alone cannot bear children.

The blade and the haft are essential complements of a functional ax. Like other objects showing the same kind of linkage (e.g., the adz and its haft, the needle kept in a monkey's tibia, the raffia fibers in a large pod), the ax blade (*isaga*) and the haft (*mwini, nkubu, kamima*) into which it fits are symbolic of penis (*nsuka*) and vulva (*butuka*), of man and woman, and even more strongly of the initiated couple: "Whatever is done, Kamima and Isaga must not separate."

When no ax blades are used in a rite, the texts may refer to the sound of axes and evoke the rhythm of bwami drums, which indicate the advent of danger: "Kimpe [bird] listen! In the [village] Deciduous-Tree, Isaga [Ax; the music accompanying the rites] sounds."

It is noteworthy that the adz (*nkondo*) mentioned during the rites is represented, not by its miniature replica, but rather by a small gaff (*igobo*). The small bent stick thus illustrates concepts about both the gaff and the adz. When the stick symbolizes an adz, the dancers manipulate it with chopping movements as they do with ax blades. One set of aphorisms on the adz praise the strength, support, and achievements of father: "I remember [fondly] the big things which Adz, Mr. Arms, did"; "At the bottom of the slit-drum where adz has arrived, arms do not arrive." In contrast, another set of texts allude to negative characters. The adz metaphorically represents a phallus in the aphorism "Father's wife is not shown *nkondo*; the wound of *nkondo* does not heal," and a weapon that can hurt people: "In the men's house of Ibanganguma [lit., slashing a knife at someone's face], an orphan does not dwell."

Billhooks

Most billhooks (*mugusu* or *kagusu*) are made of elephant bone, in sizes ranging from 23 to 31 cm. They are often decorated with circle-dot designs (pls. 82–83; Biebuyck, 1973a, pl. 103; Fagg, 1968, pl. 277; Museum of Primitive Art, 1966a, pl. 232). Basically symbolizing diligence, they occur in association with ax blades in the ngandu and the *mpunju* rites and also in kindi. In one ngandu performance, a group of initiates danced with bunches of leaves, while a preceptor holding the billhook simulated chopping at the leaves. A young man was criticized for failing to pick up the billhook and finish the clearing work his father had told him to do. This kind of criticism is formulated in an aphorism: "Mugugu [Chameleon] sings for [the bananas of] Mpombo [field prepared during the period of heavy rains]; he does not have his billhook." Mugugu did not prepare a field during the relatively dry *kilimo* season when most people clear the land; he has been waiting for the *nzogo* period, when only very enterprising people make ready an additional field.

In a kindi rite the preceptor simply danced with the billhook, singing: "He who does not have many [kin, followers] does not clear the inextricable forest of vines." It is impossible to perform a difficult task without the help of others. In another rite the preceptors first danced with the billhook, repeatedly making chopping motions in the air, and then showed it to the other participants, as if it had been broken: "The small billhook of Big-One cultivates for you and hides the fracture [i.e., the place where it is broken] from you." The preceptor continued to chop and then ran around haphazardly: "Mr. Clearer will not go to Mamba [the inextricable forest]; he [now] clears Mamba and something [else] that is said." A person who refused to perform a task ran into trouble, and then he was forced to do it; the text criticizes a person who does not listen to what is said in the village.

Blades, Chips, Slabs, and Disks

In some communities narrow, flat blades made of bone, some with marvelous dark-brown patination, are shown at the end of the *kinsamba* rite of kindi. Elsewhere the blades are replaced by oblong whitened pods similar in form to the bone blades. Men and women of the highest grade, seated on their stools in a circle or a row, pass the blades back and forth behind their backs. The accompanying text, "Hide your children, Kasusuma [one who is always sick; one who presses his colleagues] comes to arrive," means that although noninitiates and junior initiates may be awed by a truly great kindi, he does not frighten or chase them. The sharing movement indicates that in the extensive kindi distributions of fees, gifts, and food, which reach a climax at the end of the initiations, no differences separate kin from nonkin: all must share without regard for the depletion of personal wealth. In a few communities, somewhat similar bone carvings (Biebuyck, 1973*a*, pl. 106) are used instead of sticks or axes as percussion instruments in the kongabulumbu rites. In one place a recent *bubake* initiate, who is making courtesy calls to villages, sits on a chair and beats two elephant bones to solicit gifts.

Thin blades in ivory or bone, sometimes shaped like the knives (*kimungu, kaluga*) used for banana stipe planting (pl. 84), may be worn by kanyamwa women, who hang them from their belts along with *katimbitimbi* figurines. The blades symbolize the assiduous work performed by initiated women. Similar miniature knives, made entirely of wood or bone, are used in ngandu and bombwa rites, often in conjunction with miniature axes and billhooks, to emphasize the virtues of industriousness: "My *kaluga* knife, I plant with it banana stipes in the inextricable growth." The *kaluga* knife is an essential tool for a woman, who receives it from her family upon marriage together with other symbols of good homemaking, such as a small knife for plucking the eyebrows, an ax, a broom, a dustpan, mats, pots, baskets, and fishing nets.

Oblong chips of ivory, less than 10 cm long, are hung from their belts by kanyamwa women as the equivalents of the small phallic and anthropomorphic sculptures called *katimbitimbi*. They are sometimes decorated with incised parallel or hatched lines or with bands of punctured circles.

Small ivory or bone chips, varying in shape from rectangular to ovoid, flattened on one side but sometimes convex on the other, may be strung together on raffia fibers and worn as a wristband. One chip may also be attached to a necklace as a pectoral. These chips may be embellished with circle-dot or dot designs. When the convex side has a crosslike division in light relief, the chip resembles a miniature shield. In rare examples the chip forms a rudimentary outline of a rounded, faceless bust.

Oval slabs, slightly convex, of ivory, bone, or wood (*lubiga*) are used in rites that mimic the game of dice. A preceptor, acting as the thrower (*mukubi*) of the dice, holds a disk in his open hands. Initiates, representing the players, each place a well-polished oval, concave piece of giant snail shell (*mbale*) or of bone (*mulika*) on the disk, while wagering and placing their stakes on the ground. The basic rules of the game are simple: when the "dice" are thrown, the position of *lubiga* is decisive; if *lubiga* falls on its back, each subsequent *mbale* shell that falls on its back marks a loss, and vice versa. Initiates are strictly prohibited from throwing dice, a restriction often dramatized during rites. Some are passionate players who lose or gain large sums and put virtually all their possessions at stake.

Large polished ivory and bone disks, called *kibukilo*, are used during kongabulumbu rites when initiates reenact a conventional divination scene (*bugila*). A disk serves as a support on which small tusks of wild pigs are placed before the diviner throws them on a hide and then reads meanings from the configuration. The interpretation is focused, not on the object, but rather on the implications and the results of divination. The scene most frequently presented leads to contention, false accusations, quarrels, poison ordeals, and death. In one instance, however, the divination ended on a positive note. An initiate had come to consult the oracle because his hunters were lost in the forest. The diviner, enacted by a preceptor, placed the tusks on the disk and then threw them. He explained that the men were not lost but that they simply had to be called. He then shouted several times until a voice was heard. As he continued to call, two initiates, stumbling along with walking sticks, arrived on the scene; they were carrying a small bundle of four pieces of wood hanging over their shoulders from a feather rope. The newcomers were quickly given food and attention. The entire scene was accompanied by the song: "The Batwa [Pygmies, Hunters] are lost in the forest; the diviner consults the oracle; subsequently they become visible [show up]." The performance glorifies the virtues of hospitality, which must be extended to the old and to those in distress. In yananio initiations, a mock divination is enacted when a woman is accused of having used witchcraft to kill her husband, but here the conventional type of oracle with *kibukilo* and pieces of tusks and bones is criticized for producing the wrong conclusion.

Dugout Canoes

The dugout canoe (*bwato*), carved in miniature form from wood, appears in the rites (*mutanga*) that precede bwami and in the lowest kongabulumbu initiation. It turns up again at the highest kindi level in modified form, either as a wooden canoe-shaped sculpture with large clitoris indications (part of the kindi basket) or as a piece of ivory (individually owned) suggestive of a vulva with a penis carved in relief on top of it (pl. 86).

In the kongabulumbu rite, the preceptor dances with the canoe and makes paddling movements.

> "A child [is] a dugout canoe; you will carve it, it will take you across [the river]." The aphorism, addressed to a man, relates that his early investments and labor in bringing up a son will be amply rewarded, for the son will take care of his father in old age. When the father is dead, the son will continue his good works.

> "My maternal uncles have carved very light canoes [in *musage* wood], and I linger [night falls, day breaks, and I am still here] at the wading place." A young man desiring the initiations complains that he has procured the necessary valuables but has received no other help. His agnates do not cooperate, and his powerful maternal uncles, who were high initiates, are dead.

> "Female [left] and male [right], on each side the Lwindi [large river] is traversed." The text warns against placing all one's expectations on one side of the kinship structure. One must cultivate relationships with the maternal uncles as well as with the father's group.

> "Big-Musage [tree] is light among others [in another land], is heavy in my own wading place [village]." One who is powerful in his own group complains that he is scorned elsewhere.

The flexibility of Lega symbolism is evidenced when the dugout, carried in the hand and beaten by a small pounder (*mombo*), is identified as a slit-drum (*lukumbi*).

> "They beat the lament of Yano [and] you have not asked me." An initiate complains because he was not consulted about the initiation of a member of his own group.

> "Lukumbi [Slit-Drum] would not have spoken; pounder tells him what to say." The text emphasizes that without the help of tutors one will fail in his attempts to be initiated into bwami.

> "The slit-drum of Kasala Malungu [lit., a vine used to perforate the pipe-stem; One-Who-Goes-Far] beats in Ikutu [lit., a crop of hair; a village]." This text criticizes a vagrant woman.

In a musage wa kindi rite, the wooden dugout with clitoris indication is held against a wooden phallus (*katimbitimbi*) after two preceptors, one of them holding the phallus against the lower belly, have executed coital movements. The object symbolizes a preferred wife (*kilanga*) "who removes the mixture [of sperm] from herself." The reference is to a woman who sleeps with a member of her husband's village but then quickly goes somewhere else, to imply, if she is accused, that she slept with someone not closely akin to her husband. This exegesis is amplified in a second aphorism that focuses on the wooden phallus: "Child of your father rots in the house, [he] Fornicator of women with fallen breasts." This text alludes to someone who committed adultery with the wife of a close kin (e.g., a son with one of his father's wives who is junior to his mother). Women (particularly if they are pregnant) magically destroy their husbands through this act. If a person dies as a result of such ritual pollution, the adulterer will not dare enter the deceased's house or participate in the rite of "jumping over the corpse."

Hammers

Hammers (*nondo*), made of ivory or bone, sometimes with a beautiful deep-red patina (pl. 87), belong to high-ranking initiates. Like iron hammers and bark beaters, they have a somewhat phallic form and lack handles, and so there may be only a minimal difference among a hammer, a phallus, and a bark beater. The term *nondo* may be applied to most types of insignia and initiation objects left by the dead to their successors; it evokes ideas of creativity, progenitorship, and continuity.

The most frequently recurring aphorisms sung in dance context about the hammer are the following:

"Kasesele [Little-Hammer] has forged Nondo [Big-Hammer]; Big-Hammer does not forge himself." A man alone cannot bear children; father was poor but his son is a master of the land.

"One hammer forges the iron [but] does not place the designs." One man alone cannot exercise all authority or wield all power.

"What were hammers are now old used objects." This text emphasizes the transience of things.

"The hammer that remained with [the] children breaks the *nkola* snail shell [or *nkumbi* nut]." Youth left on their own destroy the land.

"[The hammers] that were with Blacksmith turn into something that pounds the ground." If the master of the land dies, the children will remain without knowledge.

"In the place of Blacksmith is sought the hammer, in the place of Straightener-of-Irons." Wisdom is sought in bwami.

Axes or pegs are often substituted for hammers and identified as such. Handclapping or chopping movements with joined hands may also suggest hammers: "They sound in the forge: two hammers" is a reference to the two membranophones used in the rites, and "Kasesele [Little-Hammer] begins to clear the dense forest growth of vines" denotes a father who is happy because his son shows strength.

Knives

Lega blacksmiths manufacture a variety of knives to be used in hunting, killing, and cutting up animals, planting, trimming eyebrows, and shaving, and also for domestic purposes. The initiates own and use several types of knives as status and initiation objects. Knives, billhooks, axes, and spears are potentially deadly weapons of aggression. The bwami rites explicitly emphasize the avoidance of all sources of possible violence. Two aphorisms sung at the beginning of the lowest kongabulumbu rites stress that initiatory experience and violence cannot be reconciled: "A staff of raffia wood and a little spear together" refers to a master of the land who would be violent; "Katungulu [Phrynium] dances in a manner Isumo [Spear] does not dance." When these tools and weapons occur in the initiations, therefore, they are normally replaced by replicas in wood, ivory, and bone. Initiation knives are made entirely of ivory and bone, or they have copper blades and wooden or ivory handles.

In some areas, however, large knives are displayed at the lower grades. They are of two types. The first type (*menge, kimbelwa*) has a double-edged, pointed, iron blade and a short ivory or wooden handle. The ivory handle may be decorated with circle-dot designs; the wooden handle may be wrapped in copper wire. The knives are placed in a sheath (*buyamba*) made of parasol wood covered with antelope leather and adorned with copper bands. A leather strap is attached to two rings fixed on the sides of the sheath so that the knife can be slung across the shoulders. In some areas these knives were presented in ngandu, together with a billhook, an ax, and a planting knife, to inform the initiate that a person who acquires all these tools and still lacks food is stupid. These knives were rare in Legaland, and I saw them mostly in the northwestern region where they were owned by initiates and seemed to have been insignia of the master of the land.

The second type of large knife, called *kabemba,* has a double-edged, pointed, iron or copper blade and a wooden handle carved in the form of a human figurine or a bust (pl. 88). In some eastern Lega groups, these rare knives belong to *katangatanga,* the most senior initiate of the highest grade. In a kongabulumbu rite, the knife and a torch were placed near the feet of this senior initiate. Dancers simulated attempts to take the torch, and the exegesis noted that initiates do not steal.

The most commonly used knives are of two varieties: small knives called *bubenga* with double-edged pointed copper (rarely iron) blades and wooden or ivory handles; and miniature knives in ivory and bone (pl. 89; Biebuyck, 1973*a*, pl. 102), sometimes decorated with circle-dot designs. The latter are called *mwene,* the general term for knife; *kene (kele) ka mungu,* Little Knife of Big-One; or *kabala ngombe.*

The copper-bladed knives have various uses and meanings. They are symbols of initiates who have the "right of the knife of the pangolin," that is, those who have the privilege of proceeding with the cutting up of the pangolin and other sacred animals. I studied this aspect in detail in one Lega group. Some lineages possess the knife by virtue of an old, untraceable tradition. Others have bought the right from another group in exchange for valuables, including shell money, a cloth, a spear, a razor, a needle, a knife, and a chicken or a goat. The knife may be obtained only when a pangolin is killed within the territory of the acquiring lineage. The person who is actually granted the right on behalf of his group is a ngandu or yananio initiate. A goat, which is part of the payments, is ceremonially killed and distributed together with the pangolin among a large number of male and female initiates of the seller's and buyer's own lineages and of related groups. In fact, initiates from all lineages in the purchaser's clan are invited.

When an owner of a knife moves up to kindi, he transmits it to another initiate of his lineage, since he cannot own both the pangolin knife and the ivory knife of *ibago lya nzogu* (skinning of the elephant rite). When the owner dies, the knife is passed on to an agnatically or cognatically related initiate. He holds it on behalf of his own lineage and retransmits it to the deceased's rightful successor when a pangolin has been killed within the territory of his group. The new owner is not necessarily the son of the former owner, but rather a person in seniority position (one who is classified by all members of his group either as little father or as grandfather). The number of knives belonging to any one group differs, but it is certain that a maximal or major lineage will have several knives, depending somewhat on its internal structural division. In one instance each of the four minor lineages composing a major lineage had its own knife. Within the minor lineage, the knife circulated among its subdivisions, depending on seniority. For example, the Kisago minor lineage included the recognized subdivisions Isamigia, Pindi, and Samwangu. When the owner of the knife in Isamigia died four generations ago, the knife was temporarily kept in trust by an in-law of another group. It was then transferred to an initiate in the Pindi lineage, and after his death to one in the Samwangu division.

The copper-bladed knife is not used for the actual cutting. When the animal is brought to the village where it is to be distributed, the knife is inserted between the scales of the pangolin while elaborate dances are performed around the animal. When the animal has been singed and its scales have been removed, a cross is drawn with the knife on its back and the distribution of the meat can then begin. (Regular hunting knives are used for this purpose.)

In kongabulumbu rites the copper-bladed knife usually appears with a *ka-suku* torch. Kasuku is presented as the animal or the person who falls victim to the knife, which is also referred to as a spear (the blades are similar in shape to spearheads). The knife has ambiguous connotations in this context. When used with the torch it symbolizes achievement: "Little-Spear hits Nkenge [bongo antelope], the big animal of the hunting grounds." Little-Spear stands for a forceful and strong-willed person who completes the initiations. When the knife is used alone it connotes violence and its consequences, as in the following aphorisms:

> "Your child dies because of violence, it does not die in the cresting river." Kin who fight within their own group cause the death of a relative for whom not even blood payments will be made.
>
> "As dies Sanda [snake] so dies Ngomo [only child in a family]." A person who disturbs many others is killed like a snake.
>
> "The bad child, may it not have a mother, he Nyabambaluka [one who jumps up and leaves without listening]."
>
> "The little knife which the woman with fallen breasts has brought will destroy the reciprocal visits of kin." A woman who has a child from a previous marriage or out of wedlock will leave if the child is mistreated.
>
> "The iron is sharp [bitter], it is not tested [by making incisions] on the body." One must not show kinsmen a knife used for fighting.

Miniature knives carved from ivory or bone are usually owned by kindi, but initiates holding the *lutala* bag of *kansilembo* (connected with circumcision rites) may also possess them. The knives are manipulated mainly in the kindi rite of *ibago lya nzogu,* the skinning of the elephant, one of the final ceremonies during which the initiation house (i.e., the elephant) is partly demolished. The knives, as well as ivory spoons (assimilated with knives for the occasion), are used here for symbolic cutting. As the initiates are dancing around the house they sing: "Give me my little knife; I am participating in the skinning of the elephant"; or "Give me my little knife, let portions from the elephant come [loose]." Then they stick the knives into the roof of the initiation house while shouting their drum names. The action suggests that the initiates have caught an elephant in the trap and are distributing him, signifying that the candidate may be proud of his achievement: he has finished all the initiations and may now dispense the remaining goods. The initiates finally withdraw their knives and start cutting and pulling leaves from the roof in a haphazard manner—"The Banamulua skinned the elephant in a confused manner"—a final reminder that the group will fall apart without leadership and that the leader, a man of poise, arbitrates disputes without causing confusion.

In other rites the ivory knife or spoon is used in a mock fight. In one performance diviners have falsely accused a man's wife of witchcraft. The man brandishes a knife and simulates an attack on those who administered the poison during the ordeal. The rite criticizes the *bugila* divination that leads to further strife and turmoil.

Pegs

The beautifully patinated pegs (pl. 91; Biebuyck, 1973a, pl. 104), carved mostly from bone, are sometimes topped by a cone or a lozenge. The names of the pegs differ from community to community: 'a'unyi, nseti, kituta, kinsamba (lit., quill), and nondo (lit., hammer). The pegs have multiple uses and meanings at different levels of the initiations: they are frequently stuck into the ground to replace sticks, gaffs, quills, poles, or walking canes; a feather rope is attached to them to make a sacred fence; a rope may be tied from a fence or from the roof of the initiation house to a peg. In the kansilembo rites, a flattened ivory peg symbolizes the small hammer that every autonomous lineage possesses for petty jobs. In some areas the preceptor gently beats the chest of the candidate with a peg while inculcating bwami principles, as among some eastern Lega and the Bembe: "Put your heart down, you are beaten with your own hammer." Two pegs are beaten together to serve as percussion in kongabulumbu or to imitate the sound of hammers. While manipulating two scepters in a percussion rhythm, a preceptor sings, "In the forge, the hammer sounds," and "There sound hammers, in the place of Mutumbi [Blacksmith] they forge," to note that the master of the land is like the blacksmith, who attracts everybody. Emphasis occasionally focuses on the elephant bone of which the pegs are made: "Where Elephant rots, there are many ribs"; "Where Elephant eats, there are many leaves." When the senior, the initiate, or the master of the land dies, there are plenty of goods to share.

Phallic Sculptures

Small phallic sculptures, already noted as a subgroup of kalimbangoma figurines, are emblems of the virile status of kanyamwa women (pl. 92; Biebuyck, 1973a, pls. 80, 99; Burland, 1973, pls. 139–140). The phallic sculptures discussed here include large pieces in wood, ivory, or bone which have differing functions. Those in wood often realistically imitate a phallus with fire-blackened gland and urethra. They are usually part of the collectively owned baskets of the two highest grades, but they are also used in ngandu rites. The phalli are called katimbitimbi (lit., what shivers of desire) or kizingio (lit., a spear that only skims the animal; a penis with insufficient erection). The sculptures, when replaced by bark beaters, pointed stipes, or torches, are known as nkingi, yango, or kasuku.

In one rite the object is simply shown. "They cut [the prepuce] in the circumcision rites, the Stupid-Ones arrange [cut evenly] the penis that will seduce," criticizes ungrateful persons; "Strong Phallus does bear twins" praises the achievements of a strong person. The phalli, however, are manipulated most often in a highly suggestive manner. They are frequently used together with a feather hat, a perforated mussel shell, and a miniature slit-drum or dugout canoe. Holding the sculpture against a miniature canoe, the preceptor sings, "The preferred wife [tries to] get herself out of the mixings of sperm," to criticize a woman who sleeps with people of her village and then runs elsewhere to pretend that she was with outsiders. Another text, "The child of your father rots in the house, [you] Fornicator of women with fallen breasts," informs the initiates that one who slept with a relative's wife will not dare to enter the house where the kinsman lies dead.

In one rite two preceptors respectively hold a phallus and a perforated mussel shell against their pubic areas. The second preceptor is then pushed with coital movements against a pole of the initiation house. This action contrasts the faithful initiated wife with an adulterous woman, as explained in the songs: "Katimbitimbi, Little-Penis that has not seen the circumcision ceremonies"; "The woman with fallen breasts removes her husband from the heart, [she] Nyalukambula [Mrs. Remover; here, one who mixes the sperm]."

In one community a small phallic stick and a miniature slit-drum are part of the yananio basket. During the dance the slit-drum is beaten with the phallus, but only one of several texts sung has sexual implications: "The slit-drum of Kasala Malungu [*kasala*, lit., a vine used to perforate the median rib of a banana leaf used as a pipestem; Malungu, a plural personification of *idungu*, far] sounds in [the village] Ikutu [Much-Hair]." This text describes women who run to faraway places to look for men.

Yango is one of the most complex characters appearing in initiations. Although sometimes presented as a phallus, a pounder, or a hammer, he is usually suggested by a freshly cut piece of *kyombi* wood or a section of banana stipe without artistic value. The small pole, sometimes called Sabeina, Father-of-Black-People, is handled in various ways to symbolize several different personages: a great initiate who visits many places (Isamalomengi); a child who must not be neglected by Nyamalendelo (a woman who always runs off); a person who flees from poverty, settles elsewhere, and then returns home a rich man but loses his wealth because of debts; a corpse (*kitumba kya Nkutu*). When Yango is depicted by a realistic phallus carved in *kabungwe* wood with the gland blackened by fire, the focus is completely different. The sculpture is held below the beaded diadem of a kanyamwa: "The wife of a Big-One may be alone in the glen; she does not call you"; "The wife of a Big-One does not remain outdoors [for] the foot surpasses the arm." The emphasis is on the diadem (i.e., the woman), which Yango tries in vain to reach. A *yango* pole made of something other than ivory is usually owned by a ngandu initiate who represents a distinct lineage of the local clan community. In one large group, I found nine *yango* poles belonging to each of the recognized major lineages.

Pounders

Pounders (*mugumo, nkingi*) in hardwood (*kabungwe* or *butulo*), rarely in ivory, are used by men to beat soaked bark (pl. 93). In kongabulumbu rites a warthog tusk evokes the idea of the pounder: "Ngulube [Pig] who gave you the striations of Nkingi [Pounder]" reminds the candidate of the persons who gave him bwami. In higher initiations the ivory pounder is sometimes used as the equivalent of wooden or ivory phallic carvings. In one community the action centering on the ivory pounder illustrated several characters. Dancers carried it around to represent Isamalomengi, Mr. Many-Halting-Places, the great initiate who visits numerous villages where initiations are held. A preceptor rested the pounder on his shoulder while other dancers tried to grab it to symbolize Mulamba, the woman who is taken by others. Supported on both hands by a preceptor who rocked it like a child, the pounder portrayed a child whose mother, Nyamalendelo, had run away. When placed against the dancer's penis in coital movement, it was Kisesa, the slanderer who destroys the village. It was held in the hand with the butt down, dropped repeatedly on the ground, and finally placed near the candidate to represent Nkingi, a person who dies in a foreign place and whose corpse nobody wants to bury. Finally an initiate took care of it.

Spear and Shield

In most communities a spear (*ishumo, ikemelo*) and a shield (*ngabo, katenge*) are part of the collectively owned yananio baskets. The short spear made entirely of wood is a small, sometimes whitened, pointed stick, which may be replaced by a short beam called *mutondo* (lit., ridgepole). The shield is either an ovoid piece of ajouré wickerwork (pl. 11) or a small rectangular object made of *musage* planks. As a miniature replica of a plank door, the latter is sometimes simply called *keibi*, door.

When male and female initiates make their ceremonial entry into the village, they march slowly and silently in a long row; the men shake their reed swatters and the women carry their husbands' shoulder bags and the covered initiation baskets. They are preceded by an initiate who carries a drum and beats it with one stick. Another drum hangs from a pole near the initiation house, where the candidate and his tutor are waiting. On stools placed between the latter two and the initiates sit two high initiates, bent over so that their foreheads touch. An initiate, called *mukemezi*, runs around the file of incoming initiates while brandishing the wooden spear and parrying imaginary attacks with the shield. He is an aide-de-camp (*kalombola* or *kalia*) of a kindi. The scene symbolizes warfare: it is as if the initiates arriving in the village were bringing a form of war—not a real war, of course, but a danger that emanates from the presence of many initiates and initiation objects, a warning that henceforth no one must infringe upon the laws and prescriptions of the association. The two seated initiates represent protection from and defense (*kikinduko*, lit., stumbling stone) against the coming war. A preceptor leading the row approaches the seated initiates and asks them: "Shall we engage in a fight or not?" "What is the situation here?" Receiving no answer, he withdraws, while the *mukemezi* initiate runs around waving the spear and shield. Another initiate leaves the row, approaches the two seated initiates, talks with them, and receives a reply: the intentions are good, everything is ready, and there is no threat of violence. A shouting dialogue (*mbila*) develops between the leading preceptor and the tutor to ensure that indeed everything is well prepared and that there is no basis for offense. The initiates did not beg to come to the initiations but rather were invited. The candidate's village is compared with an inextricable forest, a difficult area to clear and to pass through, an area full of potential dangers. The initiates filing in then enter the village and dance with the reed swatters and with the spear and shield.

In some groups, after these preliminaries, the row of initiates moves toward the building where the candidate has stored food supplies, gifts, and payments. An aggressive mood is expressed in one of the songs: "The Red Ants enter into the house *zogozogo* [onomatopoeia]." This notifies the candidate that the initiates, like red ants, will devour everything in sight and that they will destroy the house if the goods stored inside are not plentiful.

The spear and the shield are occasionally used in other contexts. For example, a preceptor dancing with a chimpanzee skull is attacked by a dancer who wields a spear and a shield. The chimpanzee counterattacks; the spear holder flees, leaving his spear behind, but he soon regains his courage, returns, picks up his spear, and kills the chimpanzee: "I came having been talked to [invited]; Nkamba [Chimpanzee] bites me a wound." The chimpanzee represents a person whose goods were taken by another (the spear holder); the thief passes through the chimpanzee's village, where the people now want to attack and kill him in revenge. The thief is smart enough to escape the attack (a thief threatened by retaliation from the injured party placed a fresh banana leaf on his head to indicate that he knew they wanted to "skin" him; this forewarning helped him to escape retaliation) and later causes even more harm.

In some dances a stick identified as *mutondo* (ridgepole) is used instead of a spear. A preceptor makes a mock attack against the candidate, then holds the stick horizontally and turns it again vertically: "Let Wakasili [one who has a spear that kills right then and there] who kills me with hatred, let him be with ten wounds"; "He who gives you the little spear with the sharp point and smooth shaft gives you war; he who gives you the walking cane [made] of a raffia [midrib] gives you greatness." The preceptor continues to assault the candidate, but others stop him: "Katungulu [a leaf] dances, let Kasumo [Little-

Spear] not dance." The nonviolent nature of bwami is dramatically emphasized in this dance action: the initiates are not men of the spear but rather of the smoothly carved walking stick.

In other dances the wooden spear appears in a mock attack against a person carrying a small plank door. The exegesis centers on the door: "What has emaciated a mwami [is] to close and to open." This often quoted aphorism applies overtly to a bachelor who must do all the work alone. When the spear is emphasized, the text has covert sexual overtones and criticizes a man who runs around with too many women.

The wooden spear may also serve as a flagpole. In some rites the preceptor dances with the spear to which bark or raffia cloth has been fastened; he brandishes it in the air while other dancers vainly attempt to seize it. The emphasis on the high and almost unreachable cloth symbolizes the bwami initiations: "The fruit of *mulanga* [tree] makes my saliva dry up." The pole may refer to a person who had prepared for the initiations but died prematurely and left his valuables to be used by others: "The cloth of *koku* tree; the fruit becomes the share [the part] of others."

Spoons

The ivory and bone spoons (*lukili, kalukili*) made by the Lega in a wide variety are not discussed in detail here. (For a description of them see Biebuyck, 1981c.) The spoons, measuring 13 to 19 cm, have an oval, concave, rather shallow, unadorned bowl, a stem, and a knop. The knop is sometimes replaced by a second bowl, by legs, or by a human face (pls. 94–95; Biebuyck, 1973a, pls. 95–97). The stem is carved in ajouré or as a full human figurine, a bust, or a wedged knife; it may be broad and straight, scalloped, wedged, elliptical, or oval. The marvelous patinations are light yellow, yellow-brown, red, or reddish brown; even the bone spoons are well polished and smooth.

Like other sculptures, the spoons are owned by members of the bwami association as status symbols and initiation devices. During the rites spoons are simply danced with, carried on the shoulder, or caressed; they are used for symbolic cutting and scraping, or for symbolically feeding a masker. In some contexts the spoons allude to sex and women, to transgenerational continuity, and to specific uses (e.g., the spoon that a relative places in the mouth of a person to save him after he drinks poison during an ordeal).

Stools

Large four-legged spherical stools in polished wood have enormous significance as initiation objects. The data I have presented elsewhere (Biebuyck, 1973a, pl. 101; 1977c) are not repeated here. Rarely used miniature stools in wood appear in the women's *muzigi* rite of yananio. The exegesis is based on only one of the scores of aphorisms reserved for the larger stools: "Kisumbi [Stool] smells the rotten odor of the buttocks." The text has a double implication: a man accuses his wife of adultery and wants to chase her, but the initiates say that is not the proper way to act; a young man sent on an errand by a senior refuses to go because, he says, it is too dangerous, but the initiates urge him to go anyway. Among the Nyindu, miniature stools are made of leopard or lion bone and are wrapped in the hides of these animals. The Nyindu stool relates to a junior who received the stool (i.e., authority) but sits uncomfortably on it: he is unprepared for the exercise of authority.

Miniature stools in bone or ivory have a very different meaning in other Lega areas. They usually belong to a person who owns the *lutala* bag, which contains a variety of objects related to circumcision: a knife (to circumcise), a spoon (to be placed in the mouth of the young man undergoing the operation), a sachet with a razor (to shave the pubic hair), a calabash (called the testicle of *kansilembo;* to catch the blood dripping from the wound), a feather rope (called the penis of *kansilembo;* to make all sacred enclosures), a small oblong copper blade trimmed with beads (called *kalambo ka kansilembo;* representing a vulva), and a miniature replica of the stool on which the boys sit for the operation. These bags are owned only by certain lineages. The *lutala* holder is always an initiate, although not necessarily a high-ranking one, and he has the authority to construct a separate circumcision lodge. Even if the owner is not a kindi, he still has the right to own some ivory objects "because he is a sororal nephew of the kindi." His extraordinary privileges are also reflected by his right to guard the belt and the kanyamwa wife of a deceased kindi. Kindi sleep in his hamlet when they journey to the initiations.

The only miniature ivory stool I collected (Biebuyck, 1973a, pl. 100) illustrates a change of function because circumcision rites were no longer systematically organized. It belonged to a yananio who had received it through his own senior brother (a kindi) from a deceased classificatory senior brother (a kindi and a *lutala* holder). The man kept the stool and used it as a *kalimbangoma* in the yananio display of those objects.

Walking Canes or Staffs

Walking canes, generally called *mukulu* or *mulonge,* are of different types. Some are simple uncarved sticks (*nkoma*) used as supports by invalids or disabled persons: "The *nkoma* of the invalid, of the leper, is the thing with which he defends himself." The initiates have five varieties of carved walking canes or staffs, all linked with particular statuses. The unadorned but well-polished and highly patinated *kitendele* or *mukulu wibondo* is made from the median rib of a raffia tree leaf; it may be owned by any initiate of ngandu grade or higher (pl. 4). *Mukulu wa kansilembo* is carved in *kansilembo* wood and is linked with the kansi-lembo initiation. The *lutala* cane, made of *muntonko* or *ibesebese* wood, flattened at the end and blackened by fire, is owned by initiates who have the *lutala* right associated with the organization of circumcision ceremonies and with certain ritual distributions of animals. When this cane is used as a secret percussion instrument in circumcision rites and in kongabulumbu and kindi, it is called *sabukyangwa. Matakale* is a stick, sometimes made of *kitankondo* wood, adorned with a hollow ivory figurine (into which the top of the stick is inserted; Olbrechts, 1946, pl. 198) and owned by kindi. *Musumbo wa mizegele* or *mungema* is made entirely of wickerwork like the *mizegele* rattles; it has several superposed bulbs and is reserved for kindi (Biebuyck, 1973a, pl. 55).

An initiate carries his staff on many occasions: when he journeys to participate in the rites, when he speaks solemnly before his kin or his peers, when he gives orders or launches a prohibition. He rests his hands and his chin on the staff to show that his power comes not from physical strength but rather from the word. He separates (*kusunga*) fighters and prohibits (*kulongeka*) fighting with his staff because he has *lusungu,* the authority to decide what is right.

The walking stick of a deceased yananio or kindi is displayed together with his hats, aprons, belts, bags, and stools outside the village near the edge of the forest. This rite (*kakenge*) takes place a few months after the burial ceremonies. A sororal nephew of high status is allowed to appropriate the initiate's objects. During the ceremonial distribution and allocation of the deceased's wealth, several walking sticks are displayed on the ground to signify the categories of agnatic and cognatic kin who have rights in the legacy.

The walking canes are also used as initiation devices during the bwami rites. In some ceremonies a walking stick is placed transversally on the ground near the entrance to the initiation house, where it forms a symbolic threshold. In some ngandu rites the initiates dance with their walking canes, which they then place together and speak of as "old house poles standing up firmly in the village of Isabanabengi [Mr. Many-Children], yet the anus [i.e., the bottom of the poles] is rotten." The aphorism complains about a numerically strong but internally divided lineage group. The initiates next tie the canes together in a bundle, which one by one the dancers attempt to lift: "The bundle of rafters that my maternal uncles have tied together" signifies the power of the maternal uncles.

Untying the staffs and holding them in the air, the dancers sing: "The noninitiate is a staff [made] of raffia wood; even if it is strong it does not kill a snake." Even if a man has several wives, he amounts to nothing if he has not achieved bwami. Finally they hold the walking canes along their bodies and speak of the power and social influence of sororal nephews: "The sororal nephew is a pole of *nkenze* [very hard wood], appropriate for [supporting] the men's house."

In other ngandu rites the preceptor places a *mukulu wibondo* in the hands of the candidate and sings: "He who gives you *mukulu wibondo* gives you the land [authority]." The walking cane is a symbol of peace. The initiate is not a fighter or a warmonger, but rather an arbitrator and a peacemaker; he is not a man of the spear but of the staff. This concept is clarified even more in another text sung on this occasion: "He who gives you the little spear with the sharp point and the well-polished shaft, he gives you war; he who gives you *mukulu wibondo* gives you the land."

In kindi rites the oldest initiates in the village where the ceremonies are held stand in a circle with their chins resting on their hands, which clasp the staffs: "Basamikulu [the masters of the walking cane] set the village ablaze; they have no spear." This text reflects the good intentions of the hosts: guests arriving in the village will find food and gifts; there will be dancing and joy, and no one will think about quarrels or violence. In some *kilinkumbi* and *bele muno* rites, where the kindi display respectively ivory masks and figurines, a *matakale* staff topped with a figurine stands near the configuration of objects to symbolize the peaceful mood that pervades the rites.

Various Carvings

Armbands, Bracelets, and Bangles

These objects (*kimpondo, nsubi*), made of iron and copper, are worn mainly by women; they are more common in some areas than in others. Men have few bracelets and bangles (*bikingi*), which may be carved from ivory and are sometimes decorated around the rims with circle-dot designs. These pieces of jewelry are not the subject of elaborate interpretations during initiation rites. Persons who are born *mubake* (the result of their parents' close in-group marriage) or who are initiated to *bubake* (a preferential status conferred upon a beloved son) wear two copper bracelets on each leg. A copper bracelet is sometimes buried on the village grounds to mark "buying the village land." The bracelets are not status and power symbols, as they are in other ethnic regions (e.g., southwestern Zaire), but as an item in matrimonial exchanges they are used as adornments. The tight armbands and bangles placed just under the knee by women produce slight swellings, which are greatly admired.

Bellows

Realistic miniature bellows (*muguba*) are carved from ivory or bone and range from 7 to 13 cm. They are sometimes surmounted by a short handle in the form of a lozenge-shaped head (pl. 81) and decorated with bands of dots and zigzag designs. When placed upright, the sculptures resemble highly stylized anthropomorphic figurines. Together with other small sculptures, they are displayed on the belts of kanyamwa women to signify their outstanding achievements and impeccable character. Two major ideas are expressed in aphorisms: "Muguba lets the breast fall; it will not stand up again," notes that an inveterately bad person cannot be improved. The interpretation fits the stylized humanized form of the bellows characterized by two protruding hollowed-out rectangles or polygons. In real bellows these concave breastlike boxes are covered with antelope or goat hide and are pumped to activate the fire. The aphorism "The animal hide is smart; it will participate in a journey on which the goat has not gone" indicates that although the goat is killed and eaten, its hide survives as a membrane for the bellows. The personified hide here symbolizes a woman who accomplished more than her own mother or her tutor.

Dog Bells

Unadorned, crudely carved dog bells may simply be attached to the neck of a stylized animal figurine to identify it as a dog. The bell without clappers symbolizes the bereavement of a man whose initiated wife has died: "[Dog Bell] which chased together with Hunting-Dog has its clappers broken." In some areas the bells (*kizugu, lungungu*) are part of the lutumbo lwa kindi baskets and are usually handled and interpreted as if they were slit-drums (*lukumbi*). The opening of the initiation basket ceremony begins with the dog bell, which was beaten with a small stick.

> "How is that you intoned the refrain [of the songs] of kindi, without calling me?" The text points out that when the high initiations are organized all kindi who have kinship connections with the candidate must be invited.
>
> "Lukumbi [slit-drum] would not have spoken; Mombo [pounder] is the reason why it [he] speaks." This idea, often expressed in different ways, stresses that the initiates give meanings to objects and actions.
>
> "Lukumbi whose sound carries far has been beaten in Ikutu [Much-Hair]." This aphorism gives the answer to the question asked in the first text: the initiates called someone, but that person did not hear. This explanation is meaningless because kindi are informed through secret messages.

Horns

Short ivory horns (*mpanda*; pl. 96) with lateral mouthpieces and pierced butts for suspension are blown in war dances; they also announce the killing of an elephant. The ivory horn is occasionally mentioned during initiations, but I have not seen it used.

Leopard Teeth

The necklaces (*mwambalo*) worn by initiates are made of *kigela* (small polished disks of snail shells) and of oblong light-blue, red, and white beads (*mizaba*), which may have been imported since the earliest contacts with Arabs and Europeans. Varying numbers of real leopard teeth (*mibanga;* and sometimes buffalo, bongo antelope, crocodile, and imported lion teeth) are attached to these necklaces. Naturalistically carved imitation leopard teeth (pl. 85) may replace real ones. Although initiates of the ngandu, yananio, and kindi grades all wear genuine leopard teeth, only kindi are entitled to wear the carved ones. Leopard teeth worn as a necklace are symbols of status and power and rarely occur as initiation objects, except in a rite that is transitional between kongabulumbu and the higher levels. At that time, a father formally designates a son as his preferred candidate for the higher grades. During this rite, which signifies the son's "complete change of heart" (i.e., of behavior, of mental outlook), one necklace made of oblong beads and leopard teeth is placed around a small termitaria, and another necklace of small polished snail shells and leopard teeth is hung around a pot. The preceptor then interchanges the objects to symbolize the unity of the bwami association: "In bwami, Ntata [the highlands of the east] and Malinga [the lowlands of the west] meet around one neck."

Mancala Game Boards

The crudely carved miniature mancala game board (*lusolo*) is part of the yananio basket. The aphorisms sung when a preceptor dances with the object note that the same care, reflection, and attention needed for a successful game must also be applied to speech. The wise person "knows how to speak"; he does not get hopelessly lost in words and does not interfere unnecessarily in problems that do not concern him.

Mortars

Tubular miniature mortars (*kilunga;* about 13 to 14 cm high) are carved from ivory; some rest on a stool-like base and are adorned with circle-dots (pl. 90). They are seldom used in the rites; most commonly the mortar is associated with a miniature pestle (*mututo*). The aphorism "The moving of an Old-One: a mortar and his pestle!" refers to an old woman moving to another place and carrying a mortar and pestle as her vital, possibly her only, belongings. The text conveys the idea that a person is often unable to conquer his vices and his faults.

Neck Rests

I have never seen an ivory neck rest (*lubigo*), but Sweeney (1935, pl. 472) and Radin and Sweeney (1964, pl. 151) reproduce one with a rectangular base and slightly concave top supported by three columns and decorated with circle-dot designs. I have heard the neck rest mentioned only once in a kindi initiation: "He who died does not return; he goes and throws the neck rest away."

Sticks

Small sticks (*nkoma, mututo*) carved from ivory or bone, sometimes with striations, represent the walking cane (*nkoma*) that a sick or crippled person uses to support or defend himself. A *yango* stick or a mortar is occasionally beaten with it to criticize a man who hits his initiated wife: "The beater of women brandishes the stick and pounds it hard."

Tusks

Small, frequently very old, elephant tusks (*mulamba*) with dark-brown patination and adorned with linear designs are sometimes among the contents of the kindi baskets. The tusk represents Mulamba, who is either a woman excessively inclined to visit other places and to leave her husband behind or a restless young man looking for trouble.

Whistles

Ivory whistles (*mpingu*) have a tubular body with a rounded or obtuse conelike gland and two pierced or notched ears (pl. 97). Whistles are sometimes blown during initiations to induce the shades to avert rain. One of the most powerful actors in the dramas of circumcision and initiation is Kimbilikiti or Kingili. The singer gives instructions and sings praises with a kazoo, usually a simple reed pipe covered with a leaf or bat skin to produce vibrations, but in some groups Kingili has an ivory object that may be in the form of a whistle. In a rare rite in which a whistle is displayed, it is used as a symbol of evildoing. Witches and persons who intend to ambush someone are said to use a whistle to imitate the call of parrots in order to lure their victim: "He who will die because of *mwale* [an ambush; here, the whistle]; the parrots tell him where to go"; "The words that Parrot speaks have killed the tree climber." In the *bugila* form of divination, a whistle fastened to a hollow stick, a genet hide, or a *mbusu* pod was blown by the diviner. The object, activated by the whistle, was then given to a bystander, who was requested to designate the culprit. It is said that the object began to move and guided the person holding it in the direction of the guilty party.

PART SIX

Bwami Traditions

Lega Migrations and Internal Subdivisions

The bwami association, with its social, political, legal, ritual, economic, didactic, philosophical, artistic, and aesthetic functions, is universal among the Lega, and it has numerous ramifications among other ethnic groups. Like the circumcision rites, bwami is very old; its fundamental structure and organization seem to antedate the emergence of the Lega as a distinct people. In trying to determine the age of this basic institution, it must be remembered that bwami is a hierarchically graded association operating within the confines of autonomous clan and lineage communities. These ritually independent entities are formed by local patrilineal clan groups, which are segmented into several lineage levels. Parts of these groups, after breaking away from the main unit, settled in other communities with which they trace affinal or cognatic links. Lineages of other clan origins have been incorporated or assimilated into the local core by virtue of the same principles. The incorporated units either are of Lega and pre-Lega background or represent fragments of neighboring ethnic groups.

Autonomous communities maintain special connections with other similar groups because of their remote common origin within the Lega as a whole, their geographical proximity, and intermarriages and interdependencies resulting from the acquisition of certain bwami rites. The Banasalu, an independent ritual unit in the Beia sector of Pangi territory, for example, trace strong historical ties with the Bakyunga and Beigala communities located north of them in the Bakisi sector of Shabunda territory. The Banasalu maintain close cognatic ties with the Banakagela and the Banampompo, situated to the south in the Babene sector of Pangi territory, and consider them to be descended from two of Salu's married daughters. Segments of the Banasalu have broken off from their base to settle in other communities where new ties have been established.

The independent traditions of many of the autonomous communities place the emergence of the Lega at locations near the Lwalaba (Zaire) River, northwest of present-day Lega country. Some groups mention areas (Mateka, noted by the Liga; Bubundu, by the Ngabo and Ngoma) south of the city of Kisangani. The northwesternmost Lega groups indicate an area (Muntungu) west of the Lwalaba in regions now inhabited by the Mitoko and the Lengola. Two frequently suggested places are easily found on the maps. Ilundu or Kilundu (Kirundu on the maps), a spot near the confluence of the Luwalaba and the Lilu rivers, is the farthest point of origin recalled by the southeasternmost Babongolo. Kakono or Kakolo (Kakoro on the maps), south of Ilundu at the confluence of the Lwalaba and the Lowa, is named in the traditions of numerous Lega communities. Other suggested locations on the Lwalaba are Munginingini (near Ponthierville), Mingalangala, and Katundugulu (between the Lowa and the Ulindi, tributaries of the Lwalaba).

Early movements predating the settlement of the Lega and of Lega-related peoples on the Lwalaba River are virtually untraceable. Delhaise (1909b, pp.

47–48) recounts a tradition, probably derived from the Lega's Museme epic, that the Lega emigrated from southern areas now occupied by the Zimba (Binja). This suggestion, which contradicts traditions known to the Lega, may apply to groups that were originally in the region but are now incorporated with the southern Lega. According to Merlot (1931*a*), the history of the epic hero Museme would have centered in the region of Mount Ruwenzori, far to the northeast of Legaland. There Museme encountered and defeated a forest man, Bungoe, who resembled an enormous animal. Museme subsequently attempted to climb the mountain with the aid of a bamboo stick but, encountering strong winds and heavy snow near the summit, he fell to his death. Merlot (ibid.) also claims that the quartz stones used in the *kasisi* rite of bwami represent the two large and two small summits of Mount Ruwenzori. In another version (also noted by Merlot), Museme was a Pygmy who led a nomadic life, eating forest fruits (*makunzu*), hunting with wooden spears and clubs (*nkinzi*), and living in primitive shacks (*pala*). One day he entered into his drum and let himself float; he arrived at a great water and disappeared. Museme's son Mutua, however, met the blacksmith Lulimba during his travels in the area of Lake Tanganyika. Lulimba taught Mutua to make bridges and canoes, to build houses, and to smith. The ancestor Lega, later joining the descendants of Mutua, brought crops and the art of making fire with a fire drill. The descendants of Lega and Mutua intermarried and gave rise to the Lega clans.

Moeller (1936, pp. 39–52 and passim) says the Lega originated in the northeast mainly because fragments of groups called Lega are found as remnant populations from Mount Ruwenzori to Lake Tanganyika. According to Mulyumba (1978, p. 4), the "mythical tradition" places the source of the Lega in the region of Lake Edouard, probably in Bunyoro or Buganda. From there they moved southwestward through the high grasslands of Rutshuru into the forest regions of Walikale, and then on to the Lwalaba and the Lowa confluence. Scanty ethnohistorical evidence, however, supports this northeastern beginning. The western Lega occasionally mention as their place of origin Kitatenge (lit., what does not move), a lake (possibly Lake Edouard) or a swamp (perhaps the swamps in the Lwalaba area). The rarely specified Kyumo kya Mwiduko (translated in Swahili as Kilima ya Mungu, the Mountain of God), possibly meaning the high Ruwenzori Mountain on the Zaire-Uganda divide, is more likely. The use of large quartz stones (*kalumbilumbi, mukito*) in some of the Lega's highly secret *kasisi* rites may substantiate the tradition of an ancient northeastern origin. The initiates explicitly state that the stones come from a remote place and are not found in Legaland. In addition, numerous entities called Lega are dispersed among other ethnic groups in a huge area lying between Mount Ruwenzori and Legaland, on the boundaries between Zaire and Uganda. These groups, together with the Pygmies, have important ritual roles in the enthronement rites for chiefs.

One Lega group in the Mount Ruwenzori area in the northern region of Beni has maintained relative independence, and its cultural position is important. In this area many distinct ethnic groups have converged over a period of time;

they are identified as Bahira, Bakira, Bahumbi, Basiru, Banisanza, Banangala, Basongora, Banande, Mbuba, and Lega. The Mbuba and their Pygmies were possibly the earliest inhabitants in the region. The Mbuba are related to the Mamvu and their origins are completely different from those of the other groups mentioned. The Lega, who came next, acknowledge the initial presence of the Mbuba. The Banisanza, who arrived after the Lega, claim that the Mbuba and the Lega were already established when they entered the region. The Lega came to the Ruwenzori area as hunters (accompanied by their dog Bandurumba); in fact, they were probably called Balega because of their toughness, indicated by their preference for hunting over the agricultural life of their land of origin. These Lega established numerous linkages with the Badulu-Mbuba, whom they call their maternal uncles, and they speak a form of Mbuba. From the Pygmies via the Mbuba they learned about the circumcision rites, which they call *lusumba* (a term the Komo use to designate a variety of esoteric practices). In contrast with the many groups emerging in the region, the Lega note that upon their arrival they had no "drum" (i.e., no chieftainship), but they do not mention bwami.

The Lega, settling mainly in and near the foothills of Mount Ruwenzori, included the subgroups Bayuhu, Bamandza, Babioma, Bakiti, Babinga, Bandiolo, Bakumbule, Basilimwanga, and Bangboka. The Bandiolo are considered the traditional owners of Mount Ruwenzori, which they call Kitwa (Tall Mountain) or Bihya (Place of Cold), and they have exclusive rights over the special quartz crystals (*ntsururu*) found there. The crystals are rubbed with oil and used by many groups in rainmaking ceremonies. The importance of quartz crystals (of unknown but very ancient origin) in one of the most secret bwami rites strongly supports a possible relationship between the Lega of Mount Ruwenzori and the Lega group studied in this volume.

Whatever the Lega's place of origin, their known history shows early contacts with the Pygmies, the Mituku, the Komo, and the Songola. Genealogical recitations agree that Lega married Kakinga, a Pygmy (Twa) girl, and that early descendants of Lega (founders of large subdivisions and clan groups) were married to Mitoko, Komo, or Songola women. In the same genealogies, southern Lega groups continue to trace agnatic connections with the Mitoko and with the Kwame and the Konjo (two mixed groups situated north of the Lega), and they speak about ancient quarrels and wars with the Mitoko, Komo, and Songola. More important, the Lega bwami system is most closely affiliated with the *bukota* association of the Mitoko (the term *mukota* is sometimes used by the Lega as a synonym for a great initiate).

The major southeastward movement of the Lega started near the confluence of the Lwalaba and the Lowa rivers. (Even northeastern Lega place their beginnings on the extreme western boundaries of Shabundu territory in Bwele, Ikozi, and Ilimu.) The traditions are virtually unanimous in noting that here the Lega were confronted by a certain Kimbimbi and later by his son Bukutu. Some groups identify Kimbimbi with the Mitoko; others reject this idea but do not substitute other tribal names. The Babongolo in southeastern Legaland claim that the Lega were chased by Kaluba, the founder of Luba groups in the Kasai region. Retreating before Kimbimbi, the Lega gradually spread into the Ulindi and Elila basins. Both these rivers originate in the high mountains on the western shore of Lake Tanganyika and flow through the heart of Legaland toward the Lwalaba.

There is no unified genealogy to account for all Lega subgroups. In the late nineteenth and the twentieth centuries the political and administrative organization introduced by the colonial government heavily influenced both interdependence and differentiation by offering opportunities for new leadership and regional autonomy. Evidence provided by separately stated traditions points strongly to an original subdivision of four major complexes or groups among the Lega. This situation is reflected in the incredibly complex genealogical recitation of the northeastern (Basimwenda) and southeastern (Bakabango-Babongolo) Lega (see diagram).

1. The Shile branch is represented among the Basimwenda and the so-called Bamuzimu (both northeastern Lega), the Liga, the southern Lega, and among the Nyindu and the Bembe (the largest number of Bembe clans trace origins to Shile). The history of this branch is closely interwoven with that of several pre-established groups: Nyindu, Basim'minje, Basi'asumba, Bagunda, Bagezi, and Bainda. Some of these were Twa Pygmies; others were already mixed groups of Bantu and Pygmies (diagrams 1, 2, 3 in appendix).

2. The Kisi branch, consisting of Beigala, Banangoma, Banangabo, Bamuguba, and Bakyunga, is established mainly in a large area of northern Shabunda, but numerous offshoots live among the western, southern, and southeastern Lega. The early history of this branch is intermingled with that of the Songola and the southern Komo, with whom they have been in contact for a long time (diagrams 4 and 5 in appendix).

3. The Batukya-Ikama and Nkulu branches, often merged as the children of Lega's son Isimbio (also called Koima, Komma, or Kemma), constitute the bulk of the southern and southeastern Lega identified as Bakabango and Babongolo. There are also numerous lineages among the Bamuzimu, the Bembe, and the Lega known as Beia and Babene of Pangi territory. This group developed the closest contacts with the Zimba and Bangubangu (diagram 6 in appendix).

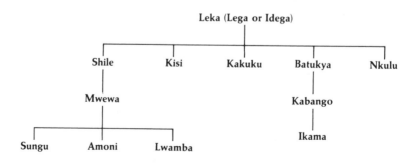

4. The Bakabango consider the Kakuku to be a branch that moved farther southwest and became incorporated with the Kusu. Fragments of the so-called Bangengele are probably an offshoot of this branch.

Three current Lega administrative subdivisions—Bamuzimu, Beia, and Babene—are not mentioned explicitly in these genealogies. They are composed of fragments of the Kisi and Batukya-Nkulu branches. The Zimu and Beia are large and powerful administrative units, whereas the Babene is a much smaller entity, and hence genealogical records have been manipulated. The Beia (diagram 7 in appendix) claim to be the descendants of Mwiya, allegedly a son of Lega, and give separate status to the Kisi and Isimbio branches. The Beia believe the Bamuzimu are descended from Mombo, one of Lega's two daughters, and her brother Isimbio. (This seems simply to be a covert reference to the mixed character of the group.) Most of the Babene are thought to be the descendants of a son of Mwiya, although some have Babongolo origins.

Traditions of the Northwestern, Western, and Southern Lega

These three communities have no theories about the origins of the lower bwami grades, kongabulumbu to ngandu. In fact, most groups have no tradition about the beginning of bwami. Oral traditions claim that the founding ancestors already had bwami grades but do not speculate on the origins of those grades. During the initiations the bami often sing the aphorism that evokes the great age of the association: "Bwami has no inventor; it is the fruit that came from above." ("Inventor" is my translation of the verbal form *wamwenne* or *wamonine*, lit., who has seen; the expression is also used for the first occupation of the land; for "from above," the term *mukyata* is used, not *mwigulu*, from the sky, or *muntata*, which when contrasted with *malinga* designates the relative eastern or western, northern or southern, position of one group vis-à-vis another.) Like a nut or a fruit on a tree, no one knows how or when bwami appeared; no one can lay exclusive claim to bwami. The name of a legendary first mwami, however, is occasionally given. He is called Katima Ngonze or Katimi of the Bokelwa, a northern Lega group. One tradition says that Katinti supposedly created bwami as a peacemaking institution in a time of war.

A curious version of the tradition was noted in 1932 by de Villenfagne de Loën. On the Lwalaba River, northwest of present-day Legaland, Muntita of the Kaluba clan had separated from the rest of the Luba, who were migrating southward toward the Kasai River, and instead followed the Lega. Muntita was poor and he looked for ways of acquiring wealth. He made a raffia hat and sold it to Nkulu, the ancestor of the Lega Babongolo division. Muntita told Nkulu not to remove the hat from his head; he promised him wealth and power if he would initiate his people to the secrets of the hat. With his son Nseti, Muntita crossed the Lwalaba and rejoined the other Luba people. Nkulu then initiated his brother Batukya-Kabango and his two sons Kaseke and Kasanza. Kabango initiated his son Ikama; several of Ikama's sons were inducted into bwami. Groups originating with Wamanila, one of Ikama's sons, spread bwami among peoples now called Beia, Babene, and Bakisi. The oral data provided by de Villenfagne de Loën were probably recorded among the Bakabango-Babongolo. Although the tradition is important, it confuses the dissemination of the highest-grade kindi with that of the lower bwami echelons.

The ideological content and procedures of kongabulumbu closely resemble, but in a more elaborate form, the circumcision (*bwali*) and the *mutanga* rites. The program of *bwali* includes intensive teaching of values and techniques. Kongabulumbu is considered a "relative" of *bwali*; for this reason women do not participate in kongabulumbu, except for a short episode in which the *kigogo* girl is introduced. Mutanga is a formal presentation of objects, whose symbolic references must be thoroughly understood by young men who have completed the circumcision rites. The procedure is simple: a large number of different objects are fastened to a long vine that is attached to two trees or poles in the village. The display includes natural objects (e.g., leaves, vines, calabashes, bark, pieces of wood, sugarcane, seeds, nuts, pods, raffia string, bananas, stipes, corn, tobacco, feathers, snail shells, and monkey skulls) and manufactured items (miniature baskets, brooms, mortars and pestles, axes, dugout canoes, shell money, pipes, potsherds, and cloth). As the teacher shows the objects one by one, pertinent aphorisms are recited. An aphorism refers to a quality, a characteristic, or a feature perceived in an object (e.g., its form, use, function, name) which is interpreted symbolically in reference to values, patterns of behavior, and standards of etiquette. In the kongabulumbu closed ceremonial setting of dance and dramatization, many simple objects, most of them not seen or interpreted at *mutanga* (e.g., mats, torches, hides, wild pig's tusks, pangolin scales, feather ropes), are explained in terms of the moral code. The initiation goes beyond *mutanga* because the new initiate views objects contained in the collectively owned *musutwa* bag of kongabulumbu. He receives the single most important emblem of the bwami association, a small skullcap woven in raffia.

It may be assumed that artworks have been used in bwami since its earliest inception. There is evidence to show that artworks were originally linked with the lower grades, for even in kongabulumbu they appear sporadically; in areas where yananio and kindi did not develop, sculptures otherwise monopolized by these grades are used in ngandu and bombwa. The striking parallels with the role of artworks in associations thriving elsewhere among Lega-related populations also indicate the great age of the traditions. There are numerous indications that bwami and the *bukota* association of the Mitoko have a common ancestry, although there is no tradition that one group borrowed from the other. Both are exclusive graded associations open to all circumcised men and based on stepwise initiations and on payments and exchanges. Although statuses in the association are not inherited—there is no guarantee that a man will achieve the grade of his father—preferences nevertheless closely favor agnatic succession. At least one and often several wives follow their husband's gradual social progression through complementary women's rites. Of the many types of valuables paid and exchanged during the rites, shell money (*musanga* of the Lega; *viringi* of the Mitoko) is the most essential; it consists of perforated fragments of giant snail shells strung on raffia fibers. The rites take place mainly in a closed men's house in the center of the village. The ritual performances in initiations include the display, interpretation, and transfer of many natural and manufactured objects. Information on the Mitoko, although inadequate, suggests that many objects they use are similar in form, function, and meaning to those used by the Lega (e.g., *kasuku* torches, mats, hammers, knives, axes, stools). Male and female figurines, some double, are revealed to elucidate aspects of the moral code. Plaited and fur hats with ornaments (shells, teeth, scales), leopard teeth necklaces (*mubanga* in both groups), and bongo antelope belts are some of the insignia. Elaborate burial ceremonies are held for high initiates, and figurines are temporarily displayed on the tomb. Members of both associations have exclusive rites over certain animals, which for both peoples include the giant pangolin, the eagle, and the leopard. Special status holders (*kasimbi, musimbi*) in the associations organize and preside over circumcision rites. The term *mukota*, which among the Mitoko designates a high-ranking member, is also used by the northern, western, and southern Lega for a high initiate.

The history of bwami includes expansion and growth as well as local elaboration or attrition of rites. Some groups never had yananio or kindi; in others those grades are of relatively recent origin. Some local clan groups never developed kindi because of a *kitampo* taboo: individuals with yananio who were ready to begin kindi died before the initiation could take place; or several who acquired kindi died soon thereafter. Entities such as the Bakyunga assert that they originally had an organization similar to the Songola's *kilemba,* which was partly supplanted by bwami introduced by other Lega.

Traditions collected independently among autonomous communities provide a more detailed picture of the rise of kindi. Three persons are mentioned as the first kindi: Kitoba of the Bokelwa, Musuli of the Babongolo, and Kabimbi of the Beigala-Banakitundu. The Babongolo, descendants of Nkulu, state explicitly that they began yananio and kindi in Ilundu, their farthest point of origin near the Lwalaba River. They passed it on to the descendants of Batukya, to the Banakimane (a small group among the Beia), the Bokelwa (among the Banangoma), and the Balobola.

Diagram 8 (in appendix) synthesizes the data provided for the origin of kindi by different communities. It does not list the spread of kindi among the Bakabango-Babongolo themselves but among groups now identified as Bakisi, Babene, and Beia. Many components of the heterogeneous Bamuzimu (Bakuti,

Bakunga, Basisemu'a Basi'asa, Banamputi) have grades below yananio level. Those like Basimbi, who have yananio and kindi, trace the grades back to the Babongolo. Nyindu-related units (e.g., Balinzi) have the *mukwendekwende* variant of bwami, and Bembe-related groups (e.g., Basi'umbilwa) have grades up to ngandu, including the typical Bembe levels. The Basi'asumba of pre-Lega origin have only the lowest bwami initiation. Yananio and kindi do not exist among the Basimwenda.

When kindi was introduced into a group, it started within a particular lineage and eventually spread to others. The diffusion is illustrated by the Banasalu, who trace an unusually large number of kindi (diagram 9 in appendix). Settled in eight villages, the autonomous ritual community of the Banasalu suffered in the 1950s from depopulation, as many young men left to work elsewhere in Legaland, mainly in the mining centers. The Banasalu were so close to the Banakagela, who were considered sororal nephews of all Banasalu (descendants of Salu's daughter), that high-level rites were never held without Banakagela representatives. The Banasalu also claimed early agnatic connections with the Baseide and the Basumbu, two Bakyunga subdivisions in the northwesternmost part of Legaland, as well as with the Bakonjo, a semi-independent unit north of the Lega. The Banasalu felt that in general the patterns of their bwami association closely resembled those of three other communities in their proximity. When they settled in their present area, they had lutumbo lwa yananio, which they had obtained before emigration from the Basumbu-Bakyunga. After they had established themselves, a certain Kamambalu (no. 1 in diagram 8 in appendix) acquired kindi from the Beigala, an independent community situated north of them near the area whence the Banasalu emigrated southward. Kamambalu stood in a *buyukulu* (grandchild) joking relationship with these Beigala.

The Banasalu trace the names of forty-two persons (including Kamambalu) who achieved lutumbo lwa kindi in their group. Four of them (nos. 37, 38, 39, and 41 in diagram 8), all in their sixties, were alive at the time of my research. Kamambalu's son Kinda (no. 2) was initiated to kindi before his father died. During Kinda's lifetime kindi was conferred upon Kibisama (no. 3), a descendant of Musombo (i.e., a representative of a major lineage in another maximal lineage; in other words, kindi spread from Ninda to Lusumbasumba maximal lineage). From Kibisama, kindi went to Mungana (no. 4), a member of the minor lineage Koka in Ninda; then to Kokonyange (no. 5) of Kabungulu minor lineage; to Kamambalu's grandson Mulingwa (no. 6), whose father Kinda was then dead; and to Kokonyange's son, Bikenge (no. 7). Only later was kindi passed on to members of the two other maximal lineages, Mugila (no. 10) and Kibondo (no. 11). Diagram 8 sketches the resultant sequences of kindi transfers. At the time of my research two persons had been initiated to kindi in Kibongo maximal lineage, fifteen in Mugila, seventeen in Lusumbasumba, and eight in Ninda. The four surviving kindi were from two minor lineages in Mugila (nos. 41 and 38), one minor lineage in Lusumbasumba (no. 39), and one in Ninda (no. 37).

In the long history of kindi distributions among the Banasalu, few sons had succeeded their fathers; kindi had largely been transferred to classificatory ag-

natic relatives. The unity of kindi had been maintained: there was one collectively owned lutumbo lwa kindi basket, one central mother figurine in ivory,
and one *kalombola* aide-de-camp shared by the four living kindi. In other communities the unity of kindi was symbolized in a similar manner.

A further analysis is made in diagram 10 (in appendix) to show how a person
like Mindo (no. 37) achieved lutumbo lwa kindi when no one else in his minor
lineage did. Mindo achieved the lowest kongabulumbu and kansilembo grades
upon the advice of oracles when his father Mukulimina became very sick. At
that time his father was already a musage wa kindi; his first senior half brother
Kyemba was musage wa yananio; his second and third senior half brothers
Kikuni and Mutumbi were not initiated (note that they were senior to Mindo by
structural position but younger by birth). The kongabulumbu and kansilembo
initiations were closed group affairs: Kyemba acted as Mindo's tutor; Mulanda,
a classificatory little father of ngandu grade, brought the *musutwa* bag with
initiation objects. Mindo's father died soon after Mindo had been initiated, and
during the mourning period Mindo did the bombwa rites "on the grave" with
his first wife; his third junior half brother, Mutumbi, completed kongabulumbu. The group left the old village of Bikombola and settled in Kakuku. Here
the first senior brother Kyemba moved up to lutumbo lwa yananio, while
Mindo did the ngandu and the bulonda initiations. In ngandu, Kyemba was his
tutor; Igulu of Kagala major lineage (in Mugila), Mindo's classificatory grandfather, brought the collectively owned objects. The bulonda rites were done for
Mindo's first wife; the wives of Kyemba and Igulu acted as her tutors and provided the initiation objects. The group now resided in a third village, Kisuku.
Kikuni, Mindo's second senior half brother, received kongabulumbu and kansilembo at Kyemba's initiative. They moved to a fourth village, Kitunga, where
Mindo reached both musage and lutumbo lwa yananio. In musage, Kyemba
acted as his senior tutor; Kibonge, a classificatory little father of Koka lineage (a
subdivision of Ikwa minor lineage in Ninda), was junior tutor; the initiation
objects were brought by Kasusuma, Mindo's classificatory senior brother of
Muligi minor lineage (in Ninda). For lutumbo lwa yananio the senior tutor was
Musoma, a classificatory senior brother of Muligi lineage (in Ninda); the junior
tutor was Lukelwa, a classificatory senior brother of Ikwa/Koka minor lineage.
Mwambila, a senior classificatory brother of Ikwa/Koka minor lineage, was in
charge of the collectively owned objects. After Mindo's initiation, his senior
half brother Kikuni moved up to bombwa, ngandu, and musage wa yananio.

Mindo's group now settled in Masanganjia village. As Kyemba, Mindo's first
senior half brother, was old and ill, he invited Mindo to advance to kindi. Mindo
first did kyogo and *kantamba*, two preliminary stages in kindi. His senior tutor
was the kindi Kilungulungu, a classificatory little father of Ikwa/Koka minor
lineage (no. 8 in diagram 9 in appendix); the junior tutor was Muningwa, a kindi
(no. 29) and classificatory brother of Walangwa (in Ninda) major lineage; Lukelwa, a musage wa kindi in Ikwa/Koka lineage, brought the collectively owned
initiation objects. By the time Mindo reached musage wa kindi, Kilungulungu
was dead, so his senior tutor was Kansilembo of Kagala major lineage (in Mugila; no. 31 in diagram 9). The junior tutor was Kisubi (no. 21), a classificatory

grandfather of Kabungulu lineage (in Lusumbasumba); Tubunda (no. 35) of Ngunga lineage (in Lusumbasumba) came with the collectively owned objects (no. 36 having died). The same persons functioned at Mindo's lutumbo lwa kindi, which immediately followed musage. Three of Mindo's wives entered bunyamwa (his third, fifth, and seventh wives; the other four were dead). Kikuni, Mindo's second senior half brother, now achieved lutumbo lwa yananio, with Mindo serving as his principal tutor; Mutumbi, the third senior half brother, reached bombwa, ngandu, and musage wa yananio.

The group finally moved to Alimba village, where Mutumbi received lutumbo lwa yananio; Kyemba and Kikuni died. Kyemba's oldest son went from kongabulumbu to lutumbo lwa yananio; his second-oldest son did ngandu and bulonda, with Mindo again acting as senior tutor; his senior son achieved kongabulumbu. Mindo's and Mutumbi's senior sons were also initiated to kongabulumbu. The only son of Kikuni worked in a mining center and was not initiated.

This example shows the extraordinary interdependences and solidarities created among agnatic kinsmen through the initiations. These ties operated at the yananio level within Ninda maximal lineage, but at the kindi level they involved individuals from two other maximal lineages. Interdependences, autonomy, and complementary oppositions in the Banasalu group are illustrated even more clearly when other collectively held rights are examined (diagram 9).

1. For kongabulumbu there are two bags (differently from some other groups, the bag is not transferred to the new initiate but stays in its original lineage) in a close agnatic line of descent:
   a. Mugila, Kagala, Kintonko, Ntonge
   b. Ninda, Itatua, Itumpu, Nkenze
   Mugila shares with Kibondo and Ninda with Lusumbasumba.
2. Ownership of the *lutala* bag of kansilembo in this area also means possession of the pangolin knife and the right to initiate a local circumcision cycle. The distribution is as follows:
   a. Mugila, Kilimu, Keisugwa
   b. Mugila, Kagala, Kazigwa
   c. Mugila, Nkola, Mukumbukwa
   d. Lusumbasumba, Ngunga, Kyanga
   e. Lusumbasumba, Wanwa, Monga
   f. Ninda, Itatua, Itumpu, Nkenze
3. For bombwa and ngandu there are no longer any collectively owned objects in this group.
4. In musage wa yananio, two baskets are passed around:
   a. Mugila, Kilimu, Keisugwa (shares with Kibondo)
   b. Lusumbasumba, Wanwa, Monga (shares with Ninda)
5. Lutumbo lwa yananio:
   a. The *mutulwa* basket: there are two baskets:
   Mugila, Kilimu, Keisugwa (shares with Kibondo)
   Ninda, Itatua, Muligi (shares with Lusumbasumba)

b. The *kasisi* basket: four baskets circulated:
Kibondo, Kinduka
Mugila, Kagala, Kazigwa
Lusumbasumba, Musimbi
Ninda, Itatua, Itumpu
The *kalumbilumbi* quartz stones are held jointly with the *kasisi* basket.

c. The *kampunzu* basket: originally there were two baskets, both held in Mugila, Kagala, Kintonko and in Mugila, Kilimu, Keisugwa, but only the one of Keisugwa remains. The other one was burned because of early difficulties with the colonial government.

d. The *mukumbi* basket: the only one is held in Wanwa lineage of Lusumbasumba.

6. For bulonda, each of the four maximal lineages owns a central *muzigi* object (a beaded belt adorned with a large Cypraea shell and a *kizombo* nutshell). These were held by the above-mentioned keepers of the *kasisi* baskets; in Lusumbasumba lineage, however, the belt was in the custody of the *kasisi* keeper's classificatory senior brother.

7. For kindi, as already noted, the group acted as a single unit.

It is noteworthy that the Banasalu remembered four great carvers, all of whom were dead at the time of my research, but their grandsons were alive. In Mugila, the lines of Kagala-Kintonko and Kagala-Kazigwa each had produced an expert carver. In Lusumbasumba, the Wanwa-Monga line had a famed carver and blacksmith; in Ninda, the great carver came from Itatua-Ikwa-Koka.

Although patrilineal linkages among individuals and groups are strongly emphasized for initiation purposes, the actual preparations for the rites bring in a broader spectrum of kin. For the acquisition of goods needed in kindi, Mindo relied heavily on members of Nkenze lineage, basically his father's large and powerful extended family, who provided huge quantities of shell money. The Itongwa line was numerically weak, and its only living male member contributed shell money. For labor (house building, hunting, providing wood and water) Mindo depended on the Itumpu, and the large-scale collective hunting included all hunters of Ninda. Help received from certain families in the other three maximal lineages (Kibondo, Mugila, and Lusumbasumba) of the Banasalu was conditioned not by agnatic but by affinal and cognatic bonds. As Mindo's second wife belonged to the Muligi branch in Ninda, and his third wife to the Mumema in Lusumbasumba, members of these two groups contributed goods. His father's maternal uncles, who were in the Kagala lineage of Mugila, also supplied goods. Valuable support came from the Banisangi, an independent ritual community into different branches of which Mindo's mother, his mother's mother, and his father's mother were born.

Mindo had no close sororal nephew because his only sister, though married, died childless among the Banameya. He did rely heavily on his powerful classificatory sororal nephews: one nephew was a kindi among the Banakeigo and a great-grandchild of Nkenze's sister; one nephew, a kindi among the Beiamunsange, was also the great-grandchild of a second sister of Nkenze (note that

Nkenze is Mindo's great-grandfather); one nephew, a lutumbo lwa yananio, was a descendant of the daughter of Itatua (founder of Mindo's major lineage). Mindo also solicited and received help from two powerful initiates who, like himself, were sororal nephews of the Banisangi and who both were sons of Mindo's mother's sisters.

Basimwenda Traditions

The Basimwenda, a northeastern Lega group, are in contact with the Nyindu and the Bembe in the northeast and other Lega divisions in the south and the west. They trace numerous relationships with Bembe clans and groups incorporated into the Bamuzimu administrative division, and they also claim that the Nyindu and the Basim'minje among the Bembe are close collateral relatives. This linkage is felt strongly by the Basim'minje but less emphatically by the Nyindu.

The Basimwenda administrative unit includes many related and unrelated clans (diagram 1 in appendix):

1. Descendants of the sons of Sungu and Mwenda: the Basimwenda properly speaking, the Basisunge, Bacinda, Ba'anga, Basimkobe, Basango, Basi'amena (Bamunda), and Babungwe.
2. Descendants of Lwamba, Sungu's full brother: Basi'asa, Basilubanda, Banakengela, Balimbikyi, Bazila, Basisemu'a, and Bazyara.
3. Descendants of Amoni: parts of Nyindu clans settled among the Basimwenda.
4. Groups immigrating from the Bakisi-Lega: Babundu-Bingyalugulu and Balobola.
5. The Baligi, who immigrated from the Bakabango.
6. Remnants of the Bouse (Bamulinda) and Bakeci.

Because of the history, composition, and location of the Basimwenda, their bwami institution has become exceedingly complex. The senior lineage of the Basimwenda provides a chief called Alenga (mwami), whose office, like that of the Vira and Furiiru chiefs, is inherited in the patrilineal line of primogeniture. The chief holds *bwami bwa ishungwe lya lusembe*, and the most important symbol of his status is a large Cypraea shell (*lusembe, lushembe*) fastened to his leopard hide hat. Others are not allowed to wear this shell, but some high-ranking dignitaries (*bitanda[h]o*), who often hold the *ngandu* grade in the bwami association, may display a smaller variety of the shell species (see also Mulyumba, 1978, p. 30). The chief is initiated in the *asa'o* shrine by the royal initiator (*mwo'o*); at the same time a member of the Basango clan (see Babembe Traditions, below) is inducted into the bwami association in the *lubunga* initiation house.

Among the other regalia preserved by a member of the Basango clan are a hat in eagle skin, a diadem in eagle feathers, a leopard hide, a stool studded with copper nails, a bongo hide on which the stool stands, and copper, iron, and ivory bracelets (*mitondo, ngolo;* ibid., pp. 33 – 42).

Junior lineages of the Basimwenda have a form of bwami association which closely resembles that of the Bembe; the grades are *bukila* or *bukabo, pinji,* and *itembu.* Some lineages, however, do not have the lower *bukila* or *bukabo* grade; others have also adopted *bumbwa, bubake* (or *buba'e*), and *ngandu* under the influence of the Babundu of northern Lega stock. Other descendants of Sungu (e.g., the Basisunge) and of Lwamba (e.g., Basi'asa), the Bouse, the Bakeci, and the Baligi, have the *bukila, bukabo,* and *hingwi* grades.

The immigrant Babundu have the form of bwami, sometimes referred to as *bwami bwa isengo* (lit., bwami of the sacred object), found among the northern Lega (i.e., descendants of Kisi). In contrast with the Bembe and Basimwenda variants, called *bwami bwa e'umbu* (lit., bwami of the hat), the Babundu grades include *bumbwa, bubake,* and *ngandu.* Some Babundu, however, adhere to the Basimwenda type of bwami.

A small autonomous group of Nyindu under Chief Abu'a broke away from the main Nyindu unit and formed a separate entity among the Basimwenda. The group includes members of the Batumba, Bamishungwe, Balinzi, Bashimbi, and Banyamganga clans (all Nyindu) as well as some Babundu. Hereditary chieftainship is held by Abu'a, a representative of the Batumba. Members of the other Nyindu clans follow the *'alemba, mukwendekwende,* and *'etasi* grading of the Nyindu form of bwami, but some have also adopted the Bembe and Basimwenda levels.

Few sculptures are used by the groups that have adopted the Nyindu form of the bwami association: ivory pegs (*mushumbo*), miniature stools (*ecumbi*) usually made of leopard bone, and ivory spoons (*a'ili*) and figurines (*'alembe*). Groups that adhere to the Lega-Bembe variant of bwami use ivory pegs (*a'unyi*), small elephant tusks, and ivory *yango* poles.

Bamuzimu Traditions

Until 1960 the Bamuzimu administrative grouping in eastern and southeastern Legaland included the Basimwenda-Lega. Shortly before Zaire became independent, the Basimwenda group was reconstituted as a separate administrative unit. The reduced Bamuzimu incorporate a wide variety of Lega clans, mainly of the Ikama and Nkulu subdivisions, but also of the Shile and Kisi. Also included are some Bembe, Basi'asumba, offshoots of the Nyindu and M'minje complex, and other remnants of pre-Lega groups (diagrams 1–6 in appendix). The resulting heterogeneity is reflected to a certain extent in the distribution of the bwami association among the component clans.

Among the Ikama clans (diagram 6), the Bakuti have the following grades: *bwami* (lowest grade, the equivalent of kongabulumbu), *bumbwa*, *bubake*, *mpunju*, and *ngandu*. In the nineteenth century the Bakuti tried to install the higher *yano* (equivalent of yananio) grade, but according to their own testimony they abandoned it because several initiates and candidates of that grade died in rapid succession. Other Lega clans sometimes explain the absence of higher grades in the same way, viewing such deaths as an expression of indefinable sanctions emanating from bwami.

Among the Shile clans (diagram 1 in appendix), the Basi'umbilwa (including the Banenge) of the Sungu subdivision have *bwami, bumbwa, bubake,* and *ngandu;* some lineages place the *itembu* grade (found among the Bembe) below *ngandu.* The Lwamba subdivision, which includes Basi'asa, Basilubanda, Balimbikyi, Basisemu'a, Bazyara, and Basibugembe, has *bwami, bubake,* and *mpunju.* Of the Amoni subdivision, the Balinzi, with fragments among the Banyindu and the Basimwenda, have the Nyindu type of bwami up to the *mukwendekwende* grade. The Basimbi of the Amoni subdivision, with offshoots among the Banyindu and the Basimwenda, in relatively recent times have obtained *yano* (i.e., yananio) and kindi from the Babongolo (southern Lega).

Basi'asumba (diagram 2) hunters who have lately adopted the circumcision rites have only the lowest grade.

A limited number of sculptures are used in the bwami rites of these groups. Ivory knives are used in the *itungilo* rite for symbolically cutting a string of shell money. Large *kabemba* knives with iron blades and wooden anthropomorphic handles are utilized, together with a *kasuku* resin torch (an object desired by all), in the *kasuku* rite of bwami. The knife symbolizes a prohibition: a mwami must never steal, not even things he may fervently covet. In *ngandu* small copper-bladed knives (*bubenga*) with wooden (rarely ivory) handles express the right to preside over the skinning and distribution of the sacred animals (pangolin, leopard, and crocodile). These knives are used in a mock fight in the *yano* rite. Ivory pegs (*kinsamba, nseti*), together with *ntundu* antelope horns, appear in *mpunju*. Preceptors point the objects at the candidate and then hold them against his back. The candidate is compared with a *nsoni*, one who acts as a scout in times of warfare. When the *nsoni* sees the enemy coming, he cannot flee; instead, he must run back to his village to report the news: "In the downpour, we shall go, we the children of Mpoko." The bent horns of the antelope— symbolic of a man who does not listen to the words of the elders—are contrasted with the straight peg. Ivory or bone billhooks (*muguzu*) in *mpunju* are used for the symbolic cutting of leaves; they indicate that a man must do the agricultural work demanded by his father. Small ivory tusks or poles called *yango* are shown in configurations of objects in *mpunju* and *ngandu* and are then planted in the men's house. Yango symbolizes the elder on whom the faithful candidate leans to complete the initiations. Yango is also synonymous with the knowledge of the elders: "Among the Big-Ones, Yango is hidden; let Yango come; in the hole of the riverbed, catfish is hidden."

Zoomorphic figurines are used in the *mpondo* rite of bwami. One ivory figurine represents a stylized quadruped called *mugugu* (chameleon): "Mugugu has no cheeks, his call goes far." He characterizes the power of the initiates' words: people must listen, even if Mugugu's message is delivered by a delegate. In *ngandu* a realistic carving of a turtle (*nkulu*) conveys the idea that senior or elder initiates must be peaceful.

Anthropomorphic figurines are manipulated in the bwami rites. Two ivory figurines, called Mpondo and his wife Nyabikuba, are placed on a *mpaga* hide in the *mpondo* rite. Mpondo is laid on his back and then rolled onto the hide; dancers approach the Nyabikuba figurine lying on the hide and stick out their tongues. Mpondo is first presented as the sick father, who moves restlessly on his sleeping mat. He then portrays the dead father whose corpse is turned on its back in preparation for burial. A son who seduced his father's wife (Nyabikuba) cannot see or touch his father's corpse. Mpondo, however, is also a person who scorns the seniors and seduces Nyabikuba, "the wife of the Big-One," and so must expect no help from anyone. In the *yano* rite three ivory figurines (usually called *bitumba*, lit., corpses) stand for Kakulikuli (asexual figurine), Nyansompo (a female), and Sakabaga (a male). Kakulikuli is a talkative person who always wants to participate in discussions and who, because of excessive talking, reveals secret knowledge. Nyansompo is a woman described as a mother-in-law who is too outgoing and takes too much pleasure in dancing; these traits will surely destroy her marriage. The male figurine is identified as Sakabaga (Mr. Skinner): "Mr. Skinner, the child of your father has skinned the animal [all by himself]." This aphorism indicates that a person must share with his kin. Sakabaga also depicts Kabonga (Nice-One): "Kabubi [lit., vine] fights with Bonga, he Big Kabonga." An old man is like a *lububi* vine that serves many purposes: as he can always do something for a young man, one must not scorn him. The old man can be extremely helpful if one runs into trouble.

Banyindu Traditions

The major clans of the patrilineal Nyindu, who live northeast of the Basimwenda, are Batumba, Bamishungwe, Balinzi, Bashimbi, Balambo, and Banyamganga; some Bembe, Bahofa-Shi, and Basimwenda have also settled among them. Their leaders, who claim that the Nyindu were originally Twa (Pygmies), place their local beginnings in Angele (in the Itombwe Mountains). They have historical affiliations with those Basim'minje and Balenge groups incorporated with the Bembe.

Two types of bwami exist among the Nyindu: *bwami bwa lushembe* and *bwami bwa e'umbu*. The first refers to hereditary chieftainship within the Batumba clan. The Nyindu migrated from Angele and in Kitamba encountered

Mwenembumbano, a local chief of the Batamba (of unidentified origin). According to the tradition, Mwenembumbano was sitting on a stool when it started to rain. After he stood up to take shelter, Kaluku of the Nyindu Batumba clan took possession of the stool and proclaimed himself chief. The people of Mwenembumbano fled southward among the Bouse. Kaluku was accompanied by members of the Bamishungwe, Balinzi, and Bashimbi clans whose leaders subsequently assumed the functions of ritual experts (*bagingi, bazyoga*). They were followed by the Balambo, whose leader received the title of *nakimborongo* (mock chief). Titleholders (such as Nizyembwe, Nashimbi), headed by Nyamishungwe, select, ritually capture, and enthrone the chief (mwami) in a sacred place called Kitamba ne Kanungu. As part of the enthronement ceremony the ritual experts place on the chief's head a skullcap (*'alemba*), the distinctive emblem of the bwami association, before giving him the *'etasi* (or *kidasi*) hat that is adorned with the *ishungwe* symbol (Biebuyck, 1980). The ritual experts are also in charge of the initiation objects (*bi'o'o* or *mashengo*) and of the skulls (*ilumba*) of dead chiefs. Shortly after the advent of the first Europeans, a split divided the ritual experts, and consequently part of the Nyindu (now incorporated into the Basimwenda administrative unit) came to be ruled by a second Nyindu chief.

The second form of bwami is a hierarchically graded variant of the Lega and Bembe types. Called *bwami bwa e'umbu*, it is found among most Nyindu groups, such as Bamishungwe, Balinzi, and Balambo, but originally not among the Batumba who provided the chief (in the 1950s I met several Batumba who were members of the association). The structured grades of bwami among the Nyindu are *'alemba* (or *kalemba, bugira*), *hingwi* (or *angwe*), *mukwendekwende,* and *'etasi* (or *kidasi*). The principles and procedures of initiation and the teachings in the Nyindu variant of bwami closely follow the Lega pattern in general and, in particular, the patterns found among the Basimwenda and the Bembe.

Different statuses in bwami are indicated by distinctive paraphernalia (hats, necklaces, bracelets, belts, and aprons). During the rites natural and manufactured objects (most of them used also by the Lega) and some sculptures are displayed in configurations, manipulated, and interpreted in sung aphorisms to convey the code of ethical conduct. The few sculptures I was able to observe in the Nyindu rites included awl-shaped pegs (*mcumbo*) in elephant or leopard bone, ivory spoons (*lu'iri*), ivory horns (*ihembe*), and ivory figurines (*a'inga*). Except for the horns, which were worn by initiates of *'etasi* grade, all other sculptures were used and interpreted as among the Lega. Like the chief, the members of the two highest ranks have the right to wear *ishungwe* on their hats, but this *ishungwe* is made of a piece of varan hide onto which have been fastened a leopard tooth and a horseshoe-shaped copper plate. The power of attraction exercised by high-ranking initiates is well illustrated by the Nyindu. An important initiate may have few agnates, but many affinal and cognatic kin, living with him. These are individuals of different clan origins who settle with a mwami out of friendship (*lwici*) and who remain with his successors if the latter are powerful and generous.

Babembe Traditions

The Bembe are a complex group who live east of the Lega and are in contact with them. Many Bembe clans trace their origins to the Basimwenda-Lega; others, to the Bakabango-Babongolo (diagrams 1, 6 in appendix). One large Bembe clan, the Basim'minje, and some of its splinter groups have pre-Lega origins, or at least were among the first offshoots of the southeastward Lega migration (diagram 2). Although the eastern Lega commonly place the Bembe with the Banyindu and the Basi'asumba hunters as the early branches of Lega's son Shile, the Basim'minje themselves claim their source and that of the Banyindu to be Mcwa (Pygmy) or Mcwa Nangungya. Another large Bembe clan, the Basi'alangwa (diagram 3), located mainly in southern Bembeland on the boundaries with the Boyo and the Bakwamamba-Baholoholo clusters, is sometimes linked in the distant past with the Basim'minje and the Banyindu. Other pre-Bembe and pre-Lega groups, such as Basanze, Bafulo, Basimwala, Bacimba, Basu, Bakwalumona, and Bahoma, which are scattered throughout Bembeland, assert connections with the Balumbu, Babujwe, Boyo, and Bemba-derived peoples living to the south.

In the distribution of the bwami association among the Bembe, members of the Basango clan have played and continue to play their extraordinary role as *bakyoka* initiators. In the entire Bembe area, no clan is more widely dispersed in small fragments than the Basango; this situation is owing to their multiple functions in bwami and in various other cults. The Basango are also found among the Basimwenda and act as the principal initiators of Chief Alenga, as well as among the Vira and the Furiiru.

It is difficult to trace Basango origins. The Basimwenda-Lega consider them, like some other Bembe clans, to be the descendants of Mwenda (son of Sungu and grandson of Shile). None of the Bembe clans, who have some connections with other groups, claim to be directly related to the Basango. The pre-Bembe hunters, such as Basi'asumba, Basim'minje, and Basi'alangwa, now mostly incorporated into the Bembe, do not assert close relationships with the Basango. According to one Basango version, the ancestor Mwenesango (whose ascendancy has not been traced) married one woman from the Komo and one from the Babila. The tradition is important because it was provided by a segment of Basango living near Lake Tanganyika, far away from the Komo and the Babila. Western Lega groups located closer to the Komo and the Babila often mention the marriage of their early ancestors with women of these groups. A more recent place of origin is Mwilu in the region of the southeastern Lega. From there the Basango moved northward to Lucingu-Esanga (among the Basimwenda) and to Mtombwe (among the northwestern Bembe). The Basango thus seem to be a Lega group that introduced bwami and circumcision rites to the northeastern Lega and the Bembe.

Members of the Mwo'o and Yo'a lineages of the Basango have special functions among the Basimwenda in relationship to the chief Alenga. As keeper of the royal initiation objects (*mwenelukumbo*), including the skulls of dead chiefs, a Mwo'o representative plays a leading part in the chief's enthronement and burial rites; he also handles the offerings brought to the burial site (*mabu'u*). The Yo'a member shaves the chief and preserves the hair for later burial with the corpse. When the chief is enthroned in the *asa'o* shrine, a Yo'a is initiated in the men's house to the secrets of the ritual objects (*bi'o'o*), whereas the chief is allowed only to view them. During the mourning period these Basango see to it that prescriptions are properly observed; they may, for example, take spears and crops from people who go to the hunt or to work in the fields. They accompany the chief on his travels, carry him, and prepare his food.

The Basimwenda have an explanation for the Basango's special privileges. In the beginning, the ancestor Lega had bwami and wanted to reserve it for his oldest son Shile. Because Shile was hated by his junior brothers, Lega was afraid that after his death the juniors would steal bwami from Shile. Lega therefore sent his son away under the protection of Mcanga (of the Bainda clan), who was in charge of the royal paraphernalia with which he would initiate Shile when he was of age. Several generations later the Bainda, great-grandchildren of Shile, transferred the functions they had performed to their sororal nephews, Mwo'o and Yo'a of the Basango (their father Sango was the most junior great-great-grandson of Shile). On the basis of this tradition, the Basimwenda claim that the bwami chieftainship, which they alone have among the Lega, stems from primogeniture and is not derived from other groups.

The Basango tradition, however, explains the situation more precisely and also clarifies the role of the Basango in the bwami association of the Bembe. The Basango had *butende* (circumcision rites) and bwami before "coming from far." Following the Elila River, they settled in Mwilu (an area of the southeastern Lega), where they organized the *bwali* or *butende* rites. Then moving northward to Lucingu-Esanga (area of the Basimwenda), they met Bulambo (great-grandson of Shile), the Basimwenda chief. When Bulambo asked to be initiated to their bwami, the Basango agreed on the conditions that circumcision rites be held first and that a woman be given as payment. The rites were performed by Bulambo, Lutonge (founder of the Balala clan of the Bembe), and M'mandama of the Basango. The descendants of Amoni (Sungu's brother) refused to participate: M'minje (founder of the Basim'minje clan), Enunda (ancestor of the Balenge, royal dynasty of the Vira), and Nyamigira (founder of the Bahamba royal dynasty among the Furiiru) fled to the Itombwe Mountains; Abu'a Lukanja (Batumba dynasty of the Nyindu) went even farther east and crossed the Ruzizi River into Burundi. Abu'a later returned, but because he had declined to undergo the circumcision rites he remained with *bwami bwa ishungwe lya lusembe*.

The Basango then migrated to Mtombwe (in the Itombwe Mountains). After a long settlement period, a Basango hunter happened upon people who were living in caves and reported the encounter to Mwenesango. The people the hunter found turned out to be the Basim'minje who had run away from the circumcision rites. By mutual agreement, M'minje now accepted the circumcision rites and bwami, receiving also an area of Itombwe from Mwenesango.

The Basim'minje acknowledge this tradition. When they first settled near the Mlengeci Mountain in Itombwe, they lived in caves (*mala*) and hunting camps; they did not engage in agriculture. Nor did they institute circumcision rites, but, like the Basimwenda and the Nyindu, they did have *bwami bwa lusembe*. Instead of drums they used the *lulanga* harp. The Basango tradition also says that different Bembe clans, upon a later request, received *butende* and bwami. Mwenesango delegated one of his descendants to remain with each group to build their bwami shrine.

The Basango have numerous privileges in the bwami rites of the Bembe. Prior to the initiations, Basango representatives receive a goat from the candidate as an invitation. They perform the preliminary rites on the *lulindi* (or *ilumbi*), the local lineage's ancestral shrine, by sacrificing a chicken and imploring the beneficence of the ancestors connected with the places (mostly in the Itombwe Mountains) where the immigrating Bembe and Basango resided. At the end of the *alambi* rite in the *bukabo* initiation, the candidate first undergoes an ablution ceremony. A member of the Basango then removes the candidate's feather hat and shaves his skull; he sacrifices a goat and spits banana beer on the candidate's head (to give him strength) and then crowns him with a hat made of goat hide. Toward the end of the *pinji* initiations the Basango extinguish the fire in the initiation house and rub the candidate with red clay and leaves to lift all taboos imposed upon him. During the *itimbu* initiations the candidate is led into the ceremonial house, where he finds a Basango initiate covered with leopard hides so as to imitate the animal. Distribution of meat and other valuables is the responsibility of the Basango, who receive the heads of all animals killed for the rites. The Basango also dress and bury the corpse of an initiate of the higher grades, a task otherwise reserved for a person's grandchild.

The Basango also have exclusive rights in other areas. They perform sacrifices before a circumcision cycle is started, and they often function as circumcisers. Frequently a young Basango man is the first to be circumcised among the group. The Basango also lay the groundwork for constructing the men's house in Bembe villages, and they build the lineage shrine (a spherical house) for the dead initiates of the group. An initiate who becomes seriously ill is transported to this shrine; initiates may also keep their paraphernalia and insignia there if their senior wives are not members of the *bahumbwa*, a female initiation that parallels bwami. The Basango are also called upon to skin leopards.

Among the Basimwenda, the Basango play a less important role in bwami rites. When a Basimwenda man is initiated to the Bembe grades (*bukila, bukabo, pinji,* and *itembu*), however, a member of the Basango is coinitiated without the usual payment of fees.

The Bembe distinguish two levels in their bwami association, which they obtained through the intermediacy of the Basango clan. The lower grade comprises the *bami ba bi'umbu* (initiates of the hats) or *bami ba banu'e* (the junior bami); the higher one includes the *bami ba ngoma* (initiates of the drum), also called *bami wengwe* (initiates of the leopard). There are two independent initiations for the junior bami: one leads to the grade of *bukabo* (divided into two levels, *alambi* and *sango*); the other, to the grade of *bukila* (divided into two levels, *bukila bwa lusala* and *bwangwe*). Most Bembe lineages traditionally follow either *bukabo* or *bukila*, but some initiate their members into both. The senior bami are grouped according to three levels: *pinji, itimbu,* and *biciba*.

Although in nomenclature of grades, levels, and rites, as well as in the wording of aphoristic songs, the Bembe differ drastically from the Lega, their organizational, ideological, and functional foundations of bwami are very similar. The candidate must be acceptable on moral grounds and he must be circumcised; he must also provide numerous payments and gifts. The separate rites leading to membership are structured around danced performances and configurations of objects (*bi'o'o; elu'we*) which are revealed and explained to the candidate in order to communicate the moral and philosophical principles of the association ("busu'ina ibe busu'usomanya": dancing is teaching). The bwami code emphasizes peaceful and harmonious relationships and the avoidance of all actions that would lead to conflict or strife. The basic philosophy is well synthesized in the following bwami teachings (*mahano*): "A mwami must be a peaceful man; he is coolheaded, closemouthed, and humble. A man of knowledge, he acts with circumspection in everything. He brings joy and order to the land. He is a judge. He acts with patience and without precipitation because the land is won not with the knife but with the buffalo tail. The mwami is not a fighter; he does not harbor wrathful or vindictive feelings. He may overhear words that vex his heart, but he will not have crossed two rivers before his wrath is eliminated by calm and serious thought. A mwami is not a talker or a telltale: never will he communicate to others secrets entrusted to him or divulge the mysteries of bwami to noninitiates." Bwami fosters the sense of solidarity that cuts across social boundaries: "One mwami alone cannot make the land beautiful [ensure its harmony]; the land brings us all together into one union"; "Let us join hands with those who are on the other side of the river."

Above everything else, bwami is the deep knowledge (*amanyina*) that is handed down from generation to generation. Bwami truths will guide those who know how to listen: "The ancient patrimony, bwami, comes from above, the great bwami comes from above"; "These things are not ours, they were of the ancestors"; "I cannot throw away the things of the ancestors"; "The knowledge of the drum is not with him who forgets." When I participated in their rites, Bembe initiates often told me: "We will know that you know us when you listen to the things that we say."

The initiates strongly emphasize respect (*bunyemu*) for seniors, elders, older people, and for kinsfolk. They organize the circumcision rites and play prominent roles in many other life-cycle ceremonies. They act as judges in formal court sessions (*ibulu lya makambo*), and they restore peace (*alembe*) after grave crises, such as those resulting from homicide or conflicts between lineages. To sanction their decisions, the initiates rely not only on moral authority and certain immunities but also on *'abi* poison ordeals.

Under the colonial system the bwami association suffered severe setbacks. Its members attributed all evils emerging in the society to the disintegration caused by Western control. Some of the strongest criticism I ever heard came from Bembe initiates: "The things of the leopard head that were snatched away from us! Oh! Of what greatness we were robbed!" Another sharp rebuke came from a most senior *biciba* initiate: "Since you [i.e., Westerners] arrived here, you have made us burn everything. The smoke of all our sacred bwami objects has risen into our nostrils. We die out; we lose our life-force; we become emaciated and miserable! Our ancestors are dissatisfied with us."

Membership in the association is open to all circumcised males regardless of position in the clan and lineage structure ("bwami bule bwa 'ula na bwa m'mela": bwami belongs to the firstborn and to the last born). The Bembe version differs from the Lega version in that the highest *biciba* grade tends to remain within the senior descent line of a minor or minimal lineage. The distribution of the other two higher grades (*itimbu* and *pinji*) within closely knit lineage groups also seems to follow seniority patterns. This custom probably is directly influenced by the chieftainship institution (*bwami bwa ishungwe lya lusembe*) of the Basimwenda and the Banyindu, whose succession rules are based on primogeniture, and by the overwhelming significance of seniority rules in the Bembe kinship system. The Bembe also hold coinitiations whereby several related men simultaneously enter bwami.

In contrast with the Lega practice, Bembe women are not members of bwami. They have the separate and highly secret graded *buhumbwa* association, to which at least the senior wife of an initiate must belong. Women may "borrow" initiation objects (*bi'o'o*) from the men for their own rites. A man keeps his paraphernalia and insignia in the house of his initiated wife, but if his wife is not a member of *buhumbwa* he may keep them in a *lwelo* or *asa'o* shrine.

The few artworks used as initiation objects are rarely found in world collections. At the time of my field research among the Bembe (1949–1951), their bwami association had lost the vitality and the cohesion that were still characteristic of most Lega initiates. The Bembe bwami also had to compete with other associations and cults. The Bembe, unlike the Basimwenda, had not developed the skull cult, but they did have a cult that was centered, at least among some Bembe, on wooden and ivory figurines (*tuse'a; mi'eci*). In Bembe groups, such as the Basim'minje of Itombwe who maintained close contacts with the Lega, the skulls of high initiates were preserved by their sons in private *akombe* shrines. The skulls of the highest initiates of the most senior branch of a local clan segment were guarded by a member of the Basango clan.

The extent to which sculptures were used in the past in bwami is unclear, and the collected aphorisms offer no clues. Sculptures, particularly anthropomorphic figurines, are more numerous in western Bembe groups that were either remote offshoots of the Bakabango-Babongolo or in close geographical contact with them. Sculptures I have observed the Bembe using in bwami initiations (Biebuyck, 1972a, pls. 8–10, 15–17, 24–25) are described in the following paragraphs.

Awl-shaped pegs (*mcumbo*), often with a lozenge knop, are made of ivory or of elephant or leopard bone. They usually belong to a *pinji* initiate. The well-patinated peg is used in *bukabo bwa alambi* to construct (with a feather rope) a sacred fence around a configuration of objects. In the final *ecumbi* rite of *bukila*, initiates of the three highest grades in turn beat the candidate's heart with a peg: "Appease your heart, you are beaten with your own hammer." The aphorism tells the candidate that he must be truthful and peaceful.

Ivory miniature stools with four legs (*icumbi*) are wrapped in a genet hide. The miniature stool is placed on a larger wooden stool (covered with a leopard hide and feathers) during the installation ceremonies for the highest initiates (*itimbu* and *biciba*). The carving is sometimes replaced by a simple piece of ivory, bones from a leopard's spinal column, or even by a beaded spool (a Western import). The Bembe consider the stool to be a symbol of power and authority, and it should be remembered that Basimwenda and Banyindu chiefs claim to have received their authority by taking away the stool of Mwenembumbano. Most Bembe initiations end with the formal seating of the new mwami. Acquisition of the stool symbolizes a linkage with the past and with the Bembe's Lega sources: "You see the stool, the stool, the stool that came from Macinga [the west, the lower lands] from Ikama [an ancestor of the Bembe clans]"; "It [the stool] is from the elders, from the seniors of ancient times." The small ivory stool, the most secret of all initiation objects, may never be seen by noninitiates, even though other objects are sometimes displayed (out of ritual context) to allow them to dry in the sun.

A ceremonial ax (*ahango a bwami*), worn on the left shoulder by a high initiate, is ritually conferred upon him at the end of the rites when he is seated on the stool. The handle sometimes has a cephalomorphic knop and may be adorned with animal figurines carved in high relief.

The ivory handle of a buffalo tail scepter (*m'munga*) is carved in the form of a double-faced bust. The highest initiates receive such scepters as insignia to be carried in the right hand. The initiate is an arbitrator, a judge, and a man of patience. The Bembe say the land is ruled not with a knife but with the buffalo tail: "The place to build a house is not taken with a knife."

Large wooden masks (*eluba*) are trimmed with feathers and adorned with a beaded band affixed to the nose. These masks were extremely rare at the time of my research. During the culminating rite of the *pinji* grade, a single mask is worn by a drummer. This masker, dressed in hides and a feather-trimmed snakeskin, is a member of the Basango clan. When the candidate is led into the initiation house, the masked drummer sits behind an *embe*, a screen made with bamboo, cloth, beaded necklaces, raffia disks studded with cowrie shells, and feather tufts. The screen is then slowly lifted up and down by a high-ranking initiate. The masker, trembling and moving his head up and down, is revealed (*u'angula*) to the candidate. In one instance the mask represents A'i'ungu, the legendary ancestor of the Balala clan, who migrated eastward through the Lulenge Mountains: "A'i'ungu, master of Lulenge, descends [the mountains]; the feather hat on the back rustles." In another song the masker is identified as the headman (organizer of the land), and the screen represents the people who protect him. In yet another text, the masker depicts the master of Ilungu (lit., the bush): "The voice that weeps and weeps in Ilungu; Ilungu has its master."

Wooden animal figurines representing quadrupeds are identified as *abwa a ngwe*, "the dog of leopard." Single sculptures of *abwa* are used in the *bukila bwangwe* and *biciba* rites (Biebuyck, 1972a, pls. 12–14, 24–25; Gossiaux, 1974, pls. 4, 10).

Ivory and wooden anthropomorphic figurines called *ase'a* or *ase'a a ngwe* appear in *bukila bwa ngwe* and *biciba*.

Other Bembe sculptures used in bwami include ivory bracelets and walking sticks. The latter, sometimes carried on the shoulder, symbolize the peaceful intentions of high initiates, who are not carriers of spears but rather "creators of joy, adorning the country; they are creators of order, maintaining the law in the land." In judicial affairs the *biciba* holds the stick horizontally in both hands and turns it above the heads of the concerned parties to signify that the problem is settled and that no further discussion will be allowed.

Bakanu (Kanu) Traditions

In the southern part of Walikale territory, northwest of the Lega, the Bakanu comprise a number of small clan fragments of disparate origins. The component groups are territorially mixed because of such factors as intermarriage, acquisition and distribution of land through exchanges, attraction of maternal uncles and in-laws, blood pacts, economic and politico-ritual specializations, and colonial resettlement. Members of several different units were found in any one of the forty villages and hamlets that constituted the administrative *groupement* Bakanu in the 1950s.

Of all the components, the Babuluko probably came earliest to the region. The Babuluko, whom Moeller (1936, pp. 134–135) describes as a mixture of Pygmies and Lega, claim autochthonous beginnings on Mount Lwee. They have the *bwali* circumcision rites and a reduced form of the Lega bwami association, which they call *bwami bwa kikumbu* (bwami of the hat). There are three grade levels: *kagolo, bwami,* and *kindo* or *mpuntsu*. The Babuluko introduced bwami among the Basibula (Bakanu proper) and the Basasa, who came later. These Basibula are the descendants of Katunguluyeye, a grandson of Mwezi, and, like the Basasa, Babugu, and Bisakasingo who accompanied them, trace their migration from Mount Itambi, "the mountain of the chiefs," eastward to the Havu. The Basasa, the blacksmiths (*besi*) of the Basibula chiefs, specialize in making the *rusingo* emblem worn by the chiefs (*mubake*) and by the seniors (*nkula* or *mutambo*) of local descent groups. Other segments of the Bakanu, such as the Bakonco, came from Icu Island (Idjwi in Lake Kivu) and settled with their remote kin, the Basibula. Still other groups, like the Balisa, migrated from the north among those Batembo who are situated between the Komo and the Nyanga. Three groups, Banisamazi, Bamakimela, and Banakasiga, trace connections with the northern Lega; they have circumcision rites and the lower levels of bwami, including *mpuntsu*.

The patrilineal Kanu attach social importance to mother's and mother's mother's groups. Before they were reorganized by the colonial government as a single administrative unit, the Bakanu were divided into small states headed by enthroned chiefs, who were recruited from three lines of descendants of Katunguluyeye (Basibula clan). The ritual organization of the kingship was similar to that of the Nyanga: the Pygmy Nakulumwami and his wife preserved the royal paraphernalia after the chief's death and also secured the flying squirrel hat for the new chief. Other groups performed special functions and held separate titles, some as blacksmiths of the chief and others who were in charge of his burial. All dependent local groups were headed, like the Nyanga, by a council of three elders: the senior (*nkula* or *mutambo*), the second in seniority (*mungatyangatya*), and the most junior (*bela*). Grades of the bwami association were reserved among the Babuluko and Basibula for the seniors of the local descent groups and for the nonruling members (*baluzi*) of the dynasties.

Among the Bakanu, the Babutetu, a small but separate group, inhabit one village. They are descendants of Hii, founder of a hunters' group with possible origins eastward on the island of Idjwi. The Babutetu settled near the Basibula but retained their own chiefs (*mubake*); later, under Babuluko influence, they adopted the *bwali* circumcision and the lower bwami rites.

The Kanu use no sculptures in bwami, although it is more than likely that they did use some in the past.

Bakonjo (Konjo) Traditions

The Bakonjo comprise at least five separate groups, all of them small. The Konjo living in seven villages among the Bamuguba (northern Lega) have direct relationships with Konjo established in twelve villages among the Kanu (Walikale territory) and in some villages among the Batiri (Walikale territory), with the Kwame (Shabunda territory), and also with the Busi on the Shi-Havu boundary.

The twelve autonomous Konjo villages among the Kanu are inhabited mainly by representatives of three independent clans—Batulanga, Bananziga, and Basengele—which do not trace a common ancestry. The Batulanga say they emerged in Kakono (a place important in the Lega migrations), at the confluence of the Lwalaba and Lowa rivers. They have their own *bwali* circumcision rites and the lower grades of bwami (including *mpunju*), which they say were not borrowed from other groups.

The Bananziga and the Basengele place their beginnings slightly southward, downstream on the Lugulu River in the area of contact between Songola and northwestern Lega (Bakyunga). Both groups have the *bwali* circumcision and the lower levels of bwami (up to ngandu for the Basengele). The Banaziga's justifications for becoming initiated into the bwami association reveal patterns followed by the Bembe. The reasons include sickness that results when a person does not try to reach the grade levels achieved by his deceased father, dreams in which the deceased father manifests his will, and transgression of prohibitions.

The Konjo established among the Bamuguba (northern Lega) have the lower bwami rites.

The Konjo organize the *bubake* initiation to purify related persons who are joined in normally prohibited marriages. After the wife has given birth to a child, she settles as a "free woman" in a special house at the outskirts of the village. Some eastern Lega groups have retained *bubake* as a bwami initiation. In one group the son or the daughter of a woman who is pregnant during her initiation with her husband receives the title of *mubake* and also a personal name to indicate the special status. The person who is born *mubake* cannot go to war and is closely protected in times of warfare.

No bwami sculptures are known to be used by any of the Konjo subgroups.

Bakwame (Kwame) Traditions

Although there are no Bakwame artworks in collections, the group is important because of its unique cultural and historical position. Located northwest of the Lega in Shabunda territory (between the mining center Kasese and the Lugulu River), the Bakwame inhabited twelve villages in the early 1950s and formed an autonomous group under the Ndeke. The Bakwame trace genealogical origins that are different from those of the Lega (see diagram). Twelve major lineages claim descent from the ancestors Samugobe or Abumma: Banammia, Banamukitilo, Banabeida, Banandoba, Banancake, Banasilimma, Bakukwe, Banakinene, Banakabango, Bananyama, Banamukulumanya, and Bapeino. Each village is identified with one of these lineages.

Both Samugobe and Abumma branches claim to have migrated from Kakolo, which is also mentioned by the Lega, at the confluence of the Lwalaba and Lowa rivers, northwest of their present areas. They were forced to leave there because of the war with Kimimbi (or Kimbimbi, as noted by the Lega). The Bakwame do not identify Kimimbi with a particular ethnic group, but they do say that his warriors used whitened canoes and wore large red hats. Driven

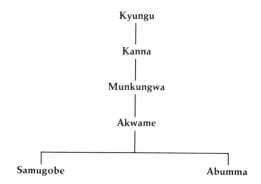

from Kakolo, each Bakwame branch followed a separate route. The Samugobe went up the Lugulu River and settled in Butula among the Songola of Nkumba. Chased again by Kimimbi, they established themselves in Ibandangulu, near the Mmi'a waterfalls of the Lugulu River, in present Bakwame country. Fragments of the eight lineages descending from Samugobe subsequently took up residence among the Komo, Songola, or Konjo as the result of internal conflicts or cognatic relationships. The Samugobe branch maintained relationships with the Abumma through intermarriages. Pursued by Kimimbi, the Abumma went up the Lowa River to Butwaankima and Makoa (among the southern Komo) before settling in their present territory. The Abumma branch was involved mainly in conflicts with the Komo, whom they call Babila. The Komo fought with bow and arrow; the Abumma, with spear and shield.

The Bakwame are in immediate geographical contact with the Komo of Lubutu, the Konjo (of Bushi in Shabunda territory), the Bakyunga (Lega), and the Songola (in Kindu territory). They identify with certain lineages found among these neighbors and even among the Nyanga. Bakwame culture reflects a remarkable synthesis of Nyanga, Komo, Songola, Konjo, and Lega patterns and institutions. The descent system is patrilineal but the Bakwame, like the Lega, attach great social importance to relationships with the maternal uncles, including not only mother's brothers but also male relatives of mother's mother, father's mother, father's father's mother, and father's mother's mother. The kinship terms are strikingly similar to those of the Nyanga, and the system of kinship classification also incorporates many Nyanga principles. Special status is accorded the position of *mubake*, a person born of patrilineally close spouses. A corresponding institution is found in different forms among the Nyanga, the Konjo, and some Lega. Among the Bakwame a *mubake* may be the son of a classificatory brother and sister linked over three agnatic generations, or the offspring of a marriage between a man and his father's mother's brother's daughter or his father's mother's brother's son's daughter. Such a marriage requires special payments to the grandparent generation. The spouses and their son wear special copper bangles.

There are no chiefs among the Bakwame. Villages identified with particular major lineages include many accretions from other lineages. The largely autonomous villages are each headed by a man called *mokota* or *mwinubungu*. Their headmen do recognize seniority linkages with other groups and refer to the senior of the larger segment as *mwisa kyuku*.

Many cults and initiations prevalent among Bakwame groups are also found among the Komo, Songola, Nyanga, or Lega. With the Komo, the Bakwame share *yaba, ndiba, bopompo, amaloto;* with the Nyanga, the *mukumo* circumcision rites and the *mpuncu* association; with the Songola, the *kilemba, zumbi, mubanga, ukanga,* and *nsinga* institutions. Other rites such as *nongi* for women and *tubanga, kabuke,* or *nyoni* for men seem to be unique to the Bakwame. Rites connected with the killing of an elephant (*mala a butuma*) or a leopard (*mukimbi*) are also significant; they are found over a wide region that includes Pere, Nyanga, Komo, Konjo, Songola, and Lega. Some cults and initiations are exclusively male and others female, while still others apply to both sexes. Configurations of initiation objects (*bitiko*), including masks and figurines, are used in virtually all rites, but none are documented.

The distribution of cults and initiations among the Bakwame follows an irregular pattern. Some villages have the three major initiations (*bwami, mpuncu,* and *kilemba*) obtained through different channels. *Kilemba*, for example, was introduced to the Banamwimma-Bakwame by a Basongola man. Other villages may have none of the three, but all observe the autonomous and patrilineally inherited circumcision rites. Skull cults (*idumba, kanga*) practiced by the Kano and the Konjo do not appear among the Bakwame. Although bwami initiates were buried in their houses, the corpses of men who had finished *kilemba* and of women who had completed the *makengelo* rite of the *zumbi* initiation were exposed in the forest on high tables (*katampi*).

A bwami association of the Lega type exists in eight of the twelve villages. The other four villages, which are in close contact with the Komo or the Konjo, are all descended from the Abumma branch. Where the bwami initiations exist, they do not go beyond the ngandu grade. There is a precise tradition of the origin of bwami. A certain Isimbasimba of the Banakoudo sublineage of the Banammia maximal lineage (Samugobe branch) obtained bwami about a century ago from the neighboring Bakyunga. Isimbasimba had seduced a Bakyunga woman (of Banalukima lineage) who had been initiated to the bulonda grade and was married to a Bakyunga initiate (Banakaninkia lineage). Isimbasimba married her, but he was first compelled by her father to accept initiation from kongabulumbu to ngandu. Isimbasimba and his successors then conferred bwami on other lineages. In 1952 there were twenty ngandu among the Bakwame, representing six maximal lineages of the Samugobe branch and some of the Abumma.

Baleka (Leka) Traditions

There are at least four groups of Leka, all situated near the Lwalaba River. The northernmost group lives west of the Lwalaba near the Ubundu administrative center. The two central groups are contiguous, east of the Lwalaba. Both the northern and central Leka neighbor on the Komo, the Lengola, and the Mitoko, and they are often merged with the Mitoko. The southern group is established in the Punia Zone near the confluence of the Lwalaba and Lowa rivers.

Spokesmen of the southern Leka claim that a European called Polepole gave the name Baleka to heterogeneous groups of peoples whose lives centered on the Lwalaba and the Lowa rivers. Among the Baleka I have found groups, such as the Baundulu and the Babondo, who call themselves Enya (Bagenia). Coming from Kirundu, they traveled down the Lwalaba and Lowa rivers in canoes, and some crossed the Lengola area. The Babondo and others say they are the descendants of Kimimbi (a tough warrior); some of their relatives probably live among the northern Songola, particularly the Babiri or Babile of Nkumba. The name and attributes of this Kimimbi bear a striking resemblance to the Kimbimbi war leader who animated the Lega migration on the Luwalaba River. Other Baleka components, such as the Bangatu, originate in the Mitoko area; others like the Baboko and the Bagundwa come from among the Lengola-Bafulamba; the Batikabagu and Banambulue have ties with the Songola, and there are also Komo and Babemo offshoots. At least some of the so-called Baleka subgroups have, like the Komo, a gerontocratic system. Clans (*kitutu*) form dispersed totemic patrilineal groups. Residential lineages and clan segments (*kisili*) are the core political units, each headed by a *mukota,* a term used by the Mitoko, Lengola, and Songola to designate a person in a position of authority. The *mukota*, also called *fumiasu,* is the oldest member of the oldest living generation.

Stools collected among a northern Leka group have the basic form of the typical Lega *kisumbi* stool: a concave spherical seat and convex base connected by four slightly outward-bent legs. Before 1910 Dargent, a *chef-de-zone* in Ponthierville (*secteur* Lubutu, *poste* Walikale), collected three horned wooden masks (Tervuren, no. 2465) which he attributed to the Leka. The masks, which Dargent called *kongu* (a term also known to the Lega), resemble the horned *kayamba* masks used by the Lega bwami association. Dargent (Tervuren, Dossier 148) believed the masks were worn by circumcisers, but they are carved more crudely than the *kayamba* and exhibit distinctive morphological features (e.g., the faces are convex; one mask has large, open, oval-shaped, slanting eyes; one mask shows the large open V-shaped mouth found in some Lega figurines).

Bakomo (Komo) Traditions

The Komo, scattered over an enormous forest area from Kisangani to the northern rim of Legaland, are divided into numerous dispersed patrilineal totemic clans (de Mahieu, 1975; 1980, pp. 1–96). Residential groups composed of clan segments and lineages are the basic political units. The exercise of political authority within these units is determined by age: the lineage head or the village headman is the oldest representative of the oldest living generation, and on his death authority passes to the next-oldest person of his generation. He is called "our old man" (*mgbega ndeesu*) or "possessor of the village" (*menandji*).

Sociocultural integration is achieved through control over the *esomba*, a term applied to several ritual institutions and their offices as well as to material objects, including sculptures, which are revealed and explained in the initiations. The word *esomba* (*lusumba, kasumba*) is used with similar meanings by many ethnic groups, ranging from the Mbole and the Nande to the Lega. It is noteworthy that the appellation Basumba, widely applied to Pygmy groups, may be related to this concept. Persons become officials of the *esomba* rites (*ab'esomba* for men, *am'esomba* for women) through initiation. The force inherent in the *esomba* may inflict illness upon people who do not observe their proscriptions. Many noninitiates declared by diviners to be afflicted can therefore be cured by *esomba* treatments (simple purifications or extensive cures), which may last for weeks.

Men are ranked into three internally subdivided age classes: the noncircumcised, the circumcised, and those who have children. Transition from the lowest to the second class is ensured through elaborate circumcision rites (*gandja*). Passage from the second class to the class of "men with children" is ritualized through the *umba* ceremonies, which are of Pygmy origin. Regardless of sickness, all men who have children are initiated into *umba* and have the right to participate in all major ceremonies. *Gandja* and *umba*, mandatory rites of passage par excellence, are controlled respectively by the *menegandja* and the *abaka-umba*, high ritual dignitaries also called *moame*.

The position of *moame* is not determined by age and seniority as is that of the lineage elder. Not every autonomous group has one of these officials, although every village aspires to have a *moame*. Ritual functions, however, tend to remain within a close-knit agnatic branch and are passed on to sons of the same father before being transferred to the sons of another man in the unit. Moral considerations govern the selection of the "master of the circumcision" and the "father of the *umba* rite." The candidate must show moderation, prudence, wisdom, generosity in sharing, and hospitality (qualities also rated high in a Lega initiate). As the *moame* shares his ritual responsibilities with his first wife (called *ama-moame* or *ngole*, the latter term applied to the senior wife by the Pere and the Nande), these qualities are also assessed in the candidate's wife, who in addition must show absolute fidelity to her husband (also required of an initiated wife among the Lega). Other criteria guide the designation of a *moame* candidate: he must have children and his father must be deceased.

The *moame* dignitaries are organized into confraternities, which function at the regional level (i.e., groups of neighboring and interacting villages with boundaries that are not strictly delineated). There are competing confraternities of *menagandja* and *aba-ka-umba* in one location. Each autonomous regional confraternity has its own hierarchical structure, which is determined by years of service and its historical development among component lineages. Successors of the person who first introduced the function into the region, therefore, have precedence over the successors of those who were initiated by him. Persons who are both "master of the circumcision" and "father of the *umba* rite" hold the highest socioritual status in the regional community and are regarded as the most accomplished Komo. This social hierarchy is reflected in the seating arrangements when regional dignitaries meet in the special rectangular house with two lateral doors. Dignitaries of the circumcision and *umba* rites own similar insignia: a large shoulder strap of bongo hide with an attached, sheathed *pindi* or *mbotea* knife, a wide loincloth in bark trimmed with chicken feathers and decorated with geometrical designs, a necklace of leopard teeth, an *aphapha* swatter, and a walking cane (*motumbo*). The latter is the most important emblem; only the *moame* may touch it, and there are numerous prescriptions about its use. The walking sticks are tied together around the central pole of the initiation house to symbolize the unity of the dignitaries and, less overtly, their union with the sky (de Mahieu, 1975, p. 245).

The *moame* dignitaries may act as individuals for the lifting of maledictions or for the rendering of oaths, or as a college for invocations that begin all healing, purification, and passage rites. Through their ritual structure and powers of intervention, the *moame* confraternities thus constitute the most powerful integrative element in Komo society. Their activities transcend clan and lineage divisions, and their authority is derived from their control of the *esomba*, "a power that emanates from another world."

The Komo use anthropomorphic figurines in several rites (Biebuyck, 1977*b*, pp. 54 – 58). Of major significance are the ivory figurines and small ivory tusks appearing in their *mpunju* initiations. *Mpunju* (*mpuncu, mbuntsu*) rites are widespread among the Pere, some Nyanga, and the Bali and the Rumbi in the north; in several Lega communities, they are incorporated into the bwami association. According to Galdermans (1934), Moeller (1936), and Gérard (1956), the figurines, otherwise kept secretly, are revealed, contemplated, and interpreted during the *mpunju* rites. These procedures offer a striking parallelism to the Lega methods of using the ivories.

Masks are rarely used. One pair of masks (*nsembu*) is linked with rites organized by an association of diviners (*babankunda*). The large polychrome rectangular or oval face masks are characterized by open oval, square, or crescentic eyes, a long, narrow nose, and a wide-open rectangular, square, or crescentic mouth, sometimes showing sharpened teeth. The male mask (*biangolo*) and the female mask (*ibole*) are thought to be the father and mother of Ongondo, a character not represented by a mask. De Mahieu (1973) suggests that these masks are the archetypes of the initiator and his wife and that Ongondo is the neophyte.

The few *nsembu* masks in existence, owned exclusively by descendants of the earliest initiates of the *nkunda* association of diviners, are seen only at a diviner's initiation, often celebrated in conjunction with commemorative ceremonies for a deceased colleague. Before the rites begin the masks are wrapped in bark cloth and covertly transported to the neophyte's village by a young relative of the owner. In a preliminary ritual the young man is purified to protect him against the power of the masks, which are welcomed with offerings of honey and salt and with words of appeasement. For the climactic nocturnal ceremony in the village, the maskers are secretly dressed inside a specially built circular house which, according to Moeller (1937), has a conical roof adorned with a bird sculpture. The house itself is intricately decorated with painted and sculptured panels, polychrome plank doors, and garlands; miniature spears, knives, axes in parasol wood, animal tails, and feathers hang from a vine (Tervuren, Dossier 522). The maskers, surrounded by acolytes, then emerge, accompanied by the sound of horns. After being seated on a bench in the village they execute movements with heads and arms, which have been lengthened by a cloth-covered reed framework. After a brief performance the dancers are led back to the house.

Although Komo tradition holds that the *nkunda* divination techniques and the masks were invented by Abalambu in a peripheral area of northeastern Komoland, the similarities to the large *muminia* masks used in some Lega initiations are striking. The rare *muminia* are owned by representatives of select lineages associated with the origin of certain rites. In some ceremonies the maskers perform head and arm movements while seated in a corner of the initiation house. One rite symbolic of honey harvesting is called *nkunda*. This ancient bwami tradition seems to be linked directly with that of the *babankunda* masks.

Bazimba (Southern Binja) Traditions

Situated in Kasongo Zone, the Zimba or southern Binja are divided into two groups separated by the Kunda River (tributary of the Lwalaba). Those west of the river are called Wazimba wa Maringa; those east of it, Wazimba wa Mulu (Boone, 1961, pp. 23–26). The ethnic composition of Kasongo Zone is particularly complex, including Enya riverain populations, Songye, Hemba, Bangubangu, Mamba, Kasenga, Nonda, Kwange, and Zimba. Many groups have a mixed character; some have also been influenced by the Lega, others by the Luba, Songye, and Kusu (see Moeller, 1936, pp. 138–164). Some Zimba groups have institutions in common with the Lega (*bwali* circumcision, bwami) or with the Luba (*luhuna* or *bufumu*). The Zimba themselves probably emigrated from areas to the east and southeast near Lake Tanganyika, whence they were chased by the Tunguti or Tuwari. As noted earlier, small entities called Zimba or Cimba are found among Bembe, Basikasingo, and Boyo. There is also an important group of Zimba (Chief Manda) situated more southward on Lake Tanganyika in the former Baudouinville territory. It is likely that all these groups are offshoots of the Zimba migration. The Zimba were followed by the Mamba, Kasenga, Nonda, and Kwange, some of whom traveled along Lake Tanganyika as far as Uvira before moving southwestward through Bembeland (see Abemba, 1971, p. 35).

All the early sources (Bronchart, 1933; Martin, 1935; Soors, n.d.) mention the close relationships between the southern Binja and Songola, Bangubangu, and Lega. Binja traditions collected by Bronchart hold that their ancestor and Lega are the sons of Kakwa, who was born on the shores of Lake Tanganyika and chased from there by the Pygmies. So direct a relationship obviously pertains only to subgroups that are incorporated with the southern Lega.

A group of Zimba called Batali by the Lega and Bakudwa by other Zimba encompass fourteen villages established south of the Bakabango-Lega of Moligi (Shabunda territory). Each village is associated with a maximal lineage (*mukinda*). Although the Batali have a fairly unified genealogy and history of migration, it is doubtful if all component groups sprang from the same origins. The Batali, descendants of Kimwali's child Zimba, probably came originally from Lubumba, a region in the Itombwe Mountains inhabited by the Bembe. Chased by the Tukundugulu (whom they identify as Pygmies), the Batali settled in Kalunda na Kiganja near the Kama River in the area presently occupied by the Boyo of Kabambare territory. Two of Zimba's descendants, Kilonda and Kanga, gave rise to the Batali. Lineages beginning with these two ancestors are also found among the Bembe, Boyo, Zimba, Bangubangu, and among the Bakabango of Pangi, and the Batali have particularly close relationships with several western Bembe subgroups. The Batali intermarry with various Bakabango-Lega and Bangubangu subgroups, but not with the Boyo and other Lega units.

The Batali have no centralized political system. Their sense of unity vis-à-vis surrounding groups is fostered in common genealogical and migration traditions and in the recognition of a common taboo, the *mukulungu* tree (which may be used only to impale a leopard on a branch for display). The core political unit is the village, which is inhabited by a patrilineage and its accretions and headed by the *mwicambuga*, the village leader. The Batali are strongly influenced by the Lega, and their patrilineal descent system shows traces of an earlier matrilineal organization (e.g., in its emphasis on a Crow-type system of kinship terminology).

The Batali have two types of circumcision rites, *kalomba* and *lwira*. *Kalomba*, for young men of two or three adjoining villages, is held in conjunction with the killing and ceremonial display of a leopard. The *lwira* circumcision is derived from the Bweku, a group partly incorporated with the Babongolo-Lega and known among the Bembe as Obekulu. This cyclical rite is held periodically in all Batali villages. One village inhabited by a fragment of the Balambo (a group widely scattered among the eastern Lega, Nyindu, Bembe, and Basikasingo) has the exclusive right to initiate a circumcision cycle. Both rites are presided over by the *kilanda,* a status holder who probably wore a mask of hide and feathers similar to those used by the Bembe *elanda* association. *Kilanda* also performed when elephants or buffalo were killed.

The Batali do not have bwami, but those established among the Bakabango by virtue of affinal or cognatic relationships may be initiated to the lower grades.

The southwestern Lega are in contact with other Zimba subgroups: Byale, Langilwa, Gunga, and Tuku. The first three perform the bwami rites up to ngandu, and the Tuku have only kongabulumbu (see Moeller, 1936, p. 411).

A few of the sculptures attributed to the southern Binja may be linked with the bwami association. Before 1911 Populair, a *chef-de-poste* in Warumba, collected five wooden figurines, four female and one male (Tervuren, nos. 1498 4/1–4/4, 1585), among the Binja (see Maes, 1911). The roughly carved, standing figurines differ in size (43, 38, 31, 26.5, and 29 cm respectively) and in the superstructures adorning their heads (a four-pronged crown; a bulbous excrescence; mortarlike extensions). Their overall style, however, shows similarities: arms carved loose from the body and hands touching the hips or the lower abdomen; concave, heart-shaped faces with narrow slit eyes, replaced in one specimen by real cowries and in another by shell inlay. Populair described the figurines as "dolls." One is identified as *kese,* and another as *tambue.* The objects are said to be protectors of children and of the house, but this information may be incorrect because they closely resemble the larger wooden figurines used in certain Lega bwami rites.

A crude ivory bust (Tervuren, no. 19987; 10.2 cm) ending in a knop has oval slit eyes, pupil indication, and arms in light relief on the sides; it resembles some Lega carvings even more closely. A female bust in ivory collected before 1922 by Ricciardi (Bassani, 1977, pls. 437–438; 16 cm) has few Lega features (circle-dots on the coiffure, arms, chest, and abdomen; hands near the navel), but it is the type of object that would fit into the context of the bwami initiations. Marijnissen et al. (1975, pl. 101) attribute to the Zimba a marvelous prognathic ivory head on a short pole (11 cm). If correct, this designation indicates that some southern Binja had adopted sculptures in pure Lega style for their bwami rites.

Three standing wooden figurines (Tervuren, nos. 12050–12051, 12053; height 18.5 cm, 25.5 cm) collected by Ooms in the Itombwe area (inhabited by Bembe and offshoots of the pre-Bembe hunters) are ascribed to the Bangubangu. With their typical concave, heart-shaped faces, they are stylistically close to the sculptures described above and thus may illustrate the intertribal spread of Lega-style carvings linked with bwami.

Outside the area where bwami is prevalent, a number of ethnic groups possess voluntary associations similar to bwami in structure, ideology, and purpose. They include the *bukota* association of the Mitoko and the Lengola, the *lilwa* of the Mbole, the *nsubi* of the Songola and the Babemo, and the *esambo* (*kisambo*) of the Ngengele and the Bashiluamba. Furthermore, some ethnic groups developed centralized political systems under the authority of sacred chiefs and kings called *mwami* or *mubake*. Among them are subgroups of the Nande, Pere, Nyanga, Hunde, Tembo, Havu, Shi, Vira, Furiiru, riverain groups of Lake Tanganyika, and the already mentioned Nyindu and Basimwenda.

Bukota among the Mitoko and the Lengola

The Mitoko (Mituku) are established in Ubundu Zone (former Ponthierville) between the Lomami and the Lwalaba rivers, on both sides of the Lilo. Some Lega traditions call them the descendants of one of Lega's sons and place them at the same level as other large Lega subgroups, such as Babongolo and Bakisi. Small clusters of Baleka settled on both banks of the Lwalaba are in contact with the Mitoko, the Lengola, and the northern Komo. The Baleka are often thought to be riverain Mitoko, but the Enya (Wagenia) ethnic element is strongly represented among them. Numerous groups of Enya live along the Lwalaba River between Kisangani and Kasongo. Some are said to be of Luba origin; others are linked with the Mongo. The northern Enya situated between Kisangani and the Lwalaba-Lowa confluence, however, claim they are of eastern origin and are related to the Mbole-Bayembo through the mother of their earliest leader (Droogers, 1974, p. 25). The Lega traditions mention early contacts with the Enya of Kilimono, who demanded compensation to help them cross the larger rivers.

The Mitoko are surrounded in the north, east, and south by the Lengola; in the west they border on the Mbole and the Balinga. It is sometimes said that the Mitoko were pushed west of the Lwalaba by the Komo and the Lengola. Their presence in that area, however, must date from ancient times, as Lega subgroups like the Bakyunga, who have close connections with the Mitoko, claim that they left the Mitoko in Muntungu, west of the Lwalaba, before migrating southeastward. The Mitoko have numerous cultural features in common with the Lega, and their language clearly belongs to the Lega group (Stappers and Agbamubi, 1970, p. 211).

The patrilineal Mitoko, divided into six partly dispersed clans, have a segmentary lineage organization. A group of villages inhabited by related lineages constitutes a *kisi,* an autonomous localized clan group with numerous accretions (maternal uncles, sororal nephews).

The *bukota* association cuts across the lineage structure to serve central political, social, economic, jural, and ritual functions (Marmitte, 1934). A tradition brought to light by Van Belle (1926) and Aurez (1930) claims that *bukota* originated with Mpumba, one of the first ancestors. In order to discipline his recalcitrant son, Mpumba invented initiation to *otamba,* a lower level in *bukota,* and forced his son to accede. The legend simply reinforces *bukota*'s social control functions, also heavily stressed by the Lega.

Membership in the *bukota* association is achieved through initiations, which several sources say are held in the forest. Selection of a candidate presupposes observance of kinship principles, moral acceptability, tutorship, payment of fees, and distribution of gifts. At least one wife must be coinitiated with her husband. *Bukota* has three basic grades—*bukota* itself, *kasimbi*, and *nkumi*—which seem to be subdivided into numerous inadequately known levels and phases (Moeller, 1936, pp. 293, 421–432). Initiation to each level centers on the revelation and interpretation of basic objects, including figurines, and carries special privileges and duties. The members of *kasimbi*, for example, organize the circumcision rites; the *nkumi* guard the highest initiation objects, including the sculptures. All members of the association have the right to be buried in the village men's house.

As among the Lega, several animals, including the eagle, pangolin, python, civet, and leopard, are reserved for the members of the association. A special relationship exists between the highest initiate (*nkumi*) and the leopard. When a leopard is killed, it is placed on stakes in front of the *nkumi*'s house and dressed with the *nkumi*'s paraphernalia (necklaces with leopard teeth, large knife, beads, and shell money). After a day of dancing, the leopard is transported outside the village to the circumcision house and is secretly distributed by members of the *bukota* association (Moeller, 1936, pp. 401–404).

Mitoko wooden sculptures (Biebuyck, 1977*b*; Leiris and Delange, 1967, pl. 110; Bascom, 1967, pl. 180) have many morphological features in common with Lega sculptures, including the heart-shaped, concave or flat face. The statues, however, are often much larger (some are close to 1 meter tall) and show traces of polychromy. Some figurines and masklike faces carved on poles have a long, narrow wooden beard, which is not found in Lega sculpture. The exact relationships between the sculptures and the *bukota* association are not known, but high-ranking initiates owned the figurines as marks of status (Marmitte and Van Belle, 1932–1934). There is evidence that sculptures used as initiation objects had distinctive names relating to characters and that some were placed on the tombs of high initiates and subsequently discarded. Some sculptures were also used in the circumcision rites and in peacemaking activities, which were organized and controlled by *bukota* members. A mask (*nduku*), perhaps similar to the Mbole mask used in *lilwa*, is said to have appeared in a funerary dance held for *bukota* members (ibid.).

The Lengola of Ubundu Zone are settled on both sides of the Lwalaba River, bordered by the Komo and Leka to the east, a group called Bira (but unrelated to the Bira located eastward of Mambasa Zone) to the north, the Linga and Mbole to the west, and the Komo to the south. Mbole and Komo offshoots are found among the Lengola, who seem to be a heterogeneous ethnic group, or at least one marked by considerable cultural differentiation because of influences from their neighbors. Jak (1938) distinguishes between Lengola-Bira, who are forest-oriented, and Lengola-Leka, whose lives center on the great rivers. This division is accepted by Stappers (1971, p. 257), but in between these two he places a third group, the Bavalongo. The name Lengola is probably a nickname (Van Belle, 1932). Those on the left bank call themselves Bahuse; those on the right bank identify themselves as Bayangwa, but the left-bank Lengola, the Mitoko, and the Leka also designate them as Bahuse (Marmitte, 1933). The Lega use the term Bahuse (Bouse) to refer to an ancient hunting population they encountered and who still survive in Legaland. Moeller (1936, pp. 52–56) says the Lengola are forerunners of the Komo, who came from the east, but this claim may apply only to some Lengola components. Rommes (1951) discovered Lengola relationships with the Mabudu of the Wamba Zone far to the northeast of them, and he notes that some groups seem linked to the Komo and others to the Mitoko.

In many ways the Lengola of the left bank of the Lwalaba are different from those of the right bank. The clans and lineages of the left are less scattered than among those of the right, and the *bukota* association is more developed among the Lengola of the left bank. Each of the three basic titles in *bukota—mukota, mokoli,* and *dumanga*—has numerous levels. Men enter *bukota* with some of their wives, and there are specific female grades. The members of the association wield political, legal, and economic power; they also organize healing and circumcision rituals as well as leopard and burial rites. Komo influences among the Lengola of the right bank are strong in the *esumba* healing and initiation practices, such as *lilwa*, in which masks are used, and *biaba*, which utilizes figurines of Komo type (Jak, 1938).

Lengola sculptures (Biebuyck, 1977b; Cornet, 1975, pp. 124–127; Leiris and Delange, 1967, pl. 163; Maesen, 1960b, pl. 42) have morphological features in common with Lega sculptures, such as concave, heart-shaped faces, bifrontal form, superpositions of multiple faces, and busts. Some wooden figurines, however, are slender and elongated and are covered with dark resin and white dots. At least one Lengola figurine (Maesen, 1960b, pl. 42) is stylistically very close to some Lega wooden statues. There is no documentation on the precise connections of the sculptures with the *bukota* association. Some figurines are revealed and interpreted during the *bukota* rites; some are placed on the graves of high-ranking members or used during circumcision and peacemaking rites organized by members of the association. Where Komo influences are strong, however, other figurines seem to be linked with healing practices. Exquisitely carved wooden cups with cephalomorphic handles, highly stylized anthropomorphic-zoomorphic figurines, and double stools (some adorned with masklike faces) are also connected with the circumcision rites and the *bukota* association.

Of special interest is a Lengola type of facial tattoo called *lukamba*. It is formed by a double line that runs from ear to ear above the eyebrows and ends at the base of the nose to look like an open V. It is possible that this mode of facial adornment originally had a much wider distribution and that it profoundly influenced the characteristic heart-shaped, concave face in many sculptures of the Lengola and of the Mbole, Mitoko, Komo, Lega, and Bembe.

Lilwa among the Mbole

The Mbole are settled east and west of the Lomami River and overlap into the Opala and Isangi zones. They live to the west and the northwest of the Lengola and the Mitoko. Mbole language is usually linked with the Mongo group, which extends west and southwestward over a huge forest area, but there seem to be major linguistic and cultural differences within the Mbole.

Although early reports by Van De Capelle (1915) and an anonymous source (n.d.) agree on the importance of the *lilwa* association, the information they give is so conflicting that they might be describing separate peoples. The two sources are in fact discussing distinct Mbole subgroups, one located in the southwest and the other in the northeast of their region. The social system described by Van De Capelle resembles a patrilineal segmentary clan and lineage organization that absorbed many cognatically related people. There are five levels of lineage segmentation, and the heads of each unit are selected on the gerontocratic principle (in each instance the leader of the group is the oldest representative of the oldest generation). Any leader is called *afa* or *ise* (father), and he makes all decisions in consultation with the council of elders. The anonymous writer explains the organization of the northeastern Mbole by presenting an interesting example.

The key political groups are autonomous local communities whose members are settled in several villages and hamlets within a common territory. These communities are composed of a number of agnatic maximal lineages that do not trace common origins but rather have occupied, either simultaneously or consecutively, the same territory in the course of migrations. Each maximal lineage is divided into smaller units, some agnatically related and others incorporated into the group. Each of the smaller lineages is headed by an *oli*, whose selection is based on gerontocratic principles. Maximal lineages constituting the local community are ranked according to titles, which are vested in the group and reflect the chronology of settlement within the region. The head of a maximal lineage is known by one of two titles: *nome* is the elder representing the senior maximal lineage that preceded all others in occupying the territory; *lisomba* is the elder of each maximal lineage that came later. The *lisomba* is considered to have received his title from the *nome* and is therefore dependent upon him. Some *lisomba* rank higher than others, depending on the historical sequence in which their groups arrived and were accepted into the political community. The situation is complicated, however, because all groups have other elders who are not in a seniority position but who have received these titles.

Initiation, and not merely structural position, seems to be at the basis of succession to titles, although almost nothing is known about the initiations. According to some sources, all youths first pass through the *lilwa* initiations, which may coincide with or follow circumcision rites but are distinct from them. The males later undergo the *ekanga* initiation to become full-fledged adult members of the group. These rites are required for initiation to political office (*oli, lisomba, nome*) or to special ritual positions linked with *lilwa*. There are four major male offices in *lilwa*, known under different regional names: *lehile* or *esoya*, *lokulama* or *yekama*, *lofinga*, and *lokolo*. Each dignitary has a particular function in the passage rites for young men, who receive moral teachings from *lofinga* and instruction in the secret language from *lokolo*. The *nome* is frequently also the *lehile* of *lilwa*, the supreme ritual leader. Women may occupy high offices, such as the most prominent *lomongo* (*lumungu*) and *asele*. *Lomongo* is the wife of a *nome* and is indissolubly married to her husband through initiation to *lilwa*. *Asele*, married to a *nome*, is selected by the *nome* college because of her outstanding arbitrative abilities. She holds the *lilwa* stick, intervenes in disputes, and has the power to stop feuding. *Asele* has little interaction with other women; when sick she must be treated by the *lilwa* men, and when she dies she is secretly buried by them.

Kalala Nkudi (1979), whose research is based mainly on the Balinga, provides a new nomenclature and new insights into the structure of *lilwa*. The association, which performs educational, jural, political, economic, and ritual functions, is structured hierarchically. All young men and some women (daughters of the highest initiates) are obligatorily initiated to the lowest level (*likomela*). On the initiative of the elders (*wilangi*) of residential groups, the neophytes are isolated in a forest lodge and, guided by a ritual expert (*onanga*), pass through a series of trials. They also learn basic social and ethical precepts. At the final rite they are allowed to see and touch the symbolic objects of *lilwa*, which include figurines representing ritual victims and condemned persons. The ritual leaders show *ofika* figurines and warn the young initiates: "Watch out; if you scorn the customs of the ancestors, we will kill you and fix you in a statue, as we did for the son of X and Y" (ibid., p. 30).

The *likomela* rites are preliminary to numerous initiations leading to higher office in *lilwa*: the specialized singers, sculptors, and blacksmiths; the *opinga* aides and messengers of the highest initiates; the *ikoni koy*, charged with the hanging of ritual victims and condemned persons; the *kanga*, diviners who also impose mystical sanctions upon evildoers; and the *yeni*, the supreme initiates. Although these positions are achieved within distinct lineages according to patterns of agnatic inheritance, they are also conditioned by initiation. Most lineages have a *kanga* and a *yeni*; when a person of either grade dies, the funerary rituals close with the initiation of his successor. On the death of a *kanga*, the corpse is suspended from a pole in his house and the liquids are collected before he is buried in a termitaria. The successor is asperged with the liquids and must then find the ritual objects owned by the *kanga* and hidden in the forest. At the final stage of the ritual, the new *kanga* rushes into the forest where he is said to encounter an albino woman with whom he mates and who reveals the place where the objects are concealed. When a *yeni* is moribund, he is isolated by his aides in the forest and killed. After the corpse is exposed in a giant tree, his successor is initiated.

The power and authority of high-ranking members of *lilwa* are symbolized by the exclusive possession of the famed polychrome *ofika* statues (Biebuyck, 1976*c*; Rouvroy, 1929). The figurines are said to be conventionalized images of persons hanged for transgressions against *lilwa* laws (e.g., seduction of an *asele* woman, infringement of proscriptions and prohibitions) and the public order (e.g., homicide, incest, proven witchcraft). Kalala Nkudi (1979, pp. 20 – 21) says some sculptures represent sacrificial victims secretly hanged in the forest on the occasion of a *yeni*'s initiation. The sculptures were carved after the hanging at the request of the senior head (*wilangi*) of the local group. The objects are carefully hidden by their owners, who show them to young men during the passage rites to explain the consequences of immoral conduct, to inculcate respect for elders, to transmit concepts about etiquette, and to warn against adultery, thieving, lying, and witchcraft. The *ofika* are also displayed during executions by hanging, in times of persistent bad hunting, when oaths are taken, or when serious conflicts between parties are settled (Abbeloos, 1949). On such occasions the arrival of the figurines is announced with drumming; women and children are not permitted to see them.

Nsubi of the Songola and the Babemo

The name Songola was probably given in the nineteenth century to peoples living in the eastern part of Kindu Zone, mostly on the eastern side of the Lwalaba River between the Lwalaba-Lowa confluence in the north and the Lwalaba-Elila confluence in the south. The heterogeneity of the population was recognized early by Delhaise (1909*a*, p. 45), and Schmit (Tervuren, Dossier 718) described a mixture of Mongo, Zimba, and Lega. Meeussen (1952) found two distinct linguistic communities among the Songola: the Ombo in the north who speak a type of Mongo, and the Binja in the south whose language is related to the Lega language. These Binja also have cultural affinities with the Zimba (southern Binja; Abemba, 1972). The Songola are in contact with the Baleka and the Babemo in the north, the Lega in the east, the Zimba in the extreme southeast, and the Ngengele in the west. The southern Songola are called Babile by the Lega and share numerous cultural features with them. Songola men married Lega women and sometimes settled with Lega in-laws and cognates. They could then be initiated to the lower grades of bwami, and in exceptional circumstances a man of Songola origin could be initiated to kindi. In one instance a Songola residing in a Lega village was forced to take kindi because he was accused of being responsible for the burning of a house that contained the grave and initiation objects of a Lega relative with kindi. Numerous trade and exchange relationships linked the Songola and the Lega. The Lega obtained camwood powder and palm oil from the Songola; the Songola, iron and bark cloth from the Lega. The western Lega, for example, purchased pots of oil with axes, knives, spears, and hunting nets. Like the Lega, the southern Songola had the long type of house with walls made of bark sheets (Delhaise, 1909a, p. 159), and they also played the *mbale* dice and the *lonze* ball games.

The Songola are probably organized in segmentary lineages and achieve social integration through a graded association generally called *nsubi,* about which there is little information. Delhaise (1909a) lists a hierarchy of eight "spirits," the three superior ones named *kilimba, mukalu,* and *nsubi.* Bronchart (1931) and Moeller (1936, pp. 446–450) discuss four stages or grades of membership: *ludzikilo, lupukupuku, butamba,* and *lokengo.* Data that I obtained among the western Lega indicate regional differences in the organization, but the terms used overlap with Delhaise's nomenclature. The Lega mention *kilemba, mukalu, tulumbu,* and *nsubi* grades, equating them respectively with kongabulumbu, ngandu, bulonda, and yananio-kindi. Each *nsubi* level is associated with special insignia, such as hats, hides, bracelets, belts, and leopard teeth necklaces. Accession to the grades is accomplished through payments and through initiations which take place in the forest and do not require the use of sculptures (Delhaise, 1909a, pp. 195–196). Women seem to be coinitiated with their husbands.

Persons who achieve the *nsubi* grade apparently wield great power and authority, and they also have numerous privileges. The distribution of certain animals (pangolin, aardvark, eagle, crocodile, python, genet, leopard, bongo antelope) takes place under their supervision in the men's house (*kibulu*). Extremely elaborate ceremonies having to do with the leopard, the pangolin, and the aardvark are held in the forest and in the village, where the animal is dressed in the *nsubi* paraphernalia before being distributed (Moeller, 1936, pp. 446–450). A *nsubi* member is buried by colleagues in a hole dug under a termitaria behind his house. Axes and knives are buried with the body; the deceased's paraphernalia and other belongings are displayed in a large hangar built above the grave. A *nsubi*'s son must be initiated without delay after the burial ceremony (Delhaise, 1909a, pp. 134–135).

No sculptures from the Songola are known. The Bakyunga, a northwestern Lega group that had adopted *kilemba* from the Songola, told me, however, that figurines were utilized in this initiation. The western Lega confirmed the use of a mask in the Songola *nsubi* rites.

The Babemo are located west of the Kwame and, like the Leka and the Bira, are not regarded as "authentic Komo" (de Mahieu, 1980). Groups of different origins constitute the *chefferie* Babemo. The Babemo properly speaking followed the Lwalaba southward and passed through Lengola country. They trace relationships with Kimimbi's descendants, whom they call Babiri (among the Songola or the Bira?), and they speak a mixture of Songola and Komo. Other groups incorporated with the Babemo, such as the Basupala and the Bapondoba, claim linkages with the Baundulu-Bagenya; others such as the Balika-Lupepo, with the Lengola; and the Bapomongo, with the Komo. The senior of a Babemo lineage group, called *mukota*, is a member of the *nsubi* association.

Esambo of the Ngengele

The name Bangengele seems to be a misreading of Asa a ngele, People of Downstream. The original name probably was Ana e nkumbi, Children of the Hawk, after a characteristic undulating tattoo in full or dotted lines on men's cheeks and abdomen (Schmidt, 1933). The Ngengele of the Kindu Zone were divided into three administrative units: the *chefferie* Bangengele, the *chefferie* Tshiambi, and the *secteur* Baombo (Lecoste, 1952). The first two subgroups, located west of the Lwalaba in the swampy plains, are in contact with the Tetela and the Kusu. The Baombo are situated almost entirely east of the Lwalaba in the rain forest near the Songola, with whom they are often confused. Ngengele is included among the large Mongo language group that extends westward through the forest belt. Jacobs (1962, p. 9 and map) places the Ngengele language in the Nkutshu (Kusu) subdivision of the Tetela complex among the Mongo. The Ngengele are bounded on north and west by the linguistically related Bakuti, Balanga, Bambuli, and Bashiluamba, who claim relationships with the Mbole (Delcourt and Dallons, 1949; Rochez, 1951a−c, 1955a−c). The Bakuti have a graded association (Rochez, 1955a, calls it *pala*) in which lineage heads achieve the highest levels (*kunga* or *kokolekota*). The Balanga and the Bambuli have forms of organization similar to *bukota* of the Mitoko (Delcourt and Dallons, 1949). The Bashiluamba have the *esambo* (*kisambo*) association in which only very few men achieve the supreme *likengo* grade (Rochez, 1955b). The Matapa and the Kusu (Nkutshu) to the south are directly related to the Ngengele, who, however, seem to have numerous cultural features in common with their eastern neighbors, the Songola and the Lega. *Esambo*, for example, has more similarities to *nsubi* and bwami than to the hierarchical *nkum'okonda* institution of the Tetela. In fact, east of the Lwalaba area there is interpenetration among Lega, Songola, and Ngengele (Aurez, 1934).

The social organization of the patrilineal Ngengele is based on segmentary lineages (*ulunga*), which are controlled at various levels by a lineage head called *mukota* (Soors, 1928; Schmidt, 1933; Lecoste, 1952, 1954). It seems that all lineage heads, as well as many other elders, are initiated to *esambo*, and that all members receive the general title *mukota*. *Esambo* is a graded association open to all men provided their behavior is compatible with its values and they make the necessary payments for initiation. From three to eight grades are mentioned for men and two for women (Schmidt, 1933; Lecoste, 1952, 1954; Rochez, 1955c). Membership in the various levels is characterized by distinctive hats, belts, hides, necklaces of leopard teeth, and copper bracelets and bangles. Materials derived from the civet, the wildcat, and the bongo antelope are extremely important. Except for this listing of paraphernalia, no other information on initiation objects is available, although Soors (1928) does note that sculptures are not included.

Initiation patterns in segmentary lineages closely follow the kinship and lineage structure (Schmidt, 1933). According to Moeller (1936, p. 294), *esambo* differs from the Lega bwami more in essential principles than in forms. Accession to the highest grade (*nsui* or *nimi*) depends on the seniority position in the lineage structure as much as on initiation and payment of fees. Others have observed that one may not be initiated to a grade superior to that held by a senior kinsman. Superficial data provided by Moeller (ibid., pp. 435–443) indicate that even numerically weak lineages have several initiated elders. A transcendent reason for membership in *esambo* is the anger of a shade or an ancestor. If a dead man's son is not promptly initiated, his shade will strike the son with illness that can be cured only through initiation. *Esambo* members, who include the heads of lineages and sublineages, obviously wield great power and influence in political, legal, and ritual matters. They organize circumcision rites (*tsuwu, kiu*), preside over all legal matters, and decide on war or peace.

Bapere (Pere, Piri) Traditions

The Pere, called Bakwa by Pygmies, are a complex group established in the northwestern part of Lubero Zone. They are in contact with various Nande subgroups and with the Komo and the Nyanga. In addition to the recent Nande immigrants, there are the Pere properly speaking, the Bapakombe (who include offshoots of the Baswaga and Bamate among the Nande), and the Batike. The Batike are related to people of the same name among the Komo and to the Batiti, an ancient group dispersed among the Pere. The Pere themselves explicitly state that they migrated from Uganda, possibly in two waves, and were accompanied by the Pygmies of Bangubaza. They claim direct relationships with the Komo, the Bira, and the Bapakombe. Precise traditions of origin and dispersal begin west of the Lindi River, which now forms the western limit of their territory. When the four children of Mabutwa (the name seems to mean kinships), a legendary ancestor, arrived at the Lindi, they were helped across the river by Pygmies. Traditions suggest that the Batiti, related to the Batike, were already settled near the Lindi. The sons of Mabutwa gave rise to the four chiefly clans: Bapaidumba, Babika, Bapukwala, and Baredje (see Moeller, 1936, pp. 72–78). Numerous fragments of other clans (some found also among the Komo and the Bira) joined the Pere and their descendants, including Bapomongo, Bapute, Bakwuu, Babolibe, Bamasangi, Batuembi, Bapungani, and Bambolu.

Political authority (*boomi*) concentrated in the four dynastic clans was soon split among different subdivisions. At a certain stage of Pere political development, all the sons of a chief could, at least theoretically, claim succession; the result was conflicts and internal wars to obtain power. The Bapaidumba and the Bapukwala were each divided into three small chiefdoms, and the Babika, into two. The Baredje, who best preserved the bwami tradition, split into Ngwisha, Limbali, and Njoma lineages. Two subbranches of the Njoma lineage, Kokodinga and Mande, each had its own chief (*moomi*). The genealogical records of each branch indicate that when the bwami chieftainship was established in a group, it was normally transmitted from the ruler to a junior son. The chief's senior son obtained the senior *bukama* status; the junior sons received the offices of *ngabwe* (war leader), junior *bukama*, and *muura* (drummer; official who conducts the chief's burial and assembles the skulls of slain enemies).

Hoffman (Tervuren, Dossier 805 of 1933–1934) provides some information about the burial and enthronement rites of chiefs. When a chief dies the genet hide (*akeka*) that he wore on his right arm is placed between his jaws. The corpse, taken out through a hole made in the wall of the chief's house, is carried on a litter to a sacred place in the forest where it is placed on a table. The sons of the dead chief stand in front of the corpse and one by one pull at the genet hide; the person who successfully removes it is proclaimed chief. This gesture is only symbolic, as the successor must be a son of the ritual wife. Because the actual successor has not yet been designated, the senior son of the ritual wife makes a token payment of respect to the pseudochief, who will retain great influence and share in the royal tribute. When the sons have left, the *muura* official who guards the corpse places fourteen (the numerical symbolism of two times seven predominates throughout the rites) goat hides under the table. He takes the genet hide, removes the chief's ivory bracelets, pulls out the beard and the fingernails, and places them in a shoulder bag, which he hides in a small house in a remote forest area known only to him. At the enthronement rites these relics will be shown to the new chief. The corpse remains exposed on the table until it has decayed, and then the bones are put into a broken drum, which is hidden in a hollow tree. After this job has been done, the *muura* and his aides return to the village to receive presents, but they settle elsewhere because they are not allowed to have contact with the chief's children. The mourning ceremonies now begin. Several months later the *mukama* (son of the dead chief's first wife, *ngole*) designates one of the sons of the ritual wife as the actual successor.

In my view the process of succession was not so simple as Hoffman's description would suggest. Selection of the new chief by the elders frequently resulted in internal strife and even in warfare when different factions of the royal house vied for power. Such struggles could eventually lead to scission into two chiefdoms or to the liquidation of one of the candidates. When the selection was completed, the chief was not immediately enthroned; as among the Nyanga he might have to prove his worthiness by remaining the non-initiated chief-elect for many years. Hoffman suggests that the chief-elect was informed in dreams about his readiness for investiture, and then he notified his senior brother (*mukama*). The chief's enthronement rites were preceded by the initiation of the *mukama*, who on this occasion received the right to wear one copper and four iron bracelets.

The investiture of the chief, organized by four ritual leaders (*basingya*) and a Pygmy (also called *moomi*), takes place in the forest near the tree in which his predecessor's bones have been hidden. The chief's head is repeatedly rubbed with *mpu*, a white powder obtained from the seeds of the wild *kasura* banana. The chief remains there in seclusion for fourteen days, sleeping with his ritual wife on a bed made of leaves and vines. In returning to the village the chief and the ritual wife walk on fourteen goat hides that are spread out before them. They are seated on stools, and their hair is shaved. (After this rite, a chief's hair normally stays uncut for the rest of his life.) The chief subsequently lives with his ritual wife in a small house outside the village. At the first new moon after his return he receives the chiefly insignia: copper bracelets, leopard hide and teeth, a genet and a bongo hide. At each new moon he is given a bracelet until he has fourteen of them, and then his investiture is complete.

The Pere chief shares power with his senior brother the *mukama*, and through him with a small council of dignitaries. The *mukama* is considered the "father" of the chief because he selects him. Secular authority rests with the *mukama*, whose decisions are ratified by the chief. The *mukama* is the "distributor of land"; as such he designates the mountains that each dignitary controls.

I was told that the *mukama* guards the *makinga*, the sacred sculptures linked with chieftainship, but nothing is known about them. It is possible, however, that the fifteen objects Hoffman (Tervuren, Dossier 805; see Biebuyck, 1976c) collected and ascribed to the *nsindi* initiation are in fact part of the royal treasure. The set (Tervuren, nos. 35478–35492) includes a miniature stool, a handle-shaped sculpture adorned with a cowrie and suggestive of a highly abstract human form, a quadruped with upright curled tail, two erect birdlike carvings, a stick glued into a piece of quartz stone, a phallic carving, and eight anthropomorphic figurines. Some objects are sculptured in soft wood and others in clay; all are covered with white and red color.

There are striking similarities between these Pere sculptures and certain Lega carvings: stylized anthropomorphic and zoomorphic figurines; erect standing birds; miniature stools; phallic sculptures; heights ranging between 14.3 and 25 cm (with only one figurine measuring 37.8 cm); full-sized figurines and busts; single and double figurines; stump arms or full arms with hands clasping the hips; massive feet. Other Pere features are found only in the visually undocumented rough figurines used by the Lega in the *kasisi* rites of bwami and in other select carvings: small heads with facial features that are barely suggested or entirely lacking, a massive nose placed high in the face, flap ears, powerful hands, and kneeless legs. The several Pere figurines with arms stretched forward and with huge hands and the seated figurine have no immediate Lega counterparts.

Hoffman notes that the sculptures are linked functionally with the *nsindi* initiations, during which they are shown and explained. Each sculpture has a distinctive name, which bears either on a particular title held by men (e.g., *mwami, shamwami, muombe*) and women (e.g., *mukali mukulu, musanduli, muole*) in the political structure, or on a status (e.g., witch). Even the birdlike carvings represent human characters. The sculptures do not represent ancestors or spirits but rather social types and characters. The formal and functional characteristics of the Pere sculptures point to very close ancient connections with Lega art. Other specific cultural features, such as the use in initiations of mirlitons, talking sticks, and bamboo horns that are blown in an empty pot, stress further the ties with the Lega.

Schebesta (1967–1968) places in the Beni and Mambasa zones a separate group called Kaego, whose members intermarry with the Bira and the Pere. In a village he studied, each of two lineages called Ndimokemo and Mopulibe had its own head (*kumu a mananji*), but both recognized a superior authority called *ebwame*. This dignitary seems to be the equivalent of officials who rule over very small chiefdoms among the Nyanga and the Pere. Although Schebesta thinks that the Nyanga or the Lega probably introduced the custom among the southern Bira, neither group could have influenced the southern Bira. The Pere, however, are located closer to the Bira, and most of the limited information on the Kaego chiefs shows strong connections with the Bira. The chiefs are "chosen" by Kaego headmen with the participation of the Pere. When the chief becomes seriously ill, he is carried ceremonially into the forest and strangulated (a rope fixed to his neck is attached to a goat). Natural death in his village would be harmful to his people, the animals, and the fields. The chief's corpse is not buried, but as among the Pere it is placed in a hollow tree and a sacred bush is planted around it. A large house (*ndekele*) for the ancestors is constructed on the site and offerings are deposited in it.

The Kaego chief wears a towering hat, copper and iron rings, anklet bells, a belt of bongo hide, a double-edged knife that hangs under his left arm, a necklace of leopard teeth, and a spear.

The use of figurines is not mentioned among the Kaego.

Banyanga (Nyanga) Traditions

The Nyanga trace their origins to the area of Bunyoro in Uganda. (For more details on the Nyanga, see Biebuyck, 1955, 1956, 1957a, 1978; Biebuyck and Mateene, 1969, 1970.) Living in the dense rain forest, this small population neighbors on Nande and Bakumbure groups in the north and northeast, on the Komo (whom they call Babira) in the west, on the Hunde (whom they identify as Bira) in the east, and on the Tembo and the Kanu (whom they call Barea) in the south. Some remaining Twa Pygmies, called Baremba, are established among them.

The Nyanga are organized in numerous small chiefdoms (*cuo*), some closely linked because of kinship relationships between their chiefs. The candidate-chief (*mwami* or *mubake*) is descended biologically or putatively from the ruling chief and his ritual wife (*mumbo*), but he is not her firstborn son. The ritual wife, who must not be a virgin, is a de facto or de jure close agnatic relative of the chief, his consanguineal sister or fraternal niece. She is selected by the elders and assigned to him during the initiation rites. The candidate-chief, said to be born holding the four sacred grains (eleusine, pumpkin, and two varieties of beans), must also possess the necessary intellectual and moral qualities to be acceptable. A person chosen for high office may therefore remain a chief-elect for many years; that is, he has received a chief's name, but he has not been fully initiated. He may lose his position if his conduct during the trial period is not acceptable. The ruling chief may have two or three ritual wives, among whom the competition is so strong that it may eventually lead to scission of the chiefdom. A chief has other wives with special statuses, such as his senior *nyabana* wife and a wife from the Pygmies. The senior son of *nyabana* has the title of firstborn-of-the-land (*ntangi ya cuo*); another son is called father-of-the-ritual-wife (*shemumbo*).

A chief's death and burial and his successor's initiation occasion extraordinary prescriptions. An ailing or weakened chief is secretly killed with a hammer or strangulated by hereditary officials. His death is not immediately disclosed, and his body is left in his house to putrify. Durable parts of the body, such as nails, hair, and teeth, are removed and placed in the *ukenye* bundle. Members of the college of royal initiators bury the skull and bones with some chiefly paraphernalia on a sacred mountain. During the long mourning period, all male domestic animals are killed, it is forbidden to work with iron tools, and only the sacred musical instruments (mirliton, bull-roarer, and talking sticks) may be played.

After an indefinitely long trial period, the chief-designate is enthroned. Secret rites are held on a sacred mountain in the presence of counselors and the college of ritual experts. The chief receives intensive teachings from the Pygmies. The initiation involves exchanges of goods, prescribed payments, consultations of oracles, offerings to ancestors, impositions of taboos, the chief's marriage to the ritual wife, and the transfer of paraphernalia. In some Nyanga chiefdoms the royal insignia may comprise as many as twenty-eight objects, including bells, drums, bow, arrows, quiver, stools, garments, hides, hats, and bracelets.

During the rites members of the college of initiators perform specific functions. Musao, for example, prepares the bed of leaves on which the chief and his ritual wife mate, and he secretly hides the leaves after the copulation rite; he and his wife prepare the ritual meal (fish boiled in water from a sacred source) for the chief and his wife. Musao also ritually kills the *rusara* goat. Muhakabi anoints the chief with oil and red powder; Minerusi, master-of-the-river, brings the fish and sacred water used in preparation of the ritual food. Mwamitwa, Chief-Pygmy, fetches a black dog, honey, the hide of a flying squirrel for the ritual wife's hat, and her *kuru* bracelet (made of hide stuffed with mosses).

The Nyanga chief has many titles designating him as the master of everything, as a giver of life and fertility, and as a person of surpassing power. Because anything that might weaken his power must be strictly avoided, there are numerous prescriptions. A good chief, some knowledgeable experts say, is a provider of hospitality; he is active and energetic, strong and firm; he is not impulsive; he does not take people's possessions from them, scorn or insult anyone, or endorse lies; he is no hypocrite; he harbors no hatred; he does not seduce women; he does not practice sorcery. He is a *kitarisa*, one who is different from all others because of his birth, his ways, and his destiny. In a Nyanga epic the chief is aptly characterized by his Pygmy as "Mr. Rejoicer-of-People, provider of conciliation, one who does not foster hatred; the good speaker who does not rest." He is also described as a person who "brings warmth to the land to make it go smoothly because of his good ways in treating people, giving good counsel, having no scorn for his people."

Few artworks are known from the Nyanga. In addition to hoods in bark and hide and the carefully carved wooden cups and lidded pots (some reserved for the chiefs), the most impressive sculptures are highly stylized anthropomorphic-zoomorphic figurines (Biebuyck, 1973b). Used in the *mumbira* initiation, the figurines have much in common with the Pere and Nande *molimo* trumpets (Biebuyck, 1974b). Some Nyanga subgroups practice the *mbuntsu* initiation in which ivory figurines are used, but there is no documentation on these sculptures.

I have seen in a private collection a large wooden mask (Tervuren, cliché no. 4849) ascribed to the Nyanga by the person who collected it. The mask has a whitened, concave, heart-shaped face, small, round, open eyes, an oval toothed mouth, and dotted zigzag lines above the eyebrows. It exhibits strong stylistic affinities with some of the wooden *idimu* masks of the Lega. There is no reason to doubt that the mask was found somewhere in Nyangaland, where the presence of some Lega in ancient times is attested. Lega-derived groups are also in contact with the Nyanga.

Bahunde (Hunde) Traditions

The Hunde, who live in the Masisi Zone, neighbor on the Nyanga and the Bakumbure in the north, west, and northeast, the Tembo in the southwest, and
the Havu in the south. The ruling dynasties and some of their followers trace
remote origins to Toro in Uganda, but their history really begins north of the
present Hunde area in Bwito (Rutshuru Zone). This territory is inhabited by the
Bakumbure, who are related to the Nyanga and to the Bamate among the
Nande. In Bwito, two related dynastic groups emerged as the descendants of
chiefs Mulungu and Kinyungu, both sons of the legendary and widely traveled
hunter Kibanga. Mulungu's son Muira and his followers settled near the four
so-called Mokoto lakes in the northern part of Hundeland, where they encountered the Batamba of Shemubembe. Muira made a blood pact with Shemubembe. When later pressed by the descendants of Kinyungu, Muira left his son
under the protection of Shemubembe, who exercised powerful magic over the
Mokoto lakes. When the war with Kinyungu had ended, Muira brought ripe
bananas and breads made of banana flour to Shemubembe, who apparently
had no knowledge of these products. In exchange, Muira was granted political
control over the Mokoto area, while Shemubembe and his descendants assumed the position of senior Shabakungu (lit., father-of-the-counselors). Although the Hunde acknowledge that the Pygmies and the Lega had been established in parts of Hundeland when they immigrated, these two groups are not
the same as the Batamba. Relatives of the Batamba are found under various
names among the Nyanga and in several Hunde regions.

Two of Muira's sons, Muritsi Mapfuno and Mpfuna Mapfuno, founded the
Bashari and Bapfuna dynasties, respectively. One of Muira's unmarried daughters, Kahindo, allegedly established the Kamurontsa chiefdom in southeastern
Hundeland. Four generations later, Muritsi, a descendant of Muritsi Mapfuno,
married two ritual wives (his half sisters; the custom for a chief to have a senior
and a junior ritual wife also prevails in some Nyanga chiefdoms). Two sons of
these women divided the Bashari chiefdom into two parts, but they remained
closely linked as senior and junior chiefs. The implication of the relationship
was that the junior must give biannual tribute to the senior and that the chief of
the junior house could be enthroned only with the consent of the senior. An
even more complex division developed in the western Bapfuna dynasty, in contact with the Nyanga. The Bapfuna created four chiefdoms with three sons of
Mpfuna Mapfuno and one of his grandsons serving as chiefs.

The Hunde chiefdoms of Bigira, Bugabo, Bunyungu, and Mwima originated
with the three sons and one daughter of Katiwa, a son of the founder Kinyungu. The chief of an area is called *mpfula ya kihuwo*, the senior of the land. If
several chiefs are descended from a single founder (e.g., among the Bapfuna,
Bashari, or Bagabo), the chief of the senior house has the title *mubake* and chiefs
of the junior houses are known as *mwami*. Some of their paraphernalia are identical, but the senior wears the *shungwe* diadem and has the *karinga* drum while

the junior chief displays the *mbake* hat made of flying squirrel hide. Both must go through enthronement rites under the supervision of a college of initiators headed by the *mwimiki,* the senior initiator, who is usually Shabakungu, the father-of-the-counselors. The positions of initiators, which are variously called *mwamitwa, mubetsi, mwamihesi, mushaho, mushumbitsa, mutei,* and *murembetsi,* are inherited patrilineally within separate clan segments. All the other clan segments in a chiefdom have distinctive titles; some, such as counselors (*bakungu*) and headmen (*batambo*) in control of regions, hills, and villages, denote high political status. Residential groups composed of small heterogeneous clan segments of diverse status are conventionally divided into five branches or clusters, whose leaders (*mutambo, muhunga, mukikulu, mubai,* and *mugembwa*) constitute the local council.

Viaene (1952*a*–*b*) notes that the chief rules with the help of three dignitaries. Shamwami, a senior half brother often called tutor of the chief, has secular authority equal to that of the chief. Shabakungu, father-of-the-counselors, is the most senior representative of the counselors and holds the high ritual office of *mushonga.* He makes sure that the chief's conduct conforms to the established custom. Shabatambo, the father-of-the-headmen, is the most senior delegate of the regional and local headmen. The chief and his council of three meet in a men's house (which has four entrances) located in the chief's village.

The successor to chieftainship is born of the ruler and his ritual wife (*mumbo*), who is usually the chief's half sister or close patrilateral cousin. The ritual wife, who does not live with the chief, enjoys high status; she has land, servants, followers, and sometimes cattle. The chief's successor, said to be born holding the sacred seeds (eleusine and sorghum), is confirmed by the ruling chief and by his elders (ibid.).

Schumacher (1949) and Viaene (1952*a*–*b*) present data on the burial and enthronement rites. When the chief is moribund, he is taken by the *bakungu* counselors to *irango,* the burial place of his predecessor. The counselors present his sons to the chief so that he may designate his successor. The chief places soil in the hand of an elder, who puts it in the right hand of the chosen one. The elder also places herbs in the left hands of the chief's two status-holding brothers, Shamwami and Muhunga. One of the designated elders then hastens the chief's death by administering hammer blows to his neck and inflicting a slight wound with the royal spear. Two elders pull out one or two front teeth of the dead chief, place them in oil, and show them to the successor. The two teeth, together with those of his predecessors and of the animal ritually killed by the chief during his enthronement, form the *shungwe.* The body of the dead chief is placed in a beer trough, over which the elders stretch the hide of the royal steer sacrificed on this occasion. The body is guarded by ritual experts led by *mutsimba,* the guardian of the royal tomb. When a worm emerges from the nose of the corpse, it is deposited in a pot with milk, beer, and goat's blood. This custom is based on the theory that a leopard and a serval will develop from the worm. The corpse is then buried on a bed in a grave, its head covered with a pot. Each elder plants five species of trees around the grave. The *mutsimba* stays behind to guard the tomb. Only then is the death of the chief announced publicly. During the mourning period all subjects of the chief must shave their hair completely and observe numerous other prescriptions (e.g., all male animals are killed; no one may wear ornaments or carry spears).

The enthronement of the new chief follows at an indefinite time after the end of the mourning ceremonies. Under the direction of Shamapfumo, chief-of-the-spears (i.e., chief of the army), the chief-elect is shown the contents of two baskets, which are permanently in the custody of the elders. One by one the objects are taken from the basket, applied to the forehead of the chief-elect, circulated among all participants, contemplated, and finally placed on a mat. This royal treasure includes an elephant's molar, *mbandi* quartz stones, knives, a copper awl, copper bracelets, beads, turtle carapaces, and the scaly hides of pangolins. Oath taking and a ritual meal follow.

The actual enthronement rites (*eyimika*) are held on the burial ground of the chiefs, near a water source (*maziba*). Sacrifices are made to ensure that the source produces abundant water, regarded as a good omen for a prosperous reign. Besides the chief and his ritual wife, those participating in the secret rites include Shabakungu, members of the college of royal initiates, and the Pygmy Shakiyijiri and his wife Ngaomba. A dog and, where cattle are available, a steer and a heifer must also be present. Major phases in the enthronement include ablution of the chief-elect and his ritual wife with water from the source, blessing of the chief, sexual relationship between the chief and the ritual wife, implorations, sacrifice of animals, and imposition of the chief's name. The chief is dressed in bark cloth, a white goat hide, and garlands of leaves. The party then returns to the royal village where a group of high dignitaries await the chief; one of them, Mwiru (who took part in the burial ceremonies), is sitting on the chief's copper-plated stool. After the chief is formally presented to his senior brother Shamwami, he pushes Mwiru from the royal stool to show his superior power and is seated on it himself. The chief is wearing the *nzita* hat of monkey hide and the *shungwe* diadem. The numerous objects constituting the second royal treasure, which is guarded by the elders, are exhibited before the chief's feet. These objects symbolize the power and greatness of the chief and his mastery over major technical activities. The treasure includes bow and arrow, walking stick, spear, razors, a chisel, a mancala game board, rattles, bells, harps, ivory trumpets, the royal drum, an ivory bracelet, a shell necklace, a spear, and, where cattle are raised, a milk pot and a churning calabash. Agricultural tools are notably absent, although the chief's head is lightly touched with hoes during the earlier rites near the water source. With the spear the chief now symbolically hunts and kills a goat brought by the Pygmy. The elders assign some of their sons as royal pages and also give goats to the chief, who in turn gives women, land, goats, and cattle to particular officeholders. The chief later returns with the elders to the royal cemetery to plant sacred trees.

The Hunde chief is thought to have surpassing power. A proverb states that "even a great mountain is smaller than a chief." His power is manifested mainly in the prosperity and fertility he brings to the land, the animals, and the people. Enormous significance, therefore, is attached to the planting of the sacred trees; if they do not grow well or if they dry out, it is a sign that the chief is not good and that he will soon die and be replaced. The relationship of the chief with the fertility of the land is well evoked in the chant (Mateene, 1974, p. 41):

> alors apparut une famine
> la nourriture disparut
> le roi devint malade

Although the successful chief wields enormous mystic powers and also benefits from tributes of beer, crops, and cattle, he is in fact totally dependent on the colleges of elders and initiators: "The elders are truly powerful men, they might throw down what would stand upright."

Few if any sculptures are known from the Hunde. A special problem concerning the distribution of Lega art is posed by Rochette's data (Tervuren, Dossier 345 of 1913) on an anthropomorphic figurine in ivory (Tervuren, no. 14684; pl. 98). This beautiful old piece has all the morphological characteristics of Lega sculpture: it is 18.2 cm high, represents a standing female (genitalia indicated by a V-slit and small rounded breasts in low relief), has short scalloped arms carved in ajouré, and has circle-dot designs on the body. Rochette collected it among the Hunde in the village of Muvugni, north of Bobandana on Lake Kivu. When Rochette arrived the villagers had fled, but he was informed by a woman remaining behind that the sculpture belonged to the "chief" (or headman) Muvugni and that he used it as a "personal fetish" to protect himself against misfortune. There is no reason to doubt Rochette's unusually precise indication of place, but the rest of the information is questionable. Since to my knowledge no similar pieces have been found among the Hunde, the problem arises as to how the Hunde obtained this figurine. In their southward migration, the Lega spread widely and left behind remnant groups among the Nyanga, Hunde, Havu, Shi, Tembo, Vira, and others. Such groups continued to exercise ritual privileges mainly in connection with chiefs' enthronement rites. If the figurine belonged to a member of such a submerged Lega unit, it would obviously point to the great age of a particular Lega carving tradition. I know that similar ivory sculptures are used by the *mbuntsu* association of the Nyanga and by some Hunde. The Nyanga traditions also note that the Banampamba of Lega origin preceded them.

Batembo (Tembo) Traditions

Groups called Batembo are found among Nyanga, Hunde, Havu, Shi, and also Bakanu according to some authors (e.g., Moeller, 1936, p. 131). The Tembo represent ancient mixtures of Pygmies, Konjo, and Lega with later additions of Nyanga, Hunde, and Havu. The term Batembo may be derived from Mbo, a mountain in the Tembo chiefdom of Ufumandu west of the Hunde (Van Bulck, 1948, p. 263), or it may simply mean "people of the forest," in contrast with groups living closer to Lake Kivu (Dubuisson, n.d.). It is possible that the Tembo are akin to the Bahumbe, an ancient substratum among the Nande. The name Bahumbe may be related to *kihumbe,* the seeded wild banana, which is extremely important in Tembo enthronement rites (the flour made from it is thrown on the chief and other dignitaries while they are seated together on a log).

The most detailed information available pertains to the Tembo of the Ufumandu chiefdom (Dubuisson, n.d.; Schumacher, 1949, pp. 195–199; Viaene, 1952a, pp. 20–22). An account collected by Dubuisson claims that Mbeba (or Mbega) was the first chief of the Tembo. He came from Kangeli Kanyonyi ya Kalonge in the Itombwe Mountains of the Nyindu and the Basim'minje; many dynasties among the Shi, the Vira, and others are also said to have originated there. Crossing Chime Island in Lake Kivu, an ancient Lega center, he moved northward to Njovu and Kikomo, where he married a Pygmy girl and received from her people the so-called *m(w)iga* amulet. Mbeba's sons Kishoko and Katwa founded Tembo chiefdoms in Hundeland and among the Baroba in Nyangaland.

The chief-elect of Ufumandu is the son of the ritual wife (*mumbo*) of the ruling chief. The ritual wife is the chief's half sister and lives in a separate village (Schumacher, 1949, p. 200). In general the enthronement rites for the chief of Ufumandu follow the pattern outlined for the Hunde (Viaene, 1952a, pp. 20–22), but more data are available on the Ufumandu rites. Among the college of ritual experts (*bahingi, bayingi*), many of whom represent ancient Lega groups, the *mwamihesi* (lit., Chief-Blacksmith) forges on a new anvil some of the insignia used during the rites: iron marbles for the mancala game board, billhooks, hammers, knives, awls, hoes, razors, and copper bells. After the chief has been formally seated on a stool and has been given his new name, all objects made by the Chief-Blacksmith are placed before him. The supreme counselor consecutively plants the anvil, the hammers, the billhooks, and the hoes in the ground; the chief removes them and in turn fixes them in the soil. The awls are used in a symbolic hunt during which the chief and the Chief-Pygmy kill a goat that is clothed in a piece of pig's hide so as to represent a wild pig. Afterward these tools remain in the custody of the supreme counselor (Shabakungu).

Using a special ritually treated wood, a carver (*mubeci*) prepares the mancala game board, plates, a spatula, goblets, and the *mwiga* or *ngisha ya matwa*, which are also held by Shabakungu. Viaene characterizes the *mwiga* as a magical whistle, but Schumacher (1949, p. 198) calls the 60-cm long object a "horn" that resembles a pipe with rounded head and two prongs on each side. I have seen no examples of this horn, which is blown to produce the voice of the ancestor Kifumandu. This vague description suggests that the piece resembles the *mumbira* anthropomorphic-zoomorphic figurines of the Nyanga (Biebuyck, 1974*b*). When the selected tree is felled, the carver first makes a libation of beer on the trunk and says: "May you cleave in half if the chief will not rule long or if the ritual wife will not give him an heir." After the tree is cut, the carver kills two chickens, a black one and a white one, and lets their blood flow on the trunk. The animals' failure to produce sufficient blood is a bad omen, and the wood cannot be used to make the objects. During the rites all food is prepared with the wooden utensils by the wife of Mwamitwa, the Chief-Pygmy. At the initial ceremonies the chief is "bitten" by *mwiga;* the sculpture is applied to his chest and small incisions are made with a razor.

Some of the Tembo carve masks that closely resemble those of the Komo. The carefully carved chiefs' stools consist of large, concave, spherical seat and bottom interconnected by a massive column decorated with waffle designs.

Banande (Nande) Traditions

The Nande, called Konzo or Konjo in western Uganda, occupy most of the territory in the Beni and Lubero zones. All the large Nande subgroups, identified as Bamate, Batangi, Baswaga, and Bashu, immigrated from Uganda. The Bamate and the Batangi who are in contact with the northeastern Nyanga are discussed in this section.

The Bamate trace close relationships with the Bakumbure (found among the northern Nyanga and the Bamate and in the Bwito area of Rutshuru Zone) and with the Banyungu (a ruling group among the Hunde). One Bamate tradition I collected claims that the ancestor Mubesebese (son of Kabubuto) and his followers crossed the southern part of Lake Edouard and arrived in Kyambi. Of Mubesebese's eight sons, the second became chief (*mwami*) at his father's request, and four others (founders of three Bakumbure groups and of the Banyungu) left because of a quarrel about circumcision rites. The remaining groups developed autonomous chieftainships. The Bamate were separated administratively into the three *groupements* of Hutwe, Tama, and Luenge, but these divisions only partly reflected the traditional organization of chiefdoms. The *groupement* of Luenge incorporated the separate chiefdoms of Luenge, properly speaking, Birwa, Irindya, and Bahira (an ancient group with origins northward in areas now controlled by the Bashu).

The internal politico-ritual organization of the Bamate chiefdoms is extremely complex and varies from one to another. The Hutwe chiefdom, for example, comprises four regions, each ruled by a titleholder called *ishemumbo, ishemwami,* or *mukulu wa kisokolo.* Each region is subdivided into several levels of smaller segments headed by dignitaries. A similar system prevails among the Batangi. Each chiefdom, headed by a *mwami,* is divided into regions placed under officials called *shemwami, shemumbo,* and *mukulu wa kisokolo.* These dignitaries are usually chosen at the enthronement of each new chief from among his senior and junior brothers. Those who held the same titles under the chief's predecessor, however, continue to be influential and exercise control over subregions. Senior headmen (*mukama*) who have legal control over landed estates depend on these dignitaries; junior headmen (*basoki*) are dependent upon the senior headmen from whom they have obtained land. The Baswaga have a similar organization, but some of their chiefs are ranked as seniors (*mwami wa mbita*) and others as juniors (*mwami wa misege*). In general, the ritual role of chiefs is strongly emphasized. As intercessors with ancestors, chiefs watch over the fertility of the land and the well-being of the people; they make sacrifices and offerings and also dispense medicines to ensure the success of the crops.

Debatty (1951) has sketched the selection and enthronement of a *mwami* among the Bamate and the Baswaga. The candidate is the son of the deceased chief and his ritual *mombo* wife. The chief's death is followed by an interregnum that lasts until a claimant presents his candidature to the elders. After the candidate is accepted, there is a long preparatory period marked by dances, festivities, distributions of food, and libations. During this time the elders make further decisions about the candidate's qualifications, and they select persons to perform specific roles during the rituals. The first part of the initiation lasts only two days and is accompanied by strict sexual taboos for people and animals. The candidate is subjected to a ritual burial: under the supervision of the *musingya* official and his aides, he spends the night naked in a specified place in a *ndiba,* a large pit. The bottom is covered with malodorant, venomous, prickly leaves, a bark cloth, and a leopard hide on which the candidate sleeps. He is accompanied by a woman (*musumbakali*) chosen from the descendants of the wife of the first *mwami.* According to information I received, this woman is a descendant of the Basumba Pygmies, at least in some chiefdoms. No sexual relations are allowed. In the morning the candidate and the woman are removed from the pit and given food; the candidate is given a new bark cloth to wear. The leaves are secretly discarded by the *musingya* in a quarry; the leopard hide will later be included in the royal insignia. In another initiation spot, the candidate sits on a palm branch in the company of five high dignitaries. He receives serpentine and reed bracelets made especially for the occasion by the *musingya.* After a period of contemplation, an official orders the bracelets to be removed and disposed of in a quarry.

The candidate and the dignitaries then leave the isolated initiation place for a house in a newly built village. Another dignitary, *isemombo,* presents the candidate with the ritual wife (*mombo*), whose son will succeed to the chieftainship. Following a ritual seating on a stool and a ritual meal, the candidate and the *mumbo* are left alone. In the morning the *musingya* verifies that sexual relations took place, and then drums are beaten to announce the news. People arrive in the village and all food and sexual interdictions are lifted. The *mwami*, now dressed in full regalia, is presented to his people. He wears a *mbita* crown (of *muhahya* leaves; I was told that *mbita* are made from the hide of a flying *mbake* squirrel) and a diadem of monkey and leopard teeth. He displays a genet hide on his arm and a leopard hide on his body, bracelets and bangles, some sculptured in yellow copper, and necklaces of cowries and blue glass beads.

The *mwami*, surrounded by dignitaries and accompanied by his first wife, sits on a stool to receive gifts. Elaborate dances are performed throughout eight days, and on the final day the *mwami*, again attended by his *musumbakali* wife, the *musingya*, and the *muhula* and his wife, withdraws into the bush. After *muhula* and his wife have had sexual relations, the *mwami* mates there with the *musumbakali*. *Muhula* is a sacred person; he lives in a separate village and must never again meet the living chief. He is responsible for severing the head from the chief's corpse and preserving the skull in a basket. He guards the *mbita* and other objects (chiefs' skulls), which he brings to the initiations.

The final rites are held about eighteen months later. A preparation of oil and various crops is carried around on a wooden plate. Some of the food is thrown to the chief's cows, and the rest is given to *kati*, a high official who is connected with the magic of the seasons and the crops. The chief then travels throughout the chiefdom with the plate to receive gifts. During this concluding rite, dignitaries display their sacred objects (*eusumba*), such as the circumcision knife, the *kima* stone, and the *isindi* sculptures. The word *isindi* resembles *nsindi*, a term used by Hoffman to characterize initiations that utilize the earlier mentioned Pere figurines. To my knowledge, these *isindi* sculptures of the Bamate and the Baswaga are not documented, but a wooden horned quadruped (Tervuren, no. 51.6.1) may fall into this category.

The exact functions of stylized wooden trumpets (Tervuren, nos. 35475–35477), called *mulimu, kaniamakende,* and *kazoni* among the Batangi, are not known; they may have been used in both circumcision and enthronement rites. They closely resemble similar carvings among the Pere. Wooden staffs topped with carved heads (some exhibiting the characteristic concave, heart-shaped faces) were owned by chiefs and other titleholders.

Conclusion

Among the Lega, sculpture is an integral part of the bwami association: it supports and illustrates the basic structure and the ideology of bwami.

In the Lega social system, which is based on a segmentary lineage organization, the universal bwami association constitutes a cohesive force that both consolidates and transcends the lineage structure and the spatial layout of the villages. The initiates are keenly aware of bwami's unifying pan-Lega role, which at times is vividly illustrated in the initiations. In one rite the initiates place together a necklace of small polished shell fragments and one of oblong *mizaba* beads, both adorned with leopard teeth and commonly worn by bami. They sing "A shade of Malinga [the west] and a shade from Ntata [the east]" to signify that customs developed by the western and eastern Lega are fused together in bwami.

To discharge their functions effectively and to preserve their unity, the bami have clearly envisaged and solved the problems of their own internal solidarity. They have achieved their objectives through elaborate rules of organization, a unique ideology and exclusive symbolism, and the rule of secrecy. Grade levels must be observed, and they are systematically attained through step-by-step initiation rites (*mpala*). Initiation requires the participation and interaction of many initiates, adequate preparation, kinship support, observance of statuses and kinship relationships, appropriate mental attitudes and moral conduct, and the distribution of wealth. Although kinship patterns must be respected, they are not the sole determinant of access to and progression in bwami. The internal structure of clans and lineages and their interconnections must be acknowledged, but they may not restrict the wider ramifications of interpersonal linkages created through bwami. Monopolization of the high grades and the top offices by one lineage or family at the expense of others is made impossible by the complex rules of eligibility, grade succession, and transfer of initiation objects.

Initiations are structured on procedures and principles that are exclusive and, for the most part, secret. For neophytes and noninitiates the *mpala* is described as something awesome, like "climbing the slopes of the sky"; the true contender must "not die of fear." The rites are intended to destroy all sources of evil by straightening "those who have a hunchback." They are predicated on the deliberate search for harmony and peaceful interrelationships.

All levels of initiation are conceived as dramatic performances that combine dance, song, music, theatrical enactments, display and manipulation of initiation objects, distribution of payments and gifts, and group interaction. It is inconceivable that an initiation would lack any of these ingredients.

Regional and local differences in the modus operandi are tolerated, but the fundamental principles of organization and structure, as well as the ideological patterns, are constant. The types of initiation objects used in the rites leading to the achievement of a particular grade level are strictly prescribed in every ritually autonomous community, but local groups have added (through borrowing, modification, and elaboration) or eliminated certain items. The objects (their nature, purposes, uses, and meanings) are kept secret from noninitiates and from initiates who have not yet achieved the level of initiatory experience at which different sets of objects are revealed. One of the major aims of each rite is to show the objects to the candidate, explain their symbolic references, and make them available to the neophyte. In all Lega communities, initiation objects include sculptures. Whether masks, figurines, or other carvings, they are displayed, interpreted, and transferred only in select rites. Most of the rites in which sculptures are so used occur at the culminating stages of the initiations that lead to the highest levels of yananio and kindi for men and kanyamwa for women. Although the initiates state explicitly that even the simplest items have purpose and meaning, they implicitly rate the sculptures highest by associating their ownership with the top initiatory levels and their revelation with the highest rites. The stylized masks and figurines therefore seem to constitute the supreme syntheses of the rules adhered to and the values cultivated by the members of the association, to mark the highest personal achievements, and to serve as the ultimate source of prestige.

These values are formulated and illustrated throughout the initiation cycle by an infinite number of actions accompanied by aphoristic songs and the manipulation or display of objects. Stated positively and negatively in an endless variety of formulations and performances, the values center on the moral qualities of male and female initiates and on the state of ignorance and the abjection of noninitiates or of initiates who do not live up to the standards of bwami. Moreover, the values stress the role of the initiate and of the association, the glorification of bwami and of the virtuous initiate, and the need for and the permanence of initiation objects. The manner in which these values are symbolically expressed and the contents of the messages conveyed are "secret"; they are not easily traceable or understandable by the noninitiate or by an initiate who is not of the appropriate grade level. The explanations do not pertain to a secret, privileged code of knowledge, such as an esoteric myth or cosmology. Instead, the thousands of cryptic formulations are meant to be understood only in the closed action context. The simplest verbal messages abound with metaphors, metonyms, allusions, suggestions, evocations, and elliptical expressions, while the pertinent objects support, illustrate, or clarify these statements in the most unexpected and unfamiliar ways. Except for high initiates and preceptors, no one can predict or know with certainty what exegesis will be provided for a particular object.

The cryptic character and the ambiguity of the words and objects produced in action context are best illustrated by the following example. At one time during the kindi rites, the initiates sing: "Mulambu of Kwidombe, wherever he goes, he has his Kalembe, [it] does not remain behind." Mulambu refers literally to a net hunt that lasts for several days, but here Mulambu is personified as a hunter. Kwidombe is the state of polygamy; the locative prefix *kw-* indicates that Idombe is conceived here as the name of Mulambu's village. Kalembe is the large hunting net that is wound in wide loops and can be hung from the shoulder. The text may then be understood to refer to the hunter of Idombe village: whenever he goes on a net hunt, he has the hunting net with him. The text is sung, however, while the kindi initiates dance with their ivory masks hanging over their shoulders from strings. The real interpretation of the aphorism and the related action is that whenever the kindi initiate (individualized as Mulambu) goes to the initiations, he is accompanied by at least one initiated kanyamwa woman (individualized as Kalembe) from among his many wives. In addition, Kalembe does not merely relate to Mulambu's initiated wife but also to his initiation objects (represented by the mask). This exegesis informs the neophyte that an initiate should never go to the rites without his initiated wife or his initiation objects.

The secrecy of the messages is effectively ensured by the multiplicity and the ambiguities of forms, their substitutions, their schematic simplicity, their non-descriptive properties, and by the focus placed on unexpected aspects in the action context of the rites. For these reasons it is simply impossible to guess what the sculptures represent. The uncertainties are enhanced because scores of objects (of similar and dissimilar form, and with conflicting meanings) are presented and then interpreted in a nonsystematic, fragmentary manner in different performance contexts. Although virtually all objects used in the initiations may have surprising interpretations, the figurines, masks, and other sculptures are the most unpredictable and mysterious of all. Knowledge associated with them is thought to be of a higher order.

The masks and figurines are not representations of divinities, ancestors, and spirits or media through which these powers are approached and placated. They are not devices through which undefined powers are harnessed for divining, healing, inflicting harm, oath taking, or cursing. The messages conveyed through the sculptures are anthropocentric, that is, they relate to concepts about good and bad people. In the didactic and moralizing context of the initiations, the sculptures illustrate with an infinite variety of images the virtuous persons whose conduct leads to harmonious social interaction and the nonvirtuous ones who disrupt the tenuous equilibrium of these relationships.

The masks and figurines, however, are not devoid of mystique. Because they are exclusive and secret objects, they are obviously regarded as dangerous for all those who have no right to own, touch, or see them. A noninitiate who profanes the sculptures is guilty of transgressing a major proscription. He would be considered a witch or a sorcerer and would have to face all the consequences (sickness, exclusion, death) that follow his misdemeanor. All objects used in bwami are thought to have a power that "kills" those who profane them and "protects" those who are properly introduced to their secrets. In bwami ordeals, persons are offered a drink of water in which a kindi had washed his hat or placed his bracelet. Dustlike scrapings from the ivory figurines are served in water as the ultimate cure for a sick person. Even the dead body of a high initiate is *isengo,* something dangerous and powerful. In the *musile* rites that follow the death of a high initiate, women thought to be "killers" were served bananas that had been placed in the mouth of the dead person or water with which the corpse had been washed. In simpler rites women had to step over the corpse, while initiates beat the ground with banana stipes and swore that any evildoer crossing the corpse would die. Men and women also had to eat meat from antelopes that had been hung above the grave of an initiate. It was assumed that persons who had "killed" the initiate through witchcraft, sorcery, cursing, or ritual pollution would refuse to participate because they would "die." Those who objected were administered the poison ordeal. In addition, persons found guilty of major offenses could be forced to be initiated—the initiation itself was thought to be a cure or a method of redress.

The initiates speak highly of the sculptures. In different rites they frequently stress their permanence, durability, and transcendence in pertinent aphorisms such as "Muntonko [a tree species used for many carvings] has no imputrescible core; Nkondo [the adz] is its big hard core." The wood rots easily but, when shaped into a mask, a drum, or a stool, it acquires permanence.

The sculptures made and owned by the dead predecessors and transferred to the living initiates are considered to be extensions of their being. Not merely reminders of the high virtues for which the predecessors strived, the objects are also media through which their presence is maintained and perpetuated. This point is constantly emphasized during the display of masks, figurines, and spoons, as in the aphorisms: "The spoon: those who have carved it [shaped it] are dead long ago!" "Each thing rots, the limb of the arms does not rot [because it has left behind permanent works]"; "The core of a [dead] tree is visible, of a human being it is not visible." The texts note that the tree rots but its core remains; a person dies and disappears but his works survive. The symbolic presence of the dead exhorts the living to follow their example; the masks are identified as "hammers of the dead" which awaken and encourage the living to meet their obligations.

The sculptures are always possessed by individuals; the right of ownership follows initiation to certain grade levels. The ownership of sculptures is determined by a combination of well-established rules that recognize the graded structure of bwami as well as seniority in grade levels, special statuses and sexual differences, and the structure of autonomous lineage groups and ritual communities. The sculptures thus are part of the insignia linked with specific grades and statuses. Individuals who hold the artworks, however, never have exclusive control over or ultimate claim to them. These objects are not randomly acquired or inherited, and they must not be lost, abandoned, destroyed, or damaged. In the aphorism "The nest of the egg is not for breaking; it does not belong to the owner of the chicken," the initiates state that the sculptures do not actually belong to any particular person since they are to be transmitted under specified conditions. A person acceding to lutumbo lwa yananio, for example, temporarily receives the basket containing sculptures and other initiation objects; it will be surrendered when another member of his autonomous community is initiated to that grade. On finishing lutumbo lwa yananio, a person also is given a wooden mask through the intermediacy of his principal tutor. This mask usually belonged to a dead kinsman of that grade or to a living kinsman who moved up to kindi. When a yananio dies, the mask is entrusted to the guardian of the tomb who keeps it until someone has been designated to "succeed" him in the yananio initiation. The successor may be a son, a junior brother, or a nephew (real or classificatory), but the consensus of the local membership is needed. A person of a specific grade level therefore must hold certain sculptures, but he is not free to do whatever he wants with them. An autonomous community must possess certain sculptures, but these cannot be monopolized by one family or lineage and must be passed around as new initiates are accepted. The only exceptions pertain to control over single ivory, sometimes wooden, figurines and masks owned by specific lineages to mark their role in the local origin of a rite.

Because of the underlying transfer system, the sculptures are not only personal status insignia but also media through which linkages between persons and groups are established and maintained. Interpersonal and intergroup dependencies and solidarities are symbolized through initiation objects. At least some of the most important sculptures are also manifestations of the unity and autonomy of groups; possession of these carvings establishes such groups as independent ritual units and also necessitates concerted action by their members. Certain high-level rituals cannot be held unless these particular sculptures and their trustee are present.

The sculptures described in this volume are not part of permanent public or private displays in shrines or palaces, in houses or villages, or at crossroads or in the fields. The sculptures, kept hidden in shoulder bags and baskets in initiates' houses, are presented only in the closed context of certain rites. The only exceptions are the small ivory and wooden phallic and nonphallic figurines that kanyamwa hang from their belts as symbols of high status. Most of the displays take place at culminating yananio, kindi, and bunyamwa rites and, where these do not exist, at the ngandu level.

At yananio, kindi, and bunyamwa levels, all the objects contained in the collectively controlled baskets are shown as a whole; in some rites all participants exhibit wooden or ivory masks, in others they show the ivory figurines, and in still others they display all the sculptures they possess. Artworks are presented in different ways. An initiate may carry his own mask; sometimes all masks are displayed on the ground or on a fence in a configuration of objects. Wooden or ivory figurines may be arranged on the ground, either in a single group or with each item placed in front of its owner. In a rite that precedes the displays, the sculptures are invariably treated with white clay or with oils mixed with colorants.

The presentation is accompanied by dramatic action, dance, music, and sung aphorisms, regardless of whether or not the initiates actually carry or handle the objects. The masks are manipulated in unexpected ways; handling of the figurines is less diverse. During dramatic performances the exegesis centers not merely on the object itself, on its form, or on its role, but also on its name, on the material of which it is made, on its actual use, and on its relationships—whether of opposition or complementarity—to other objects. The aesthetic qualities of the sculptures are rarely placed in perspective, although in a major kindi rite the collection of artworks displayed is likened to the shining mass of a white mushroom patch in the forest. Their beauty is simply a reflection of the harmony, good order, and peace that underlie the rites.

The display and exegesis of the sculptures have much in common with procedures followed in the presentation of clay, wood, bark, and wicker images in puberty rites for girls and boys among peoples (Bemba, Bira, Lala, Lamba, Kaonde, Sambaa, Zigua, Nguu, Pare) situated in southern Zaire, Zambia, and Tanzania (Richards, 1945, 1956; Cory, 1946). The Bemba, for example, show pottery images to an initiated girl during the final stages of the *chisungu* ceremony; the mistress of the ceremonies takes each object, sings appropriate songs, and moves in rhythm with the drums. The images and songs explain the legal, moral, economic, and procreative aspects of marriage.

Writers on African art like to think that Lega art influenced that of the Mitoko, Lengola, Mbole, Komo, Bembe, and so on (Maesen, 1950; Cornet, 1978*a*, p. 162) or that Lega art diffused among these peoples (Maesen, 1960*a*, p. 238). In fact, the Lega trace ancient and even more recent historical connections with segments of these populations, interpreting such bonds as agnatic, cognatic, or affinal. Ethnic maps are merely approximations of the intricate cultural interconnections that have developed over wide areas. Thus they cannot do justice to the mixtures of and the divisions among groups that are discussed in this volume. Virtually every group in the enormous region between 1 degree north and 5 degrees south latitude and between 24 and 30 degrees east longitude has a composite ethnic background. Certain subgroups among the Lega, for example, trace ancient links with subunits of Mitoko, Lengola, Enya, Leka, Komo, Songola, Ngengele, Bembe, Vira, Nyindu, Binja, and Bangubangu. In other areas, groups identified as Lega among Nande, Pere, Nyanga, Hunde, Havu, and Shi seem to be remnants of Lega migrations. Separate groups such as Bakumbure, Baasa, Batiri, Bakwame, Bakonjo, Bakanu, Batembo, Baleka, Babile, and Batali are, because of cultural mixtures, transitional among larger ethnic entities. That kind of interlinkage makes an immense region in eastern Zaire a cultural continuum. Early ethnographic sources acknowledge general cultural connections among many populations as well as specific ties arising from voluntary associations.

Indeed, these voluntary associations, though many of them are imperfectly known, do show uniform structural, organizational, and ideological principles. Societies with statelike systems, such institutions as initiation, enthronement, and burial rites for chiefs, exhibit striking similarities to their counterparts for high-ranking members of voluntary associations. Some bwami rites, such as *mpunju* and *bubake,* turn up as independent institutions elsewhere, even as far north as the Lengola and the Nyanga. Sculptures used in the bwami, *bukota, lilwa, nsubi, esambo,* and *mbuntsu* associations have stylistic (e.g., concave, heart-shaped faces) and thematic (e.g., plurifrontality) characteristics in common, as well as closely related functions: they are owned by initiates; they are revealed and explained in initiations as symbolizations of moral and legal codes; they denote individual status and rank; they are symbols of group autonomy or of group interdependence; they are secret and sacred; they signify transgenerational linkages with ancestors; they have a role in funerary functions. Sculptures used in chiefs' initiations among Pere, Batangi, Tembo, and possibly other groups are similar in function to the rudimentary figurines in clay and *ntutu* used in the *kasisi* rite of the Lega. Masks manipulated by Komo diviners show strong stylistic and functional affinities with the large Lega masks. Figurines close in form and function to those of the Lega have been found among the Nyanga and the Hunde.

These and other cultural similarities among the groups studied in this volume are not accidental. They are not merely the result of local diffusion of cultural traits; they are also the product of common origins. Voluntary associations—bwami, *bukota, lilwa, esambo, nsubi, mbuntsu*—and chiefs' initiations are regional variations of common ancestral institutions introduced during the migrations by Lega and Lega-related populations but modified by rituals already known to preestablished Pygmies and Pygmy-influenced hunters. Virtually all traditions attest to the early presence of these hunters. Although Pygmies have disappeared in most areas (except among the Nyanga), groups identified as descendants of Pygmies or of Pygmy-influenced hunters are numerous and widespread. The Lega story runs as follows. A compact mass of Lega and Lega-related clans established themselves near the Lwalaba River in regions still inhabited by Mitoko, Lengola, Leka, Enya, and some Komo, with whom they had common origins or close relationships. The settlement of these other groups possibly followed the Lega migration from the Ruwenzori range in the east to the Lwalaba. They had brought the circumcision rites and the rudiments of bwami initiations with them when they settled near the Lwalaba. By the time the Lega began to move southeastward to their present territory, at least some Lega groups (the Babongolo) had developed bwami into a full-scale hierarchical association culminating in kindi. The sculptural traditions linked with voluntary associations were probably invented by Lega and Lega-related peoples. The wide distribution of Lega-like arts used by the voluntary associations of various peoples attests to the antiquity and common origin of these arts and of the institutions in which they prevail.

As they entered the forest regions they now inhabit, the northern, western, and southern Lega encountered Pygmies and Pygmy-influenced hunters (e.g., the Bouse), some of whom were probably offshoots of an earlier Balumbu migration. To the south they met with Binja and Binja-derived groups that had migrated from the southeast. Prior to this massive movement, splinter groups of Lega who originated in the Ruwenzori area had moved directly southward, leaving behind smaller units still found among Nyanga, Hunde, Havu, and Shi. The spearheads of these factions encountered, in the Lwindi-Itombwe region, large groups of Pygmies and Pygmy-influenced hunters, such as Basim'minje, Basi'asumba, and Banyindu, all claiming local origins, and many others who were moving eastward toward Lake Tanganyika. These groups were already using a type of bwami based on clan seniority, and the Lega, upon coming into contact with them, adopted the same form. The huge Lega movement later emanating from the northwest reestablished connections with the splinter groups and reintroduced their own form of bwami via some of their forerunners (e.g., the Basango).

Familiarity with the sculptural arts used in ancestral cults by preestablished peoples undoubtedly affected formal aspects of the wood, ivory, and bone carving traditions that the Lega brought with them. This influence is reflected in two diverging stylistic characteristics of some Lega sculptures: the angularity of some forms and the fullness and roundness of others.

Because of the expansion of the top grades of bwami and the continuing increase in the number of high initiates, the volume of artworks must have shown steady growth, culminating in the early twentieth century. Both the ideology and the structure of bwami favored this development: high individual status was earmarked by the required ownership of certain artworks; local autonomy of ritual communities was symbolized by the obligatory possession of certain sculptures; autonomous communities had the freedom to expand art-using rites; local variability was a hallmark of the association.

APPENDIX

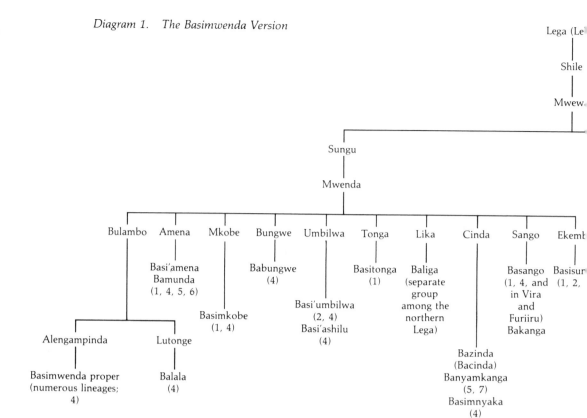

Diagram 1. The Basimwenda Version

KEY

Groups established among the

1. Basimwenda
2. Bamuzimu
3. Bakabango-Babongolo
4. Bembe
5. Nyindu
6. Shi
7. Barhinyi

NOTES

The Basimwenda properly speaking place their origin in Bwele (west of Shabunda).

Shile was hated by his brothers; in order to save him from their wrath, Lega sent Shile away under the protection of Mcanga and the Bainda. When Shile had his son Mwewa in Ikozi, he received his father's bwami from Mcanga. This led to numerous wars, mainly between the Shile and Ikama factions.

When his sons were grown, Mwewa decided to organize the circumcision rites for his three sons, Sungu, Lwamba, and Amoni. Before entering the enclosure, however, Amoni was sent to fetch salt; his two brothers were circumcised. In the meantime Amoni's mother had learned what was happening in the lodge, and when her son returned she hid him. The descendants of Amoni (Nyindu and M'minje) thus did not have the circumcision. The Basim'minje later acquired it from the Basango (descendants of Sungu).

In the Basimwenda version, Mambwe, the ancestor of the Basim'minje, is listed as both

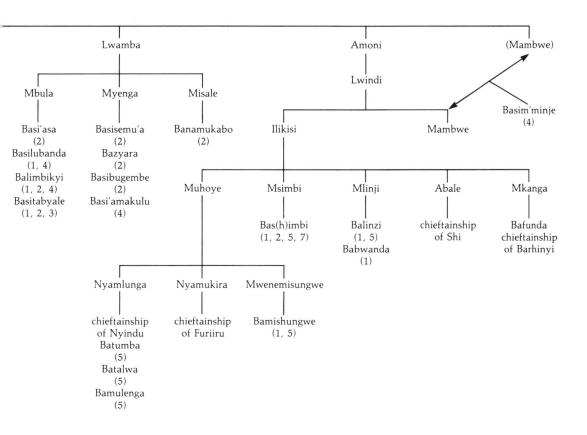

a son and a great-grandson of Mwewa.

Some groups encountered among the Basimwenda, Bembe, and Nyindu are not mentioned in this genealogy:

1. Basi'asumba, also called Batwa or Bambote, are hunters generally claimed as collateral relatives by the Basim'minje. The Bakeci are included among them.

2. Bamulinda are the Banamusanze of the Ikama subdivision.

3. Basyele, originating among the Shi, but claimed in the Basi'alangwa group (diagram 3).

4. Babundu, Bazila, and Balobola are from the Kisi division.

5. Bouse (2, 3) sometimes referred to as descendants of Mwenembumbano (diagram 2).

   Bonga and Baelekya groups, preceding Balimbikyi, who claim an independent origin.

   Baongo (1) and Bainda-Basilwinda (2, 4), related to Bahese, descendants of Ebamba, their chief Nyarubamba was chased by the Nyindu (?).

6. Bakunga (Bagunga). Basim'minje tradition establishes an early affinal link with the Bakunga.

Diagram 2.   The Basim'minje Version

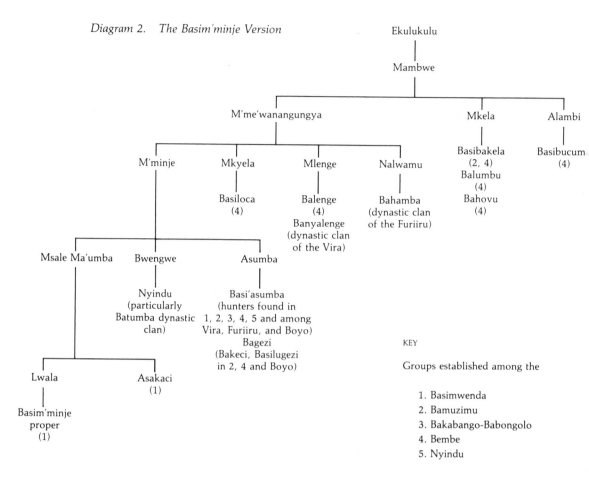

KEY

Groups established among the

1. Basimwenda
2. Bamuzimu
3. Bakabango-Babongolo
4. Bembe
5. Nyindu

NOTES

The M'minje version claims local origin in Aseka (Lwindi) for several groups now among the Lega, Bembe, and Nyindu.

Mambwe has early contact with the Bakunga (Bagunga still among the Bamużimu), located south of them. Mambwe marries among the Bakunga.

Move to Apembwe and dispersal (because lightning struck many people): Mkyela and Alambi move eastward, following the Elila River; M'minje and Mlenge move to Angele (Lubumba in Itombwe).

Bwengwe leaves Angele and returns to Lwindi. He encounters Mwenembumbano, who gives him his daughter and his chieftainship because Bwengwe hunted wild pigs that were destroying Mwenembumbano's fields. Bwengwe is followed by one of Mlenge's children.

Asumba becomes a famed hunter in Angele; his group disperses.

Lwala moves to Mlengeci (Itombwe) and encounters the Basango.

The M'minje claim they had *bwami bwa ishungwe.* The Basango brought *butende* and *bwami bwa e'umbu.*

Diagram 3.   The Basi'alangwa Version

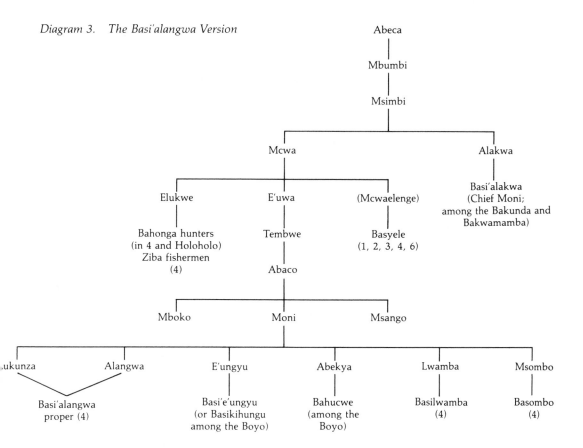

KEY

Groups established among the

1. Basimwenda
2. Bamuzimu
3. Bakabango-Babongolo
4. Bembe
5. Nyindu
6. Shi

NOTES

The Basi'alangwa trace their origins to Tonga, an area between the Elila and Lwindi rivers. Close and remote kin are found among the Boyo and the Baholoholo.

The Basi'alangwa received bwami from the Basango through Babungwe influence. The Basi'alangwa trace most of their relationships with hunters and with groups located south of them among the Boyo, Bujwe, Bakwamamba, and Baholoholo.

Diagram 4.   Banangabo, Banangoma, and Bamuguba Versions

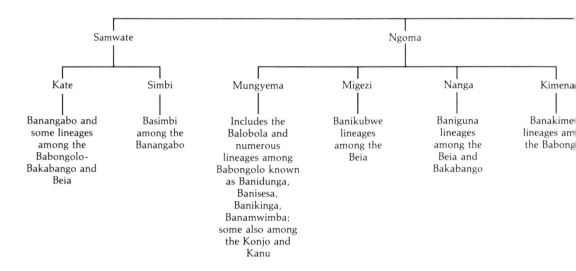

NOTES

The Banangabo, Banangoma, and Bamuguba form large autonomous groups among the northern Lega. As the chart indicates, however, they claim numerous relationships with lineages scattered among the western, southern, and eastern Lega, and with some incorporated among the Kanu, Konjo, and Bembe.

The Bakyunga (diagram 5), have close relationships with the Bamuguba but consider the Banangabo and Banangoma to be ancient descendants of their ancestor Kyunga.

The Banamunwa among the Babene trace origins to Muguba through his son Kinza (not mentioned on chart).

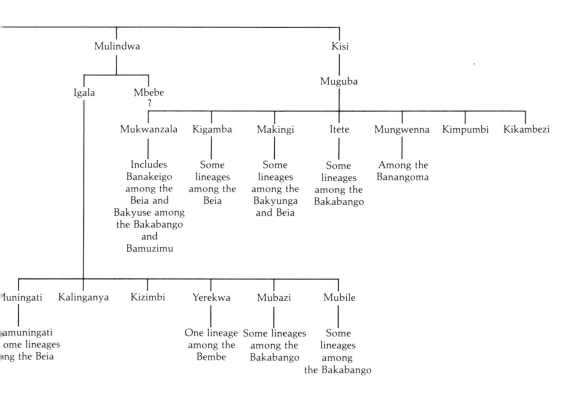

Diagram 5.   The Bakyunga Version

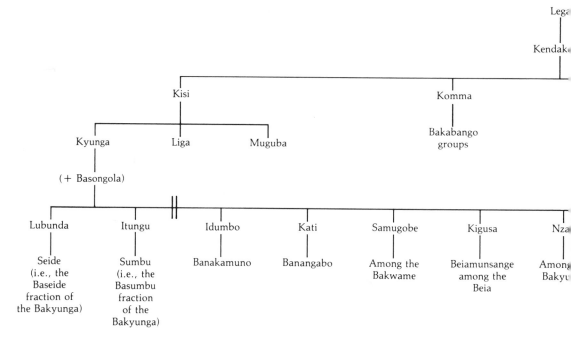

NOTES

The Bakyunga view the Banangabo and Banangoma (diagram 4) as the descendants of their ancestor Kyunga.

The Baliga, claimed by the Basimwenda to be the descendants of Mwenda's son Lika, accept close relationships with the Bakyunga and Bamuguba, as indicated here in the Bakyunga version. They also accept close historical connections with the Basimwenda, the Basimbi, the Bagalia, and other groups among the Banangoma, Babongolo, Bamuzimu, and Shi.

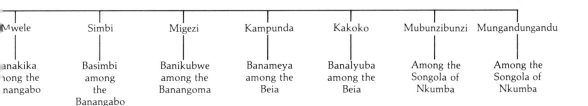

The Banasalu among the Beia perceive strong relationships with the Bakyunga and Bakonjo but are not mentioned in this chart.

The Beiamunsange, Banameya, and Banalyuba referred to here do not agree that they are the descendants of Kyunga but claim separate origins with Lega's son Mwiya (diagram 7).

Diagram 6.   The Bakabango-Babongolo Version

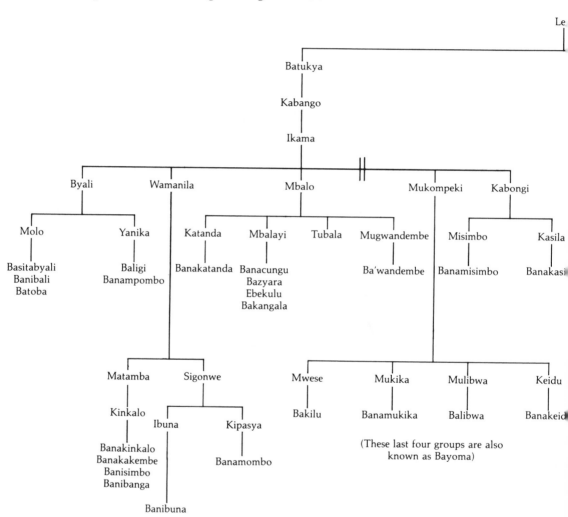

(These last four groups are also known as Bayoma)

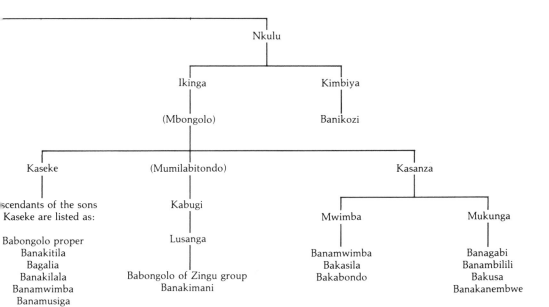

Nkulu

Ikinga   Kimbiya

(Mbongolo)   Banikozi

Kaseke   (Mumilabitondo)   Kasanza

Descendants of the sons   Kabugi
of Kaseke are listed as:

Babongolo proper   Lusanga
    Banakitila
    Bagalia
    Banakilala   Babongolo of Zingu group
    Banamwimba   Banakimani
    Banamusiga

Mwimba   Mukunga

Banamwimba   Banagabi
Bakasila   Banambilili
Bakabondo   Bakusa
           Banakanembwe

NOTES

Representatives of the groups mentioned on this chart are widely scattered among the Lega; major concentrations are among the Bakabango-Babongolo of Moligi and of Kasambula, in the *secteur* Kama, among the Bamuzimu, and some in the Beia and Babene sectors of the western Lega. The Ebekulu are among the Bembe.

Clans of the Kisi division among the northern Lega trace numerous linkages with lineages mentioned on this chart.

The Banakasyele (also in Kama) trace relationships with the Bamuguba.

The Balambia and Banakalobia among the Babongolo of Kasambula trace their origins respectively to the Basimwenda and the Pygmies.

Diagram 7.   The Beia Version

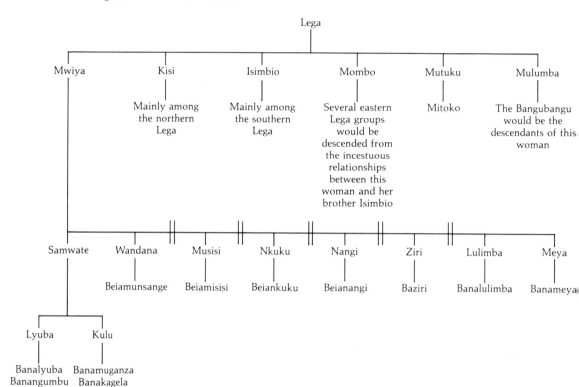

The groups mentioned here constitute the bulk of the western Lega.

Among the western Lega groups not indicated, the Banasalu trace relationships with the Bakyunga (who also claim connections with the Banalyuba, Banameya, and Beiamunsange), the Banakeigo with the Bamuguba, the Bakangala (who are partly also among the Ngengele) with the Bouse, the Banisanga with the Babongolo, and the Batoba with the Bakabango.

Some constituent units deny separate origin for the Baziri among the children of Mwiya.

There are small groups of Bouse, descendants of ancient hunters, and of Enya riverain populations.

Diagram 8. Spread of Kindi from the Babongolo
to the Northern and Western Lega

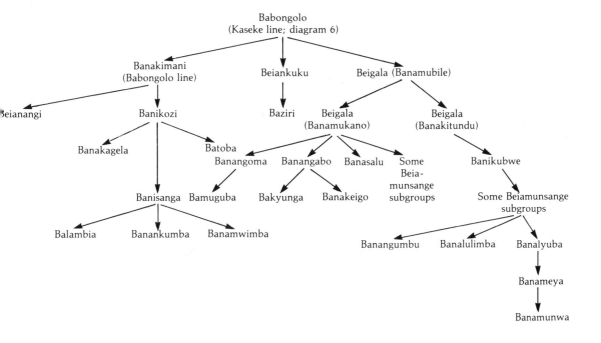

Diagram 9.   *Distribution of Kindi*
in the Banasalu Clan

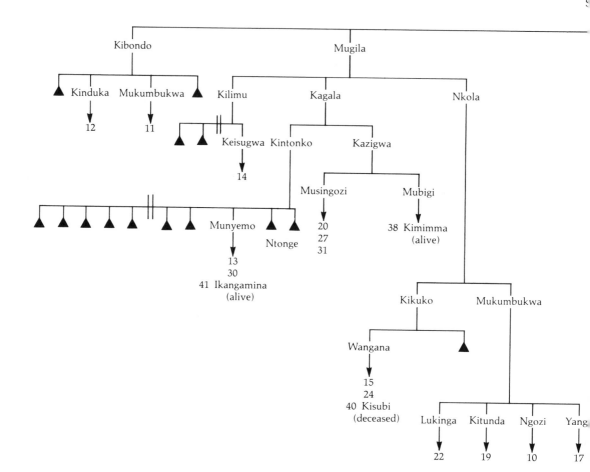

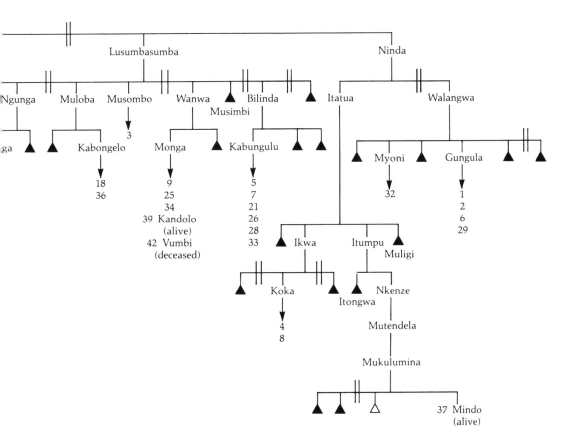

NOTES

In the diagram, only the names of the founders of lineages and sublineages whose members achieved kindi are indicated, together with the names of the most recent kindi. The founders of other lineages are simply marked by ▲ (for deceased persons) or △ (for living persons).

The numbers 1 to 42 refer to the sequence in which individual members of the Banasalu lineages achieved kindi.

Diagram 10.   Distribution of Bwami Grades in Itumpu Lineage
of the Banasalu Clan (see diagram 9)

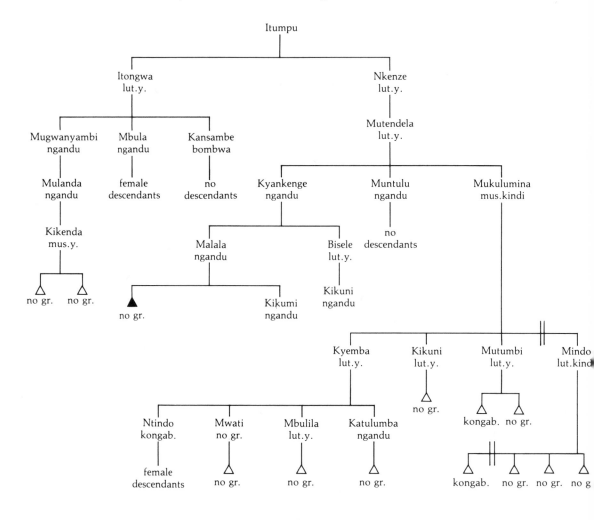

Bibliography

NOTE: Most of the colonial administrators who wrote ethnographic
reports (Documents A.I.M.O.) are known only by their surnames.

Abbeloos, R. V. "De sekte 'Lilwa.'" *Band* 8 (1949):311–313.

Abemba, Bulaimu J. *La collectivité locale des Wasongola (territoire de Kindu, Zaïre).* Brussels: Les cahiers du Cedaf, 1972.

———. *Le mode de production lignager face à la traite arabe et à la colonisation. Le cas des collectivités locales au Maniéma.* Brussels: Les cahiers du Cedaf, 1979.

Abemba, J. I. *Pouvoir politique traditionnel et Islam au Congo oriental.* Brussels: Les cahiers du Cedaf, 1971.

Agnuzzo. *Meisterwerke altafrikanischer Kultur aus der Sammlung Casa Coray.* Bellinzona: Instituto grafico Casagrande, 1968.

A.I.M.O. "Sectes Wabembe, territoire de Kalembelembe." Fizi, 1918.

———. "Rapports spéciaux sur l'état d'organisation des secteurs et juridictions indi-gènes." Province du Kivu, 1923.

———. "Rapport de sortie de charge." Lubutu, 1927.

———. "Historique du territoire des Babembe." Fizi, [1932].

———. "Liens qui rattachent la chefferie Asekunda à d'autres groupements indigènes, territoire Kibombo." Kibombo, n.d.

———. "Liste des secteurs, chefferies, sous-chefferies, territoire Kindu." Kindu, n.d.

———. "Liste des secteurs et chefferies." Kabambare, n.d.

———. "Liste des secteurs, territoire Bakusu." Kibondo, n.d.

———. "Liste des secteurs, territoire Kasongo." Kasongo, n.d.

———. "Moeurs et coutumes des Babembe." Fizi, n.d.

———. "Notes ethnographiques sur la peuplade des Bambole." Province Orientale, n.d.

———. "Rapport d'enquête sur la chefferie des Bahutshwe." Kabambare, n.d.

Allison, Philip. *African Stone Sculpture.* New York: Frederick A. Praeger, 1968.

Altman, Ralph C. *Balega and Other Tribal Arts from the Congo.* Los Angeles: Dickson Art Center, University of California, 1963.

Anderson, Richard L. *Art in Primitive Societies.* Englewood Cliffs, N.J.: Prentice-Hall, 1979.

Art Institute of Chicago. *Collection of Mr. and Mrs. Raymond Wielgus.* Chicago, 1957.

Aurez, F. J. "Etude sur les bakota des Beniamituku." Province orientale: Documents A.I.M.O., 1930.

———. "Etude de la partie du territoire des Wagengele située à l'est du Lualaba." Kindu: Documents A.I.M.O., 1934.

Bailleux. "Territoire de Beni." Kivu: Documents A.I.M.O., 1950.

Baltimore Museum of Art. *The Alan Wurtzburger Collection of African Sculpture.* Baltimore, 1954.

Bascom, William. *African Arts: An Exhibition at the Robert H. Lowie Museum of Anthropology of the University of California, Berkeley, April 6 – October 22, 1967.* Berkeley: University of California, 1967.

Bashikwabo Chubaka. *Notes sur l'origine de l'institution du "Bwami" et fondements du pouvoir politique au Kivu oriental.* Brussels: Les cahiers du Cedaf, 1979.

Bassani, Ezio. *Scultura africana nei musei italiani.* Bologna: Calderini, 1977.

Baumann, Hermann, ed. *Die Völker Afrikas und ihre traditionellen Kulturen.* Wiesbaden: Franz Steiner Verlag, 1975.

Bercoux. "Uvira. Saturation des terres." Kivu: Documents A.I.M.O., 1949.

Bergmans, L. *L'histoire des Baswaga.* Butembo-Beni: Assomption, 1970.

Bergmans, L., and Marcel Joniaux. *Onder de zon van de vrees.* Butembo-Beni: Assomption, 1969.

Biebuyck, Daniel P. "La monnaie musanga des Balega." *Zaire* 7 (1953a):775–786.

———. "Répartition et droits du pangolin chez les Balega." *Zaire* 7 (1953b):899–934.

———. "Signification d'une statuette Lega." *La revue coloniale belge* 195 (1953c):866–867.

———. "Function of a Lega Mask." *Archives internationales d'ethnographie* 47 (1954a): 108–120.

———. "De verwording der kunst bij de Balega." *Zaire* 8 (1954b):273–278.

———. "De mumbo-instelling bij de Banyanga (Kivu)." *Kongo-Overzee* 21 (1955): 441–448.

———. "L'organisation politique des Nyanga: la chefferie Ihana." *Kongo-Overzee* 22 (1956):301–341; 23 (1957a):59–98.

———. "La société kumu face au Kitawala." *Zaire* 11 (1957b):7–40.

———. "Effects on Lega Art of the Outlawing of the Bwami Association." *Journal of the New African Literature and the Arts* 1 (1967a):87–94. Also in *New African Literature and the Arts,* ed. Joseph Okpaku, pp. 340–352. New York: Thomas Y. Crowell, 1967b.

———. "The Didactic Function of African Art." *African Forum* 3 (1968):35–43.

———. "The Problem of the Function of African Art." In *Contributions to the Colloquium on the Function and Significance of Negro-African Art in the Life of the People and for the People,* Présence africaine, pp. 278–282. Paris, 1971.

———. "Bembe Art." *African Arts* 5 (1972a):12–19, 75–84.

———. "The Kindi Aristocrats and Their Art among the Lega." In *African Art and Leadership,* ed. D. Fraser and H. Cole, pp. 7–20. Madison: University of Wisconsin Press, 1972b.

———. *Lega Culture: Art, Initiation, and Moral Philosophy among a Central African People.* Berkeley and Los Angeles: University of California Press, 1973a.

———. "Nyanga Circumcision Masks and Costumes." *African Arts* 6 (1973b):20–25, 86–92.

———. "Mukumbi: une configuration d'objets d'art." *Africa-Tervuren* 20 (1974a):30–38.

———. "Mumbira: Musical Instrument of a Nyanga Initiation." *African Arts* 7 (1974b):42–45, 63–65, 96.

———. "Textual and Contextual Analysis in African Art Studies." *African Arts* 8 (1975):48–51, 90.

———. "The Decline of Lega Sculptural Art." In *Ethnic and Tourist Arts: Cultural Expressions from the Fourth World,* ed. N. Graburn, pp. 334–339. Berkeley and Los Angeles: University of California Press, 1976a.

————. "Sculpture from the Eastern Zaire Forest Regions." *African Arts* 9 (1976*b*):8–15, 79–80.

————. "Sculpture from the Eastern Zaire Forest Regions: Mbole, Yela, and Pere." *African Arts* 10, 1 (1976*c*):54–61, 99–100.

————. "Schemata in Lega Art." In *Form in Indigenous Art: Schematisation in the Art of Aboriginal Australia and Prehistoric Europe,* ed. Peter Ucko, pp. 59–65. Canberra: Australian Institute of Aboriginal Studies, 1977*a*.

————. "Sculpture from the Eastern Zaire Forest Regions: Lengola, Metoko, and Komo." *African Arts* 10, 2 (1977*b*):52–58.

————. *Symbolism of the Lega Stool.* Philadelphia: ISHI Publications, 1977*c*.

————. *Hero and Chief: Epic Literature from the Banyanga (Zaire Republic).* Berkeley and Los Angeles: University of California Press, 1978.

————. "The Frog and Other Animals in Lega Art and Initiation." *Africa-Tervuren* 25 (1979):76–84.

————. "The *Shungwe* Diadem of the Vira Chief." *Africa-Tervuren* 26 (1980):38–41.

————. "*Buhabo* Statues from the Benembaho (Bahoma)." *Africa-Tervuren* 27 (1981*a*): 18–31.

————. "Dress as Cultural Artifact: A Case from the Lega." 1981*b*. Manuscript.

————. "Lega Spoons." In *Liber Memorialis for Professor Vandenhoutte,* ed. H. Burssens, pp. 51–66. Ghent: State University, 1981*c*.

————. "Plurifrontal Figurines in Lega Art (Zaire)." In *The Shape of the Past: Studies in Honor of Franklin D. Murphy,* ed. G. Buccellati and Ch. Speroni, pp. 115–127. Berkeley and Los Angeles: University of California Press, 1981*d*.

————. *Statuary from the Pre-Bembe Hunters: Issues in the Interpretation of Ancestral Figurines Ascribed to the Basikasingo-Bembe-Boyo.* Tervuren: Musée royal de l'Afrique centrale, 1981*e*.

Biebuyck, Daniel P., and Kahombo Mateene. *The Mwindo Epic from the Banyanga.* Berkeley and Los Angeles: University of California Press, 1969.

————. *Une anthologie de la littérature orale Nyanga.* Brussels: Académie royale des Sciences d'Outre-Mer, 1970.

Bonew, Alexis. "Patines." *Connaissance des arts, Supplement Benelux* 1974:iii–xvi.

Boone, Olga. *Carte ethnique du Congo: Quart Sud-Est.* Tervuren: Musée royal de l'Afrique centrale, 1961.

————. *Carte ethnique de la République du Zaïre: Quart Sud-Ouest.* Tervuren: Musée royal de l'Afrique centrale, 1973.

Borms. "Reconnaissance du pays Bango-Bango et d'une partie de l'Uzimba." *La Belgique coloniale* 8 (1902):255–257, 268–270.

Bragard, P. "Les Bavira." Uvira: Documents A.I.M.O., 1937.

Brain, Robert. *Art and Society in Africa.* London: Longman, 1980.

Brizzi, Bruno. *The Pigorini Museum.* Rome: Quasar, 1976.

Bronchart, P. "Le Luhuna." Bukavu: Documents A.I.M.O., 1931.

————. "Les Wazimba." Kasongo: Documents A.I.M.O., 1933.

Bryan, M. A. *The Bantu Languages of Africa.* Oxford: Oxford University Press, 1959.

Buccellati, G., and Ch. Speroni, eds. *The Shape of the Past: Studies in Honor of Franklin D. Murphy.* Berkeley and Los Angeles: University of California Press, 1981.

Burland, Cottie. "Africa, South of the Sahara." In *Primitive Erotic Art,* ed. Philip Rawson, pp. 197–251. New York: G. P. Putnam's Sons, 1973.

Burssens, H. *Yanda-beelden en Mani-sekte bij de Azande (Centraal-Afrika).* Tervuren: Musée royal de l'Afrique centrale, 1962.

Burssens, H., ed. *Liber Memorialis for Professor Vandenhoutte*. Ghent: State University, 1981.

Cambron, L. "La circoncision dans la région de Beni et des environs." *Congo* 1923, 1: 708–711.

Cardinal, J. "Règles de succession chez les Yeyango [Mbole-Lomami], deuil, investiture du chef." Opala: Documents A.I.M.O., 1938.

Carière. "Bashu (territoire Beni)." Kivu: Documents A.I.M.O., 1951.

———. "Groupement Isale Muhahirwa (Bashu, territoire Beni)." Kivu: Documents A.I.M.O., 1952.

Carnegie Institute Museum of Art. *The Art of Black Africa, Collection of Jay C. Leff.* [Pittsburgh], 1969.

Celenko, Theodore. *Selections from the Harrison Eiteljorg Collection of African Art.* Indianapolis: Leah Ransburg Art Gallery, Indiana Central University, 1980.

Celis, J. "Enkele nota's over den godsdienst der Vanande." *Kongo-Overzee* 2 (1935): 100–105.

———. "Nota's over de plechtigheid der manddraging bij de Zuid-Vanande." *Kongo-Overzee* 9 (1943):176–182.

Centre d'information et de documentation du Congo belge. *Les arts du Congo et au Ruanda-Urundi*. Brussels, 1950.

Cerulli, Ernesto. "Sacralita della fucina e degli strumenti di lavoro del fabbro in Africa." *Annali Lateranensi* 20 (1956):29–59.

Chabry, J. *Panorama du Congo No. 4. Des Falls à Bukama*. Brussels: Malvaux, n.d.

Chauvet, Stephen. "Les arts indigènes d'Afrique et d'Océanie." *Variétés* 2 (1930): 849–855.

Chernova, Galina A. *The Art of Tropical Africa in the Collection of the Soviet Union*. Moscow: Moscow Soviet Artists, 1967.

Chrétien, Jean-Pierre, and Emile Mworoha. "Les tombeaux des bami du Burundi: Un aspect de la monarchie sacrée en Afrique orientale." *Cahiers d'études africaines* 10 (1970):40–79.

Christoffels, Hildegard. "Über afrikanische Holzschnitzerei." *Jahrbuch des Bernischen Historischen Museums in Bern* 39–40 (1961):457–463.

Claerhout, Adriaan. *Het Masker. Le Masque. The Mask. Die Maske*. Antwerp: Royal Museum of Fine Arts, 1956.

———. *Tentoonstelling. West-Zuid-Oost. Etnografisch Museum*. Antwerp: Ville d'Anvers, 1960.

———. *Tussen schepper en mens. Het dier in de niet-Europese kunst*. Antwerp: Ville d'Anvers, 1968.

———. *Afrikaanse kunst. Nederlands en Belgisch bezit uit openbare verzamelingen*. Nederlandse stichting openbaar kunstbezit en openbaar kunstbezit in Vlaanderen, 1971.

Clarke, A. Stanley. "The Warega." *Man* 29 (1929):66–68.

Cleire, R. "Talen van het Kivu-meer." *Aequatoria* 5 (1942):44.

———. "Talen en taalunificatie in het Vicariaat Kivu." *Kongo-Overzee* 17 (1951):32–37.

Clouzot, H., and A. Level. *Sculptures africaines et océaniennes: Colonies françaises et Congo belge*. Paris: Librairie de France, n.d.

Colle, R. P. "L'organisation politique des Bashi." *Congo* 1921, 2:657–684.

Corbisier, F. "Rapport d'enquête sur la chefferie Luhindja." Kabare: Documents A.I.M.O., 1933*a*.

———. "Rapport d'enquête sur la chefferie Lwindi." Kabare: Documents A.I.M.O., 1933*b*.

———. "Rapport d'enquête sur la chefferie Nindja." Kabare: Documents A.I.M.O., 1933c.

———. "Les Bashi." *Bulletin des juridictions indigènes* 20 (1952):197–205.

Cordella, Ernesto. "Ricognizione nel Bacino dell'Elila (Stato indipendente del Congo)." *Bolletino della società geographica italiana* 7 (1906):864–878, 963–978.

Cornet. "Note sur la chefferie des Bahina." Kibombo: Documents A.I.M.O., 1933.

———. "Dawa la ohamba." Kibombo: Documents A.I.M.O., 1935.

Cornet, Joseph. *Art de l'Afrique noire au pays du fleuve Zaïre.* Brussels: Arcade, 1972.

———. *Trésors de l'art traditionnel.* Kinshasa: Institut des musées nationaux du Zaïre, 1973.

———. *Art from Zaire: 100 Masterworks from the National Collection.* New York: African-American Institute, 1975.

———. *A Survey of Zairian Art: The Bronson Collection.* Raleigh: North Carolina Museum of Art, 1978a.

———. "Das zentrale Afrika." In *Kunst der Naturvölker,* ed. Elsy Leuzinger, pp. 156–172, pls. 96–133. Berlin: Propyläen Verlag, 1978b.

Cory, H. *African Figurines: Their Ceremonial Use in Puberty Rites in Tanganyika.* London: Faber and Faber, 1956.

Coune, H. "Notes sur les Batwa installés en chefferie des Bahina." Kibombo: Documents A.I.M.O., n.d.

Coupez, A. *Esquisse de la langue holoholo.* Tervuren: Musée royal du Congo belge, 1955.

Crédit communal de Belgique. *Arts premiers d'Afrique noire.* Brussels, 1977.

Crine, B. *La structure sociale des Foma (Haut-Zaïre).* Brussels: Les cahiers du Cedaf, 1972.

Crine-Mavar, B. *L'avant-tradition Zaïroise.* Special issues of *Cultures au Zaïre et en Afrique* 3 (1974).

Cunard, Nancy, ed. *Negro Anthology Made by Nancy Cunard, 1931–1933.* London: Wishart, 1934.

Cuvelier. "Notice sur les croquis de tatouages Kusu et Songye." Kasongo: Documents A.I.M.O., n.d.

Czekanowski, Jan. "Die anthropologisch-ethnographischen Arbeiten der Expedition S.H. des Herzogs Adolf Friedrich zu Mecklenburg für den Zeitraum vom 1 Juni 1907 bis 1 August 1908." *Zeitschrift für Ethnologie* 41 (1909):591–615.

Daggers, H. "Notes sur la circoncision des Wazimba et Warega." Kindu: Documents A.I.M.O., n.d.

Debatty, René. "Etude des coutumes des Wanande en territoire de Lubero." *Bulletin des juridictions indigènes* 19 (1951):174–188.

De Croock, E. "Ngitse (Bashu, territoire Beni)." Kivu: Documents A.I.M.O., 1953.

———. "Kasine (Bashu, territoire Beni)." Kivu: Documents A.I.M.O., 1954.

Dedave, André. "Les pêcheurs de Stanleyville. Quelques aspects de la vie sociale et coutumière des Wagenia." *Africa* 27 (1957):262–267.

de Heusch, L. "Autorité et prestige dans la société tetela." *Zaire* 10 (1954):1013–1027.

De Kesel, P. C. "De Kunst bij de Bashi." *Nieuw Afrika* 55 (1939):232–235.

De Kesel, W. G. *Bindingen. Kultuurhistorische bijdrage over de bindmiddelen in kunst en magie.* Wetteren: Cultura, 1980.

de Kun, Nicholas. "L'art lega." *Africa-Tervuren* 12 (1966):69–99.

Delange, Jacqueline. *Arts et peuples de l'Afrique noire. Introduction à l'analyse des créations plastiques.* Paris: Gallimard, 1967.

———. *African Sculpture from Canadian Collections.* Winnipeg Art Gallery, 1973.

Delcourt, L., and A. Dallons. "Les Mongo du Sankuru." *Bulletin des juridictions indigènes* 17 (1949):137–163, 165–189.

Deleu. "Benia-Baya (secteur Wazimba wa Mulu, territoire Kasongo)." Kivu: Documents A.I.M.O., 1953.

Delhaise, Le Commandant. "Moeurs des peuplades du Tanganika." *La Belgique coloniale* 11 (1905):184–186, 195–198, 206–208, 220–222, 232–234, 245–246, 255–257.

———. "Ethnographie congolaise. Chez les Warundi et les Wahorohoro." *Bulletin de la société royale belge de géographie* 32 (1908):429–450.

———. "Ethnographie congolaise. Chez les Wasongola du Sud. Bantu ou Ba-Bili." *Bulletin de la société royale belge de géographie* 33 (1909a):45–58, 109–135, 159–206.

———. *Les Warega.* Brussels: Albert de Wit, 1909b.

Delsupehe. "Wanande du Bas-Tama (territoire Lubero)." Kivu: Documents A.I.M.O., n.d.

Delvaux. "Kasongo." Kivu: Documents A.I.M.O., 1950.

de Mahieu, Wauthier. "Het Komo masker oorsprong en functie." *Africa-Tervuren* 19 (1973):29–32.

———. "Cosmologie et structuration de l'espace chez les Komo." *Africa* 45 (1975):123–138, 236–257.

———. *Structures et symboles. Les structures sociales du groupe komo du Zaïre dans leur élaboration symbolique.* London: International African Institute, 1980.

De Meirsman. "Benia-Kasenga." Kivu: Documents A.I.M.O., 1951.

———. "Etude politique foncière Nonda (territoire Kasongo)." Kivu: Documents A.I.M.O., n.d.

De Pélichy. "Plan de campagne pour l'Urega." Kindu: Documents A.I.M.O., 1926.

De Rop, A. "Lilwa-Beeldjes bij de Boyela." *Zaire* 9 (1955):115–123.

de Saint Moulin, Leon. "Mouvements récents de population dans la zone de peuplement dense de l'est du Kivu." *Etudes d'histoire africaine* 7 (1975):113–124.

de Sousberghe, Leon. *Unions consécutives entre apparentés. Une comparaison de systèmes du Bas-Congo et de la région des Grand-Lacs.* Louvain: Desclée de Brouwer, 1969.

———. "Union structurale et alliance en Afrique centrale." *Anthropos* 68 (1973):1–92, 491–536.

———. "Le problème de l'anthropologie: Repenser et réobserver la parenté et le mariage." *Anthropos* 70 (1975):461–512.

de Villenfagne de Loën. "Warega." Kindu: Documents A.I.M.O., 1932.

Dorsingfang-Smets, A., and A. Claerhout. *Masques du monde. Het masker in de wereld.* Brussels: Société générale de banque, 1974.

Droogers, André. *De gevaarlijke reis. Jongensinitiatie bij de Wagenia van Kisangani.* Amsterdam: Vrije Universiteit, 1974.

Druet. "Itombwe." Kivu: Documents A.I.M.O., 1950.

Dubuisson, M. "Rutshuru." Kivu: Documents A.I.M.O., 1931.

———. "Légende sur l'origine des Watembo." Masisi: Documents A.I.M.O., n.d.

Einstein, Carl. *Negerplastik.* Munich: Kurt Wolff Verlag, 1920.

Elisofon, Eliot, and William Fagg. *The Sculpture of Africa.* London: Thames and Hudson, 1958.

Eloy, J. "Benia-katembo (secteur Wazimba wa Maringa, territoire Kasongo)." Kivu: Documents A.I.M.O., 1951a.

———. "Benia-Lubamba (chefferie Bakwange, territoire Kasongo)." Kivu: Documents A.I.M.O., 1951b.

———. "Benia-Mwendzi (chefferie Bakwange, territoire Kasongo)." Kivu: Documents A.I.M.O., 1951c.

———. "Wazula (territoire Kasongo)." Kivu: Documents A.I.M.O., 1951d.

———. "Benya-Kibumba (secteur Bangobango de Wamaza, territoire Kabambare)." Kivu: Documents A.I.M.O., 1952a.

————. "Etude politique et foncière des Benia Lusanga." Bukavu: Archives du district du Maniéma, 1952*b*.

Encyclopaedia Britannica. 1969 ed. S.v. "elephant."

Encyclopedia Americana. 1978 ed. S.v. "elephant."

Encyclopédie du Congo belge. Vol. 3. Brussels: Bieleveld, 1952.

Engels, J. "Enquête sur le droit coutumier des Benia Beia, territoire Kihembwe." Pangi: Documents A.I.M.O., 1939.

Fagg, William. *Afrique: Cent tribus, Cent chefs-d'oeuvre.* Paris: Musée des arts décoratifs, Palais du Louvre, 1964.

————. *African Tribal Images: The Katherine White Reswick Collection.* Cleveland: Museum of Art, 1968.

————. *African Sculpture.* Washington: International Exhibitions Foundation, 1970.

————. *African Sculpture from the Tara Collection.* University of Notre Dame Art Gallery, 1971.

Fagg, William, and Margaret Plass. *African Sculpture: An Anthology.* London: Studio Vista, 1964.

Fassin, A. T. "Rapport sur les moami des Warega." Bukavu: Documents A.I.M.O., 1918, 1920.

Fivé. "Rapport sur le moami." Bukavu: Documents A.I.M.O., 1922, 1923.

————. "Etudes Bamanga." District de Stanleyville: Documents A.I.M.O., n.d.

Flament-Carière. "Groupement Buniuka (Bashu, territoire Beni)." Kivu: Documents A.I.M.O., n.d.

Fontaine. "Codification des coutumes indigènes." Kalehe: Documents A.I.M.O., 1925.

Fourdin, M. "Etude de l'unité foncière de base Kalero." Kivu: Documents A.I.M.O., 1955.

————. "Etude de l'unité foncière de base Malihi-Ilambula-Ngebo." Kivu: Documents A.I.M.O., 1956.

Fraser, D., and H. Cole, eds. *African Art and Leadership.* Madison: University of Wisconsin Press, 1972.

Frobenius, Leo. *Kulturgeschichte Afrikas.* Zurich: Phaidon-Verlag, 1933.

Fröhlich, W., ed. *Exotische Kunst im Rautenstrauch-Joest Museum.* Cologne: Greven und Bechtold, 1967.

Fry, Jacqueline (Delange). *Vingt-cinq sculptures africaines. Twenty-Five African Sculptures.* Ottawa: National Gallery of Canada, 1978.

Fuhrmann, Ernst. *Afrika: Sakralkulte. Vorgeschichte der Hieroglyphen.* Hagen and Darmstadt: Folkwang, 1923.

Gabus, Jean. *Art nègre: Recherche de ses fonctions et dimensions.* Neuchâtel: Editions de la Baconnière, 1967.

Gaffé, René. *La sculpture au Congo belge.* Paris and Brussels: Editions du cercle d'art, 1945.

Galdermans, G. "Crimes et superstitions indigènes." *Bulletin des juridictions indigènes* 2 (1934):221–222.

Gérard, J. "La grande initiation chez les Bakumu du Nord-Est et les populations avoisinantes." *Zaire* 10 (1956):87–94.

Gilson. "Histoire du Tanganika-Moero." Kabambare: Documents A.I.M.O., 1922.

Glorie, Lieutenant. "La marche du Lieutenant Glorie contre les révoltés de l'Est." *La Belgique coloniale* 4 (1898)a:605–606, 616–617; 5 (1899a):3, 5, 7.

————. "L'expédition Glorie de Riba-Riba au lac Kivu." *Le mouvement géographique* 16 (1899b):61–64.

Goldwater, Robert. "From . . . by . . . and for . . . Ralph C. Altman." *African Arts* 1 (1968):36–39, 78–79.

Golovanova, I. N. "Statuettes des Warega dans la collection du M.A.E." *Africana. Etnografia, Historia, Linguistica, Akademia Nauk* 93 (1969):227.

Gossiaux, P. "Recherches sur l'art bembe." *Arts d'Afrique noire*, 11 (1974):26–40.

Graburn, N., ed. *Ethnic and Tourist Arts: Cultural Expressions from the Fourth World*. Berkeley and Los Angeles: University of California Press, 1976.

Griaule, Marcel. *Arts de l'Afrique noire*. Paris: Editions du chène, 1947.

Guthrie, Malcolm. *The Classification of the Bantu Languages*. 1948. Reprint. London: Dawsons of Pall Mall, 1967a.

———. *Comparative Bantu*. 4 vols. Hants, England: Gregg Press, 1967b, 1970a, 1970b, 1971.

H. U. H. "A Batetela Image." *University Museum Bulletin* 2 (1931):155–157.

Hardy, Georges. *L'art nègre: L'art animiste des Noirs d'Afrique*. Paris: Henri Laurens, 1927.

Harries, Lyndon. "Kumu: A Sub-Bantu Language." *Kongo-Overzee* 24 (1958):4–5, 265–296.

Hautefelt. "L'initiation de la puberté chez les Baenya." *Congo* 1923, 1:207–210.

Hellings. "Kaniengele (secteur Bangobango de Wamaza, territoire Kabambare)." *Kivu: Documents A.I.M.O.*, 1955a.

———. "Mwambao (secteur Bangobango de Wamaza, territoire Kabambare)." *Kivu: Documents A.I.M.O.*, 1955b.

Herskovits, Melville J. *The Backgrounds of African Art*. Denver: Art Museum, 1945.

Himmelheber, Hans. *Negerkunst und Negerkünstler*. Braunschweig: Klinkhardt und Biermann, 1960.

Hombert. "Renseignements sur la naissance des rois ou moami." *Kabare: Documents A.I.M.O.*, 1925.

Hôtel Drouot. *Collection G. De Miré: Sculptures anciennes d'Afrique et d'Amérique*. Paris, 1931.

———. *Ancienne collection Paul Guillaume: Art nègre*. Paris, 1965.

Hudson River Museum. *African Art in Westchester from Private Collections*. Yonkers, New York, 1971.

Hulstaert, G. "Grafbeelden en Standbeelden." *Congo* 1938, 2:94–100.

———. *Carte linguistique du Congo belge*. Brussels: Institut royal colonial belge, 1950.

———. "Les langues de la cuvette centrale congolaise." *Aequatoria* 14 (1951):18–24.

———. "Der zentrale Teil." In *Die Völker Afrikas und ihre traditionellen Kulturen*, ed. Hermann Baumann, pp. 722–746. Wiesbaden: Franz Steiner Verlag, 1975.

Jacobs, John. *Tetela-Grammatica (Kasayi, Congo)*. Ghent: Wetenschappelijke Uitgeverij en Boekhandel, 1962.

Jacquot, Cécile, et al. *Les ivoires*. Part 2. Paris: Tardy, 1977.

Jager Gerlings, J. H., et al. *Schatten uit de tropen*. Amsterdam: Koninklijk instituut voor de tropen, n.d.

Jak, J. "De initiatie-ritus tot de Lilwa bij de Bambole." *Het Rijk van het Heilig Hart van Jesus* 35 (1936):86–88, 118–121.

———. "Eenige ethnographica over de Walengola-Babira." *Congo* 1938, 1:13–21.

———. "De Walengola." *Congo* 1939, 2:47–55.

Jenssen-Tusch, H. *Skandinaver i Congo. Svenske, Norske og Danske Maends og Kvinders Virksomhed i den Uafhaengige Congostat*. Copenhagen: Gyldendalske, 1902–1905.

Joset, P. E. "Historique du territoire de Beni." *Beni: Documents A.I.M.O.*, 1939.

———. "Les Baamba et les Babwizi du Congo belge et de l'Uganda Protectorate." *Anthropos* 47 (1952):369–387, 909–946.

Kalala Nkudi. *Le Lilwakoy des Mbole du Lomami: Essai d'analyse de son symbolisme*. Brussels: Les cahiers du Cedaf, 1979.

Kataliko, Emmanuel. "Les croyances traditionnelles Nande." *Annali Lateranensi* 28 (1964a):55 – 73.

———. "L'homme tel qu'il est conçu par le Munande." *Annali Lateranensi* 28 (1964b): 75 – 84.

Kjersmeier, Carl. *Centres de style de la sculpture nègre africaine.* Vols. 3, 4. 1937, 1938. Reprint (4 vols. in 1). New York: Hacker Art Books, 1967.

Kochnitzky, Leon. *Negro Art in Belgian Congo.* New York: Belgian Government Information Center, 1948.

Krieger, Kurt. *Westafrikanische Plastik.* Vols. 1, 3. Berlin: Museum für Völkerkunde, 1965, 1969.

Krieger, Kurt, and Gerdt Kutscher. *Westafrikanische Masken.* Berlin: Museum für Völkerkunde, 1967.

Lake Forest College. *African Art: The Herbert Baker Collection.* Lake Forest, Ill., 1962.

Laude, Jean. "Le Musée du Congo belge à Tervuren." *L'oeil, revue d'art* 13 (1956):32 – 39.

———. *Les arts de l'Afrique noire.* Paris: Librairie générale française, 1966.

Laurent. "Rapport sur le moami du territoire de l'Elila." Bukavu: Documents A.I.M.O., 1916.

Lauwers, S. "Procès-verbal relatif aux Mboso, Topoke, Bambole, territoire Yanonge." Isangi: Documents A.I.M.O., 1931.

———. "Notes sur la peuplade des Bambole." Stanleyville: Documents A.I.M.O., 1932.

Lavachery, Henri. *Statuaire de l'Afrique noire.* Brussels: Office de publicité, 1954.

Lecoste, Baudouin. "La justice coutumière chez les Bangengele." *Bulletin des juridictions indigènes* 20 (1952):231 – 241.

———. "Bangengele et Wasongola contribution à l'établissement d'une carte des groupes ethniques du Congo belge." *Bulletin des juridictions indigènes* 22 (1954): 241 – 243.

Leiris, Michel, and Jacqueline Delange. *Afrique noire: La création plastique.* Paris: Editions Gallimard, 1967.

Lema, Gwete. *Kunst aus Zaire. Masken und Plastiken aus der Nationalsammlung I.M.N.Z.* Bremen: Uebersee Museum, 1980.

Lenaers, Constantin. "Chez les Warega." *Grands lacs,* nos. 82 – 84 (1946):65 – 69.

Leruth, A. "Paysannat indigène en chefferie Bena-Kuvu." Katanga: Documents A.I.M.O., 1952.

———. "Etude monographique et instauration du paysannat indigène en chefferie Muhona." Katanga: Documents A.I.M.O., 1954a.

———. "Paysannat indigène en chefferie Bena Mambwe." Katanga: Documents A.I.M.O., 1954b.

Leuzinger, Elsy. *African Sculpture, a Descriptive Catalogue (Museum Rietberg).* Zurich: Atlantis Verlag, 1963.

———. *Villa Hügel Essen. Afrikanische Kunstwerke, Kulturen am Niger. Handbuch zur Ausstellungen. 25 März bis 13 Juni 1971.* Zurich: Verlag Aurel Bongers, 1971.

———. *The Art of Black Africa.* Greenwich, Conn.: New York Graphic Society, 1972.

———. *The Art of Black Africa.* New York: Rizzoli International Publications, 1977.

Leuzinger, Elsy, ed. *Kunst der Naturvölker.* Berlin: Propyläen Verlag, 1978.

Liétard, L. "Les Waregas." *Bulletin de la société royale belge de géographie* 3 (1924):133 – 145.

Lobho, Jean-Pierre. "Impact de la colonisation belge sur les structures socio-politique au Congo: le cas de la société hema en Ituri." *Revue congolaise des sciences humaines* 1971:85 – 102.

Lobho lwa Djugudju. "La vie socio-politique dans les chefferies traditionnelles Hema du Bulega." *Cahiers zaïrois d'études politiques et sociales* 2 (1974):121 – 147.

Locke, Alain. *Blondiau Theatre Arts Collection of Primitive African Art.* New York: New Art Circle, 1927.

Lokomba, Baruti. *Structure et fonctionnement des institutions politiques traditionnelles chez les Lokele (Haut-Zaïre).* Brussels: Les cahiers du Cedaf, 1972.

Loons, R. "Etude sur l'origine des Bafulero." Uvira: Documents A.I.M.O., 1937.

Louillet. "Notes sur le dawa la nkinu." Kasongo: Documents A.I.M.O., 1932.

Lunsford, John. *The Clark and Frances Stillman Collection of Congo Sculpture.* Dallas: Museum of Fine Arts, 1969.

Maes, J. "Kese et Tambue fétiches des Wazimba." *Man* 11 (1911):18–19.

———. *Aniota-Kifwebe, les masques des populations du Congo belge et le matérial des rites de circoncision.* Antwerp: de Sikkel, 1924.

———. "La société des mwami." *Pro Medico* 10 (1933):109–111.

Maes, J., and Olga Boone. *Les peuplades du Congo belge: Nom et situation géographique.* Brussels: Musée du Congo belge, 1935.

Maesen, A. "Un art traditionnel au Congo belge: la sculpture." In *Les arts du Congo belge et au Ruanda-Urundi,* Centre d'information et de documentation du Congo belge, pp. 9–33. Brussels, 1950.

———. "La sculpture décorative." *Les arts plastiques* 5 (1951):16–30.

———. *Arte del Congo.* Rome: De Luca, 1959.

———. *Encyclopedia of World Art.* 1960a. S.v. "Bantu Cultures."

———. *Umbangu. Art du Congo au Musée royal du Congo belge.* Brussels: Cultura, 1960b.

———. *Art of the Congo.* Minneapolis: Walker Art Center, 1967.

Marijnissen, R. H., et al. *Afrikaanse beeldhouwkunst: Nieuw zicht op een erfgoed. Sculptures africaines: Nouveau regard sur un héritage.* Brussels: Philippe Guimiot, 1975.

Marmitte, H. "Notice sur les origines et la migration des Bambole." Opala: Documents A.I.M.O., 1931.

———. "Notice sur les origines et les migrations des populations Walengola, Wasongola, Mituku." Ponthierville: Documents A.I.M.O., 1933.

———. "Rapport sur le bwami." Bukavu: Documents A.I.M.O., 1934.

Marmitte, H., and A. Van Belle. "Baleka-Mituku." Ponthierville: Documents A.I.M.O., 1932–1934.

Martin, R. "Le régime foncier en Uzimba." Kasongo: Documents A.I.M.O., 1935.

Massart, A. "Chefferie de Lumbu." Kabambare: Documents A.I.M.O., 1931.

Masui, Lieutenant. *Guide de la section de l'état indépendant du Congo à l'exposition de Bruxelles-Tervueren en 1897.* Brussels: Monnom, 1897.

Mateene, Kahombo. "Trois poèmes hunde chantés par Fatuma wa Bacira." *Journal of African Languages* 11 (1974):21–44.

Meauzé, Pierre. *African Art: Sculpture.* Cleveland and New York: World Publishing Co., 1968.

Meeussen, A. E. *Esquisse de la langue Ombo (Maniéma).* Tervuren: Musée royal du Congo belge, 1952.

———. "De Talen van Maniema." *Kongo-Overzee* 19 (1953):385–391.

———. *Linguistische schets van het Bangubangu.* Tervuren: Musée royal de l'Afrique centrale, 1954.

———. "De Talen van Kongo." *Congo-Tervuren* 1 (1955):147–150.

———. "Aktiespreuken bij de Lega." *Kongo-Overzee* 25 (1959):73–76.

———. "Een en ander over Lega-muziek." *Africa-Tervuren* 7 (1961):61–64.

———. "Lega-teksten." In *Africana Linguistica*, Musée royal de l'Afrique centrale, pp. 75–97. Tervuren, 1962.

———. *Eléments de grammaire lega*. Tervuren: Musée royal de l'Afrique centrale, 1971.

Merlot, J. "Etudes sur les Wangania, Baombo, Wasongola." Kindu: Documents A.I.M.O., 1930.

———. "Notes complémentaires sur les Warega du territoire de l'Elila." Bukavu: Documents A.I.M.O., 1931*a*.

———. "Notes préliminaires à la réorganisation des Warega." Shabunda: Documents A.I.M.O., 1931*b*.

Metropolitan Museum of Art. *Art of Oceania, Africa, and the Americas from the Museum of Primitive Art*. New York, 1969.

Milingo, Valérien. *Les rites matrimoniaux des Bahemba*. Brussels: Les cahiers du Cedaf, 1971.

Miller, Joseph C., ed. *The African Past Speaks: Essays on Oral Tradition and History*. Hamden, Conn.: Dawson-Archon, 1980.

Moeller, A. *Les grandes lignes des migrations des Bantous de la Province orientale du Congo belge*. Brussels: Institut royal colonial belge, 1936.

———. "Danses." *Les Beaux-Arts* 7, no. 227 (1937):18–19.

Moons. "Babindja, secteur Baombo." Kivu: Documents A.I.M.O., 1951.

Morigi, Paolo. *Raccolta di un amatore d'arte primitiva*. Bern: Kunstmuseum, 1980.

Muensterberger, Warner. *Sculpture of Primitive Man*. London: Thames and Hudson, 1955.

Müller, Ernst W. "Le rôle social du 'Nkumu' chez les Ekonda." *Problèmes d'Afrique centrale*, no. 38 (1957):281–289.

Mulyumba, Barnabé. "La croyance religieuse des Lega traditionnels." *Etudes congolaises* 11 (1968), 3:1–14; 4:3–19.

Mulyumba wa Mamba Itongwa. *Les proverbes, un langage didactique dans les sociétés africaines traditionnelles. Le cas des Balega-Bashile*. Brussels: Les cahiers du Cedaf, 1973.

———. *Aperçu sur la structure politique des Balega-Basile*. Brussels: Les cahiers du Cedaf, 1978.

Musée de Rennes. *L'art nègre*. Rennes, 1966.

Musée royal de l'Afrique centrale. *Africana Linguistica*. Tervuren, 1962, 1970, 1971, 1975.

———. Dossiers ethnographiques. Tervuren. Manuscripts.

Arnold, Secrétaire général, no. 378 (1917)

Baude, no. 557 (1931–1932, 1934)

Biebuyck, no. 55.3 (1955)

Dargent, no. 148 (1910)

de Kun, nos. 54.131 (1954); 55.17, 55.37, and 55.78 (1955); 62.46 (1962); 74.21 and 74.22 (1974)

de Limelette, no. 52.29 (1952)

Frateur, nos. 55.42 (1955), 56.3 (1956)

Glorieux, no. 50.2 (1950)

Hautmann, no. 51.35 (1951)

Ledocte-Corbisier, no. 534 (1930)

Lemborelle, no. 51.11 (1951)

Passau, no. 55.134 (1955)

Prigogine, nos. 62.44 (1962), 63.50 (1963), 64.53 (1964), 66.18 (1966)

Rochette, no. 345 (1913)

Van Hooren, no. 1051 (1939)

Walschot, nos. 51.41 (1951), 53.43 (1953), 73.36 (1973), 75.51 (1975), 80.2 (1980)

Zographakis, no. 561 (1931)

Museum of Primitive Art. *The Lipchitz Collection (Jacques, Yulla and Lolya)*. New York, 1960.

———. *Traditional Art of the African Nations in the Museum of Primitive Art*. New York, 1961*a*.

———. *The Traditional Sculpture of Africa*. New York, 1961*b*.

———. *The John and Dominique de Menil Collection*. New York, 1962.

———. *The Robert and Lisa Sainsbury Collection*. New York, 1963*a*.

———. *Sculpture from Africa in the Collection of the Museum of Primitive Art*. New York, 1963*b*.

———. *African Sculpture from the Collection of Jay C. Leff*. New York, 1964.

———. *Masterpieces in the Museum of Primitive Art: Africa, Oceania, North America, Mexico, Central to South America, Peru*. New York, 1965.

———. *The Clark and Frances Stillman Collection of Congolese Sculpture*. New York, 1966*a*.

———. *Masks and Sculptures from the Collection of Gustave and Franyo Schindler*. New York, 1966*b*.

———. *African Tribal Sculpture from the Collection of Ernst and Ruth Anspach*. New York, 1967.

———. *The Herbert Baker Collection*. New York, 1969.

———. *Robert Goldwater: A Memorial Exhibition*. New York, 1973.

Newbury, David S. *Kamo and Lubambo: Dual Genesis Traditions on Ijwi Island (Zaire)*. Brussels: Les cahiers du Cedaf, 1979.

Newton, Douglas. *Masterpieces of Primitive Art: The Nelson A. Rockefeller Collection*. New York: Alfred A. Knopf, 1978.

Neyt, François, and Louis de Strycker. *Approche des arts hemba*. Villiers-le-Bel: Arts d'Afrique noire, 1975.

Noll, Colette, et al. *Sculptures africaines dans les collections publiques françaises*. Paris: Editions des musées nationaux, 1972.

Obenga, Théophile. *Le Zaïre: Civilisations traditionnelles et culture moderne*. Paris: Présence africaine, 1977.

Oberlin College. *Allen Memorial Art Museum Bulletin*. Oberlin, Ohio, 1955.

Okpaku, Joseph, ed. *New African Literature and the Arts*. New York: Thomas Y. Crowell, 1967.

Olbrechts, Frans M. "La statuaire du Congo belge." *Les arts plastiques* 5 (1951):5–15.

———. *Plastiek van Kongo*. Antwerp: N. V. Standaard, 1946. Translated as *Les arts plastiques du Congo belge*. Brussels: Erasme, 1959.

Olbrechts, Frans M., et al. *Kunst in Kongo. Algemene wereldtentoonstelling te Brussel, 1958*. Antwerp, 1958.

Olderogge, Dmitry. *Afrikanische Kunst*. Hanau: Verlag Werner Dausien, 1969.

Olderogge, Dmitry, and Werner Forman. *The Art of Africa: Negro Art from the Institute of Ethnography, Leningrad*. London: Paul Hamlyn, 1969.

Packard, Randall M. "The Study of Historical Process in African Traditions of Genesis: The Bashu Myth of Muhinyi." In *The African Past Speaks: Essays on Oral Tradition and History*, ed. Joseph C. Miller, pp. 157–177. Hamden, Conn.: Dawson-Archon, 1980.

Pahaut. "Basikalangwa (Mokanga-Kalembelembe)." Kivu: Documents A.I.M.O., 1951.

Palmaer, G., ed. *Mästaren på Kongos Stigar. Fran Svenska Missionsförbundets Arbete i Kongo. Aren 1881–1941*. Stockholm: Svenska Missionsförbundets Förlag, 1941.

Parke-Bernet Galleries. *African and Oceanic Art: The Property of Arman.* New York, 1967.

Pauwels, P. Marcel. "Le Kalinga, tambour-insigne du royaume et de la dynastie des rois Banyiginyo (Abasindi) du Rwanda." *Annali Lateranensi* 26 (1962):221–256.

Peneniembo. "Rapport d'enquête, chefferie Pari, territoire de Walikale (Bakusu Arabisés)." Kivu: Documents A.I.M.O., 1955.

Penniman, T. K. *Pictures of Ivory and Other Animal Teeth, Bone, and Antler.* Oxford: University Press, 1952.

Périer, Gaston D. "Artisanats et arts populaires." In *Encyclopédie du Congo belge,* vol. 3, pp. 799–814. Brussels: Bieleveld, 1952.

Pestiaux, A. T. "Rapport sur le moami." Bukavu: Documents A.I.M.O., 1927, 1929.

Plass, Margaret. *African Tribal Sculpture.* Philadelphia: University Museum, n.d.

Polak-Bynon, Louise. *A Shi Grammar: Surface Structures and Generative Phonology of a Bantu Language.* Tervuren: Musée royal de l'Afrique centrale, 1975.

Préaux, G. "Etude sur le bumbuli des Bangubangu du territoire des Bangubangu-Babuie." Kabambare: Documents A.I.M.O., 1932.

Présence africaine. *Contributions to the Colloquium on the Function and Significance of Negro-African Art in the Life of the People and for the People.* Paris, 1971.

Radin, Paul, and James Johnson Sweeney. *African Folktales and Sculpture.* 2d ed. New York: Pantheon Books, 1964. (1st ed. New York: Bollingen Foundation, 1952.)

Rahm, U. *Les mammifères de la forêt équatoriale de l'est du Congo.* Tervuren: Musée royal de l'Afrique centrale, 1966.

Rawson, Philip, ed. *Primitive Erotic Art.* New York: G. P. Putnam's Sons, 1973.

Richards, A. I. "Pottery Images or *Mbusa* Used at the *Chisungu* Ceremony of the Bemba People of North-Eastern Rhodesia." *South African Journal of Science* 41 (1945):444–458.

———. *Chisungu.* London: Faber and Faber, 1956.

Rivière, Marceau. *Les chefs-d'oeuvre africains des collections privées françaises.* Paris: Philbi, 1975.

Robbins, Warren. *African Art in American Collections.* New York: Frederick A. Praeger, 1966.

Robert. "Associations secrètes, territoire de la Lueko." Kibombo: Documents A.I.M.O., 1925.

Rochez. "Chefferie Mukoko, territoire Kindu." Kivu: Documents A.I.M.O., 1951*a.*

———. "Chefferie Tshiambi (territoire Kindu)." Kivu: Documents A.I.M.O., 1951*b.*

———. "Secteur Balanga (territoire Kindu)." Kivu: Documents A.I.M.O., 1951*c.*

———. "Bakuti (territoire Kindu)." Kivu: Documents A.I.M.O., 1955*a.*

———. "Bashiluamba (territoire Kindu)." Kivu: Documents A.I.M.O., 1955*b.*

———. "Clan Tshiambi (territoire Kindu)." Kivu: Documents A.I.M.O., 1955*c.*

Rommes, M. "La situation linguistique dans les vicariats de Stanleyville et de Wamba." *Kongo-Overzee* 17 (1951):240–249.

Roosens, Eugeen. *Images africaines de la mère et l'enfant.* Louvain: Nauwelaerts, 1967.

Rosefielde, Susan J. *African Sculpture and Artifacts in the Collection of the William Hayes Ackland Memorial Art Center.* Chapel Hill: University of North Carolina, 1977.

Rouvroy, V. "Les Bambole." Stanleyville: Documents A.I.M.O., 1927.

———. "Le 'Lilwa.'" *Congo* 1929, 1:783–798.

Roy, Christopher. *African Sculpture: The Stanley Collection.* Iowa City: University of Iowa Museum of Art, 1979.

Roy, Claude. *The Art of the Savages.* New York: Arts Inc., 1958.

Roy, R. "Le Mubande." *Missions d'Afrique des Pères Blancs,* no. 42 (1926):65–68.

Salmon, Jacques. "La polygamie en chefferie Wamuzimu." *Bulletin C.E.P.S.I.* 16 (1951):114–147.

Savary, Claude. *Collection Barbier-Müller Genève. Sculptures d'Afrique.* Geneva, 1978.

Schebesta, Paul. *Les Pygmées du Congo belge.* Brussels: Institut royal colonial belge, 1954.

——. "Die Bira-Waleseneger am Oberen Ituri (Kongo)." *Wiener Völkerkundliche Mitteilungen* 14–15 (1967–1968):105–123.

Schmalenbach, Werner. *African Art.* New York: Macmillan, 1954.

Schmit. "Les Bagengele." Kindu: Documents A.I.M.O., 1933.

Schouteden, H. *De zoogdieren van Belgisch-Congo en van Ruanda-Urundi.* Tervuren: Musée du Congo belge, 1947.

Schumacher, Peter. *Expedition zu den zentralafrikanischen Kivu-Pygmäen. II. Die Kivu-Pygmäen (Twiden).* Brussels: Institut royal colonial belge, 1949.

Schwers, A. T. "Rapport sur le moami des Wabembe." Bukavu: Documents A.I.M.O., 1917.

Segy, Ladislas. *African Sculpture Speaks.* 3d ed. New York: Hill and Wang, 1969. (1st ed. New York: A. A. Wyn, 1952.)

Sieber, Roy. *African Furniture and Household Objects.* New York: American Federation of Arts, 1980.

Sieber, Roy, and Arnold Rubin. *Sculpture of Black Africa: The Paul Tishman Collection.* Los Angeles: County Museum of Art, 1968.

Sigwalt, Richard D. "The Early History of Bushi: An Essay in the Historical Use of Genesis Traditions." Ph.D. dissertation, University of Wisconsin, Madison, 1975.

——. "The Kings Left Lwindi; the Clans Divided at Luhunda: How Bushi's Dynastic Origin Myth Behaves." In *The African Past Speaks: Essays on Oral Tradition and History,* ed. Joseph C. Miller, pp. 126–156. Hamden, Conn.: Dawson-Archon, 1980.

Société générale de banque. *La maternité dans les arts premiers.* Brussels, 1977.

Société nationale d'éditions artistiques. *Le miroir du Congo belge.* Vol. 1. Brussels, 1929.

Soors, M. "Note générale sur les Bakumu." Province Orientale: Documents A.I.M.O., 1924.

——. "Renseignements sur les Bagengele." Kindu: Documents A.I.M.O., 1928.

——. "Essai de codification des coutumes locales (Bagengele), territoire Bakusu." District du Maniéma: Documents A.I.M.O., 1931.

——. "Etude sur les Bakusu du Lomami, dits Bakongola." Kindu: Documents A.I.M.O., 1932.

——. "Note générale sur les Wazimba." Kasongo: Documents A.I.M.O., n.d.

Sotheby, Parke Bernet. *African, Oceanic, and Pre-Columbian Art.* New York, 1978.

Sotheby and Co. *A Highly Important Collection of African Art Chiefly from the Belgian Congo.* London, 1960.

——. *Catalogue of Important African Sculpture, Pre-Columbian, Oceanic and Indian Art.* London, 1965.

——. *Catalogue of Primitive Art and Indian Sculpture.* London, 1967.

Soupault, Philippe. "L'art africain au Congo belge." In *Le miroir du Congo belge,* vol. 1, Société nationale d'éditions artistiques, pp. 203–250. Brussels, 1929.

Spa, J. "Vocabulaire Enya." In *Africana Linguistica,* Musée royal de l'Afrique centrale, pp. 159–185. Tervuren, 1975.

Städtisches Museum für Völkerkunde. *Plastik der Afrikaner.* Frankfurt, 1968.

Stappers, Leo. "Esquisse de la langue lengola." In *Africana Linguistica,* Musée royal de l'Afrique centrale, pp. 255–307. Tervuren, 1971.

Stappers, Leo, and I. Agbamubi. "Textes mituku." In *Africana Linguistica*, Musée royal de l'Afrique centrale, pp. 209–222. Tervuren, 1970.

Starr, Frederick. *Congo Natives: An Ethnographic Album*. Chicago: Lakeside Press, 1912.

Stas. "Balega (Shabunda)." Kivu: Documents A.I.M.O., 1950.

———. "Bahavu du Mbinga et de Idjwi." Kivu: Documents A.I.M.O., 1954.

Stavelot. "Groupements des Wasongora, secteur Ruwenzori, territoire Beni." Kivu: Documents A.I.M.O., 1951.

Stradiot, F. "Rapport concernant l'origine des populations Barumbi et Bakumu des territoires Makala, Wandi, Lubutu et Ponthierville." District de Stanleyville: Documents A.I.M.O., 1931.

———. "Notes complétant l'enquête sur le bumbuli et concernant certaines pratiques de sorcellerie, guérison, fétichisme et magie." Kabambare: Documents A.I.M.O., 1932.

Strauven. "Fuliru." Kivu: Documents A.I.M.O., 1950.

Sweeney, James Johnson, ed. *African Negro Art*. New York: Museum of Modern Art, 1935.

Syracuse University School of Art. *Masterpieces of African Sculpture*. Syracuse, 1964.

Taylor, Brian K. *The Western Lacustrine Bantu (Nyoro, Toro, Nyankore, Kiga, Haya, and Zinza, with Sections on the Amba and Konjo)*. London: International African Institute, 1962.

Teeuwen, A. T. "Rapport sur le moami des Wabembe." Bukavu: Documents A.I.M.O., 1917.

Thilmany, R. "Rapport d'enquête sur la chefferie des Bakalanga." Albertville: Documents A.I.M.O., 1932.

———. "Chefferie Bango-Bango." *Bulletin des juridictions indigènes* 7 (1939):185–188.

Thompson, Robert Farris. *African Art in Motion: Icon and Act in the Collection of Katherine Coryton White*. Berkeley and Los Angeles: University of California Press, 1974.

Tollet, M. "Notes sur les droits coutumiers des Wasongola." Kindu: Documents A.I.M.O., 1938.

Trowell, Margaret. *Classical African Sculpture*. London: Faber and Faber, 1954.

Ucko, Peter, ed. *Form in Indigenous Art: Schematisation in the Art of Aboriginal Australia and Prehistoric Europe*. Canberra: Australian Institute of Aboriginal Studies, 1977.

Uyttebroeck. "Situation ethnographique et politique des groupes Babui du territoire de la Luama." Kabambare: Documents A.I.M.O., 1932.

———. "Rapport d'enquête sur la chefferie des Basonga, territoire Bangobango-Babuye." Kabambare: Documents A.I.M.O., 1933.

———. "Notes sur les Warega du territoire de Kihembe." Kindu: Documents A.I.M.O., 1935.

Van Belle, A. "Les Mituku." Province Orientale: Documents A.I.M.O., 1925.

———. "Renseignements sur les Bakota-Mituku." Ponthierville: Documents A.I.M.O., 1926.

———. "Etudes Walengola, territoire Walengola-Wasongola-Mituku." Ponthierville: Documents A.I.M.O., 1932.

———. "Les Bakota chez les Mituku." Province Orientale: Documents A.I.M.O., 1938.

Van Bulck, G. *Les recherches linguistiques au Congo belge: Résultats acquis. Nouvelles enquêtes à entreprendre*. Brussels: Institut royal colonial belge, 1948.

Van De Capelle, E. "Les Bambole." Opala: Documents A.I.M.O., 1915.

———. "Les Topoke." Opala: Documents A.I.M.O., 1922.

———. "Organisation du territoire ethnique des Boyela." Ikela: Documents A.I.M.O., 1923.

Van de Ghinste, C. D. "Rapport sur le buami des Wabembe." Bukavu: Documents A.I.M.O., 1918, 1923, 1927.

Van Den Dries. "Rapport d'enquête sur la création du secteur Bapere." Lubero: Documents A.I.M.O., 1941.

Van Geluwe, H. *Les Bira et les peuplades limitrophes*. Tervuren: Musée royal du Congo belge, 1956.

———. *Art africain. Afrikaanse kunst (J. Van Der Straete Collection)*. Brussels: Musée d'Ixelles, 1967.

Van Overstraeten. "Mwa Muhia I (secteur Saramabila, Bangobango, territoire Kabambare)." Kivu: Documents A.I.M.O., 1954.

———. "Groupement Kitababeia (Benya-Kibumba, territoire Kabambare)." Kivu: Documents A.I.M.O., 1955a.

———. "Mwa Muhia II (secteur Saramabila, Bangobango, territoire Kabambare)." Kivu: Documents A.I.M.O., 1955b.

Vatter, Ernst. *Religiöse Plastik der Naturvölker*. Frankfurt am Main: Frankfurter Verlags Anstalt, 1926.

Verbeke, A. "Rapport d'enquête sur les M'Bole, territoire Isangi." Isangi: Documents A.I.M.O., 1928.

Verplancke. "Etude sur l'unité de base du Buirima." Kivu: Documents A.I.M.O., 1954.

Viaene, L. "L'organisation politique des Bahunde." *Kongo-Overzee* 18 (1952a):8–34, 111–121.

———. "La religion des Bahunde (Kivu)." *Kongo-Overzee* 18 (1952b):388–425.

Vleugels, A. "Etude sur l'unité foncière de base de Selemani." Kivu: Documents A.I.M.O., 1955.

———. "Unité foncière de base de Vutshumbwa." Kivu: Documents A.I.M.O., 1956.

Vogel, Susan, ed. *For Spirits and Kings: African Art from the Paul and Ruth Tishman Collection*. New York: Metropolitan Museum of Art, 1981.

von Sydow, Eckart. *Handbuch der westafrikanischen Plastik*. Berlin: Dietrich Reimer, Ernst Vohsen, 1930.

———. *Kunst der Naturvölker und der Vorzeit*. Berlin: Sammlung Baron Edouard von der Heydt, 1932a.

———. "Negerkunst in europäischem Privatbesitz." *Atlantis* 2 (1932b):112–128.

———. *Afrikanische Plastik aus dem Nachlass herausgegeben von Gerdt Kutscher*. New York: George Wittenborn, 1954.

Vorblicher, Anton. "Die Herkunft der Bira linguistisch gesehen." *Anthropica* (1968):408–420.

Voukovitch. "Le Moami du territoire de l'Elila." Bukavu: Documents A.I.M.O., 1923.

Walthoff. "Renseignements concernant les chefferies Wazimba du territoire de l'Elila." Kindu: Documents A.I.M.O., 1930.

Wardwell, Allen. "The Herbert Baker Collection." *African Arts* 3 (1970):30–35.

Weis, G. *Le pays d'Uvira*. Brussels: Académie royale des sciences coloniales, 1959.

Weiss, M. "Die von der Expedition des Herzogs Adolf Friedrich zu Mecklenburg berührten Völkerstämme zwischen Victoria-Nyanza und Kongostaat." *Zeitschrift für Ethnologie* 41 (1909):109–113.

Willett, Frank. *African Art: An Introduction*. New York: Praeger Publishers, 1971.

Wingert, Paul S. "Congo Art." *Transactions, New York Academy of Sciences* 1947:320–337.

———. *The Sculpture of Negro Africa*. New York: Columbia University Press, 1950.

———. *Primitive Art: Its Traditions and Styles*. Cleveland: World Publishing Co., 1962.

Wouters, L. "Groupement Bolema, territoire Beni." Kivu: Documents A.I.M.O., 1951.

———. "Etude de l'unité foncière de base de Kahendo (Bashu, territoire Beni)." Kivu: Documents A.I.M.O., 1952*a*.

———. "Mugheri (Bakira, territoire Beni)." Kivu: Documents A.I.M.O., 1952*b*.

———. "Wahumu (territoire Beni)." Kivu: Documents A.I.M.O., n.d.

Wynants. "Rapport d'enquête sur la chefferie des Bahemba." Kabambare: Documents A.I.M.O., 1933.

———. "Rapport d'enquête en vue de la création du secteur Bahemba." Kabambare: Documents A.I.M.O., 1936.

———. "Rapport d'enquête sur le secteur des Bangobango de Wamaza." Kabambare: Documents A.I.M.O., 1937.

Wynants, and R. Wauthion. "La dance kikwayaba ou kindalala." Kasongo: Documents A.I.M.O., 1932.

Yakusu, Jean. "Histoire des Wagenia." District de Stanleyville: Documents A.I.M.O., 1948.

Yogolelo Tambwe ya Kasimba. *Introduction à l'histoire des Lega. Problèmes et méthodes.* Brussels: Les cahiers du Cedaf, 1975.

Index

Designer: Lisa Mirski
Compositer: Innovative Media
Text: 10/13 Palatino
Display: Optima
Printer: Malloy Lithographing
Binder: Malloy Lithographing